RAMBLES
IN
THE PEE DEE BASIN
SOUTH CAROLINA

By
HARVEY TOLIVER COOK
Professor Emeritus, Furman University

VOL. I.

This volume was reproduced from
An 1926 edition located in the
Publisher's private library,
Greenville, South Carolina

All rights reserved. No part of this publication
may be reproduced, stored in a retrieval system,
transmitted in any form, posted on to the web
in any form or by any means without the
prior written permission of the publisher.

Please direct all correspondence and orders to:

www.southernhistoricalpress.com
or
**SOUTHERN HISTORICAL PRESS, Inc.
PO BOX 1267
375 West Broad Street
Greenville, SC   29601
southernhistoricalpress@gmail.com**

Originally published: Columbia, SC 1926
Reprinted by:
Southern Historical Press, Inc.
Greenville, SC
ISBN #0-89308-447-6
All rights Reserved.
Printed in the United States of America

PREFACE

The first inhabitants of the eastern part of South Carolina were choice emigrants from England, Scotland, Wales, Ireland and France. South Carolina was called the Home of the Huguenots and it was even more appropriately the home of the Scotch, who formed the larger part of the population in the distant sections of the state. It was also the home of a Welsh colony in Cheraws District. The intervening spaces between Georgetown and the colony at Williamsburg and at Long Bluff were filled up with the English, predominant in number and in language. The great Pee Dee River was the central way of access to these parts of the state, where there were no powerful Indian tribes to molest the planter and the farmer. For forty or fifty years the upper parts were neither in nor out of the government's control. After 1768, it had sufficient representation to make it feel that it was a small part of the government. This continued till 1776, when the exigency of the times broadened the narrow basis of the government and it so continued until 1790, when the State Constitution was formed.

Among the writers outside of the Pee Dee Basin who referred to this section in their larger works were Wood Furman and Benedict in their histories of the churches, (1811-15), Dalcho's History of the Church in South Carolina (1822) Howe's Presbyterian Church in South Carolina (1870).

The Journal of Bishop Asbury, 1785-1815, as well as Carroll's Collections, Drayton's Memoirs, Gibbes' Documentary History, McCrady's volumes up to 1783, The South Carolina Historical and Genealogical Magazine and others, are among the essential authorities on our early history.

Preface

The dwellers within the Pee Dee Basin have shown much interest in the preservation of their past history, the literature on the subject being, A Memoir of Edmund Botsford, a minister at Society Hill and Georgetown over thirty years, by C. D. Mallary (1832), A Tradition of the Old Cheraw by A. D. Sims of Darlington, The History of the Old Cheraws, by Bishop Gregg (1868), Historical Sketch of the Welsh Neck Church (1888), Chronicles of St. Mark's Parish, Williamsburg County, Etc., by James M. Burgess (1888), History of Marlboro County, by J. A. W. Thomas (1897), Narrative of Reminiscences of Williamsburg County, by Samuel D. McGill (1897), History of Marion County, by W. W. Sellers (1902), Methodism on the Pee Dee, by R. E. Stackhouse (1904), The Ebenezer Church, by W. A. Brunson (1909), the Williams Family of Society Hill, by Joseph S. Ames, with introduction on Life on the Old Plantation, by N. Williams Kirkpatrick (1910), Hartsville, Its Early Settlers, by J. L. Coker (1911), Harmony Hall, Recollections of an old Southern Home, by E. C. Dargan (1912), Life and Legacy of David Rogerson Williams (1915), Sketch of Old St. David's Church, by W. R. Godfrey (1916), Sketch of Old Marlboro, by D. D. McColl (1916), The Register Book for the Parish Prince Frederick Winyaw, by Mrs. Elizabeth W. Allston Pringle (1916), and a History of Williamsburg County, by W. W. Boddie (1923).

The Parish Church Book is the only one found on the history of Georgetown County. Its great value was enhanced by materials found in the London Museum in the Archives of the Society for the Propagation of the Gospel in Foreign Parts. The long list of writers in the Pee Dee section made a choice necessary between drawing heavily from preceding historians or the making of ram-

Preface

bles in search of what enterprising predecessors had overlooked, gleaning as it were, like Ruth, the wheat left ungathered, or to do both. The difficulty of the task was not lightened by the isolation of the section in its early years and its successive subordinate positions, first in respect to the state and then to the state and the United States after 1789.

The Charleston Library, the Winyah Indigo Society Library at Georgetown, and the offices of the Secretary of State and of the Historical Commission in Columbia, have been the main sources from which materials have contributed to our story. To their courteous and efficient assistance special acknowledgements are here accorded. Among the individual helpers must be mentioned Messrs. William Godfrey and B. F. Pegues of Cheraw, D. D. McColl of Bennettsville, J. J. Lawton of Hartsville, W. D. Morgan, Walter Hazard and Mrs. Elizabeth W. Allston Pringle of Georgetown, S. A. Graham of Heinemann and Langdon Cheves of Charleston. The last to be mentioned are Maj. James L. Coker, the President of the Pee Dee Historical Society, now no longer with us, and Mr. Bright Williamson, his successor in spirit and in service, to whose benevolent encouragement and beneficent assistance this work has been prosecuted and thus far accomplished.

Greenville, S. C., September 3rd, 1924.

CONTENTS

	PAGE
INTRODUCTION - - - - - - - - - - Pages	XVII-XXIV

CHAPTER I

Crossing over the Santee and going up the Winyaw, on the Black River—Settlement north of the Santee forbidden in time of danger—The site of Georgetown—"Advice for rich and poor"—Real Estate advertisement, 1712—Virgin pines near Georgetown—Indian traders—War with Indians—Desperate straits of the Colony, Prince George's Parish, Winyaw erected—Leading settlers, land and negroes in 1731—The Huguenots and other settlers—The Pawleys and the Screvens. - - - - - - - - - - - 1

CHAPTER II

The Board of Trade—Robert Johnson, the first Royal Governor—His plans for laying out townships approved and carried out—Trouble with the Indians—Trouble with Indians on the Waccamaw and with the Tuscaroras in North Carolina—Running the line between North and South Carolina - 18

CHAPTER III

The founding of Georgetown—Reopening of the Land Office—The rush across the Santee for land grants; also on the Wadmacon, Cedar Creek, Wittee Creek—Petition to form a port of entry—George Hunter's map—The new town laid out in 1729 and depth of water measured—Reports of commercial transactions by naval officer, imports and exports—Sale of lots interrupted by the claims of the Perrie heirs—Georgetown's future shown by purchasers of lots in the new town—The Pee Dee and Waccamaw rivers—The tributaries in between them and the early land grants on Bull Creek, Wando, Squirrel Creek, and Jericho Creek, Long Bay, Collins' Creek and Little River—The journey of a young Englishman through this section in 1734—Kingston Township—Description of Georgetown and of a party sailing up the Waccamaw to view the land just after Kingston (now Conway) had been laid out into lots—The land near the borders applied for, and settlement begun by poor Protestants. - - - - - - 25

CHAPTER IV

The Sampit and Black rivers, and their early inhabitants—Improved farms for sale—Incomers numerous—Settlers on

Contents

PAGE

the water courses—The churches on the Black visited by water—Settlers in the bend of the river near Potato Ferry—Black Mingo Creek with its numerous settlers—Daniel and Thomas LaRoche—Meredith Hughes, Alexander Parris, George Morley, Col. George Chicken, William Brockington, Joseph Johnson, etc.—The settling of the Williamsburg Colony—The cause of the emigration of these Scotch-Irish—The laying out of Kingstree—Some of the lot owners—The remonstrance of the people of Williamsburg—Ill treatment in their allotment of lands—Commissioner McCullough presents their just complaints—Several members of the Council or Commons House who had taken up some of the best land, opposed any action which would lay burdens on themselves.   -   41

CHAPTER V

Up the Pee Dee—Land owners on the Western side—Earliest grants—Queensborough Township—The rush of emigrants up all the rivers, especially the Pee Dee—West of Little Pee Dee—Traditions about early settlements, Lynch's Creek, Catfish, its barony which eluded the tax collector—Jeffries' Creek, Mars Bluff, Toby's Creek, Sandy Bluff, Black Creek, Cashua or Cashaway Ferry, the Long Bluff, "Charraws Old Town"—The Welsh Tract about sixty miles along the Pee Dee—The large tracts granted outside of the Welsh tract—Robert Hume—Blue Laws, three departments of the government.   -   57

CHAPTER VI

Stock raising and agriculture—A high type of men in the forest—Hunters, shepherds, agriculturalists, all at once—A fine country for hunting, fishing, cattle and horse-raising—Description of an evening scene on a farm and also of a chicken yard and a dairy scene on the Santee—A circular of 1682—Introduction of cotton—Wine from grapes, liquor from corn, silk production, rice and rice lands, indigo—The Sea Nymph—Peter Sinkler—Hard times, farmers elated by high prices, caught in the severe deflation—The first attempt by the planters to seek pecuniary aid from the government—They were interested in a lower rate of interest and in a proper sum of money to be stamped and lent to farmers on the best security—Raw silk, indigo, hemp, flax or cotton to be the security—The result of the agitation.   -   -   -   72

CHAPTER VII

Life in the backwoods—The family the unit—Absence of schools—The Welsh agreement—Dissoluteness after wars—Marriage and divorce—Economic marriages—Parish registers—Grander and shabbier family life—Hospitality—English language prevailing—The Huguenots—The Scotch-Irish, the Welsh, the Germans—Amalgamation of good races.   -   87

VIII

CONTENTS

PAGE

CHAPTER VIII

Stagnation of trade during the wars in Europe before the peace of 1748—English settling farther inland—Preparation for a struggle with France—Gov. Glen a foreseeing Governor—Treaty with the Indians at Saluda Old Town—The Governor unpopular with some designing persons and removed by the complaints lodged with the Board of Trade by the Governor of North Carolina—Did not aid Braddock—He was looking out for South Carolina—Peace with the Indians of the first importance—The French defeated to the Northward make their last stand against South Carolina—Gov. Lyttelton a failure—The province suffered by his hard-headed ignorance of the savages—The expedition by Col. Montgomery, by Col. Grant, who brought the issue to a close—The gates of Janus closed in 1761. - - - - - - - - - - - - - - 96

CHAPTER IX

Education in South Carolina—No schools above the Santee save the one at Georgetown (1755)—The testimony of Charles Woodmason—Neither the province nor the Society for the Propagation of the Gospel was interested in secular education in the upper parts—A free school in Georgetown—Interest abated in 1772—Interest in a college increasing as trouble with England deepens—A bill to establish one, read twice and then suddenly abandoned—The credit due to Ninety Six. - - - - - - - - - - - - 107

CHAPTER X

The Parish Churches in Craven County—The formation of Prince George's Winyaw Parish,—Petition of Representatives, Church Wardens, and Vestrymen—Rev. Thomas Morritt's letters—Prince George's Winyaw Parish,—The letters of his successor, Rev. John Fordyce—Rev. Michael Smith's letters and bad conduct—Lay readers, Charles Woodmason and others—Their successors in the ministry—Church building—The bricks for the church at Georgetown collected in 1739—Apply for a pastor in 1742—Duty on goods imported into Georgetown (except negroes) turned over for five years to the church commissioners to help build the church, walls going up in 1745—The "joining, carpentry, plastering, glazing and painting" still to be done in 1755—The rectors, Alexander Keith, Fayerweather, Pearce, Stuart, St. Mark's Parish-Search for a minister, Charles Woodmason, St. Mark's Parish 1757, an itinerant minister—His testimony on important subjects—St. David's Parish 1769 - - - - - - - 113

IX

CONTENTS

PAGE

CHAPTER XI

Presbyterian Churches in Craven County—On the Black Mingo—Rev. Samuel Hunter, Rev. William Knox—First Scotch Presbyterian Church, its pastors, discipline and mortality—Rev. Robert Heron, Rev. John Rae, Rev. David McKee, Rev. Hector Allison—Church at Indian Town—Hopewell Church up the Pee Dee and Aimwell—More active in preaching than in education. - - - - - - - - - 148

CHAPTER XII

Early Baptist congregations and churches—The Welsh Neck, 1738, the first on record above the Santee—Was one of the three churches to form the Charleston Association—The visits of Rev. John Fordyce to the Welsh—Primitive in church building and doctrine—The names of the early members—Puritan in characteristics—A great revival in 1779—Rev. Edmund Botsford—The Cashaway Church built up by Rev. Mr. Pugh—Its earliest list of members—Seven new light Baptist churches, Rev. Joseph Reese, Rev. Richard Furman and Rev. Timothy Dargan. - - - - - - 156

CHAPTER XIII

Pre-Revolutionary Methodism—The spurious Methodist—The first one named Pilmoor, a follower of Mr. Wesley, 1773—The first Conference—The society, divided into bands, a weekly experience meeting of a religious character and for stated contributions—Itineracy to prevent independency—Duties of ministers—Four years trial preceding ordination—Smallness of salary, business of the bishop, Quarterly meetings composed of ministers, leaders and stewards and other invited guests—In the District meetings was lodged the authority to deal with immoral or unfit preachers—The conference—Wesley's advice—Wesley and Whitefield. - - 166

CHAPTER XIV

The Poor of the Province—South Carolina of the 18th Century, their paradise—Slavery in South Carolina not the main cause of the prevailing poverty—The cause in England and in the glut of gold and silver carried back to Spain, and lack of work for the people, taxation necessary in addition to church collections—The colony of Georgia, for the poor, to help them and relieve the people at home—Cost of the poor 1670-1725, one million pounds annually—The poor in Purrysburg, Kingston, Williamsburg, Amelia Township, Fredericksburgh, Londonderry, New Bordeaux, etc.—The North of Ireland drained—Generously treated—The Sand Hill region, the western part of North Carolina—The true cause of their backwardness. - - - - - - - - - - 172

X

CONTENTS

PAGE

CHAPTER XV

Friction between Charles Town and the upper people—The provincial government encroaching upon the prerogatives of the Crown and negligent in its attention to the upper parts—Infested with thieves—Pee Dee petition slighted, the people neither represented nor protected from lawlessness—An opinion from the forks of the Saluda and the Broad—Might overcoming right—More radical views of itinerating preachers—Act to punish stealing of horses and neat cattle—The beginning of Lynch law—Circuit Courts not favored—The pen used in a Remonstrance signed by representatives of the back inhabitants—Its authors were four persons, but its composition is almost certainly the work of Woodmason. - - 181

CHAPTER XVI

The friction continued—A change of mind in regard to Circuit Courts—Yielding somewhat to pressure from above—Short-sightedness—Many above had reason to feel like sheep to be sheared—In the meantime the Regulators were acting promptly and in contempt of the Government below—Circuit Courts ratified in England—Provincial Government steering between Scylla and Charybdis—"A numerous democracy" still feared—Regulators more determined—Proclamations unheeded—Regulators at Mars Bluff ready to join battle with the officials if necessary—Col. Powell's account of it—Rumor that the Regulators in great numbers were coming down in September—Woodmason's account of the conduct at an election—Both sides drawn up for battle—An end to the reign of the Banditti—Gov. Bull, an excellent and wise Lieut. Governor—Woodmason's activities with the pen. - - - 219

CHAPTER XVII

The Stamp Act—America to be an English Colony, South Carolina's debt—England in debt—Success in war often more hurtful than defeat—The greatest power on earth drawing the reins tight to curb independence—Conflict between governor and council and the representatives of the people—The assembly usurping the functions of the governor and council—The Stamp Act—Remonstrance from South Carolina, Virginia, Massachusetts—Delegates to a convention—Reception of the Stamps—Act repealed—Its decisive work—St. David's Parish, Church and Courts—Commissioners to build church and parsonage—Lot presented by Ely Kershaw—Its slow erection—No rector in the years 1768-1818—First election of a member of the assembly—Claudius Pegues the first, George Gabriel Powell, the second representative—1768 a year beginning Circuit Courts and representation—Struggle for the site of the Court House, Long Bluff, Greenville or Society Hill, later names, selected as the site—Judge William Henry Drayton's charge to the juries—As "Freeman" and Provincial Congress. - - - - - - - 234

CONTENTS

PAGE

CHAPTER XVIII

Rejoicing over the repeal of the Stamp Act—Gov. Montagu kindly received—Restriction on the trade not hurtful to South Carolina—Mass meeting to form importation agreements—Much talk about economy, industry, home manufactures—Encouragement to makers of linen and thread—The grievances, wrangling between the governor and assembly, misappropriation of funds—Deadlock lasting about five years—The governor solidifying the opposition—Duty on tea—A call for the meeting of the inhabitants of the whole province, the union of all the colonies felt to be urgent—A committee of ninety-nine—The granting to the inland people representation in the assembly—Nov. 9, 1774, the day of election—The association—Secret Committee—Special committee—Provincial Congress to meet in June, the province to be placed in posture of defense—Two regiments of infantry and a million of money voted, William Henry Drayton the soul of the movement—The Up-Country pacified—General Assembly ceased to exist—The General Committee *functus officio*, Council of Safety soon to yield to a Constitutional government—McCrady's observations—The Pee Deeans also in harmony with the patriots, names of soldiers, trouble with Cuningham the Tory—Col. Richardson, Col. Powell and Maj. Hicks of Cheraw in the field—Officers commissioned—The battle of the Cane Brakes, the Tories scattered—The noble character of Gen. Richardson—The lack of eagerness to extend the northern limits of the State. - - - - - 246

CHAPTER XIX

The Council of Safety preparing to defend the City—Advised to form an independent government—South Carolina drawn into the conflict, and independence mentioned—The new government formed and officers elected—The new government too narrow—Agitation which leads to a more representative government—President Rutledge resigns and is succeeded by Rawlins Lowndes—Troops by land and sea converging around Charles Town—Battle of Fort Moultrie—The Indians on the warpath—Treaty with Indians at DeWitt's Corner—William Henry Drayton's foresight—Lowndes' uneasy year—Charles Town threatened by Prevost—Offers of peace rejected and a siege by land and water begun—Lincoln surrenders and Gov. Rutledge leads the opposition to the English. - 266

CHAPTER XX

The capitulation of Charles Town followed by effective garrisons—The leading men prisoners—All not lost—Gov. Rutledge's letter—Worthless proclamations—The State prostrate before the various garrisons—Flight of leading men, Tarle-

Contents

PAGE

ton's cruelty—The stirred-up Scotch-Irish—Wemyss before Tarleton in his incendiary work—Tarleton and Wemyss, the precursors of Sherman and Howard—McArthur at Cheraw—not so barbaric as Wemyss—Unable to overtake some of the rebels who dared to defy him—The affair at Hunt's Bluff—Other important skirmishes—The rout of Gen. Gates' army—Sumter's narrow escape, Gov. Rutledge's wise course—Capt. Ardesoif, Maj. James—The brave men of Williamsburg and their officer, Marion, sent by Gen. Gates—Marion's activity—Marion's flight—His return and frequent battles—Battle of King's Mountain—Col. Kolb enters the field—Lord Cornwallis retreats and camps at Winnsborough—Tarleton's pursuit of Marion, called off to fight Sumter—The respective forces in the field—Gov. Rutledge much discouraged, undervalued the small successful skirmishes—Charles Town the height of his wishes—Gen. Greene, a new factor, in the war—Sumter and Marion made Brigadier Generals. - - - - - 285

CHAPTER XXI

Greene's difficult task to feed his forces, watch the enemy and keep the peace in his independent forces—Battle of Cowpens—Greene's retreat—Marion's forces active, attack on Georgetown—Lee recalled and Marion still, like a hawk, pouncing upon his unprotected enemies—The armies being in North Carolina, the partisan troops had the advantage—The chase after the Swamp Fox—Col. Ervin's defeat changed Marion's plans—Jenkins Narrative—The battle of Hobkirk's Hill—Col. Kolb's expedition and murder—Versions of the event—Siege of Ninety Six—A disastrous month to the British—Skirmishes in various counties—No organic connection between the militia and the Continental Army before April 1781—Greene a great general—Sumter's raid—Capture of Dorchester—Wade Hampton's valiant services—Marion thanked by Congress—Battle of Eutaw Springs—A drawn battle, victory claimed by both sides—Rutledge called it a glorious victory—Tories alert on the Pee Dee—Greene's situation like Cornwallis' had been—enemies in his front and tories in his rear—The legislature called to meet—Parting with Gen. Sumter—Marion still the daring officer—A contrast in character with that of Sherman—The end of the war—Two journeys over the desolated country—Poverty, missing members of the family, slaves abducted, hates and murders, and a general demoralization in the State—Judge Burke's address to the jury—A gradual return to temperate conduct, Justice Champion and Rev. Mr. Botsford. - - - - 310

CHAPTER XXII

First session of the legislature—Liberal treatment of Gen. Greene—Gov. Mathews succeeded Gov. Rutledge—People running into debt to British money lenders and for slaves—Refusal of Whigs to pay British creditors—Judge Burke on the situation, and the Pine Barren Act—Timothy Ford on the situation. - - - - - - - - - - 342

CHAPTER XXIII

Sub-entries, Large Slave holders in Prince George's Winyaw and the names of men and their services to the Cause—Also the same of Prince Frederick's and of Cheraws District. - 351

CHAPTER XXIV

An able legislature—In great straits financially but lenient toward tories—Care for disabled soldiers and their families—Forward movement along many lines—A digest of the laws, a more central seat of the legislature mentioned—Dark days, laying out Districts, and a committee to digest the laws finished in 1789—Judge Henry Pendleton. - - - - 363

CHAPTER XXV

A more democratic trend—Judge Pendleton's reform program, Districting the upper parts, and equalizing the representation—Objections and debate—A question whether 40 or 50 who objected or 300 should prevail—It was finally decided by a vote of 65 to 61 in favor of Columbia—The Convention to form the Constitution at work—Discussion and voting, 109 to 105—The site fixed at Columbia was subject to removal by a two-thirds vote—Representatives reduced to 125, senators to 36—The compromise committee recommended dual departments of the treasury and arrangements to suit Beaufort, Georgetown and Charleston in reference to the Courts—Recapitulation. - - - - - - - - - 369

CHAPTER XXVI

Doings in Congress of the Confederation—Forming the Constitution of the United States—The thirteen isolated states driven by England's cupidity into a desire for union—Massachusetts outgeneraled—Commerce at the mercy of foreigners in South Carolina—Virginia the first to act, aided by Washington—Virginia and Maryland's cooperation started the idea of a greater union of efforts—Washington's influence for the union—The fear of the people seen in not enlarging the articles of Confederation—The perils of the new form known by a thinking few—May 1787 the meeting of the Constitutional Convention—Randolph of Virginia, James Madison and Charles Pinckney, the leaders—The extreme views of Hamil-

Contents

PAGE

ton rejected—Patterson of New Jersey offers a substitute for Randolph's resolutions—Charles Pinckney's draft—Small and large states to be equal in the Senate—Ben Franklin's wise words—The question how the slaves should be regarded—A compromise settled the question—Charles Pinckney's wise motion about two-thirds vote on all acts regulating the commerce of the United States—Defeated by C. C. Pinckney—Idealism unable to stand among practical politicians—Madison's good opinion of the work of the convention—His foresight short as compared with that of William Henry Drayton, Rawlins Lowndes and Charles Pinckney—Three-fifths of the slaves to be counted—No agricultural exports taxable—Charles Pinckney's draft—The mystery of the Pinckney Draft 382

CHAPTER XXVII

Adopting the Federal Constitution—Delegates' report to the legislature—Charles Pinckney's Eulogy of the Constitution—Opposition by Rawlins Lowndes—Gen. Pinckney's reply—Lowndes' reply—Edward Rutledge's speech—Lowndes' last reply ending with his hoped for Epitaph: "Here lies the man who opposed the Constitution because it was ruinous to the liberty of America"—James Lincoln's warning—Vote to assemble in Charleston gained by one vote—The convention—Charles Pinckney's speech—Rather optimistic in his views, and biting in his remarks on the State's commercial honesty—William Gilmore Simms' apology for the State's mistake in entering the Union, which abridged the energies of the South—Passed 149 to 71—Honored names of those who voted "no." 397

APPENDICES

Appendix I
Major James Lide Coker 413

Appendix II
Bright Williamson 441

Appendix III
K. Kinloch 446

Appendix IV
A description of an Old Field School during the Revolution 447

Appendix V
A discussion of variations in certain spellings 453

INTRODUCTION

The system of rivers which converge near Georgetown, South Carolina, and pass through Winyah bay into the ocean includes that part of the State east of the watershed of the Santee and Wateree rivers. The lower part of it was known as Winyaw in the early period, but no specific name was given to the whole. For convenience it may be referred to as the Pee Dee Basin; for the great Pee Dee touches Chesterfield, Marlboro, Darlington, Florence, Dillon, Marion, Williamsburg, and Georgetown Counties and, through its tributaries, Sumter and Lancaster. To the early emigrants, the province appeared to be lying in the river systems, whose central streams and larger tributaries formed inland high ways. The large rivers west of the Pee Dee came down through the three natural divisions, the upper, middle and lower sections; but the great Pee Dee passes through one homogeneous region, a coastal plain, as may be conjectured from the relative elevations of Georgetown, 12 feet above the tides, Conway 25, Kingston 54, Marion 68, Mars Bluff 98, Florence 135, Darlington 155, Society Hill 91, Cheraw 150, and Bennettsville 155, the rise from Georgetown to Cheraw being less than that from Charleston to Orangeburg. Greenville in the northwest, in nearly the same line of latitude as Cheraw, is 1066 feet higher than Georgetown and 924 feet higher than Cheraw.[1] Craven County, never laid out, vaguely embraced all this well-watered wilderness, which for two generations formed a frontier to the settlement at Charles Town. It was named in honor of William, Earl of Craven, one of the noblemen whom Charles II "of his own free and ample grace, certain knowledge and meer motion" made Lords Proprietors of that vast tract which lay between 29 and 36½ degrees of north latitude, and extended within

---
[1] U. S. Geological Survey No. 160.

INTRODUCTION

parallel lines from ocean to ocean. It was one of the original counties named in 1682, and the third to receive an influx of inhabitants. It was selected for the home of the French Protestant refugees, who with others gradually occupied the space south of the Santee, known as the St. James Santee parish, but the greater part of the country north of the Santee was left untouched for a generation. It was waiting for an overflow from Berkeley with its fortified capital and for colonists from the mother country. But that overflow was held back and influenced, when it began, by the stress of events. There were at this time twelve colonies and all of them were open to the enterprising emigrants. The colony at Charles Town had advantages of a peculiar kind, but its climate was less adapted to the European laborer than that of other colonies, and there was a lack of harmony in the little England transplanted on the Ashley and the Cooper. The people had brought over their civilization and their discordant religious beliefs, which gave color to their practical politics. About twenty years were consumed by the Lords Proprietors in trying to set up their fundamental constitutions and by the effort the colony was divided into two parties, one of which wanted a larger share in the government. Disquietude and distrust were engendered, and the people being headstrong as well as patriotic, found in the friction with the deputies of the Proprietors a discipline in the science of government, in which there was a general leaning in the direction of self government.

In the last years of the seventeenth century, the smallpox broke out in the town and continued more than ten months to levy its toll of more than two hundred victims. While it was raging, a fire destroyed fifty houses, which were thought to be nearly equal in value to the unburnt residue; and upon the heels of the disaster, another con-

INTRODUCTION

flagration augmented the number of sufferers. The yellow fever which had no respect for age, sex, or condition, laid low officials, legislators, ministers and merchants as it did others in the common walks of life. A hurricane, murrain among cattle, shortage of vessels to remove the rice crop, stagnation in business caused by epidemics or the activity of pirates, kept filling the cup of adversity; but these were resolute men who were to wring out success where others might have failed. The slaves were soon equal in number to the whites and in addition there were 1400 Indian slaves in 1708. These savages from Africa and from the American forests being facile tools in the hands of the Spaniards at St. Augustine, became a source of danger and of anxiety and made necessary a form of service and police, not known in other colonies. The people were soon spread over a frontage of 150 miles and a depth not less than 35 and thus scattered, they were subject to marauding expeditions which decimated their number and wasted their possessions. The Spartans, to whom South Carolinians have been likened, rented their farms to slaves of the state and lived in camp in times of peace but the citizens in the colony lived on the plantations, owned their slaves, provided for their families and all of them from sixteen to sixty years of age were liable to be called out in times of public danger. The white population in 1700 was conservatively estimated to be 5500, but in 1708, according to the estimate of Governor Johnson and his council, the white population numbered only 4080. Legal restrictions were thrown in the way of those who wanted to abandon the province and by legislation it was undertaken to render more compact the inhabitants in times of pressing danger.

The Yamassee war began in 1715 when about 1200 soldiers could be mustered to meet an enemy seven or

INTRODUCTION

eight times as numerous. The gravity of the situation was fully realized, but the colony was saved from extreme peril by the lack of central authority to combine and direct the confederated Indians. The Yamassees were defeated and driven from their homes across the Savannah and deprived of their valuable lands. About 400 whites were cut off in this war, houses were burned, cattle driven off and plantations rendered unproductive, and a debt of about 100,000 pounds was incurred. A possible recompense from the loss of lives was looked for in a large accession of European immigrants to take up the Indian lands on the Savannah. They were offered to actual settlers, but when they had arrived at great expense and found that the Proprietors ordered 180,000 acres of the best land to be laid out for themselves, they began to depart. The accounts differ as to the number of emigrants who were thus lost to the colony by the arbitrary orders of the Proprietors, but there is no doubt that the incident along with other serious grievances, such as the closing of the land office, prepared the people, without bloodshed or violence, to throw off the yoke of the Lords Proprietors. England, however much the province was coveted, had too much regard for law to take possession by force. At the close of September, 1729, all the obstructions were removed and seven of the eight Proprietors surrendered their vast estate for 22,500 pounds, a sum which could not now change the ownership of not a few individual holdings.

One other temporary check to provincial growth was the altercation in the assembly and among the citizens on the subject of the Establishment. That feature in the constitution had been published in the beginning as one of the fundamentals, with the promise of toleration to all; but the Proprietors in setting up their government for more than one reason allowed self in-

INTRODUCTION

terest and the welfare of the colony to postpone action in ecclesiastical matters. Intolerance and persecution had driven over to Charles Town a number of dissenters whose wealth, ability and character were recognized and called into service. Sayle, Morton, Smith, Archdale,[2] Blake and West had been governors by or before 1700. But about this time the Proprietors were quickened into new interest by the formation of the Society for the Propagation of the Gospel in Foreign Parts, which aimed to reach the Indians and relieve the religious destitution of the colonies. The Lords Proprietors were also desirous of putting an end to the strife of parties in Charles Town, which promised to be unceasing. William III, who favored the Whigs, died in 1702 and was succeeded by Queen Anne who favored the high church party of which Lord Granville, then Palatine of South Carolina, was a zealous member. In her speech at the close of the first parliament, Queen Anne said: "My own principles must always keep me entirely firm to the interests of religion of the Church of England and will incline me to countenance those who have the truest zeal to support it." The appointment of the deputies and other colonial offices foreshadowed coming changes in 1704, when by an act of the Assembly with a majority of one vote, provision was made and perfected in later sessions by which churches were built, ministers maintained and teachers provided. Parishes were laid out and made election districts and the basis of representation in the Assembly, and church officers were made supervisors of the poor with power to levy taxes for their support. The contemporary writers Archdale (1707),

---

[2]Archdale was a Quaker and he fully deserved the eulogy of Gov. R. F. W. Allston who referred to him a century and a half later as "That good Governor." His administration forms a striking contrast with Gov. Lyttelton's, by the success of its efforts for peace with the Indians on a basis of justice.

INTRODUCTION

Oldmixon (1708), DeFoe (1708) and later historians are full in their treatment of this legislation which as the sequel will show, vitally affected the history of the people in a large part of the period covered by these rambles; and it is not yet fully expended in its force. It had something to do with the declension of population in 1708, already referred to, and in contrast with the laws of Pennsylvania, Maryland and other colonies, it must in a period of intense conviction have turned away for some time the stricter dissenting emigrants from the old world. Whether or not the legislation was expedient and right and profitable, it must be classed with things that were inevitable. It was catching step with the great dominant party in England which has ruled the empire since 1660 and does not yet hesitate to subordinate the theological and educational to the national feeling by making the church an engine of the State.

Some statistics were found in the chest of William III which throw light upon the religious composition of the English people at this time. As the result of an investigation[3] set on foot by him, it was found that out of 2,599,786 freeholders, 2,477,254 were conformists, 108,676 non-conformists, and 13,856 Catholics. The colony as planned and initiated was a genuine offshoot of the England of the Restoration or of the half century succeeding the accession of Charles II to the throne. A large majority of the people were one with the philosopher Locke in the conviction that an aristocratic element was necessary to curb an arbitrary sovereign and to serve as a bulwark against democratic innovating tendencies; or as Fox explained its function, "the balance which equalized and meliorated the forces of the two other extreme branches and gave stability and firmness

---

[3]*Southern Review*, May 1831.

INTRODUCTION

to the whole." Locke's Constitutions were rejected, but the Church Act incarnated its essence in the government, which was thenceforth to be modeled more closely after the one in the mother country; and it is to the persistence of this masterful, aristocratic spirit, with its marked political capacity, that one must look for the elucidation of anything political, regarded by outsiders as peculiar to South Carolina. Shaper in his *Sectionalism in South Carolina* finds in the economic system the causes of what seem to be eccentricities and McCrady states that the social order is the "outgrowth of her peculiar circumstances." And yet one may see a major cause in anterior times. The background of our religious and civil development is in England herself. The Puritans in New England, the Catholics in Maryland, the dissenters in upper Carolina and the Churchmen in Charles Town, show that their inherited characteristics were more potent than any environment. The negro and rice and cotton buttressed but no more created the aristocratic feature than the Alleghany range with its cool springs and bracing atmosphere breathed the democratic spirit into the people under its shadow. Indeed emigrants from a nation which seceded from the Catholic communion, and then while remaining under the same government seceded from one another and created governments within the government, must have brought to the new world a predisposition to antagonize arbitrary power, to nullify unjust laws and secede or revolt as occasion might prompt, and set up a government of their own. Being under an aristocratic regime, South Carolina, like the Quakers in the matter of dress, speech and religion, lagged behind the procession and found safety in resisting changes. Change meant self-effacement and the institution of slavery served so effectively as brakes to the wheels and as support of centripetal ideas, that the part played in ante-bellum times has caused it to be regarded a prime rather than a powerful subordinate factor. The city of Charleston has suffered from epidemics, fires, hurricanes, bombardments, and earthquakes. George Whitefield's comment on one of these disasters is still pertinent, "chastened but not changed!"

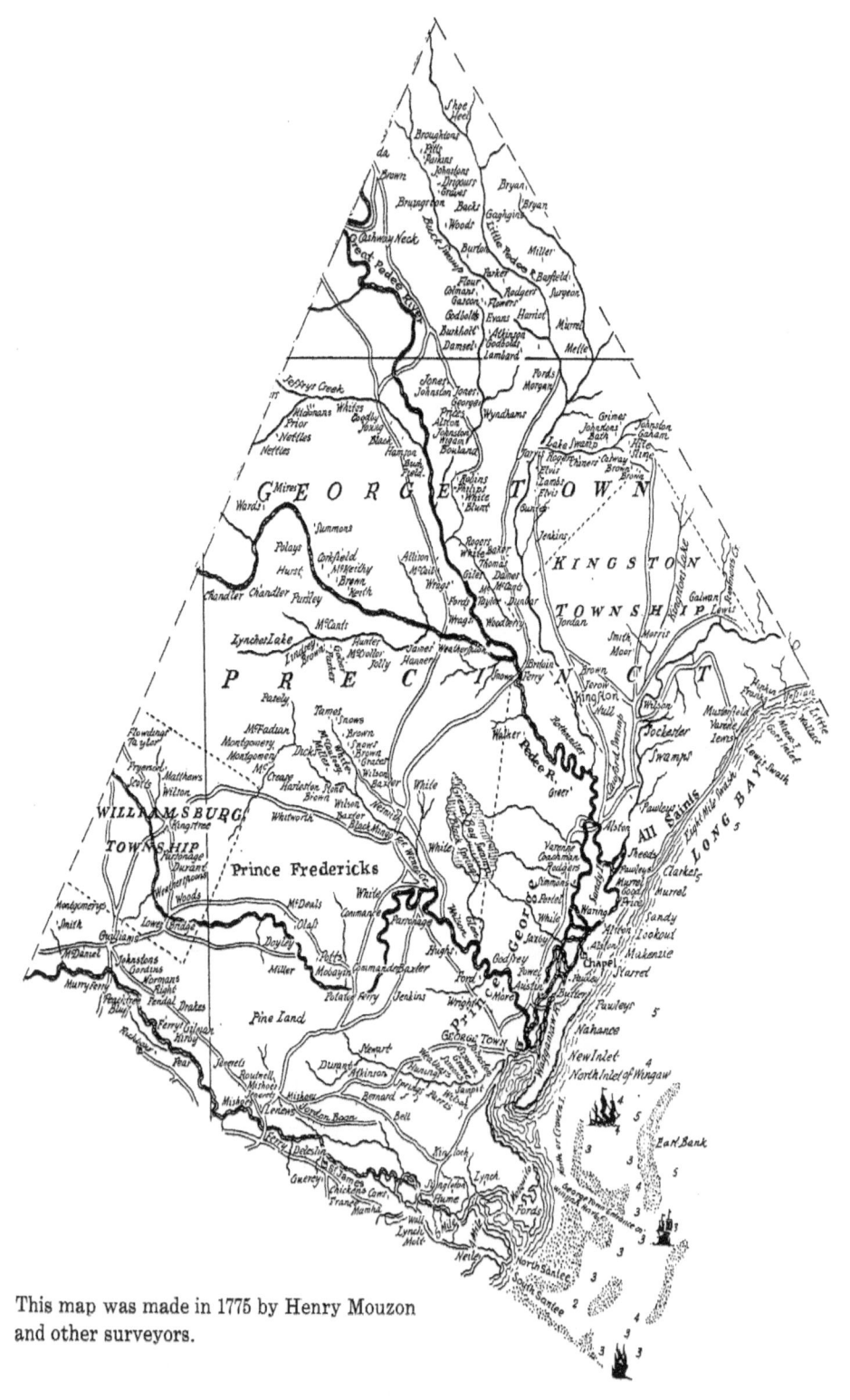

This map was made in 1775 by Henry Mouzon and other surveyors.

CHAPTER I

CROSSING THE SANTEE AND GOING UP THE WINYAW.
1700-1730.

Only a single homesteader has been definitely located north of the Santee at or before the beginning of the eighteenth century, January 1, 1701. Edmund Bellinger and John Bayly were made Landgraves in 1698, but years passed before parts of their baronies were laid out on the Santee and the Black. It is stated in a standard work[1] that Rev. Samuel Prioleau died on his farm on Black River in 1699, but it is a misprint apparently for Black River, near Goose Creek. It was in the last month of the century that Lawson went up the Santee and spent nights on both sides of the swollen river, finding shelter on the north side under the roof of Bartholomew Gaillard. There is also a verisimilitude in the tradition that the vessel, the *Rising Sun*, found about A. D. 1700 nobody on the Sampit except Indians.

As might have been expected, the first to cross over were the men who lived on the lower bank, fished in the stream and reconnoitered on the other side; but they were soon reinforced by merchants and capitalists, who had seen their plantations double in value. Among the first to go over in 1704 with warrants for land were Benjamin Schenckingh, George Montgomery, Patrick Stewart, Daniel McGregor, and Paul Bruneau. In July John Bell, Sr., John Bell, John Jeffries and John Sauso selected large tracts on the north branch of the Santee. John Jeffries took up 1300 acres and John Bell bought other tracts and made his home on the river. He was one of the first actual settlers in the new country and with his wife Martha were among the first members

---

[1]Howe's *History of the Presbyterian Church in South Carolina.*

of the parish church. In October, James Child reached the Winea, Indian name for the Black, prepared to run out 500 acres. He lived in St. John's Parish and became the founder of Childsbury, later Strawberry, and left in legacies the nucleus for the settlement of a school, chapel and cemetery. In December Col. Thomas Cary, John Cary and George Sterling secured each 500 acres on the Winea.

In 1705, George Montgomery, John Abraham Motte, Michael Pequott, Peter Stewart, John Sauso and Benjamin Schenckingh took up large tracts on the Santee. John Abraham Motte, a Huguenot, who held various responsible positions in the province, acting at this time as agent of John Perrie, Esq., went up the Winyaw with warrants for 3300 acres, to be surveyed in lots for John Perrie, Edward Perrie, and Madam Elizabeth Elliott. The Perrie tracts rested on the Sampit and on the Pedee and westward of them was Mrs. Elliott's tract. Motte's were north of Wehaw Creek and west of the Perrie tract. John Perrie's land became the site of Georgetown as will be seen. Aaron Screven early in the next year got a grant for 100 acres of land "on the uppermost bluff on the south side of the Black on the Winea" and another for 500 acres "on the Bluff below." The next reinforcements on the Black were Samuel Milner, William Furbush and Robert Screven, William Tarbiau and Richard Brusian. These were not far above the junction with the Pedee. The last three secured lands lying in a body. When groups of men got warrants on the same day, there was not unfrequently a relationship of some sort, ecclesiastical, social or industrial, which cannot always be made clear. The last group were probably dissenters. The Black was now becoming attractive to home-seekers. In 1707, Henry Bruneau went up stream "to the northward." Richard Nixon had his land surveyed on the lower part of the Black whence his numerous descendants appear to have spread to Williamsburg County. In 1708, Benjamin Schenckingh in behalf of himself and James Moore, got warrants for 1500 acres on the north side of the Santee. Schenchingh was "the beloved uncle" of Thomas Smith and James Moore was the brother-in-law, of the man of that name who was more prominent in the political scrambles of the time. Schenckingh and Moore were of the "Goose Creek Men" and it appears from the North Carolina Records that there was an intermarriage of the families, some of whom went to Cape Fear in 1725. Richard Brier got warrants for two tracts on the Black from Landgrave Smith, Daniel Huger an inland tract. On the Santee, Philip Gendron, Noah Serre, Peter and John Gaillard and John Bell, continued their raids on the public domain. Francis Courage took up land not far from Lenud's ferry. An act was passed by the Assembly prohibiting settlement north of the Santee and south of the Savannah, with a penalty of fifty pounds attached for non-observance. The object was to avoid the danger which was looming up on the Indian frontiers. The law was not in force a long time; for warrants continued to be issued. John Holland and John Stanyarne acquired lands butting easterly on the Pedee[2] and five on the Santee added to their possessions. Maurice Murphy purchased on the Black not far from Lane's Creek.

In 1710, Rev. William Screven took up two hundred acres butting southward on the Sampit. He also got possession of a part of the Motte-Perrie-Elliott land granted in 1705. Robert Screven who lived and died on James Island purchased 950 acres in the neighborhood, bounding to the northward on the Black, a part of which

---

[2]This is an early use of the name of the river already well known in 1709. Spelt Peedee, Pede, P. D., now Pee Dee.

is included today in Mr. C. P. Allston's[3] plantation known as Windsor. He also acquired 500 south of the Sampit opposite Georgetown. 1711 was a banner year. Twenty tracts were taken up. Lady Blake, Percival Pawley, John Allston, John Stanyarne, Thomas Diston, Jacob Staur and Samuel Wragg had extensive tracts run out on the Pee Dee, on the western side not far above its junction with the Black. The last three mentioned were residents of St. Andrew's Parish and were associated a few years later as Church Commissioners in St. George's. Waccamaw on the south side was encroached upon by Thomas Stocks, Dr. John Huthinson of Charles Town, John Clark, Michael Brewton, a captain of militia, James and Ann Howell, Anthony Shorey, grandfather of the Pawleys, William Porter, a Congregational minister, John Gaillard, Philip Gendron, Andrew Allen, Samuel Masters, an inn-keeper, and John W. Laws. John Green acquired 1000 acres on the Black and on a stream which bore his name and served in 1734 as a boundary line between the two parishes. The granting of a barony to Robert Daniel, Landgrave, was an event among these pioneers on the Winyaw. He transferred the titles immediately to Landgrave Thomas Smith for a consideration. This barony was on the west side of Winyaw Bay, two to eight miles from Georgetown.

About this time appeared a booklet in England with the title "Advice for Rich and Poor, a Dialogue between James Freeman, a Carolina Planter and Simon Question, a West-Coast Farmer." James Freeman was acting as agent of a large land holder who wanted indented servants to bind themselves for four or five years to cultivate his land. In order to get the ear of the people who were willing to emigrate, these questions and answers

---

[3]His demise occurred since the above was written.

were so arranged as to put all needed information in a form most easily understood. Question: What price may a man purchase a slave for at the best hand? An Indian man may cost 18 or 20 pounds, but a good negro is worth more than twice that sum. What sorts of money is current for payment, and what value is it in proportion to money here in England? We have passing as current amongst us Spanish money, pieces of different value, according to its weight, the smallest money that we have is called half a Ryall, in value with us, three pence three farthings, then a whole Ryall seven pence half penny, and double Ryall fifteen pence, all of which passes by tale, so does Dutch Dollars at five shillings and half dollars at $2\frac{1}{2}$ shillings and six pence, but all others, except milled money, go by weight, either silver or gold; the English Crown is there worth seven shillings and six pence, and other money, whether silver or gold, by weight or tale, is valued at near the same proportion in all our payments, we have also, of late, stamped bills of credit on the public, payable and current as money from hand to hand. These bills are of several values, and, at least, payable out of the public treasury of the country." A slave may die, objected the West Country farmer, and then all his money is lost! A man's slave will by his labor, pay for his cost in about 4 years at most, so, the remainder of his life, you have his labor free. If a man purchase cattle or horses, how can he be assured of their lives . . . We esteem their eating and wearing as little, for that raises on the plantation, and is little cost out of the pocket . . . A slave's work may be worth 25 or 30 pounds. There are some in the Country that make 1000 or 1500 pounds of rice a year which their slaves doth plant, hoe and manage for them . . . I never yet saw there, any man, woman or child, in the country, beg an alms, neither do I know any family so poor and in want but that, if a small gift of any kind of provisions was offered them, because 'twas supposed they could not subsist without such helps, they would refuse it, and scorn the acceptance thereof; for I fully affirm that a laborer and industrious man, being settled for himself, may, with his own labor and industry, maintain a wife and ten children, sufficient with corn, peas, rice, flesh, fish and fowl, without such assistance from Charity." A good negro man was valued at 45 pounds, an Indian woman 18, a cow and a calf one pound and fifteen shillings, two mares and a stallion at 40 pounds, a yoke of oxen five pounds, a canoe four pounds, a farrowing sow one pound. The cost of building in the woods was also given, etc. The inducement offered the indented servant was a promise to pay necessary wages for necessary clothing, to treat them friendly, to provide passage and a kind reception into his service. After the expiration of four years, fifty acres of good land was to be measured out as a plantation for the said servant, and on land so measured out a lease of not more than 99 nor less than 30 years was to be granted to the said servant, without pay of any fine for the same, provided of course he should prove faithful and honest in his undertakings."

The war in 1712 with the Tuscarora Indians made the year unfavorable for immigration, and in the next year there was some traffic in real estate by William Screven, Robert Sinclaire, John Shaw, and John Lane, whose first grants have not been found. John Lane is the first on record to have been visited by a minister and may therefore be regarded as the starting point of Prince Frederick's Church, in 1713. John Green, another leading man in the community and church, appears both from the records and from the *Gazette; and Country Journal* to have been one of the first settlers and of the first church of England communicants. He lived in Christ Church Parish but married on James Island and moved to the Black. When his wife Elizabeth died in 1766, it was stated that she came from Bermuda as a young girl "and removed to Winyaw several years before the Indian war of 1715."

John Lewis,[3] an Indian trader, sold his real estate to Alexander Widdicomb. He may have been the Indian dancing master in Craven County whom the Indians are said to have treated more liberally than it was the good fortune of missionaries to experience either among the red men or pale faces. In this year William Screven died and his estate passed to his widow and children, except 400 acres devised to William Forbush, who appears to have followed him from Maine, and 200 acres to Joseph Watters of Cape Fear. Robert Sinclaire settled on Black River not far from the mouth of Black Mingo. A few years later he lost a slave by drowning and found about twenty alligators around the body. 200 years make many changes. Even some of the streams then advertised as navigable will not now bear a batteau. An act was passed by the Assembly in 1714, appointing a packer for several ports, including Winyaw, to prevent "deceipts" in selling and buying beef, pork, tar, and turpentine. The enumerated articles of export, show that cattle and swine and products of the pine, rather than of the field, were the sources of ready money. When Whitefield came to America, about 1740, he travelled in the woods and made fires at night to ward off the wild beasts, which lurked around the camp. On his return to England, he eulogized the hospitality of the Americans and declared that one could travel "hundreds yea thousands of miles," looking up into tall green

---

[3]John Lewis was a moonshiner and was ordered to close shop.—Indian Book.

trees. On a part of the Screven tract, purchased through John Abraham Motte and on land adjoining, is still a large body of virgin pines, about 5000 acres, in which the woodman's axe has never resounded. Here one may in the twentieth century, stroll and meditate as William Screven and John Abraham Motte did over 200 years ago and calculate the possible value of the timber or slide into the reverent mood as he gazes at the tall sentinels with their evergreen crowns reaching heavenwards. It has already been stated that through John Abraham Motte, a large area of land, covering the site of Georgetown was deeded to John and Edward Perrie and their sister Madam Elizabeth Elliott in 1705. John Perrie left the lands in South Carolina to his daughter Mary in his will written in 1707. Mary married John Cleland and moved to South Carolina and eventually left the real estate to their only daughter Anna Isabella Cleland, who, in 1715, married Francis Kinloch,[4] sometime President of H. M. Council of South Carolina.

These lands passed to their two sons, Hon. Francis Kinloch, member of Congress, 1782, who had Kensing-

---

[4] Francis Kinloch died in 1767 at his plantation on the Santee, a successful indigo planter.

Most of the lands, says Mr. Langdon Cheves, were sold at various times. But a tract of 1800 acres of the lands, including Wehaw and Kensington was settled on their only child Anne Isabella Cleland, who married in 1751 Francis Kinloch, only son of Hon. James Kinloch, President of the Council, South Carolina. These settled parts passed to their two sons, Hon. Francis Kinloch (member of Congress 1782), who had Kensington, and Cleland Kinloch, Esqrs., who had the Wehaw part and added extensive pine lands to it. Mr. Cleland Kinloch left, by his will, these lands to his son Francis Kinloch, and daughter Harriott, who married Henry A. Middleton, Esqr., and ultimately inherited from her brother who died unmarried. Mr. Middleton became possessed of Kensington also, but later sold it to Mr. William Allston. After Mr. Middleton's death in 1887, the Wehaw lands came to three of his daughters, Mrs. Isabella Cheves and Misses Harriott and Alice Middleton. The property is therefore still in the descendants of the original grantee, in the female line."

ton, and Cleland Kinloch who had the Wehaw parts, and added extensive pine lands to it. Mr. Cleland Kinloch left by his will these lands to his son Francis Kinloch and daughter Harriott, who married Henry A. Middleton, Esq., and ultimately inherited from her brother who died unmarried. Mr. Middleton became possessed of Kensington also but later sold it to Mr. William Allston. After Mr. Middleton's death in 1887, the Wehaw lands came to three of his daughters, Mrs. Isabella Cheves and Misses Harriott and Alice Middleton. Thus the property bought in 1705 or part of it, is in the descendants of the original grantee, in the female line and that which attaches more than usual interest to it, is the seventeenth and eighteenth century aspect which it is thought to have preserved. In this year Samuel Wragg on the Pedee, John Shippey and Richard Wigg on the Black, Peter Robert, Bartholomew Gaillard, James LeGrand, Peter de St. Julien and Peter Perdrieu on the Santee made investments. Mary Sheppard's sale of land to Maurice Murphy on the Black is the only one noticed in that ill fated year. 1715, when the Yamassee war spread terror everywhere in the colony. All the males of military age were called out in this great crisis, but it does not appear that the homes above the Santee were molested. Bartholomew Gaillard and William Gibbon got warrants for land on the Santee; Thomas Smith, Jr. and John Hays, on the Black; Noah Serre sold land to Col. William Rhett on the same river. In 1718, John Green located land on a barony on the south side of the Black. George Smith, William Drake and Maurice Murphy were among the traders in this live community.

The afternoon of July 10th 1716 was spent by Indian Commissioners, Ralph Izard, John Barnwell and Charles Hill, in discourse with Landgrave Smith whose possessions above the Santee and his acquaintance with that part of the province made him a discreet counselor. He had been trading with the Indians through William Waties, and advised the Commissioners to open a factory at Winyaw and commended William Waties as one suited to be factor. They got Waties' consent to act, with William Waties, Jr. as security, and sent up a cargo worth about £1200 for the trade with the Waccamaws, etc. They chose for the factory the Casekey's house on the Black.

Waties advised that the factory be opened at Saukey as more convenient for trading with the Waccamaws and Pedees. £50 was allowed for building a log house 25 x 14 for the factory. About this time Bartholomew Gaillard informed the Commissioners that a part of the Winyaws were seated on the Santee and were found beneficial, as their presence awed the negroes. He prevailed on the Commissioners to open a factory at his house, but he had to carry back the goods as the Indians found moonshine traffic more profitable. A tanner named Rogers was found with 13 raw deer skins which ought to have passed through legitimate channels. These Indians were farming as well as hunting and decided to go back to their abodes because Mr. Weekly demanded 2 deer skins apiece as rent. Some of the Santee Indians treacherously fell upon and murdered some of Mr. Summer's family; but they were caught and convicted.

Corn was scarce and high and the Indians at the Winyaw were in want. Mr. Waties was directed to get what was needed from Mr. Webb at Seawee. There was none in town. At the close of the first six months, the factor sent down 202 dressed deer skins, 50 raw hides. He reported the "Indians to be peaceable, obedient and well affected to the government." Coats, blankets, shirts, knives, buttons, beads, tools and other things for building a house, besides guns and powder sparingly offered, were for sale. In 1717, Mr. Waties Sr., resigned and was succeeded by his assistant, Meredith Hughes.

Hughes had to report that the Indians were now buying little else than ammunition and that the whites complained that the Waccamaws were continuing to prey upon their cattle. Hides raw and dressed and slaves were the articles bartered for. And the slaves were to be branded not by iron but by powder or other means. The factory was at Andrew Collins' place at one time and 540 skins was the highest number sent down.

The factory was moved to Euavenee the great bluff, a name which seems to have passed through many changes until it reached Euhany. One such point was on the ocean near the Wineaus, but there are reasons why the Euhany, miles above Georgetown was the place selected. He was annoyed by illicit white traders whom the government pursued but could not repress. The Charraws however, and the weak Indian tribes found discretion the better part of valor in their intercourse with the Whites and kept at peace with them.

A nation on Winyaw river called Vocarnas not above 100 men took up the tomahawk in 1720 "but, the gentlemen have paid for it, said the governor, for there are sixty men, women and children of them killed and taken, and we have lost not one white man, only one Winyaw Indian and they now petition for peace which will be granted to them."

The following depicts the situation after the Indian wars had exhausted the resources of the colony:—

> Charlestowne, South Carolina in
> America June 26th 1718

Rev[d] Sir

....The Circumstances of this Country in Generall are very Dismal, wth regard both to Spiritual & temporal af-

fairs, as to yᵉ former we have few of yᵉ Clergy of the Province living but 5 besides myself; & these Under such hard conditions of Subsistance, by reason of the great fall of yᵉ value of our current Species.yᵗ I fear, wee yᵗ are here will be oblig'd to quit our Livings. ......
and as to yᵉ temporall concerns of yᵉ country they cannot be reduc'd to a lower Ebb, for yᵉ Merchants are quite Discouraged from venturing their effects abroad by reason of yᵉ Pyrates.....and what is as bad, our home trade wᵗʰ the Indians behind us is sunk to nothing & we are likely to lose our correspondence wᵗʰ yᵐ, the french & Spanish-Settlements being abler to secure their friendship wᵗʰ yᵗ barbarous people, (by large present yⁿ the people of this province, who are very much immers'd in Debt to their own people who assisted yᵐ in Carrying on the late warr wᵗʰ indians, A Calamitie wᵗʰ this settlement, (if itt shou'd Stand longer) will feell in a fatal manner

We are just now ye poorest Colony in all America, & have both before us at Sea & behind us at Land very appearances of ruine   Wᵐ Wye

....

     The Rev.Dr.Astey
        at the Bishop of London's house &c

It was a serious time in the province generally. In May 1718, Rev. Mr. Bull wrote to Bishop of London that

	£	s	d
Candles per lb. cost		7	6d
Soap " " "		5	
Wheaten flour per h.	4	10	
Butter, salt		5	
Fresh		7	
Mutton, veal or pork per lb.		1	3
Black worsted stockings		3	
Black Cloth 14 s. in Eng.	7	10	
Making coat, waistcoat & breeches	10		

South Carolina

The Assembly merged the part of Craven County above the Santee into the Parish of St. James Santee and allowed the Parish two representatives. A Barony containing 12,000 acres was granted to Lord Carteret, on the Waccamaw River southeast of Georgetown. In 1721, "The parts of Craven County, bounded to the south on Santee River, to the north of Cape Fear, to the east on the Atlantic, and to the westward as far as it shall be inhabited by his Majesty's subjects," were erected into the Parish of Prince George Winyaw, Craven County of which it was a part, was thus automatically extended so as to stretch out indefinitely in the westward direction. The Land office being closed in 1719, local trading became more active. In 1722 Meredith Hughes and Samuel Miller, William Brockington and Thomas Potts bought land twenty miles from Georgetown on the Black, in 1724 William Howell and Nathan Ford on the Waccamaw, William Swinton and Anthony White, north of the Sampit, were trading in real estate. In 1725, Alexander French, agent of John Bayly, disposed of tracts to Thomas Peacock, John White on the Black, Dougal McKichen near Black Mingo, Richard Wigg, and J. P. Summerhoff. Isaac Lesesne, John Lloyd, John Ridley were trading on Sampit, Robert Daniell and Richard Smith on the Waccamaw. In 1725, the land around Cape Fear being thrown open, a number of investors were attracted thither. The sons of Governor Moore of South Carolina, James and Maurice, being led into North Carolina in the Tuscarora war joined with some of their kindred and friends in settling the Cape Fear Country. In South Carolina the Moores belonged to the Goose Creek men, in North Carolina they were styled by Gov. Burrington "the pestiverous Moore family." In 1729, William Allston bought on the Waccamaw. John Lane and Meredith Hughes, bought near the Prince

Fredrick Church. The Smiths too numerous to classify and William Waties were among the purchasers in the closing of the decade. There were seventy families in the parish in 1727. Isaac Lesesne in March 1728 got 500 acres bordering on Richard Smith and Robert Daniell, below the Sampit. (There were parts of baronies above and near the Sampit, also on the south side of the Black and on Peter's Creek and Black Mingo). "There is not extant in this province," said Henry McCullough, Esq. in 1742, "any correct or regular account of the registry or other memorials of the lands surveyed, laid out or granted under the authority of the late Lords Proprietors." It is probable that John Thompson, Daniel Shaw, Anthony Atkinson, Benjamin Avant, Benjamin Roberts, Joseph Port and Thomas Jenkins, nearly all of whom came into the space between the Sampit and the Black, or north of the Black, got their lands either from the agents of the Landgraves or in some way not now manifest. The alleged land frauds do not appear to have been committed in this part of the province. There were no land taxes after 1725 and before 1731. In the last named year, it transpired that 290,556 acres had been granted in excess of what had been granted in 1720 when the taxpayers in the whole province numbered 1305 and their possessions amounted to 1,163,319 acres and 11,868 slaves, being an average of less than 100 acres to one slave. Out of the 1305 Landowners, 42 were credited with 117,274 acres and 584 slaves in Craven County, an average of 14 slaves and of 2792 acres. One of 31 of the taxpayers were in Craven County, one slave in about 20 was owned there. The baronies would make the average of acres large, but they were not improved and settled. George Hunter, Surveyor and later Surveyor General, says in his map of 1730 that not more than five families were above the

Santee "about 1712." The number of tax payers placed at 42 and the number of families above the Santee about 1712 at 5 appear to be under-estimates; but it must be admitted that the number of purchasers was more numerous than the actual settlers for a long time. The dwellers on the south side of the Santee invested early on the north side and there is no way to decide when they began to change their residences. There were also merchants of Charleston who invested on all the rivers and in some of the first towns laid out. At least 100 warrants for land, granted in this period, have been found besides those which have escaped notice or have been lost, at the close of which in 1730, George Hunter made the militia company at Georgetown number 170.

The Huguenots Philip Gendron, the Gaillards, Horrys and Noah Serre appeared to be thrifty amidst many that were less ambitious. Noah Serre was a man of some note, who served this parish in the Assembly and in his church. He bought on the Santee, Black and left a less noted son bearing his name. John Gaillard died early in the century and left his widow Mary Esther a valuable estate. She married James Kinloch who became president of the Council. He was living on the Santee when he lost his promising son, James Kinloch, just after his return from touring Europe. Jacob Satur and Benjamin Schinckingh were wealthy merchants of Charles Town who chose to invest in lands above the Santee. Both of them died about 1733. Maurice Murphy came into the light in 1709 as a purchaser on the Black. He is classed as one of four brothers, but he was probably an uncle of the other three who settled afterwards on the Pee Dee, and became influential citizens. The father was named Moses who in his will mentions only Moses, Michael and Malachi. Maurice died at an advanced age on the Pee Dee in 1757.

Percival Pawley had been a mariner, lived in Berkeley County but invested in the Winyaw and left his property to his sons, George, Percival and Anthony and daughters, Susannah and Anne. The Screven family in South Carolina was a large and honorable one, all of which appear to be descended from William Screven who arrived in the colony in the last quarter of the seventeenth century, being one of the first to come with an organized congregation to Charles Town. In consequence of his banishment from Maine, he became the first pastor of a Baptist Church in South Carolina and continued in that relation till the close of 1706. He then retired to his farm near Jameston, the town laid out on the Santee for the Huguenots. Here, in 1707, he decided to return to Charles Town and act as supply to the church left vacant by the death of his successor. So great was the scarcity of ministers in England and New England that a church in Boston also invited him to become its pastor. When relieved of this last trust, he moved to Winyaw and purchased land about 1709, and later bought, as it is supposed through John Abraham Motte, a part of the Perrie tract, now the site of Georgetown. Here he died in 1713 and left a considerable estate to his family and two friends. Some earlier writers made Mr. Screven the founder of Georgetown. But the honor of founding that town belongs to his youngest son Elisha who had the first lots laid out in 1729[5]. Mr. Screven lived in an obscure period, but as the rays of the sun are some times penciled on the western sky after sunset, so after the lapse of more than 200 years, Mr. Screven's friction with the Magistrate in Maine, his leadership of a congregation in South Carolina which he styled "Anti-Pedobaptist" and his transactions in real estate, all con-

---

[5] See George Hunter's map, published by A. S. Sally, Jr.

vergent, point to him as a man of more than ordinary worth. Little is known of him in his private life, but a line of worthy descendants to the third and fourth generation is a reminder that the source is always higher than the stream. Aaron, Robert, Elisha and his grandson William were the early ones out of perhaps fifteen children who owned land in Craven County. His grave is still pointed out in Georgetown on the west side of Prince Street near the court house, in part of lot 66. According to the deed and plat which is yet in existance, it has never been conveyed to another.

NOTE: The literature which touch upon Rev. Wm. Screven's Life are Backus' History of New England Baptists, Morgan Edwards' Manuscript History, 1772, Richard Furman's Answers to Dr. Ramsay's 7 Questions in 1807, given by his daughter, Miss Catherine to the Charleston Library Society, Dr. Basil Manly's Discourses, 1832, The History of the First Baptist Church, 1882 and The S. C. Historical and Genealogical Magazine. The last mentioned see Vol. IX, 87, 88, 230, 231 and Vol. XVI, 93.

CHAPTER II
1729-1732

The Lords Proprietors gave place nominally to the King, but practically to the Board of Trade in England, which served as eyes to the King. To them were intrusted the general management of all the colonies, the nomination of members to the Council and other provincial officials, subject to the King's approval. The Board held the reins and tried gently to mould the colonies according to one and the same imperial pattern. The first aim was to make the colonies profitable to the mother country as producers of what was not made but needed at home; and also as a market for English manufactures. Because of its climate, products and necessities, the colony at Charles Town fitted well into the scheme of the Board. Under its general supervision, each colony grew up in isolation, yet all of them were curbed, shaped and moulded by the same laws, by repealing or disallowing those considered repugnant to the laws of England or to the unwritten interests of merchants and manufacturers. Besides these commercial interests the Board had a corresponding supervision of the churches and of the great financial and moral problem, the care of the poor, both of which left an abiding impression in the state. As the care of all the colonies rested upon the Board, there was a need of a practical statesmanship in dealing with the jealous, independent spirit of the colonies and in preparing for eventualities with the Spanish and French neighbors and the Indians under their influence. Then as now the English were slow to face unpleasant facts, but energetic and pertinacious, when once aroused. To keep the peace with the Indians, while emigrants were being sent over to fill the inland sections, was a duty as well as a problem not to be deferred in its judicious handling. An agent was sent to the Cherokees who persuaded them to become subjects of Great Britain and to send six of their number to visit the great King.

The first royal governor, Robert Johnson, came to Charles Town with these returning Indians and began his term of office with a wise council, which soon established public confidence and unanimity among themselves; but some of his wisest planning had been done previous to his embarkation to America. The favors granted the colony in respect to quit rents and the shipment of rice and hemp as well as the activity in laying out townships can be traced directly back to his promptings. In 1729 he offered some proposals to the King for the better settling of South Carolina which after some modifications were adopted:[1]

1. That His Majesty be pleased to grant 200,000 acres of land for Townships, three on Savannah, one on Ponpon, two on Santee, one on Wateree, one on Black river, one on Pee Dee and one on Waccamaw, and that no person be allowed more than one lot in the said Townships and that the said person be a resident, and that each of these townships have the privilege of sending one or two members duly qualified to represent them in the Assembly.

2. That all lands outside of these townships pay 2-6 proclamation money per annum and that no person hereafter be allowed to take up more than 640 acres in these townships and that the land revert to the King unless it be settled within two years.

3. That no person possessed of any land in South Carolina be allowed to take up any more unless the said person settles it within one year.

4. That all lands on any navigable river, creeks, lakes, bays or seas do not exceed $\frac{1}{4}$ part in front, excepting

---

[1] The Council in South Carolina, it appears, made these proposals for Governor Johnson, not yet arrived.

that the townships which shall be laid out in the advantageous manner that's possible for the inhabitants of said townships.

5. That no person be allowed to take up any lands on any of the said rivers till the said townships be laid out and that these townships be laid out immediately.

6. That no person possessed of grants of large tracts of land, by the late Lords Proprietors, be allowed to take up more than 640 acres by virtue of such grant within ten miles of these townships.

7. That all foreigners as well as his Majesty's subjects be allowed reasonable quantity of lands and have the same privilege of voting for assemblymen as if born in any of His Majesty's dominions.

"The proposed townships were to contain 20,000 acres, laid out in square tracts, in the centre of which were to be little towns of 250 lots and a common.

Six months after these proposals had been received, instructions from the King embodying them with slight modifications, were sent to the Governor. One paragraph in the instructions beginning with "Whereas it has been found by long experience in our province of New Hampshire and Massachusetts Bay, that ye settling of such persons as were disposed to become planters there in townships doth redound very much to their advantage, not only with respect to ye assistance they have been able to afford each other in their civil concerns, but likewise with regard to the security of ye neighboring Indians," was a translation of Council's experience in South Carolina into the experience of the Board of Trade, which held the reins over all the colonies. One writer[2] draws the conclusion that the success of the township in New England caused it to be

---

[2]Shaper's Sectionalism in South Carolina, p. 265.

tried in South Carolina. But the authorities gave it a different reason, "Newcomers should be encouraged to settle in townships on the frontier and to fortify and defend themselves in their small towns," and they based this opinion not on the experience in other colonies but upon the colony's history in the Indian wars and the dangers still to be feared from the French, Spaniards and Indians. The language of the Board of Trade which had a general acquaintance with all the colonies must be considered as an endorsement and amplification of the Council's reasons rather than an effort to introduce the township system of New England.[3] Governor Johnson was the moving spirit in this renewed activity, though current histories give the credit to the King. The townships of Williamsburg, Queensborough and Kingston, with which our narrative is concerned, existed first in his mind; and in another way he was serving the Pee Dee inhabitants especially.

The Tuscarora Indians of North Carolina, who had ceased to murder the whites, made occasional excursions down the Waccamaw, and killed or took away friendly Indians residing in the heart of the settlement. Gov. Johnson, deciding to act in a spirited manner with this remnant of Indians, sent Capt. Watis with a letter to Gov. Burrington, who assembled the Indian head men for a conference with Capt. Watis. He questioned them about the slave taken from Summerhoof's, three miles west of Georgetown, Mr. Pawley's cattle and horse and Mr. Bell's clothes taken out of the wash in the sight of persons, and they admitted the mischief was done as he

---

[3] In the midst of Indian depredations one Stephen Crell of Saxe Gotha advised Gov. Glenn that the close settling of a number of people on the frontiers, was the best means of defending the country against the encroachments of the Indians, and mentioned the lands lately purchased about Ninety Six as being fertile and well adapted to close settlement.

narrated but claimed that it was done by the Senecas and not by themselves. When it was demanded of them to restore or pay for the stolen goods, emphasized with threats about what would be done if they did not, they withdrew and after consideration reported that they could not be unanimous in their voting to restore the things stolen, but they would promise to make no more expeditions in that direction, and thus they parted as enemies.

With respect to the line between North Carolina and South Carolina, Gov. Burrington of North Carolina entertained some decided convictions. He thought that the Pee Dee River was the line made by nature and could be adopted without expense or danger; but when summoned to appear before the Board of Trade which desired to settle the controversy (about the line) and put a stop to tax-dodging, he laid before that body Mosely's map of Cape Fear and Waccamaw rivers and advocated the Waccamaw as the boundary. Gov. Johnson favored the resolution that a line should be run, beginning at the sea, 30 miles distant from the mouth of Cape Fear on the southward side thereof keeping the same distance from the said river as the course thereof runs to the main source or head thereof. With this understanding the question was amicably settled, but when instructions came, Governor Johnson was surprised to find in them, "But if Waccamaw lies within 30 miles of Cape Fear river, then that river to be the boundary from the sea to the head thereof and from thence the distance parallel from Cape Fear river to the head thereof." Gov. Burrington at once advertised in Timothy's Gazette that "all land on the north side of Waccamaw is by the King's instructions, in the North Carolina government and whoever has a mind to take up land there, must take out the grants in North Carolina." Gov. Johnson replied with a counter proclamation stating what had taken place in the presence of the Board of Trade when both governors had been summoned before them and saw no explanation in the change made in their agreement unless the word "mouth" in the phrase "If the mouth of the Waccamaw" had been inadvertently omitted in the instructions. "We have a great settlement (at Winyaw) said Gov. Johnson, and a collector of customs, who can't prevent illegal trading if that be. An order from the Board caused Commissioners from each province to be appointed to attend the matter. These Commissioners appointed by the two colonies met and agreed that a due west line should be run from Cape Fear along the sea coast for 30 miles, and from thence proceed north-west to the 35th degree of North latitude and if the line touched the Pee Dee River before reaching the 35th degree, then they were to make an offset at five miles distant from the Pee Dee and proceed up the river till they reached that latitude and from thence they were to proceed due west until they came to Catawba town, but if the town should be to the northward of the line, they were to make an offset around the town so as to leave it in the South government. A copy of this agreement, duly signed and sealed was deposited in the Secretary's office in each province. They began to run the line May 1, 1735 and proceeded 30 miles west of the Cape Fear which fell 10 poles of the mouth of Little River, and then went north-west to the country road and set up stakes there for the boundary of the two provinces and then separated, agreeing under hand and seal to meet again on the 18th of September, and if either party failed in coming the other was to continue the line, and it was to be binding on both. In September the North Carolina Commissioners attended and ran the line about

70 miles. The South Carolina Commissioners arrived in October and followed the line about 40 miles and finding the work right so far sent a draught to the Lords of Trade. A deputy surveyor, however, took the 35th parallel and set up a mark which was from that date deemed to be boundary at that place.[4] The cause of the conduct of the South Carolina Commissioners, as found in the North Carolina records, was their not being paid for their trouble. It should have been stated "Not being adequately paid." Seven weeks were spent in making the line through uninhabited woods, crossing rivers and creeks and other almost impassable places; and they ceased only when it was difficult and dangerous to go forward or to retrace their steps. So at least it was reported by the surveyors, Pawley and Abercrombie, when they were petitioning the government for reimbursement, the cost having been £250 instead of £50 apportioned for defraying the expenses of the survey. In 1737 the line was extended to a stake in a meadow supposed to be at the 35th parallel of north latitude. By an error in the calculation the line fell short by 11 or 12 miles, as was afterwards discovered. This error, never corrected, cost the state about 600,000 acres but in the running of the later lines, a subject outside the compass of the present work, a larger acreage above the 35th degree of north latitude compensated in part for it.

---

[4]This is the version of the running of the line found in the Saunders Records of North Carolina, Vol. V, XXXVII.

CHAPTER III

THE FOUNDING OF GEORGETOWN

The first applicants for land warrants in Craven County, when the land office was opened in 1731, would have been valuable accessions to any country but some of them never became actual settlers. The individual was actuated like the governments. Spain, France and England were planning to hold or get hold of as much of the new world as possible and in the same spirit enterprising men saw the opportunity for getting control of more and better land. Conspicuous among these far sighted men were Thomas Lynch, who was easily foremost outside of the Landgraves, in the amount of land acquired. He was living below the Santee when he purchased during 1732-3, eight thousand one hundred acres, between the branches of the Santee and adjoining the Smith barony. He was probably led in this direction by the trend of his neighbors northward. He was followed by John Vanderhorst who secured 500 acres in the neighborhood. It was perhaps this family which furnished the mother of the more celebrated son of Revolutionary fame, Thomas Lynch. Col. Lynch found a number of men settled or having land in their possession in advance of his large investments. These were Thomas Jones, Thomas Threadcraft, Anthony Simmons, a freedman, William Rae, Philip Cheever, Charles Hill, Noah Serre, John Brunston, John Pritchard, Francis Britton, Joseph Wragg, Ralph Jirman, Robert Stewart, Mrs. Martha Bell, James Higgins, Phineas Spry, Edward Weekley, Daniel Horry, Fork Island, Susanna Mayrant and Isaac Mazyck. Mrs. Martha Bell represented one of the families longest in possession of a home in the new country. Francis Britton had been in Colleton

County in the preceding century and was probably turned northward to the lands free from Indian depredations. Three or four young Brittons, presumably his sons, were at the first of this period living north of the Sampit in a few miles of Georgetown and before its close they had gone up the Pee Dee and made new settlements. Joseph Wragg, merchant of Charleston, member of the Council, owned 2500 acres north of the Santee. It contained 700 acres of good rice land. Near Col. Lynch's, Charles Hill had secured on Wasso Creek 500 acres. He was a member of the Council in 1717 and Secretary of the province, when the Lords Proprietors were overthrown.

Others who came in or invested in adjacent plantations were Capt. Richard Smith, on whose 1800 acres was a good dwelling which had a fine view of ships moving down or up the Winyaw and out of the Santee; Thomas Schoolcraft, John Achison on Six Mile Creek, Mrs. Susan Mayrant, who bordered on Daniel Horry with his large tract in the forks of the Santees; William Drake opposite Malassa Creek and 500 acres on Charles Hart.

On the Wadbaccan or, as it is now called, the Wadmacon were the Guerrys, James, Peter, Daniel and Thomas. Also Isaac DuBose, Isaac LeGrand, Peter Robert, Abraham Satur, Isaac Chaudon, Noah Serre, Ralph Izard, William Satur, John Summers, Elias Horry, Anthony Bonneau, Robert Brown, John DuBose, Theodore Gaillard, William Lewis and John Deliesseline. Some of these were adding to land already improved. The others were coming in. Isaac DuBose bordered northward on glebe land, Andrew Rembert rested southward on the same. This was on the Santee and it was probably land held in vain in anticipation of a church.

A chapel was built in 1767 at Murray's Old Field. Samuel Clegg, Theodore Gourdine, Samuel Newman, William Michau, and J. Perrot, church commissioners.

On Cedar Creek, Paul Mazyck, Abraham Bruneau, Nicholas LeNud, Andrew Rembert, Andrew Delorillet, Daniel Williams, Peter Mazyck, James Kinloch, and John Barnet found and appropriated vacant lands. James Robert lived on this creek 17 miles of Georgetown. The great preponderance of French names on these two creeks is what might be expected as an overflow from St. James Santee.

On Wittee Creek and lake, William Drake, Frances Herres, George Brown, Francis Pearce, Samuel Wigfall and Daniel Gibson possessed themselves of more or less ample tracts. Also Isaac Chardon, William Waties, Abraham Michau, Edward Thomas, Elias Ball, Daniel Williams. At or near Mt. Hope near the line of Williamsburg and near the Santee, William Cleiland, Richard Butler, Richard Rotan, Henry Toomer and Joseph Cantey were the first in securing land in this period.

In November 1726, the representatives of Winyaw Parish, Richard Smith and James Nichol, united with the vestry and church wardens in a letter to Governor Nicholson: "Your Excellency having consented that instructions should be given to messengers Yonge and Lloyd, when they went to Great Britain, agents to solicit that a port of entry might be made in our parish, it being so highly reasonable, we pray that when your Excellency's tho'ts are employed in the service of this country that you will be so good as to remember so important an affair. You will be pleased to remember we are at least 100 miles from Charles Town, where we are obliged to carry our goods to market and to cross several large and dangerous sounds which subject our industry to many great hazards and occasions us to pay great and unreasonable prices for freight which abates greatly the profit of our labor and pains. And we presume there is as much if not more reason that we should have a port than Port Royal on this account, that our inhabitants are more numerous there being now settled upon several rivers in Prince George Parish, at least 100 families, many of which are good settlers and have large gangs of negroes and make large quantities of produce."

In George Hunter's map, 1730, further information is found: "At the Winneaw Bar I sounded the channel and at low neap tides found 10 foot water. At high water spring tides there rise $16\frac{1}{2}$ feet and the same water has at Georgetown in Sampit creek 4 fathoms. Georgetown was laid out in lots and sold last year (1729) to people who are obliged to build a house in 15 months." This is corroborated by Elias Horry who advertised lot 23, the one next to Georgetown Bank and offered "proper timber and cypress boards for building a house 30 x 20, and by a visitor in February 1734 who saw more houses than families. In November 1732, the Gazette announced that Georgetown has been made a port of entry.

William Swinton was at this time acting as naval officer at Georgetown, a reference to whom is found in the following:

Charles Town
May 20, 1734

My Lord

On my visitation of the port of Georgetown, Winyaw, I found the quarterly accounts by my predecessor had not been duly returned, so immediately ordered Mr. William Swinton (whom I have appointed my deputy at that port) to make out the same, which he having performed to Lady day last, I now humbly transmit to your Lordships and beg leave to assure you they shall for the future regularly come with those of the port of Charles Town, and am with all submission

My Lords
JAS. FOX.
Naval Officer, S. C.

In the third quarter of the year 1733, there were imported into Georgetown "European goods" from London, 20,000 brick, some earthen ware and one hogshead of rum from Boston, ten hogsheads from Antigua. In another ship from Boston came three hogsheads and eight tierces of rum, "two boxes of axes, six iron pots, twelve caggs of spirits." Two of the six vessels entered with ballast only, three of them were armed and the crews consisted of five to eight men. The six vessels carried out cargoes which aggregated two barrels of rice, 1977 barrels of pitch, 278 barrels of tar, 999 barrels of turpentine, three tons of brazilletto wood and one barrel of skins. In the last quarter nothing was imported, but the going out vessels carried eight barrels of rice, 1177 barrels of pitch, 300 barrels of tar, 87 barrels of turpentine and one chest of skins. Six vessels brought into Georgetown the first quarter of 1734, five barrels of sugar, two hogsheads of molasses, six barrels of flour, ten hogsheads of rum, one pipe of Madeira wine and dry goods per certificate from Charles Town. In the second quarter, 10 barrels of sugar, 17 hogsheads and 3 tierces of rum, and one cask of lime juice, all from Barbadoes; also from New London, two hogsheads of fish, 35 sheep, 10 horses and parcel of lumber. Providence sent some fruit in the sloop *Defiance*. In the third quarter, one hogshead of sugar, 7 barrels of the same, one hogshead of molasses, 35 barrels of flour, 2 barrels bread, six hogsheads and 4 tierces of rum, 50 barrels of rice, two hogsheads of deer skins, 29½ tons of Brazeletto wood, 28 barrels of pitch, 50 barrels of corn, one barrel of pork, one hogshead of platt, two casks of Madeira wine, parcel of drygoods and 77 barrels of turpentine.

Joseph Wragg, Othniel Beale, and Gabriel Manigault of Charles Town were among the owners of vessels. In the last quarter, 6 hogsheads of rum, two boxes of soap, four of candles, one dozen axes, came in from Philadelphia, ten hogsheads of salt, parcel of lumber, powder, shot, fish, iron potts from Boston. The exports of 1734 were 374 barrels of rice, 4674 barrels of pitch, 1092 of tar, 2262 barrels of turpentine, 1 hogshead of platt, 51 steer hides and 1 calf skin, one barrel of foreign sugar, parcel of Cedar, parcel of staves, some dry goods and one parcel of spirits from Charles Town.

Early in 1735, Elisha Screven, who had been advertising and selling lots in Georgetown, turned over to George Pawley, William Swinton and Daniel Laroche, trustees, all the lots unsold or not already designated for specific public or religious purposes, reserving for himself out of the sale of each lot a specific sum, and sums to be increased after the expiration of five and twelve years. These trustees were live men and they no doubt would have expedited the sale of lots by advertising and personal efforts, had not the arrival of John Cleland arrested the progress of their work. He was the husband of Mary Perrie, the heir to the Perrie lands owned in America. He seems to have found little difficulty in establishing a prior claim to the land where Georgetown was rising which had come into the hands of Rev. William Screven, through John Abraham Motte[1] who in 1710 "entered into an agreement with 'William Screven, the elder of Craven County,' to deliver in six months to him a deed of conveyance of the land at Winyaw or 1500 acres of them' from John Perrie of London." Over twenty years had passed since William Screven had taken possession of the Perrie tract and it had been willed twice and laid out into a town and lots sold before the validity of the titles was questioned. Mr. Cleland, however, seems to have acted with prudence, and to have recognized that something was due Elisha Screven whose compensations in lots, at least, four of them still in the heart of the town, was not inconsiderable. It worked a hardship on those who had purchased lots, as each owner was required to pay about $12.50 or forfeit his lot. The impression had gone abroad that there was a future for the new town as it was a port of entry and an outlet for all the products which were to come down the rivers. Lots were readily disposed of to men on the Santee, Black, Pee Dee, Waccamaw, including Kingston, and to some from Charles Town. An act was passed by the Assembly for the laying out of bouys, for erecting and supplying beacons or land marks near the bar of the harbor of Georgetown and for building pilot boats and for settling the pilotage of the said harbor.[2]

The Pee Dee and the Waccamaw are not ten miles apart twenty-five miles above Georgetown. The latter river runs nearly parallel with the ocean and is two miles of it at one point. About thirty miles up the Pee Dee, Bull Creek, an effluent about ten miles long, unites with the Waccamaw. These two rivers are connected by other

---
[1] Motte's death in 1711 may account for the entanglement.
[2] For fuller account of the founding of Georgetown, see Vol. IX, South Carolina Historical and Genealogical Magazine.

streams which form islands: Little Bull Creek 25 miles from Georgetown, the Thoroughfare or Wando, 18 miles, Squirrel Creek 15, Schooner Creek 13 and Jericho Creek 8 miles above Georgetown. The Thoroughfare or Wando was at first an attraction to new comers. Landgrave Thomas Smith had a large tract on the South side on or near both rivers. John Allston had land above and below butting easterly on the Waccamaw, William Waties, Zachariah Villeponteaux were near by. On the Pee Dee end of the stream William Swinton and south of him, James Gordon, an attorney, had lands. North of it were William and Hugh Swinton. Mrs. Elizabeth Pamur, Thomas Brown, William Poole, brother-in-law of William Allston, were also owners of land somewhere on the stream only 6 miles long. Percival Pawley was the first to invade Bull Island and take up land on its southern extremity to be followed by Andrew Broughton and Rev. Daniel Dwight. Squirrel Creek was another boundary mentioned. William Allston had the land south of it butting on the Waccamaw and south of him was Percival Pawley's. James La Bruce had the land east of Pee Dee and north of this creek, east of whom was George Pawley. Schooner Creek, supposed to be Beaver Creek, a short stream, furnished the boundary line, for Thomas Blythe, one of his tracts being a part of an island with Andrew Broughton as neighboring owner. The latter owned a number of tracts and his brother-in-law, Rev. Daniel Dwight, adjoined him, and John De La Consieliere. Somewhere adjoining one of John Allston's tracts were the plantations of Samuel Prioleau, Major Pawley and James La Bruce. Charles Hart and Peter Allston were also in this locality. The former, once the Secretary of the Province, a senator and chief justice, got warrants for 3700 acres.

On the eastern side of the Waccamaw and on the northern line of the Carteret barony rested the places of Anthony and George Pawley, James and John La Bruce, Samuel Masters, John Vanderhorst and James Gadsden, near whom were lands belonging to James Abercrombie, Attorney-general of the province, William Balloon, William Arnold and Thomas Clark.

On the Long Bay were the large areas owned by Colonel George Lucas, father of Miss Elizabeth Lucas, Isaac Lewis, who helped to defeat the pirate Stede Bonnet, Adam Stewart, Othaniel Beale, Col. George Benison, Stephen Peake, William Catchpole and on the upper swash of that bay were Alexander Campbell, William Drake, Benjamin Godwin. On Collins Creek, 21 miles from Georgetown, on the eastern side, Thomas Boone took up 1000 acres in the neck between it and the Waccamaw, Daniel Green a merchant, George Smith, John Daniel, John Bonhoste, Mrs. Sarah Raven, and John Sanders were adjacent. John Allston and William Allston looked at through nearly two centuries appear as the most striking personalities among those who made their homes in this place of streams. These brothers and William Waties were neighbors in Berkeley, not far from Irish Town (South Carolina Historical Magazine, Vol. XIII, Nov. 1, p. 8) and their purchases were interlocked as they extended from the Pee Dee to the ocean. John Allston took up 3450 acres in 9 tracts. They were near the Pee Dee, on both sides of the Waccamaw and on three or four streams. William Allston got warrants for ten tracts, 3484 acres, William Waties acquired 4805 acres in this same period some of which was west of the Pee Dee, or north of the Santee. It is pretty clear by their absence from the vestries of the churches that these men lived at homes distant from Georgetown. They were not of the church on the Black nor, it seems, of the Prince George Winyaw.

Laurel Hill, 19 miles distant was perhaps the home of William Waties; for in some unrecorded year, Robert Daniell the Landgrave, was granted 1300 acres on the Waccamaw, from him it passed to Thomas Smith, and by him it was conveyed to Samuel Eveleigh who conveyed it to William Waties in 1729. William Allston owned the land south of Laurel Hill. Toward the close of his life, William Waties offered for sale two improved tracts, one 18 miles from Georgetown, open to the sea, another 15 miles, and a third on the great sand island which contained some fine rice land.

A few purchasers located or invested on Little River: Thomas Ash, Samuel Masters, John Daniel and William Poole.

A young gentleman from London set out from Charles Town on the 10th of June 1734 with 13 companions and reached Mr. More's on Goose Creek. "The next night we reached Capt. Screen's, at French Santee, and the third reached Wineaw ferry, which is about one hundred miles from Charles Town. There we lay that night, and there being so many of us, it was the next day before we all crossed the ferry. We dined there at one Mr. Master's on the fens on the other side, and the same night reached one Muenly, who keeps another tavern on the road, about 22 miles from Masters.[3] The next morning at five we left his house, and about six came on the long bay, the tide just serving for us to get over the swashes. We had 25 miles farther to ride on the bay or sea-shore, and five miles before we came within sight of a house, so that we were obliged to ride gently for fear of our horses." Four of the horses "gave out" before they reached Ash's on Little River. On his return

---

[3]Samuel Masters, who must be meant here, owned land north of the barony, on Little River, and at least six other tracts. This account shows how the tavern was an essential part of the backwoods.

from Cape Fear, the young gentleman put up at Ash's again where he arrived in the afternoon. "At seven in the next morning, said he, I left his house and by eight reached the Long Bay—by eleven reached Bulloons or the end of the bay; by eight I reached Murrels where I met with plenty of rum, sugar and lime juice, and a good pasture for my horse, but no corn. The next morning set out from thence and by noon reached Masters' or Winneau ferry; but the ferry-boat being gone adrift, could not get over till near ten at night, after I had supped upon a wild turkey. The next morning I set out from Shingleton's on the ferry on the other side and the same night reached Daubuz... I reached Witton's by noon; the same night I reached Moore's in Goose Creek and the next I arrived at Charleston on the 7th of August, where I remained till the 23rd of November, when I set said for England and arrived safe in London on the 3rd of January 1734-35."

Some of the warrants issued in this period were for land in Kingston Township, laid out in that year. Among the most important of those who took up Kingston land were James Bodenhop, Thomas Brown, Robert Lorimer, Hugh Campbell, Thomas Blythe, Henry Christie, John Daniel, Edward Thomas, Rev. Daniel Dwight, Thomas Farewell, Hon. George Lucas, William Price, Rev. William Porter, Penelope Reynolds whose husband died before the deed was delivered, Alexander Skene, who had grants for 2000 acres, William Trinker and Alexander Wells. At this point the right of way is given to a party who went up to Kingston before the town was laid out. "Georgetown," said the visitor who was there in February 1734, "is a very plesant place ... the town is laid out very regular, but at present there are a great many more houses than inhabitants; but do believe it will not be long ere it is thoroughly settled; it being a place that has a very good prospect for trade, though I confess the land to the southward is much preferable, only in this place they say is not much danger in case of an Indian war, of which the people to the south is in daily fear. We staid there two days and on the 7th of February set out thence in a large canoe, leaving our horses behind, with an intent to take a view of the land... same night we reached Mr. Gordon's on P. D. where we slept; it was about ten miles from Georgetown. The next morning we set out to Major Pawley's on Waccamaw and from thence we proceeded up the said river accompanied them both and in which we found a great deal of good land; but it is entirely taken up for 40 miles. We slept that night on a bluff belonging to Capt. Matthews of Charleston, about ten miles from the Major's passed by several pretty settlements on the main; we found there 2 ½ barrels of pitch and being very cold, set fire to them and dressed some salt beef and rice for our supper. We left that place about four that morning and by eight came to a bluff belonging to one of Major's sisters, adjoining to which there was vacant land, which after having investigated, we took a view of it, but it proved to be mostly pine barrens and that is very inefficient, and not fit for anything but tar and turpentine, we left it for the use of those who might have occasion for it, from thence we came to another beautiful bluff, but an island and very small not being above 100 acres at most and inquiring the name of it, found it had none; so one of our company named it after him, by throwing a bottle of rum against the largest pine tree and it goes after his name to this day. We slept that night and the next morning, proceeded on our voyage and came to a beautiful bluff on the P. D. side, about two miles from the other of the opposite side, which we took a particular view of and liking the situation of the place very well we encamped there and found a good deal of good oak, hickory, and the pine land very valuable and a good deal of cypress swamp, which is counted best for rice; and having a surveyor with us, one gentleman in the company concluded to run some out, which he did next morning; but in the meantime while we were running out the land, our companions went up the said river in a boat to look for more, leaving only a bottle of punch and a biscuit apiece, promising to be back again the afternoon, but in short they never came near us that night nor the next day, in which time we had like to have been starved and not knowing what might be the occasion of their stay, we concluded to tie some trees together and make a barque, as the Indians call it, to ford over the main, where we might possibly find a house. But the next morning when we were in the midst of our work, our companions came back to us, but without one morsel of provisions, the oarsmen having eaten it all up so that we were then almost as bad off as before, save only our having our guns again which we had unluckily left in the boat. We had made shift to shoot some crows and woodpeckers, which we lived on that day; but on inquiring what might be the occasion of their staying so long, they told us one of their men had straggled out into the woods a shooting and it was with great difficulty we found him again. The next morning we went out with an intent to shoot some venison; but having hunted some considerable time and not meeting with any, concluded to return to our own company; but in our return met with a wolf in full chase of a deer, and had the good fortune to kill them both, so that we had then provisions sufficient for two days longer, which time we spent very pleasantly, and finding by our companions that there was a still better land higher up, we concluded to see it, trusting to our guns to supply us with provisions which they did very plentifully.

The next bluff we came to was the bluff on which Kingston is to be settled; but there are yet no inhabitants; the lower part of the township is not above 50 miles from Georgetown, but the tide runs 70 miles up; it is much the boldest river in South Carolina, in a parallel line with the sea coast, which runs north-east and south-west and is not above two miles in some places. But the township is settled on the P. D. side, though it was first run out half on one side and half on the other. The people have great advantages in settling in these townships, for they have no taxes for ten years nor quit rents . . . The land hereabout is for the most part very good and is not subject to overflow as on the P. D. and Santee. The next night we camped at Bear Bluff about thirty miles above the township; I think this tract is much the finest in all the river; and I believe if we had each of us a warrant, we would have fell out about the choice of it; but we had neither of us one with us; so we were obliged to leave it for some other. That night we had a very off affair happen. One of our men had killed a venison in the evening and about twelve o'clock at night, as we were all of us fast asleep, one of my companions was waked by a noise heard some distance from him, and as I lay next to him, he endeavored to wake me so gently as he could; when I waked he bid me present my piece, for he had just seen something not six yards from him, which he imagined was a bear; we lay in that posture with our pieces presented to the same place where we first saw him, for near half an hour, when we heard him coming again and soon after saw him. When we both fired and shot him dead on the spot; but instead of a bear, it proved to be a wolf that had stolen a quarter of venison before and was just then come for a second; and indeed it was very lucky for us that we killed him or otherwise we must have come to short allowance. On the 20th of February we set out on our voyage back again and the first night reached Kingston bluff where we had the good fortune to kill a bear, some of which we barbecued for our supper. The next morning we set out from thence and the same night reached Major Pawley's, where I had the misfortune to lose my pocket book with £15 in it, but could not find it again, though I offered the negroes the money, if I could have my book. The next morning we set out from the Major's and reached Georgetown the same night where we stayed two days to refresh ourselves after our fatiguing voyage."[4]

Saunders Records of N. C. Vol. IV, p. 258 gives this interesting petition for land above Winyaw:

Murray Crymble, James Huey and their Associates in the settlement of the land petitioned for 1,200,000 acres in N. C.

To the Board of Trade:
Sept. 17, 1736

Winyaw lies at a distance of about 85 miles from Charles Town South Carolina and that river is the entrance of the Pee Dee, Wackamorn and Black Rivers, there is at present settled at Winyaw, about 2500 people besides several ships with passengers that are gone this summer to Charles Town South Carolina, where there are settlements run out for them at the head of that river, almost joining to the line which is run between South and North Carolina, which is not above 50 or 60 up from Winyaw, the number gone is as follows. In

---

[4]Georgia Historical Collections. V. II.

William and Mary of Liverpool from Belfast 350 passengers and in the Oliver Capt. Walker, belonging to Messrs. Hopes of Rotterdam 360 Palatines and another small ship called the *Catherine* with about 176 passengers, all which are to be settled under the line which divides South and North Carolina, upon Winyaw River besides which was a township run out above two years ago for a considerable number of poor protestants that came into South Carolina and are since fixed there" . . .

There is a gentleman at present here who came lately from S. C. (from whom we had a great part of this information) who is willing to take up two tracts of land 12,000 acres, one upon Winyaw and settle it, and as security for his so doing, is willing to advance the Quit Rents of four shillings Proclamation money for ten years which will amount to about £360 Sterling & to pay the same immediately upon passing the grants.

CHAPTER IV

THE SAMPIT AND THE BLACK

Along the lower side of the Sampit the land was soon acquired in large amounts by enterprising men. Robert Screven owned the 600 acres in the great curve of the river opposite Georgetown. At an interval west of this tract was William Swinton's who was an alert and active man in the rising town. On the west of him, was the residence and ample grounds of Capt. George Smith. The Smith family was numerously represented on the Sampit including Rev. Josiah Smith of the Circular Church, or his son. On the Sampit and Turkey creek, the first considerable tributary on the south side, was James Stewart. George Pawley, another of the prominent leaders in Georgetown, had a tract on the south side. John Daniel, a merchant at Charles Town and Capt. Richard Smith came next. Capt. Smith had been a member of the Assembly and an officer in the militia. Here as in England large landholders enjoyed military honors. In 1735 or 6 he died and left at his sale 46 hands to be disposed of. He had offered for sale his place on the Winyaw and passed his last years here not far from Georgetown, by land or water. His land was, it appears, a part of the 48,000 acres alloted Landgrave Smith, which also extended above the stream and included tracts west of Deep Gully or Caanan's Creek. John Beamer was west of Capt. Smith and also Daniel Crawford, another merchant, with a large tract bounded by Gravelly Creek on the west. South of these last mentioned were Bentley Cooke, John Gardner, Thomas Cordes and Henry Bossard. In seven miles of Georgetown were Hon. George Logan's place and that of Martha Logan. Henry Bedon had two tracts near this limit.

Up the Sampit at further intervals were William Anderson eight miles, Edward Weekley with 2000 acres situated on both sides, ten miles up but navigable with periaugers. Near the headwaters of the Sampit were Robert Daniell with 2000 acres, part of 48,000, Robert Stewart, Thomas Bolen, John Russ, John Summers and Charles Codner of Daniel's Island. On the north side of the Sampit, seven miles, were William Whiteside, William Colt, James Withers, Widow Mary Smith, James Summers who married Rector Morritt's daughter, her tract next and west of Caanan Creek. James Summers offered in a few years these 1130 acres for sale: "There is on it a dwelling house, barn, etc. a good pasture well fenced in, with high tide lands ready for planting, also about 40 acres of other tide lands dammed in. A fence about ¾ of a mile will (with the above said two creeks) include the whole tract. Joseph DuBordieu's was next and it was thus described: "Five miles from town, many good new and convenient buildings, dwelling house, beautiful situation on fine bluff, kitchen, fowl house, smoke house, dairy, stable, two fine long barns." It became the property of Paul Trapier. Thomas Bonneau, Anthony White, William Whiteside, the Receiver General's deputy at Georgetown, John Ouldfield, surveyor, George Pawley west of White's Creek, John Peter Summerhoof who married the widow Forbush whose land was devised by Rev. William Screven, Job Rothmaler of Charleston, Thomas Cordes, James Russ and Joseph Singleterry were in the locality. Isaac Lesesne, Joseph Port, William Bonneau were also in this neighborhood, on or near the river. In August 1731, Rev. Mr. Morritt rector of Prince George Winyaw parish, reported that it was incredible to relate how people daily were resorting to his parish. In the next five months he reported 8 settlers had come among them. During this year, 1732 over fifty persons got warrants for land within about 15 miles of the church, situated not far above the mouth of Lane's Creek.

Capt. Anthony White had extensive tracts in three or four miles of the town. He was now an old resident. He served the parish in the Assembly and became a prominent member of the new society on the Winea. He acquired lots in Georgetown and was a liberal citizen. The stream on which he lived was called Three Mile Creek, or Pawley's Creek, but finally it bore his name and became noted for the murder of Gabriel Marion by the Tories where the present road crosses the stream. Some years later Capt. White offered some of his land for sale in language which showed even in large transactions that barter was possible where money was stringent: "500 and 1500 acres between 3 and 4 miles from Georgetown, joining each other and Hughes, Ellis, Gadsden, Lane, Malone, and my own land—about two miles from a landing from either Black, or Britton or Green's Creeks—proper for tar, pitch, turpentine and for corn, pease, potatoes, good summer range—to be sold for money, produce or cattle." John White had lands near by and also on both sides of the Black; but later in life he built three miles from the church a two story brick dwelling and convenient brick out-houses. He had a good landing, a fine pasture, garden, orchard and a convenient water conveyance to market. In this same neighborhood within five miles of the town, Joseph Port, James Futhy, four Brittons, William Shackelford, Thomas Bosher, Thomas Jenkins, Stephen and Thomas Ford went with the current up the Pee Dee to purchase or to live. Other large plantations were owned by non-residents—as John Ouldfield, surveyor, John Gough of a lower parish, Theodore Laws and Benjamin Laws of Christ Church parish, Morion Sarrazin, goldsmith of Charleston, and Rowland Vaughan, four miles from town, head of Green's Creek, Rev. Josiah Smith three and seven miles from town. Another group was not far from Rev. Mr. Morritt on the Black: Anthony Atkinson, George Smith, Benjamin Avant, Meredith Hughes, Thomas Hinckley, William Colt, John Richardson, John Lewis, James Lloyd, William Saxby, William Screven, Anthony White and John Green. One tract of 197½ acres taken up by John Green passed into the hands of his sons, John and William and from the latter to William Poole in 1750 and later to his son Joseph. The Screven tracts adjoining and near, containing 600 acres, were sold in 1749 to the said Wm. Poole and fell to Joseph Poole, only surviving son and heir. Anthony White was also granted a tract adjoining these of Green and Screven. By his will in 1746 Anthony White ordered this tract to be sold and it was purchased by the said Joseph Poole. He was doing just what others in all parts of the state were doing—buying up adjacent plantations. These 1177½ acres, he sold in 1757 to John Waties whose executors in turn sold 757 acres of these five tracts to Paul Trapier, which included the home of the late John Waties known by the name of Windsor plantation. It was south of Samuel Wragg, east on the Black, south on John Cleland's, now Francis Kinloch's, west on Kinloch and Mrs. Susanna Mann. John Lane was west of the parsonage and glebe, on the stream which still bears his name. He was satisfied with a small acreage. West of him was the extensive possessions of Daniel and Thomas LaRoche. This land reached north-westerly on the Black, a few miles above the mouth of Black Mingo, in the great bend northward. On the Southwest of him were William Forster, northeast William Swinton. The number of settlers or purchasers here was soon increased by Noah Serre, George Dick, Richard Walker, Edward Bullard, Edward Vanvelson, William Brockington, Meredith Hughes, Arthur Foster, John DuFarge.

Further up the stream at Potato ferry was Samuel Commander who had land on both sides of the river, Elisha Screven, his son-in-law, Peter Johnson, Joseph Johnson, Isaac David, George Morley, Provost Marshal, Landgrave Smith, Noah Serre, William Brockington, Abraham Bond, James Gordon, John Abbott, Henry Durant, Henry Lewis, Edward Simpson and Thomas Jenkins were near Commander's.[1] Further down the stream was the much resorted to Black Mingo Creek or north branch of the Black. Hereabouts were George Chicken, Dougal McKichen, George Hunter, John Nesmith, William Thomas, Paul Mazyck, Miles Sweeney, Robert How, the school-teacher who lived below, Gordon, Richard Smith, John Campbell, James Summereigh, Edward Howard, Ed Simpson, Burtonhead Boutwell, Phineas Spry, Dan Jordan, John Vickeridge, Henry Lewis, Paul Bruneau, John P. Summerhoof, Alexander Parris, Samuel Eveleigh, William Thompson, Mrs. Mary Raven, Stephen Bedon, Elizabeth and Edward Handlin, Thomas Hurst, Charles Hill, James Sinclaire. On Peter's Creek a few settlers appeared; nearer the Pee Dee were widow Sanders, John Driver, James Atkins, William Saxby, John Green and William Swinton.

Daniel and Thomas LaRoche appear to have been the foremost of the men who lived in Craven County, in property and in liberality. Thomas died early. Daniel accumulated a respectable fortune and was missed at his death. He was one of the first and best of the parish

---

[1] In 1918 a visitor to Potato Ferry said to his driver "Sam Commander lived here in 1732." He replied "Alex Commander lives here now." He turned out to be a freedman.

church at Georgetown. He left to be disposed of at his sale, 10,000 acres of land on the Black and Waccamaw, the whole of Cat Island and eight lots in Georgetown, together with 130 slaves, some cattle, horses, boats and canoes.

Meredith Hughes was a pillar in the church on the Black, a successful planter and business man. To him belongs the honor of being the first on record in the parish of devising property for the benefit of a parish church. Alexander Parris was public treasurer of the province when he invested on the Black. George Morley the provost marshal got 1000 acres beside him. John Gough, an Irishman, one of the first in Irishtown, Berkeley County, selected a large tract a short distance from the town. Col. George Chicken, who had earned his title on the field of battle, or his son of the same name, took up 1000 acres astride the Black. On it were a good dwelling house, barn and out houses. He died at Strawberry and like many who engage in politics and in military service, left his estate seriously involved.

William Brockington left his impress on the public domain, which he constantly sought to lessen. Little is known of him otherwise. He did not figure in the parish churches. He was more likely to have been a dissenter rather than a "prophane person." His son-in-law was Joseph Johnson. At his death his choice slaves numbered thirty-two. Dougal McKichen was an uneducated man who could not sign his name, but he managed by the help of certain merchants to secure a good landed property and to improve it. He lived 18 miles from town in a newly weatherboarded house in good repair, one story 28 x 18, 6 rooms, 5 fire places and a "peaatch" front. But his advertisement was accompanied by the ominous name of a merchant who was in

SOUTH CAROLINA

all probability waiting for the cash which had long been tied up in it. He moved to North Carolina. Jacob Satur who died in 1732 and Samuel Eveleigh had been members of the Council. The latter died about 1733 owning 1000 acres on the Black, with a good house, kitchen, milkhouse, 200 cattle and 30 horses.

There was another class of colonists who came from Europe in a slow moving body, to follow the suggestions of those in authority and sometimes depending upon the public treasury for transportation and maintenance for a season. The first of this character which came to the Winyaw emigrated from Ireland in 1732. They paid for their own passage to Carolina where they arrived on the 27th of October, in the ship *Happy Return* from Belfast. There were 85 passengers.[2] They went up the Black early in the next year and disembarked at Potato Ferry and set out to the Township laid out for them. There is a tradition that they sent ahead men to blaze the way and to fell trees across ponds, branches and swamps, on which their wives, children and old men crossed. When the leaders were out of sight, the hindmost ones would shout to find out where they were and would get the response, "Follow the bleezes."[3] They found the township laid out in 50 acres lots. Some of the first boat load got warrants for land at once, but they were denied the right of choosing the best and larger tracts as allowed in other localities. Among those who took up 50 acres or multiples of that number in 1733 were John Witherspoon, James Witherspoon, William James, John Mackey, John McKay, William Moore, James Moore, James Scott, Ann Donovan, Roger Gordon, Gavin

---

[2] See Gazette, October 28, 1832.
[3] Reminiscences of Williamsburg County, by McGill, p. 277.

Witherspoon, Hugh Graham, James Scott, John and James Blakeley.[4]

Another boatload from Ireland reinforced the colony at Williamsburg. It was thus mentioned by Samuel Eveleigh, merchant at Charleston to George Morley, Provost Marshal. "Last November twelve months (i. e. Nov. 1733) came over a parcel of Irish Protestants from the north of Ireland, which the governor got settled at a township called Williamsburg on Black River where the land is extraordinary good and they immediately made up some huts to cover them from the weather and then the clearing of the land which they planted and made very good crops so far, that they had corn enough for themselves and 500 bushels to spare. There are several families since arrived, gone there to settle and I believe in a short time will be a considerable settlement. I cant tell you the particular they have out of the public exactly, but I think it is a cow and a calf and a sow to two families, 100 weight of beef, half a hundred of pork, 100 weight of rice to each person and 10 bushels of corn besides tools." The immigrants continued to come in, in 1734, before the town called Williamsburg now Kingstree was laid out.

In 1735, Anthony Williams, Deputy Surveyor, laid out the town of Williamsburg. On the northeast side were the lands of Roger Gordon and John Henderson, and the south-west side David Johnson's and Jane Irwin's;

---

[4]The causes of the emigration to America in 1729 were the rise of rents, increase of tithes of Episcopacy, very unfavorable harvests of 1725-6-7, very high price of food in 1728 and disqualification for office created by the sacramental test. They looked to America as more promising investment for labor and capital and as part of the empire where religious grievances were almost unknown. In March 1729 there were seven vessels in Belfast that were to carry off about 1000 passengers, 6000 emigrants being reported for that year and 12,000 for several years in that century, nearly all Presbyterians. J. S. Reid's History of the Presbyterian Church of Scotland, Vol. III, p. 224.

South Carolina

on the south-east side Archibald Hamilton's and a swamp. 378 half acre lots were laid out, separated by 6 streets running south 15 degrees east, parallel with the river and by 10 intersecting these. The lots were numbered from the river front where it appears the first lots were sold. The following persons who also had plantations are credited with being first owners of lots:

	Lot Nos.
I. J. Fisher	1
Richard Hill	4
John Barnet	5, 6
Wm. Dexter	18
Francis Goddard	9
Thomas Lake	13
Capt. Robt. Austin	15
Capt. James Pollard	17, 26
William Dick	18
T. Monck	23
Thomas McCullough	26
Bridget Hughes	20
Thomas Dale	102, 315
John Sikes	21
Thomas Monck	23
William Henderson	25
Thomas McCullough	26
Capt. John Adams	27
James Gamble	22, 78
Henry Cristie	35
John Ryan	36
Andrew McClellan	39, 59
John Ballentine	200
William Christie	50
Hugh Copeland	45
J. Pennefather	52

Patrick & J. Dannell	76
Charles Starnes	100
J. Arnot	101
Charles Stone	100
Mathew Vanalle	103
John Scott	104
Ann Blakeway	107
Charles Starnes	110
John Barry	113
Thomas Forrest	117
Riblin Hutchinson	136
Christopher Harvey	152
Magdalene Boule	203
Benjamin Bates	201
J. Swisston	257
Thomas Rodross	279
Rev. Joseph Bugnion	301
William Williamson	310
——— Covnutt	314
Mary Gleadon	317
William Hamilton	319
John Dick	365
Anthony Williams	399

The emigrants from Ireland after the first several boatloads, continued to come in and add to the excellent class of citizens who were worthy of a home in the new world; but they were not so well treated by the authorities in the colony as the king's Injunctions enjoined. The complaint which that treatment brought forth adds to our knowledge of the first eight years much more than is known about the other two townships. It can be given in their own language in a communication to Henry McCullough, Esqr., who had been appointed commissioner by the king with power to inquire into all abuses with respect to grants of lands and toward preventing and determining all disputes concerning them

"We beg leave to represent," said the petitioners, "that by his majesty's 43rd Instruction to his governor of this province, there were 11 townships set apart for the reception of such Protestants as might come and settle in the Province.

That in consideration of the encouragement offered us by the governor and council and from the certainty we apprehended we had under his Majesty's Royal Instruction to his Governor to be secured in our properties and the remainder of our township land would remain only for the uses directed by his Majesty's Instructions which would have enabled us to have brought over our friends and relatives to settle in our neighborhood. We under these encouragements transported ourselves and our families to this province and settled in Williamsburg township.

But to our great concern, we have found the lands in this township become a common and unrestrained range for all persons whatsoever; the best lands therein taken up. Persons who have not at this day settled the same, nor in all probability ever intended to reside therein. Some of us have been sued for trespassing on land pointed out to us by the Deputy Surveyor and have been cast in considerable damages, and others became tenants rather than remove their families.

Sometime past we represented our humble petition to the Governor and Council setting forth our said grievances and praying relief, but we could obtain no answer, we therefore take leave to trouble you with a copy of the same, wherein the hardships we have labored under are enumerated which we humbly submit to your consideration.

Rambles in the Pee Dee Basin

The river by which we can have any conveyance of our goods to a market is rendered difficult in the navigation by reason of great trees which have fallen therein and which induced the General Assembly at our humble application to pass a law for clearing the same. Now the whole burden of that work falls on us the residenters, while those who are possessed of great tracts of the most valuable lands contribute nothing to it. We have letters from our friends in Ireland acquainting us of their desire of coming here, if we could in any shape encourage them, which we have hitherto declined, because of the land being run out and possessed by others. We take leave, Sir, to assure you that every fact alleged in our said petition and in this our humble representation, shall be effectually proved, with the addition of many more particulars, when you will be pleased to require it. We pray therefore that you will take the premises into consideration and that you will relieve us of the oppression and hardships we labor under in relation to our possessions, and we shall ever pray. Williamsburg Township, 9th day of May 1742.

Thomas McCree	Robert McCaughton
James Bradley	Patrick Lindsay
William Thomas	John Watson
Alexander Scott	John S. McFadding
John Beadley	William McCormick
Samuel Bradley	Asazbel Campbell
John Dick	Jno. Anderson
James Dick	David Witherspoon
Wm. Dick	James McClelland
George Burroughs	James Armstrong
John Lemon	John McCullough
Thomas Scott	Jane Blakeley
Adam Strain	John Moon

James Gamble
William Pressley
John McKnight
John James
William James
David Wilson
John Fleming
Alexander McCree
John Hamilton
Robert Mason
John Scott
Robert Witherspoon

John Liviston
John Dick
Hugh McGill
John Porter
Gaven Witherspoon
Roger Gibson
Jno. Henderson
John Givon
James Lawes
Henry Montgomery
George Montgomery
Roger Gordon

John Pressley

The first petition to Lt. Gov. Bull and the Council which had been pigeonholed was appended to this communication to McCullough, with some repetitions omitted: "The Humble Petition of the several subscribing persons, inhabitants of Williamsburg Township in behalf of themselves and the rest of the inhabitants, sheweth that your petitioners and the rest of the inhabitants of this township are chiefly Irish Protestants who came over from their native country to this province, at their own expense to settle in the said Township, encouraged by an account they received that the lands in the said township were for the most part good and fertile and the same wholly reserved for such distant Protestants as should come here from Europe to settle the same particularly for Irish Protestants. That your petitioners were informed and apprehended that the scheme of settling as well the said Township as the other Townships was strictly enjoined by his Majesty's royal Instructions to his excellent Gov. Johnson with a view of encouraging back inhabitants who would make no great use of slaves in these parts, but that from their own labors they might have a competent maintenance and upon any occasion be the more ready to unite for the public safety; for that the said Instructions as your petitioners are informed have not been altered from their first frame in that particular since the demise of the said governor, but continue still in force as his Majesty's stated plan for the settling of the province. . . . That several of the said inhabitants who first arrived the said township were obliged by the Deputy Surveyor to settle on contiguous tracts laid out for them in square forms, beginning at a certain place called the King's Tree which your petitioners at that time thought to be a great hardship to be debarred from making any choice and rather so, as the said lands were for the most part infertile pine barren lands and not likely to afford any product or profit to compensate the trouble of cultivating the same. But as they were given to understand that the said Deputy Surveyor was instructed by government to settle them in such a manner that a square of land 6 miles round the township was reserved for the further accommodation of the said township inhabitants. The said inhabitants proceeded to improve and settle the square tracts to the best of their power in hopes of being afterwards better provided out of the said reserved lands. That the second set of people who arrived in the second ship were subject to the same strictures and hardships but were nevertheless encouraged with the same hopes of having better lands in the parish lines as well for themselves as for their relatives and countrymen, who they expected would follow them. But your petitioners cannot but represent to you how greatly they were discouraged in finding as well the lands of the said Township of the said parish around the same afterwards became common unrestrained range for other people, all of the good lands of both taken up by gentlemen residing in other parts of the province who were better able to pay surveyors and were ready at Charles Town to get their grants passed for them, so that near sixty families who came last over to settle with their countrymen were greatly disappointed. Many of them were obliged to straggle off, into other parts of the province, others obliged to become tenants to gentlemen who had lands there granted them in great tracts and others who were directed by the Township Surveyor to settle with their families in particular places had the misfortune to find their possessions granted from them, so became subject to action at law attended with great expense.

Your petitioners cannot but further represent to your Honors that notwithstanding the many discouragements they have labored under, yet from their natural adherence to each other, the said township still consists of about 150 able bodied male persons, willing and ready to furnish their assistance in the defence of the Province against any of his Majesty's enemies. But must at the same time humbly desire that the scheme for settling them, directed by his Majesty be fulfilled to them. That the said Township lands be rendered wholly vacant for the township inhabitants and their township be made a parish with the privilege of sending Representatives to the Assembly as his Majesty has most graciously directed. Otherwise most of your petitioners must think it prudent to remove to some other of his Majesty's American Provinces, where they may hope to meet with less danger and more encouragement. Your petitioners take leave to set forth the names of several persons who have lands granted them in the Township and who reside in other parts of the Province, viz.:

John Harrington, George Hunter, Mr. Ballendine, Rev. Baxter, Capt. Cleland, Charles Starnes, Andrew

Rutledge, Esq., David Hartley, Thomas Potts, Mr. Monck, Bridget Hughes, Samuel Porleaine, Capt. Austin, Elisha Screven. Capt. Whitfield, Mrs. Blakeway, Mrs. Eldridge, John Wilson, Thomas Harrington, Capt. Atkins, Dr. Dale, Gibson Clapp, Mr. Morley, Mr. Fisher, John Scott, Ann Hargrave and many others.

Upon a view of which list your petitioners have reason to hope your Honors will take Premises into consideration and grant such relief as your Honors shall think most meet."

The commissioner Henry McCullough, Esq. felt the justice of the complaints from the township and proposed to the Assembly measures to remedy the existing abuses. A committee appointed by the Assembly reported favorably on the essential parts of the proposed remedy, but in the second reading at the next session, the most material parts were rejected by a majority of the House. The two reasons assigned by the commissioner for this action:—Several members of the Council and Assembly had taken up Township lands and it was publicly declared in the Assembly that they would not lay burthens on themselves and this evidently appeared to be the sense of the majority.[5]

To these Presbyterians from Ireland must be accorded the first place in making cloth called 'Hollands.' William Lowry showed the governor and council in 1742 what they declared to be the first made in the province and allowed him a bounty of 20 pounds current money.

---
[5] Vol. 21, The Public Records.

CHAPTER V

UP THE PEE DEE RIVER 1731-1740

The distance from Georgetown by water to the junction of the Pee Dee is 33 miles, to the mouth of Lynch's Creek 63 miles, to Cat Fish Creek 73, to Jeffries 88, to Mars Bluff 100, by land 65.

In 1731, the landowners on the western side of the Pee Dee already mentioned, were few and not many miles above the Black. One of the newcomers more venturesome than the rest went up the Great Pee Dee and had two tracts containing 1000 acres surveyed. It was on the western side and not far from Lynch's Creek. More than a year later it was found to be the only land granted in Queensborough township. Othniel Beale[1] for whom this land was laid out, had been a ship captain in the South Carolina trade and had the misfortune to be captured by pirates from Algiers, and the dexterity to turn it into good furtune. By the help of a storm which overtook them, he directed the vessel on which he was detained into an English port without losing the good will of his captors. The exploit led to an audience with the king and opened in Carolina a career that gained the respect of his contemporaries. He was a native of New England and died in his 85th year, after having been a member of the council 17 years and in the province 32.

In 1733 Joseph Dopson who also invested on the Black went up in advance to Cashaway in Marlboro County and had a small tract laid out on the eastern side but it remained unoccupied until Jacob Kolb took it up years afterwards. In 1732 John Ouldfield was appointed to lay out Queensborough Township on the Great Pee Dee. He promptly accomplished his task but his judgment

---

[1]Carroll's Collections, Vol. I, p. 268.

was not endorsed by subsequent events. Neither its exact location nor its contents in acres or square miles can be gathered from the conflicting evidence. Many more than the alleged 20,000 acres were granted in it. The lower and upper lines were run 45 degrees northeast and southwest across the Pee Dee. The southern line was below the mouth of Lynch's Creek and on the eastern side the Little Pee Dee was put down by the same surveyor as the boundary of one tract in the township. On the western side, a part of Lynch's Creek was included. The northern line was above the mouth of Catfish Creek and below Jeffries. Ten thousand acres on the eastern side were transferred to the Welsh Tract, laid out in 1736. Its deduction left the Pee Dee as the boundary of Queensborough Township. In 1734 scattering tracts as high as Sandy Bluff were located. In 1735 the town of Queensborough was laid out on the western side of the Pee Dee and several lots were sold; but no permanent improvements were made which prevented the site and even its name from being forgotten. James Gordon, owned the land above it. Francis Futhy and his neighbors, Jacob Moon, William Wallace and James Hepburn also touched upon it. Of the lots in the stillborn town, No. 4 was taken by William Morgan, No. 5 by Catherine Raunie, No. 6 by David Delescure, No. 49 by Elizabeth Righton, No. 64 by Thomas Goodman, No. 79 by Hercules Coit, No. 161 by Peter Hume. The Queensborough Township now began to be rapidly settled. The emigrants from the old world were going through Charles Town to Georgia, up the Savannah, Santee, Sampit, Waccamaw and the Black rivers and yet there were persons to go up the Pee Dee in this decade too numerous to mention. And many of those who can be mentioned cannot be located on lands bounded by vacant lands or other lands with no special marks to identify them.

The lands south of the junction of the Pee Dees were generally taken up or picked over before the rush set out for higher lands. The Allstons, Waties, William and Mary Drake, Charles Hart, the Swintons, Pawleys, James Gordon and Alexander Nesbit were large purchasers, but were not immigrants. Stephen Ford, Ann Donovan, Josias Garnier DuPre, Elias Foissin, William Simpson, William Leander, Thomas Hennings, James Futhy, 35 miles above Georgetown, William Leslie, Dr. J. Lupton, Joseph LaBruce, Alexander Leslie, Robert Quash, J. Thompson, William Wilson, J. McKay, Caleb Avant, Stephen Proctor, John and Thomas Conn, Robert McNott, William Saxby, James Paine, John Godbold, William Price, Ben Avant, William Adkins, Cornelius DuPre, William Shackelford and Abraham Staples appear to have been in search of homes. The Prince Frederick Church was well represented among these famiiles. Those who went up on the east side of the Little Pee Dee were few in number and some of them non-residents. This part of the state was neglected or if there were schools and churches in it, they were few and far apart. On the west side of the Little Pee Dee in the Neck there was quite an assemblage in a few years. Among them were the Brittons, Frances, Philip, Moses, Daniel and Timothy, John Arthur, Robert Fledger, William Boreland, Ann Jolly, Madam Elizabeth Bremer, Gabriel Manegault, Gabriel Marion, Elias Horry, Meredith Hughes, Joseph Robinson. Several of these never lived in the Neck. Madam Bremer had 2100 acres and tried for years to sell them. Elias Horry in partnership with Daniel Britton raised a large herd of cattle in six years. Robert Fledger got possession of about 2000 acres, lived on them and had at the sale 25 slaves, 3 riding horses, 4 mares and 50 head of cattle. In the short period of six years a wilderness had been reduced to a habitable and profitable plantation. The five Brittons were neighbors with land jutting on Little Pee Dee and being in the Neck, they were not far from the Great Pee Dee. The land was found to be fine for farming and unsurpassed for grazing purposes. Getting a living was so easy that not one fifteenth part of the land was cleared in the first generation or two except where the more energetic increased their slave forces. A daughter of one of these Brittons, Elizabeth, married as her second husband Samuel Jenkins, and the autobiography of their son Rev. Jas. Jenkins is to contribute to the interest of our story.

There is a tradition[2] that sometime in the early part of 1700 there came from Ireland some people by the name of Michaels and settled on a point of land now called Tanyard. Another tradition given in the same connection accounts for the name given to the neck in this way: "About 1710 there came over a goodly number from Great Britain and thereby they were called the Brittons." But these dates are too early, except for Indian traders. George Hunter marked the Pee Dee in his map made 1730 as "extraordinary good land not settled." In 1731 only one tract was laid out in Queensborough Township and its owner lived in Charles Town. James Jenkins said the neck was named after his grandfather whom he does not deign to name. Its name would have been quite appropriate as the neck on which so many Brittons lived. As we go up stream the Queensborough township is entered and Lynch's Creek is first to divert the stream of immigrants from the Great Pee Dee. Rev. John Fordyce halted on this creek to run out his 1000 acres, and John Pyatt also who has lived in

---

[2]Sellers History of Marion, p. 106.

worthy descendants, John Deleisseline, the Huguenot, John Cleland the quondam owner of Georgetown, Wm. Shackleford, James Gordon and Robert Wright, chief justice, with his 4000 acres were investors if not homeseekers.

The next stream, the Catfish, on the eastern side of the Pee Dee, has an interesting history. In 1736 or 7, a colony of Welsh began to settle on its banks which was then a part of the Welsh Tract. Some of them died and about 30 others having investigated the region higher up, had the good fortune to secure the extension of their tract to the North Carolina line or higher, having pulled up their stakes on the Catfish, went to the Long Bluff in the latter part of the year 1737. On the Catfish stream there was within Queensborough Township a barony which eluded the tax collector many years. It was laid out to John Roberts adjoining Monck's large acreage on the eastern side, in the year 1735. People squatted on it and refused to pay the state or the poor any contributions. Charles Woodmason being appointed the thankless task of collecting the poor tax, found about 3,000 acres owned in England, North Carolina and by tax-dodgers in South Carolina. This barony was a part of the untaxed land. The owners, Nicholas Linwood and William Baker, of London, through their attorneys, in 1769, notified the incumbents that there was trouble in store for them. The baron and the barony were supposed to have gone with the Lords Proprietors but the large tracts still retained the name. It was in this quinquennium 1735-9, that members of the council indulged in their own interests in some rather surprising violations of the King's Instructions as well as of the laws regulating the issuing of grants. According to Governor Glenn, 6000 acres were granted by the then governor to each of the 12 members of the council, 72,000 acres in all, and the council at the next meeting, not to be outdone in that species of generosity, voted the same amount to the governor. Natives never made the government of South Carolina a house of merchandise. On Jeffries Creek, on the west side of the river, the first to get grants were one Bonolas and Frances Verambaut with one Sanders. Verambaut lived in Charles Town, dyed silk and prospered. 1,100 acres in this tract, which the Pagetts bought and 500 in Irish-town in Berkeley County were turned into cash, when he went back to the old world. Thomas Greenwood got a grant for the place he had improved on Jeffries Creek by claiming that he was there long before the Welsh came.

Mars Bluff and Toby's Creek are referred to in early deeds as places already well known. The Bluff became an important place as soon as a road was made leading up and down the river. Samuel Axson was one of the first on or near the Bluff, but his land was soon in the hands of Edmund Atkins, who secured about 800 acres a mile above the Bluff with Abraham Satur of Charles Town, above him and Richard Purcell below him. Flay and Malachi Murphy were above him. Opposite the Bluff on the eastern side was a tract of 300 with two others north of it, containing over 1000 acres, which belonged also to the Atkins. Toby's Creek flows through these; Solomon Middleton may have been related by marriage to John Atkins, as their lands on another river were adjoining. This tract was next to Satur and other Middletons on Toby's Creek. Thomas Groom was on the eastern side, resting on Atkins tracts. The Middletons lived on the Pee Dee, John Atkins, an Indian agent, Edmund did not.

The next bluff near the present railroad crossing, called Sandy Bluff, attracted a number of enterprising settlers that were to figure largely in the development of the country. John Crawford, William, George and John Sanders. Gideon Gibson, and J. Keighly. Rev. Mr. Turbefield was also present in the community, whose importance will secure it further notice. Mention has already been made of the ascent of the river in 1737 by the Welsh colony. As they passed by the mouth of Black Creek, ten miles above Mars Bluff they found large tracts already occupied by Alexander Skene, Edward Satur, both of the low country, Joseph Law and James Moody and a larger acreage at Cashaway ferry 7 miles higher up. In 1736 Charles Wright had the higher parts of "Causeway Neck," now Byrd's Island, surveyed and adjoining him at the ferry was Samuel Master's tract. About two miles up stream on Muddy Creek, Col. Henry Fox and south of him Col. Thomas Hume had grants for a large body of land. Charles Irby was a later owner of the Hume tract, Col. Fox was an eminent lawyer in Charles Town. North of him was Thomas Groom's tract. Opposite these three land grabbers on the Darlington side were two other tracts laid out on Christmas day in 1736 for Bartholomew Ball, son of Elias Ball, and Thomas Heywood, the former being the only one of this company who retained the land for his descendants.

The Welsh passed on to upper Pee Dee and from 5 miles above Cheraw to three miles below Cashaway ferry they settled on the margin of the winding Pee Dee 57 miles in length. The central point of their colony was Long Bluff opposite Society Hill on the eastern side. It was first called James' Neck after the leader of the colony and then Welsh Neck, 147 miles by water above

Georgetown, 30 above Cashaway. As this colony was barely planted in this decade, the time limit has not been observed in the following investments of the men who secured grants of land: Thomas Evans, Abel Evans, Mary Evans, Philip James, John James, David Lewis, Philip Douglass, Daniel McDaniel, James Rogers were on the Welsh Neck. Thomas Evans of Plumfield, or Plumgarden, bought on both sides of the river. The name Plumfield still adheres to a plantation in the western side, once owned by Governor Williams. A little higher up the river were the lands of David James, Daniel Dousnal, Joab Edwards, William DeLoach, Thomas Evans, Sr., David Jones, Joshua Evans, John Rowell and somewhere near them were David Harry, Evan Harry, John Harry, Thomas Harry, William Einon, Daniel James, Abel James, William Tarrel, Griffith John, Thomas James, Samson Thomas, Philip James, James James, Capt. William James, Owen David, William Screven, Wm. Smith, Ben Rogers, Joseph Jolly; on Naked Creek, Richard Barrow, Samuel Hollingsworth, Samuel Greenwood.

Evan Vaughan got a warrant for land opposite the great Cheraws and Samuel Sarrence two miles below 'Charraw's old Town,' also a tract on the eastern side with Walter Downs, David Roach and Mrs. Judith Lewis as neighbors; five miles above Cheraw James Gillespie, John Brown, James Price, John Ellery, James Read, formed another group of settlers near the line of the Province; on three creeks John Newberry, Hasker Newberry, John Singleton, Daniel LaRoche, Andrew Slann, Thomas Ellerby. On the lower Muddy Creek around the Fox-Hume-Groom lands were John Newberry, Tilman Kolb, Jacob Kolb, John Cattell, John Mixon, John Singleton, near Abraham Colsons.

On the western side of the river numerous farms were run out and improved. Beginning at Pidgeon Creek, now Buckholdt's, the owners were Jacob Buckholdt, Peter Roblyn, Thomas Evans, William Evans, Daniel Roach, Henry Roach, Edward Boykin, John Cunningham, Nathaniel Evans, Samuel Wiggins, James Baber, John Evans, Thomas Ellerby, Robert Williams, James Beaver, Thomas Herrington, Ben Wall, Giles Powers, John Bowdry. Nathaniel Evans owned the land between Cornelius Reine and Thomas Ellerby. He probably never lived on it as he was buying about this time several tracts on the Catfish. Mary Evans, Francis Young, John Thompson, James Jones, Isaac Chanler, Thomas Bowen, John Rowell, Daniel Monahan had contiguous farms on the right bank also; William Evans, Hardy Council, Robert Inman, John Westfield, Simon Parsons, formed another group on the same side of the river.

At Cashaway ferry, Johannes Kolb, a Hollander, was content to settle on Causeway Neck, now Byrd's Island. The Kolb home is marked on a plat north of the loop but south of Sugar Loaf. The neck of land made by this loop in the river (marked Kolb's Neck on the Darlington side on some maps) was crowded with early settlers: Edward Lovell over against the ferry, John Perkins, William Cary, Joseph Jolly, Moses Crosby, Joseph Alison, John Ouldfield near the mouth of Hurricane Creek, John Keithy north of these encroached upon Bartholomew Ball's place and north of that land were John Brown, Abraham Colson, Penelope Davis (the wife of a Welshman who by neglecting to take out his deed lost his home) Gideon Ellis, Anthony Pouncey, John Purvis and Isaac Nichols.

Rambles in the Pee Dee Basin

On Black Creek Malachi Murphy, John McIver, Thomas Freeman, Abraham Paul were among the first grantees of land. On Thompson Creek William Johnston, Martin Johnston, Edward Sharpston, George Dubbs, John Purris, Edmund Kite, William Boatwright, John Rusting. On Cedar Creek John Jones, Samuel Sarrancy, William Hughes. On Red Bluff three miles below Cashaway John Moiden, Daniel Mooney; at Beauty Spot James Law, Anthony Simmons, and Gideon Gibson; on Duck Pond and John Hitchcock on Mars Bluff.

There were no large tracts granted in this period in the upper Pee Dee. 1000 acres was granted to one man but in the main the tracts were moderate in size averaging about 250 acres. The cause of this was the foresight of the Welsh which shut out the non-resident moneyed men who were not of Welsh extraction. This prudential arrangement had sound reasons for it. They had the benefit of the experience at Williamsburg where the immigrant for whom the township was laid out, had to yield to the non-residents in the choice of the best lands. The larger tracts on the Pee Dee and its tributaries were granted to Thomas Broughton. Lt. Gov., John Roberts, James Hammerton, Receiver General, who had more than a barony on the Waccamaw and Pee Dee, James Abercrombie, also on both streams, Joseph Wragg and Samuel Wragg, each three or four thousand acres. Robert Wright, Chief Justice, large tracts on Lynch's Creek and Pee Dee, Benjamin Whitaker, Judge of Admirality, Alexander Skene who had more than a barony, Thomas Monck, Nathaniel Broughton, Walter Good, 4000, Isaac Amyand, clerk of the Assembly, John Roberts got a whole barony and it passed into other hands and remained intact for years. Robert Hume, a lawyer of Charles Town, was perhaps the largest landowner above the Santee. He could offer a barony for sale and feel no discomfort in reckoning the diminished remainder. He died in 1739 and after a widowhood of many years, Mrs. Hume married the Provost Marshal, Roger Pinckney. James Gordon, a lawyer of Georgetown, was one of the landowners, quite energetic in his business of buying real estate at various places near the town of Queensborough, in the junction of the Lynch and the Pee Dee and on both sides of the river, was cut off in a few years with his fellow land owner Robert Hume, both of them leaving their lands to whom they knew not.

These pioneers in the woods had hardships of their own. But they were not subject to the 'Blue Laws' enacted at Charles Town in these early years, in reference to blasphemy, profaneness, bastardy, observance of the Lord's Day, and marriage, while wife or husband was still living.

For example: "Any person shall by writing, printing, teaching or advised speaking, deny one of the persons of the Holy Trinity to be God, or shall assert or maintain there are more Gods than one, or shall deny the Christian religion to be true, or the Holy Scriptures of the Old and New Testament to be of divine authority, and shall, upon indictment or information in any of the courts of record within this part of the province, be thereof lawfully convicted by the oath of two or more credible witnesses, for the first offence shall be adjudged incapable and disabled in law to have or enjoy any office, to be member of the assembly or have or enjoy any employment, ecclesiastical, civil or military. If in office, it shall be void.

For the second offence, he would be disabled to sue, prosecute, plead or use any action or information in any courts of law or equity or to be guardian of any child or executor or administrator, or capable of any legacy or deed of gift or bear any office civil, military or benefice ecclesiastical. He shall also suffer imprisonment three years. Recanting after space of four months, he shall be discharged."

The first of offence for having a bastard child was subject to a fine from £5 to £10. In case of failure to pay, the penalty was to be publicly whipped on the bare back not exceeding 31 stripes. The second offense the penalty was increased from £15 to £20 and failure to pay, punishment not exceeding 39 lashes.

The third offence, the mother of the bastard was to be tied to the tail of a cart and publicly whipped through Charles Town in as many streets as shall be ordered by the chief judge. In case the reputed father of the child was judged to be the father, he shall be fined not more than £10, not less than £5, and in case of failure to pay he was to receive 31 stripes.

If the mother of the bastard refused, she goes to prison, in case of refusal before the judge, the fine was £40 and continued imprisonment. In case of further reticence, she was to be sold as a servant four years.

In 1712, an act for the better observance of the Lord's Day commonly called Sunday was passed. All persons were required to observe it by ceasing from worldly labors, selling, buying, travelling and refraining from sports and pastimes. Strangers and lodgers were the only lawful guests on the Lord's Day. Dressing meat in families and selling milk not prohibited. The statutes (enumerated in the act) were to be in force in the province, as if they had been enacted in it. South Carolina was a genuine offshoot of England.

An act to restrain all persons from marriage until their former wives and former husbands were dead. It begins, "Forasmuch as divers evil disposed persons being married, run out of the country into another or into places where they are not known and there become to be married, having another husband or wife living, to the great Dishonor of God, and utter undoing of divers honest men's children." From the severe penalty of death only two exceptions were made: Where one did not know the other was living and those marriages declared void by an ecclesiastical court.

It will appear later that these bluish laws did not operate in the back settlements. Profaneness abounded, the church records show that bastardy was common and unpunished, that the Lord's Day was not observed generally where there were no churches. As to marriage and separation, Rev. Woodmason who travelled over several parishes in 1766, gives a rather shocking account.

The hunter in front, the cow-man second, and the land owner the third and last to arrive, was the order of advance into the interior. But in the Pee Dee the river was a highway which enabled the purchaser of land to anticipate the usual order. Only two men preceded the Scotch-Irish in their Kingstree settlement and only one Indian trader is known to have preceded the Welsh on the upper Pee Dee. A number of tracts had been laid out and bought, but the evidence that they were improved by their owners is lacking. There were many good people among the first who went up the river. No schools can be mentioned, but their morals and ability to write, indicate that they were not reverting to a savage state.

In 1739, there was an insurrection of slaves at Stono, about twenty miles from Charles Town. They killed the citizens and burnt their houses on the way towards the Spaniards in Florida, until they were overtaken and most of them killed. That event gave rise to some legislation which was the basis of the patrol system which ended with slavery in 1865.

To secure the inhabitants against the insurrection and other wicked attempts of negroes, it was enacted that every white male inhabitant of the province (except travellers and men over 60 years) who are able to bear arms in the militia of the province either in times of alarms or at common musters who shall on any Sunday or Christmas day in the year, go and resort to any church or any other public place of worship and shall not carry with him a gun or pair of horse pistols in good order, and fit for service, with at least six charges of powder and ball and shall not carry the same into the church, every such person shall forfeit and pay the sum of twenty shillings current money. This act was passed after the upper Pee Dee was in possession of the Welsh, and there is no evidence that the law was enforced in the Pee Dee Basin. That part of the state was free from Indian Massacres and the negroes were too few to create alarm. It was a habit, however, for the men to carry their arms to church long before this time. The men who put down the negro insurrection in 1739 happened to be armed at church when they were summoned to the place of the drunken negro revellers.

The thoughtful reader need not be reminded that the men who grew up as a state under arms for the defence of their family, city and country, were not likely to be patient in later times when their rights were trampled upon!

After the Lords Proprietors sold out, in 1728 the government was thus analyzed by Gov. Glen: The Constitution was formed after the model of the Mother Country. The Governor, Council and Assembly constitute the three branches of the Legislature and have power to make such laws as may be thought necessary for the better government of the Province, not repugnant to the laws of Great Britain. The Governor is Governor-in-Chief and Captain General in and over the Province. The members of the Council are appointed by the King and are twelve in number, the Surveyor-General also having a seat in the Council.

The Assembly consisted of 44 members elected every third year by the freeholders of 16 parishes, some returning five representatives, others four, three, two or one. A court of Chancery was composed of Governor and Council. The Court of the King's Bench consisted of a Chief Justice and Assistant Judges. The same persons constituted the Court of Common Pleas, and other offices were filled by the crown. The public treasurer, county comptroller, the Commissioner of Indian Affairs and others were appointed by the general assembly." A member of the Assembly, a native or naturalized, 21 years of age or over, after a residence of 12 months, must own 500 acres of land or have in his own proper person and in his own right to the value of £1,000 in houses, buildings, town lots or other lands, £1,000 in cash or stock. A settled plantation of 500 acres of land or above, and not less than ten working negro slaves, under the care of at least one white man, also was a qualification to be chosen a member of the Commons House of Assembly.

To be qualified as a voter, one had to be a professed Christian, 6 months a resident, and to own a freehold of at least 50 acres, or be liable to pay £50 in taxes. *Statutes of S. C., Vol. III, 3.*

CHAPTER VI

STOCK RAISING AND AGRICULTURE

The evening smoke was now ascending from the cabins newly erected on all the streams of eastern South Carolina and boats were constantly passing upward with their living freight. They were leaving behind schools, churches, physicians and the conveniences of life to live in log huts on lands of their own where they might exercise greater freedom than was possible in overtaxed and over governed communities. They entered at once into the three stages through which mankind passed, at long intervals, hunting, pastoral and agricultural. House keepers they were without houses, shepherds without flocks, planters without fields, citizens without citizenship. They were relatively a high type of men who set to work to transform the forests with troops of wild inhabitants into cultivated fields and comfortable homes with all the accessories of civilized life.

The question that had to be answered by all of them was: What shall I eat, what shall I drink and wherewithal shall I be clothed? Bread for the first and second year had to be imported; for other articles of food, the stream and forest were ready to respond. Many hundreds of families were wanting at the same time foundation stock of horses, cows, sheep, swine, and less universally, the goat which was not of sufficient importance to gain the notice of the census taker. Such was the success of cattle raising in the province that the demand was easily met. And it would have been met had all the cattle below the Santee been inaccessible. Long before this rush up stream, the live stock industry above the Santee was greatly developed. The business spread toward the limits of the State faster than the population. In a dialogue[1] of an early day it was stated that some men content themselves with fewer cattle than others; some may not exceed 30, 40 or 50; some may have one, three, four or five hundred cattle at a time; others again, having large tracts of land to feed them on, summer and winter, keep a thousand or more. I know a man that at his first coming into this country was a servant for four years, yet before his death it was computed he had at least 3,000 cattle, young and old, 100 horses and 300 calves yearly, which he bred without the trouble and expense of providing winter fodder for them." The same excellency of pasturage and prolificacy of animals had drawn over the Santee early in the 18th century droves of horses and herds of neat cattle owned by non-residents. Some had as many as 40 brood mares. Samuel Eveleigh offered on the Black before the tide of immigration rose so high, 200 cattle and 30 horses. Of St. Mark's parish, the first Governor John Peter Richardson affirmed that the yeomanry owned a thousand cattle on a thousand hills.

The live stock industry was a great privilege of the poor man, worth more to him than rice land. Such was the fact in the upper parts also notwithstanding the trouble and expense of marketing. The wills of such men as Thomas Evans in the upper Pee Dee, the contracts of widows with their relatives to be supported in compensation for herds of cattle and the donation of 16 cows and calves to the rector of Prince Frederick by the congregation and many other transactions, showed that cattle was abundant and of cash value. Not long after the Welsh arrived on the Pee Dee, Bishop

---

[1] Profitable Advice to Rich and Poor in a dialogue between James Freeman, a Carolina Farmer, and Simon Question, a West County Farmer, containing a True Relation of South Carolina, an English Plantation or Colony, 1712.

Rambles in the Pee Dee Basin

Spangenburg visited his Moravian brethren in Anson County adjoining them and left a word about their stock. They were at that time driving their cows and hogs to Virginia where the butcher paid for the meat but kept the hides and tallow. He reported the road to Charles Town infested with robbers and the water not good. The profits of the business were curtailed by the distance to market, sometimes as far as Philadelphia with which place a traffic was kept up till the close of the war of 1812. The stock ran out in the open, a privilege which lasted till the latter years of the 19th century in many places, and was finally forbidden by the legislature of 1921. It was on the unfenced lands free to all that the marking and branding system became necessary. It was here also that the stealing began which was curbed by legislative action time after time. All of the Pee Dee basin was a magnificent stock range, but only fragmentary notices of it survived in the traditions of the settlers. There are no statistics of cattle, horses or swine, sold at Charles Town or to the northward, only traditions remain in some families that their ancestors laid the foundation of their fortunes in the industry and "cowpens" and "horsepens" retain their names long after the cattle and their masters have been forgotten. The hides of animals slaughtered at home were sufficient to support tanneries and caused shoe shops to flourish where wax, bristles and flax were abundant. The state is still well adapted to the industry. Over 3,000,000 pounds of butter have been made in this state in one year. In 1860 there were 845 oxen in Chesterfield, 706 in Darlington, 324 in Marlborough, 569 in Williamsburg, 1452 in Georgetown and 22,629 in the state.

The domestic by-products of the table in colonial days were neither few, scant nor unimportant. Goats on account of their mischievous dispositions and sheep preyed upon by the cur, did not play as important a part in the common diet as they deserved. In six months of the years, 1771-72, Charles Town devoured 910 calves, 661 sheep, 661 lambs, 846 pigs, 2241 shoats, 456 beeves and 156 deer, numbers too small to make a ripple in the more distant parts.

The meat used everywhere and in all seasons was pork and bacon, furnished by the "prodigious" number of swine, some unmarried men raising 300 to be fattened by a feed of Indian corn in the last month. Much of it also was exported. Bacon became the staple food of the farmer and of his servants, as corn became the most important cereal for man and beast.

Horses also multiplied rapidly. According to a tradition preserved by Logan the first horse or horses came with the first people to the colony. Indians in hiding were astonished by the appearance of a horse led out and tethered to graze. Others may have come from Virginia, but there is testimony that 150 mares and some horses came from New York and Rhode Island early enough for the experiment to be found a success in the first 12 years. Wild horses were already in the land and were to be recruited from the new comers. The offspring of these imported animals were more slender and suited for the saddle or traveling than were their big headed and large boned sires and dams. The explanation of this inclination toward fleet footed horses is found in the statement of a late rambler in the state that the English part of the people were good riders, but not so with the Dutch, Irish, and Scotch. "Horses," said Peter Purry, "the best kind in the world, are so plentiful that you seldom see anybody travel on foot, except negroes. And they often on horse back; so that when a taylor or shoe maker or any other tradesman is obliged to go but 3 miles from his house, it would be very extraordinary to see him travel on foot."

The interest in horse flesh was not found restricted to one colony or to one part of it. The up country immigrants brought their horses with them and prided themselves on their good stock. The saddle horse was the precursor of the carriage drawn by horses as the carriage and buggy were of the automobile. The horse is not and may never be a discarded machine, rendered useless by steam and electricity. At any rate in that 18th century, the horse was the most important animal in the progress of the race.

A glamour is thrown over the abundance of fowl, fish and game in these colonial days. Wild geese were so plentiful that men killed enough to make one or more feather beds annually. Turkeys were so tame that the hunter shot them sitting on limbs as they looked down at the dog treeing them. Deer were numerous and wantonly destroyed for their venison, hides and many times for sport. Zamba[2] the African King, described an evening scene on the Santee at the farm of a widow owning twenty or more slaves. Among the animals which were driven from their feeding places, "came first a few cows with a bull at their head, at whose neck hung an old bell, next a flock of sheep, led by a ram, which had two plate of old iron tingling at his neck; a flock of goats followed; then a herd of swine, and lastly a whole squad of turkeys, geese, cocks and hens." The commotion and confusion recalled the saying, "The ox knoweth

---

[2]Life and Adventures of Zamba, an African Negro King, and His experience of Slavery in South Carolina. p. 138.

his owner and the ass his master's crib." The same dusky authority is responsible for the story that a white man brought to Mrs. Kennon's a wild turkey, a forty pounder, and in order to relieve his thirst told her that he had spent a long dull night waiting for this fellow. "I took it up by both legs and when I held it up higher than my face, its head lay on the ground; its plumage was really splendid; its legs were about as thick as the wrist of a boy 12 years old and its spurs were at least 4 inches long."

Another picture of a scene near the same Santee showed the poultry yard teeming with a well fed population, pastures of crab grass and cane pouring into the dairies streams of rich milk, swine in abundance, and countless fish from the inexhaustible river.

In full historic times, the simple narration of the meals enjoyed by the Winyah Indigo Society in their summer outing, to be hereafter mentioned, reads more like "the supper of the gods" was being described than what falls to the lot of men.

In a circular written in 1682, by Samuel Wilson, the question was put into the mouth of the hesitating emigrant, "What commodities will I be able to produce in South Carolina that will yield me money in other countries that I may be enabled to buy negro slaves, (without which a planter can never do any great matter), and purchase other things for my pleasure and convenience, that Carolina cannot provide?" and it was answered by a discussion of the possible profits in herds of cattle, (a word sometimes used to include horses) and swine, and in the cultivation of silk, oil, tobacco, indigo, cotton, flax, hemp, and the preparation of pitch, tar, turpentine, timber and medicinal material." In this part of the state silk and oil never secured much if any attention; nor were the pine products except near the ocean exploited in colonial days. Tobacco, especially after Virginians came to the state, was cultivated only in small quantities at first and afterwards became a money crop. Cotton, contrary to other opinions, was introduced into the Cape Fear settlement before 1670 and of course was soon tried in the Charles Town colony, and cultivated in small amounts to mix with woolen goods. Conrad Marks, a loyalist in the Revolution, gave in to the pension bureau of England 100 pounds of seed cotton among other things he abandoned in northwestern Edgefield in 1776. It is well known that cotton involved too much labor to be profitable, when ginned by human fingers. That process had a social side to it. At the fireside at night visitors, including even Bishop Asbury, joined in separating the lint from the seed, an act which did not hinder interchange of ideas. Hemp, flax and wheat were tried on these streams but they never became great sources of revenue. The lack of mills in many places and people's indifference caused wheat to be neglected, the table of farmers being without it far into the 19th century, except on Sunday or when hospitality to visitors called for it. Oats and peas were considered valuable for home consumption and in the feeding of horses and hogs. It is claimed by some agricultural editors that the pea is not a native of America. This is an error; for peas were known to the Indians and in the memory of the living, men used to plough their horses and turn them out at night to graze in the wild peas. They are still found wild in the state. Some strains of the pea, however, may have been introduced from the old world. Corn figured in a small way as an export. It was too bulky for conveyance by land and was utilized at home for food of man and beast and for whiskey. Its growing importance may be gathered from the 15,000,000 bushels made in the state in 1860 which left undetermined how many bushels in addition were imported directly or indirectly in the fat swine and mules from Tennessee. Nearly 100,000 bushels were exported one year.

Wine from the culture of the grape was never an extensive industry but brandy from peaches "a pleasant refreshing liquor," continued to be made in various localities. A dozen years had not passed over the colony in Charles Town before the thirsty Anglo-Saxon[3] had "invented a way of making out of corn good sound beer; but it was strong and heady. By maceration, when duly fermented, a strong Spirit like Brandy was drawn from it." From the beginning of the Huguenot settlement on the Santee to the times of the settlement at Abbeville much encouragement was offered and many efforts were made to increase the amount of wine and silk production, but the climate or the genius of South Carolinians made it a failure. For the cultivation of the tea plant and for running of a dairy and other things which require close attention or yield picayunish returns, they are unadapted.

Rice was not enumerated in the crops planted in Cape Fear and the Charles Town colonies as early as 1682. But it was in use within the next dozen years. The evidence is positive that rice was a commodity in 1694 and that a duty was charged on exportations to England. Rice was first planted in dry ground and in low places. The greater yield in the low ground suggested the river swamps and finally the tide lands with their great facilities for irrigation.[4] In the advertisements

---

[3]Thomas Ash in Carrolls Col. pp. 64, 68.
[4]The Introduction of Rice Culture into South Carolina by A. S. Salley, Jr., p. 16

of lands, the number of acres suited to rice culture was made prominent. It was estimated that each hand ought to make four and a half barrels of rice weighing 500 pounds each. It was for many years the principal export. In the soil survey of Georgetown it is said that generally only families with influence, who could get grants from the Royal governor of the province came into the possession of these (valuable rice) lands, some of the grants containing several thousand acres." The large tracts of land and several baronies in Georgetown were granted in the times of the Lords Proprietors. Some of them may have been included in the alleged illegally granted 80,000 acres in the period between 1720 and 1731, by the connivance of the last surveyor General of the Lords Proprietors and his Deputy Surveyor General. In Gov. Johnson's term, 1731-5, the best rice lands in Georgetown had already been granted. The large tracts on the Pee Dee began to be run out in 1735. No serious damage seems to have arisen from the large grants in these two localities. Land was plentiful. Many of the large tracts granted to men with ability to meet their obligations proved to be of little value in the lifetime of the original purchasers. To none of them was granted the perpetual right to keep them in the family. They often sought another owner. In this period Joseph Wragg offered 2150 acres land to the first purchaser. Noe Serre had 300 in a tract of 1000 acres fifteen miles below Williamsburg. Robert Austen had 1811 on the Black fifteen miles from Georgetown, 1200 of it rice land. William Bruce offered 800 acres on Lynch's Creek of exceedingly good rice land, corn and indigo. William Coachman put Hasty Point[5]

---

[5]Hasty Point is said to be so named because Marion had to get away from it in a hurry. It is here mentioned a dozen years before the Revolution.

on the market which had on it 100 negroes, stock cattle, hogs, sheep, carts, wagons and rice tanns.

Mrs. Bremer on Little Pee Dee, James and Edmund Atkins at Mars Bluff and many others were ready to part for a consideration with their valuable lands. The rice lands of Waccamaw were also frequently changing hands. The increase of the African slaves who alone could survive the rice industry was marked by increased rice production. The average of eight crops of rice was reported to be:

1747-1755	65,000 tierces
1755-1761	68,500 "
1761-1767	94,000 "
1767-1773	124,000 "

From January 1753 to January 1773, 43,965 African slaves were imported.

Indigo which was the source of great profit had been in some measure cultivated nearly as early as rice.[6] About 1746 the successful experiment with indigo incited some one to descant on the farmer's lack of diversification of crops as follows: The staple rice has already brought the planter not only a threadbare coat but many in his family to no coat at all." In trying to turn the planter's attention from his "darling rice" to the more profitable crop he continued, "One acre of indigo at the lowest calculation, yields more profit than five of rice at a middle computation. One hand in seven months can make more than two in twelve months." Stores were prepared to furnish seed, but the conservative planter with his usual reluctance to change his habits still clung to his darling crop. "Our chief and almost our sole dependence hitherto has been on rice,"

---
[6] A. S. Salley, Jr., in Introduction of Rice Culture in S. C. p. 16.

said Governor Glen in 1754, "but we now have happily found out other resources; we no longer plant indigo by way of experiment, our success in it seems to be certain and the culture and manufacture of it are nearly brought to perfection and therefore I recommend it to you to cause some short account of the whole process to be printed and to be dispersed among the people on the outer parts; and also that some indigo seed be distributed at public expense in our new townships and other parts where the poverty of the inhabitants make such supplies necessary." From this communication of the governor it is fairly inferred that in the upper parts of the Pee Dee where it became a great money crop, it had not yet been generally cultivated. From this time the prosperity of the upper parts was secure. The great profit in the crop was the cause of opening of the Winyaw Indigo Academy in 1755. The premium offered from the public treasury for every hundred pounds of indigo worked more efficaciously than exhortations and free seed and printed instructions. It was a boast in 1765 that the *Sea Nymph* carried from Georgetown 195 casks of indigo weighing 42,909 pounds besides many hogsheads and bundles of deer skins, being the richest cargo sent from that port since its establishment. Peter Sinkler[7] for example, began life on the Santee a poor man and by industry became among the wealthiest in the whole colony. He lost 20,000 pounds of indigo worth $1.50 per pound when the British came to his plantation. Up on the Pee Dee near the line, Gen. Harrington[8] sent three or four horse loads of indigo to Virginia and with the produce bought from 15 to 20 negroes. So great was the profit of the crop

---

[7]History of the Huguenots in South Carolina, p. 6.
[8]Gregg's History of the Old Cheraws, p. 112.

that the Huguenots who for the sake of religious liberty had fled from France, now relaxed in their warmth and liveliness in religion, carried lumps of indigo to church to compare and see whose was the finest. Thus one of them, James Guerry, reported to Rev. James Jenkins, an early Methodist minister.

There is nothing new under the sun, even among scattered farmers and planters in colonial days.

During the war, 1739-1746, there came an end to the prosperous preceding decade. The Board of Trade favored the colony and the merchants freely lent the planters money at 10 per cent interest. The flush times and easy money made many of the cultivators of the soil forget those primitive virtues, self-denial and economy, with a view to become independent of the money lender. They were in consequence of the war, caught by falling prices and held in a vise by their obligations to their creditors. The privateers on the ocean made imported goods high while the charge for the planters' cargo sent to Charles Town for wharfage, cooperage and storage left the planter in debt. Six years after the war had begun, the province still being free from invasion, one of these planters summed up the situation and suggested several ways in which the legislature could come to the planters' relief:

1. To disannul or very much reduce the interest of money. 2. To prevent any part of one's estate being sold for ready money (Gold and silver had been drained off.) 3. To lessen expense of lawsuits. 4. To put a stop to all suits for former debts during a reasonable time (to be settled according to the variations of the circumstances of the country) by an express law to that purpose that shall not screen any one who attempts to carry off his goods to the defrauding of his creditors;

and if possible, 5, That a proper sum of money be stamped by the government to be lent upon the best security to those that are indebted and in sums proportioned to their debts or to the whole inhabitants without distinction, but most discreetly; the interest of which money in a certain number of years shall sink the principal and shall be applied to defray the charges of the government."

This may be regarded as the forefather of the Farm Loan Board which in November 1922 had advanced 265 millions of dollars, to banking institutions, to live stock companies and to cooperative-marketing associations. On that same date repayments of these loans amounted to 109 millions of dollars leaving a balance outstanding of 155 millions. About the middle of 1921 money was lent on 200,000 bales to cotton cooperatives in Oklahoma, on 300,000 in Texas, and on 100,000 bales held by an association in Mississippi. A disturbed state of mind, a combination of hopelessness and resentment over inability to pay debts from the proceeds of sales of farm products at prevailing prices, a sense of injustice, disappointment in the past and apparently hopeless outlook for the future, were reported the salient psychological facts in the situation when the agricultural credits were initiated. The result was a change for the better set in and the demoralization began to disappear.

6. That all debtors shall give the best security they can to their creditors when required.

7. That what are not soon perishable, viz., raw silk and drawn, indigo, hemp, flax or cotton, fitted for the market be made at proper rates, tenures in Law or processes for payment of future debt and may be received for taxes." This idea too has been kept in mind in

later times when the men under an avalanch of deflation were looking for some way of escape.

8. That frugality and industry be recommended and enforced in the best manner. These points thrown out by "Nobody to Nobody" were thought so absurd by the merchants and money lenders that they passed unnoticed. But when the next election came, a majority of those elected came into the Assembly as a farm bloc and engrossed the attention of a long session and created a wide spread interest. Six petitions came in which had as a preamble: "That by the fall of the produce in value, they were reduced to the greatest straits and rendered unable to pay their debts at present and would be also to pay their taxes, quit rents, and maintain their families for the future here, seeing if timely relief was not obtained, many of them must be obliged to leave the province."

Of these petitions, one came from the inhabitants of St. Helena Parish, Granville County, signed by 93 persons, from Prince Williams Parish in the same, 62; St. Bartholomew Parish, Colleton 71, with members of the Assembly at their head. Wadmelaw in the same, 37, Edisto Island in the same, a member of the Assembly at their head, 31, Craven County which included the Pee Dee section, two members of the Assembly at their head, only 45, tho' headed by a Colonel of a regiment in that county, which contains not less, 'tis thought than 1200 men. The total number of these subscribers was 339. They spun out the session, said their critic 'Freeholder,' to the middle of June, appointed near 50 committees beside many more to bring in bills, etc, many of which never reported and of the 30, four were not passed by the upper house, 4 were neglected by the Assembly, 2 that were ordered to be brought in were not so much as read and six ordered to be brought in were not brought in at all. One of the bills rejected by the upper house provided for the stamping of £150,000. The money was to be lent only to such as would make oath that they were in such circumstances that they were under a necessity of borrowing to pay their debts.

When these members who were the first to demand pay for their services, saw that they could not succeed in all their main endeavors, they turned their backs on the Assembly and left it without a quorum. The seventeen who needed two more to get a quorum held out in order to pass a tax bill for 3 years.[9]

This was the first cleavage discovered in our history of the province between the merchants and the planters, caused by the rising prices of farm products and their fall by forces beyond the control of man. It disclosed a bitterness of feeling on the creditor side and a desire on the debtor side to put off the evil day by legislation. Happily the two classes now understand that their fortunes are bound together, but there is still need of the preaching of an ancient gospel that "the ultimate and perfected self-government begins and ends with the good behavior of the individual and that self-reliance is at the foundation of all material and moral progress.[10]

An ancient lawgiver declared that the causes of tumults and revolutions were economic—the love of money—An Apostle declared that the love of money was the cause of many kinds of evil, and an ancient poet supplemented both statements by the assertion that mankind had but one virtue—to make money.

---

[9]See S. C. Gazette, Aug. 23, 1746, and Jan. 6, 1784.
[10]See Congressional Record, Jan. 15, 1923, pp. 1775 and 1789.

CHAPTER VII

COLONIAL FAMILY LIFE

As late as 1768, the larger part of the people in the colony were passing through a modified patriarchal stage of existance. Hunting and stock raising were still receiving attention but agriculture was becoming the preeminent calling. It was as families, preyed upon by thieves and robbers, single and organized, that they were thrown upon their own resources and impelled to enter into a league in defense of their property which involved their rights as freemen. The better of the two tendencies in all human societies prevailed here in the back woods against formidable disintegrating forces and the government soon discovered that these resolute men were worthy to receive all the advantages of a protecting government. In a few years, as will be seen, they were put upon an equal footing in reference to courts and a partial representation in the Assembly; but before that justice is accorded them, their family life and customs, the most important part of their history and the most difficult to relate, must not be passed by as too obscure or insignificant.

The family is the fundamental unit in all the social and political aggregations and its importance in these distant wilds was greater than in more developed countries, where the preacher and the teacher relieve the father of the family of a part of his duty to his offspring. The home was in most places a shelter for the family, the school house and the meeting house, combined with its burial ground near by. The ordinary head of the family found his strength taxed to provide for the physical wants of his numerous children and had he been competent to teach and keep them out of crooked paths, he would have been forced to turn over the task to the mother. Not a teacher can be named who had a school above Georgetown before 1766. It is therefore to be inferred that the intelligent mothers were mostly the teachers of the larger number of well informed men and women who grew up in this period. The Presbyterian pastors were educated men, but they appear to have devoted themselves before the Revolution to preaching, an evidence that the morals of the country attracted more attention than illiteracy. The catechism doubtless was faithfully taught.

In 1760, the members of the Welsh Neck church promised, "each for ourselves that if God gives us children to bring up whether our own or others, that we will use our utmost endeavors to bring them up in the nurture and admonition of the Lord, that we will keep a strict watch over their conduct and at all convenient seasons give them such advice, admonition and correction as their case shall appear to require; and that we will take due care to have them taught the catechism; and also that we will use our authority to keep them as much as possible from wicked company and vain pleasures, knowing that a companion of fools shall be destroyed and that lovers of pleasure are not lovers of righteousness." Nothing was said about training the minds in this promise, which indicates a healthier state than that of the present crusade for mental training with secondary or less emphasis on good morals. In respect to education, the ordinary family life of this period must be classed much below par and many of the less fortunate families in morals also. But as to marriage relations there was little tendency toward the disintegration of the family by false theories and loose practices, when allowance is made for the lawlessness which made itself felt in the family and society also. There was dissoluteness in all the colony as in the old countries from which the citizens came. Such freedom as follows reformations and revolutions always gives, as it were, a new birth to multitudes who stumble around in their new world like new born calves and colts on unsteady limbs. The reformers were not to blame for the evils which sprung up. They simply uncovered them when they were in pursuit of greater freedom for the individual. The original business of mankind was to "subdue the earth" which the industrial, mercantile and commercial classes only can do. It was therefore a move in the right direction. The evils it disclosed with reference to the sexes and the confusion in the minds even of the wise men of the day about the ceremony connected with marriage and its essential nature are seen in the singular theories and loose practices which favored bigamy, polygamy and worse evils. Even Milton did not escape from the infection of his times. By the beginning of the period under review, it was undecided whether the magistrate or the established minister had an exclusive right to perform the marriage ceremony or whether it could not be performed without either, as by the poor in distant parts near no minister or magistrate. South Carolina is the only state in which the legislature has stood between the family and divorce laws. The reason why is bound up with wider questions connected with the semi-feudal character of the colony and strict interpretation of the New Testament teaching. Time, the test of all experiments, has pronounced no judgment unfavorable to legal family safeguards. The generality of the marriages were between young men and maidens, but the exposure of the husbands to malaria in the seasons of planting and harvesting, cut short their days and left widows and orphans to mourn their departure. Widows had the advantage over the spinsters in the possession of homes, lands, slaves as well as of equal personal attractions. They fared well when they could balance these accomplishments with the presence of genial companionship and good business management. The charm which led to these marriages has been stigmatized as "economic" which is nothing more than an inference where the motives cannot be known. The registers kept by the parish churches furnish data to show the number of widows whose isolation and need of protection made them know the value of a man. The widowers were also numerous. The births and baptisms show the number of the base born in the parish. In the decade 1736-1746 Rev. John Fordyce baptized about 315 infants of these 9 were recorded as "natural" sons and daughters. Children, several in number of the same father and mother come under this designation though it is possible that it was an irregular marriage as was not unknown in the interior among the poorer classes. The painful picture drawn by Woodmason in the Remonstrance of the depravity in some localities may not have been overdrawn. Some allowance must be made for the pessimism of the missionary and for the optimism of the governors who reported progress in the colony. It may be safely said of the well-constructed middle class families that the father was the head and the mother the heart of the little group. His lot was often hard and monotonous and hers was more so; but the mother's influence was a growing one with an upward tendency. Her unselfish devotion and forgetfulness of self, appreciated more justly after she was gone, was remembered by the lads and lassies who imitated her example in their own homes. Strong men, rough in appearance, have been seen to soften in their features, become husky in voice with eyes full of tears when questioned about their mothers. The women of South Carolina have been honored by spontaneous forethought in the general Assembly about their pecuniary interests and their maternal rights in the courts.

Some one has truly said that the family life at this period was grander and shabbier than it is today. Shabbier it certainly was in its primitive conveniences and sanitary arrangements, in its seclusion separated from schools and churches, and possibly in the temptation to neighborhood gossipping and small rivalries, in the absence of newspapers and books. On its grander side were the tendencies to make the home the center of the universe; just as the children at night looked up at the stars with the horizon equally distant on all sides, so when they went into their humble dwellings there they felt the cohesive tendency and fulness of affectionate family life that centered around mother and father. The manly independence encouraged on the plantation and the hospitality accorded the passing stranger at their firesides must also be included in the grander traits. Oftentimes the family felt itself the debtor when an entertaining stranger passed the hours with instructive conversation which contributed as much to the young people's enjoyment as the extra dishes prepared by hospitable mother.

The time was already at hand when the Huguenot, the Highlander, the Welsh, the Irish, Swiss, and Dutch families were to feel the assimilating force of the all conquering English language. The most powerful agency was the ubiquity and dominance of the English and their language, coupled with the interrmarriage of adjacent families which kept coming in. The Huguenots below the Santee were compact in settlement, associated in the same church and naturally intermarried; but above the Santee there began intermarriages with the other families. Noe Serre, above the average in intelligence, shrewdness and wealth, married Catherine Chicken and one of his sisters married a Shackelford. There was no prejudice against other races cultivated in his five daughters and son Noe. Contiguity as well as language furthered marriage alliances among the Guerrys, LeGrands, Gaillards, DeLeisselines, Remberts, Conturiers, Dutorques, Gendrons, &c, and on the Winyaw the Foissins and LaRoches and Trapiers intermarried, while the LaBruces and Marions became connected with the Allstons. The rare book containing contributions to the History of the Huguenots of South Carolina by Samuel DuBose and Prof. F. A. Porcher reads more like romance than sober history. Their conspicuous services to the state give them a prominence as great as their numbers were small.

A very different atmosphere meets one at Williamsburg. There was greater compactness there in settlement, clan feeling and religious cohesion, at a time when religion was at a low ebb in the mother country. The Irish were cloth makers and these Scotch Irish were led by weavers who gave the art of weaving a standing in the community and the community a standing in the colony. John Witherspoon was the founder of the well known Witherspoon family, now scattered throughout the South. He married his cousin and his daughter married John Fleming in Ireland. His son David married Ann Pressley. Elizabeth married William James, a Welshman, also in Ireland. Mary married her cousin David Wilson. These were all influential men and elders in the church. Out of 58 descendants, eight of 30 males and ten of 18 females died in infancy. So great a loss of life was the price to be paid for the acquisition of one's own vine and fig tree in this part of the new world. His grandson, Gavin Witherspoon, a brave soldier in the Revolution, an elder in the Hopewell Church, married Elizabeth Dick and their children were John Dick Witherspoon of Society Hill fame, Jane and Elizabeth. John Witherspoon, an older brother of Gavin, appears to have broken the custom in the family connection by going outside of his clan to marry Mary Conn whose ancestors probably resided on the Pee Dee not far from Georgetown. Their only daughter, Elizabeth, lost her mother in infancy and her wealthy and indulgent father in her 18th year and found in Gov. David Rogerson Williams a kind and faithful husband. Many of the Scotch-Irish at Williamsburg were poor but they were not mendicants nor brought over as redemptioners. Many of them had been tenants under landlords who knew how to keep them poor, but they were like the stunted undergrowth in forests which as soon as they are transplanted grow to fair proportions. The following commendation of two such persons is copied from the original in possesion of their descendants: "That Robert Irwin Did Live as a body servant with Mr. William Heavens seat of Belfast Merchant and afterwards with John Gordon of Belfast in the County of Antrim in the Kingdom of Ireland Esqrs and that in his service he intermarried with agnes Campbell a Tenants daughter of the Sd Mr. Gordon and lived as tenant to him for some years and that he and his wife Did behave themselves in an honest, sober well Behaved manner & Regular in the Desenting Principles Certified By us this

9th Day of October 1771 Seventy one at Loughbrickland In the Kingdom of Ireland

>JOHN GORDON
>JOHN SMITH, A. M,
>DISSENTING MINISTER
>JAS ANDERSON

The new world offered an asylum to the industrious hard pressed peasant of the 18th century. The Scotch Irish as citizens were less spectacular in their movements, self-reliant in whatever calling they followed, self-assertive and successful in business, patriotic and perhaps too bellicose for the highest type of Christianity. Their number at this time was about half of the population and their consequent weight in the Revolution must be generously acknowledged.

The Welsh on the Pee Dee were not so brilliant as the Huguenots nor so cohesive and self assertive as the Scotch Irish; but they exhibited a nobility of character all their own in their homes, churches and social gatherings. For five years they met without a minister, carried on devotional exercises with exhortations from the laymen before one of their number was chosen and ordained leader. Fewer defects and more rounded characteristics served to make them in a century appear like a higher peak in a mountain range. It was not purely a Welsh civilization, but it was one contributed to and largely aided by judicious intermarriages with the Scotch, Irish, Dutch and English.

For example, Johannes Kolb, a Hollander who came to the upper Pee Dee along with the Welsh to Cashaway Ferry, lived there with his large family of boys and girls. His son Tilman married Beersheba Watkins, his daughter Sarah married Robert Lide, Mehitabel married Charles Irby and Peter married into the leading James family. After the battle of Culloden, Roderick McIver, the ancestor of an illustrous line, married Rachel the daughter of Rev. Joshua Edwards and his son Evander married Sarah the sister of Abel Kolb, daughter of Ann James and Peter Kolb. Gen. Alexander McIntosh also married a Miss James.

The Germans were generally sent up the other rivers but a few ascended the Pee Dee. They were an addition to the agricultural forces, being industrious, economical, honest, good managers, kind neighbors and resolute in the defense of their property. They played no great part in the development of public enterprises, being like the Dutch of the 17th century who spent 360 days in the dwelling his grandfather prepared for him![1] They enlarged the exports of the colony.

Since this period a whole century has passed with a part of two others and one may now pass judgment on the prediction or claim that the amalgamation of good races produce a race superior to any one of them and that there will result a "national character having for its basis the irresistible energy and steady courage of the Anglo Saxon, in which are mingled the religious tenacity of the thrifty Scotch, the generous bravery of the quick witted Irishman, the sanguine, elastic spirit of the mercurial Frenchman and the patient persevering industry of the honest German."

---

[1] Calhoun's The American Family.

CHAPTER VIII

Gov. Glen, Gov. Lyttelton and War. 1739-1763

After all parties were weary of the long war in Europe, so eager were they for peace in 1748 that they surrendered their gains in the war; but it was only a truce in the struggle for supremacy in America. South Carolina had for about eight years suffered from stagnation of trade, and for several years yet to come the people of the state were only anxious spectators of the contest. They had a wide awake governor, Glen, who kept the Indians at peace during his long term, which ended all too soon.

The territory of the French extended from the mouth of St. Lawrence up to the lakes and down the Mississippi to the Gulf of Mexico and they exhibited great energy in building their chain of forts and tact in cultivating the friendship of the Indians. The English were pushing back their habitations further inland and even invading the valley of the rivers which emptied into the Mississippi. The French and Spaniards had been making it a matter of prime importance to stamp out heresy and did not allow heretics a shelter even in American woods. In this infatuation they were playing into the hands of the English enemies, who welcomed all the exiles and treated them as fellow subjects in England and in the colonies. Conscious that a conflict in and over America was inevitable, the English encouraged emigration and at the same time, while granting greater liberty than other people enjoyed, took care that they were subject to military training. Over against this advantage must be set down the isolation of the colonies which with their local dangers were too jealous of each other and of the mother country to unite their forces against a common enemy whose much weaker force was directed by a superior mind. Gov. Glen was an observant spectator and alert actor in these days which needed no weather bureau to forecast that a storm was going to burst upon the state. The Catawbas, Cherokees and Creeks Indians were on the borders of the colony and to keep the friendship of the chiefs and to preserve the scattered and undefended backwoods men from the tomahawks were his constant aims. In 1746, Gov. Glen sent Gen. Pawley of Georgetown with 20 men to inquire of the Cherokees and Creeks what their grievances were in order to pacify them. He was continually getting messages from the Over hill Cherokee leaders that emissaries of the French were present and trying to estrange them from the English. He called in 1753 a convention of the chiefs to renew their friendship and ward off the danger to the colony involved in a defection of these brave red men. The council was held in the country of the lower Cherokees. In it he made a treaty with them and built a fort, Prince George, on lands ceded near the Indian town Keowee. This treaty did not pacify the Indians however and Gov. Glen called another Council to meet at Saluda Old Town, for the purpose of persuading them to cede their lands to the king and come under his protection. It was at this time and place that "a territory of prodigious extent," the valuable domain embraced in the present districts of Abbeville, Edgefield, Laurens, Union, Spartanburg, Newberry, Chester, Fairfield, Richland and York, was ceded to the king. Lt. Col. Clarke of the Anson County militia was present at this Council at Saluda in June or July 1755, and reported to Gov. Dobbs of North Carolina what he heard and saw, viz., that Gov. Glen with large presents for the Indians, summoned near 700 people to attend him at their own expense, to make a show, and thus went with a great parade to the place of meeting where he was met by 1100 Indians; these he treated with meat and liquor for several days, whilst the Carolinians maintained themselves." One of the Cherokee chiefs gave him "very gross words" and refused to return to the conference. A gift of 100 pounds sterling softened the chief's resentment and in consequence of other entreaties, he ate and drank with them again. Gov. Glen exchanged his dress with this disgruntled chief and gave him a diamond, said to be worth 60 pounds to carry to his queen, "so that by repeated presents and liquor, he prevailed with them to sign a treaty by which they gave up all title to the lands they claimed toward the Mississippi to the crown of Great Britain, that he saw all the Indians sign their mark and about 700 English, with which he returned in triumph." This report of an eyewitness was not altogether friendly but in the main outlines it is historical. The last phrase "returned in triumph" is the better tradition as Gov. Glen's term of office did not expire in that year. He was at Ninety Six when Gov. Lyttelton's message reached him and relieved him of his office.

Gov. Glen was found fault with by certain men and classes connected with Indian trade and was charged with mercenary and unpatriotic motives in his negotiations with the Indians. Gov. Dobbs of North Carolina made a sinister report to the Board and Gov. Dinwiddie of Virginia thought his disregard of the instructions from headquarters inexplicable. With these governors the great fault of Gov. Glen was his slowness in forgetting the interest of South Carolina and in sending reinforcements for the defense of Virginia and of the British empire. Gov. Glen's conduct with reference to the Indians put him in line with Presidents Washington, Adams and Jefferson who bore the insults and injuries of England and France and trusted to remonstrance and negotiations rather than declare war and suffer more grievous evils. The Indian mode of warfare was peculiarly difficult to checkmate. A few thousand of them could have made an irruption in various places, kill and plunder and return home before an effective army could be raised. Therefore Gov. Glen exhausted his ingenuity in keeping the chiefs friendly and increased his patience when the hot headed youths inflamed by whiskey and intrigues of the French, made attacks by night in unguarded frontier places. He increased his rangers and called the chiefs into conference rather than declare war even on justifiable grounds. During his time the territory of the colony was greatly extended. His mild treatment of the Indians however prevented a rapid emigration into the frontiers. But a war had to be fought and in his jealous guardianship he practically assumed that the Indians were his and resented any meddling by other governors. A further evidence of his foresight was the wish to keep the Cherokees and Catawbas as a friendly outworks against the Indians in the interior under French influence. Braddock's defeat near Pittsburg on the 9th of July 1755 put a new face on affairs. South Carolina, up to this time had not been the theatre of war with the Spaniards and the French; but in close connection with this defeat was the deportation of 1020 Acadians to Charles Town whom it was the royal will the government should bind out in the parishes. These were a part of the unfortunate neutral French who were removed from their homes in Nova Scotia. It was decided to distribute them in the various parishes. Thirty-two were sent to Prince

Frederick.[1] Perhaps a larger number to Prince George Winyaw. Rev. John Baxter assumed charge of five. Charles Woodmason and Dr. James Crockatt four each, Col. John White and Andrew Burnet, two each. The remainder were assigned to persons not otherwise known. Before the year was out one fourth of these Acadians in Prince Frederick had succombed to the changes they had passed through. These men and women were designed to act as helps on the farm and in the house during the six or seven years of the war, after which time they were permitted to assemble at Charles Town and sail away in ships to Cape Francois.

The campaigns in 1756 and 1757, favorable to the French, were succeded by the fall of Fort DuQuesne and a reestablishment of the British in the eyes of the Indians as the more powerful nation and by the fall of Quebec. As the last resort the French agents went southward to stir up the Cherokees to war upon the English. Some thoughtless Virginians aided the French in their forlorn design by shooting a number of friendly Cherokees who were returning from the British army. They had appropriated wild horses, as they supposed, to be ridden on their long journey and were fired on in the act by their owners. This blunder and the skill of the French emissaries to take advantage of it, caused reprisals and inroads into the lower parts that made alarming reports reach Charles Town. There had been rejoicing and entertainments in that city over the recent fall of Fort DuQuesne; but that event transferred further South the theatre of war and disturbed the pacific Indian, Little Carpenter, as well as the people of the colony. In April 1759, he and about 90 other headmen and warriors came down to the city in the in-

---

[1]Register Book, Parish Prince Frederick Winyaw, p. 142.

terest of peace and they were followed later by Creeks who came a circuitous route, but the visits, consultations and agreements meant very little to the younger Indian warriors. In August the Assembly decided that the Indian situation called for two companies of Rangers to protect the frontiers and Adjutant General George Pawley assigned days and places for a general review of the militia—Kinloch's Old Field, Oct. 2, Georgetown Oct. 4, Black Mingo Oct. 8, Mars Bluff Oct 11, and Westfield's on upper Pee Dee Oct 13. It was in contemplation to enlist 1500 men to reduce the Indians, with the Congarees as the rendezvous. In October, the General Assembly, seeing that Governor Lyttelton was bent upon a war against the Indians, expressed to him unanimously the opinion that "declaring war at this time will be attended with the greatest evils and calamities and be productive of the most dangerous consequences." Gov. Lyttelton among other things replied, "Nevertheless, as it is my sincere intention to do nothing which may have the most remote tendency to prevent a good accomodation with those people and you so earnestly desire me in this address to defer declaring war against them, I will do so; but I trust you will enable me, by a speedy grant of the supply I have asked of you, to pursue vigorous measures in order to avert those many evils which must unavoidably fall upon this country, if these hostilities are not soon repressed."[2]

The Assembly was prorogued and notwithstanding his promise to defer war, in two weeks 113 loaded wagons were on their way to the Congarees, where two or three colonels with their battalions were already. On Nov. 4, after a review of the soldiers with Col. Powell's Pee Deeans on the left, the soldiers in line of March extended

---
[2]See South Carolina Gazette, October 11, 1759.

over two miles. The Indian chiefs who had accompanied Gov. Lyttelton to the Congarees began to desert and to prevent further desertion and though they had come as ambassadors to treat of peace, they were put under guard, and deeply incensed; and to this inexcusable blunder was added incarceration at Fort Prince George, where most of them were finally murdered. A hollow treaty was made with Indian chiefs and there followed a triumphant entry into Charles Town, which is explicable on one of the alternatives that the people and the Presbyterian clergy were either in the dark as to the facts or that they were vieing with the orientals in adulation of their ruler. The jubilation soon gave way to tidings that the incensed Indians paid no regard to the treaty and had begun at once a campaign of revenge. Fort Prince George was besieged and murders committed around it. They also came down within a month after Gov. Lyttelton's return with their tomahawks on the promising settlement of the Calhouns at the Long Canes and killed or wounded 38 and scattered the estimated 250 inhabitants.

Gov. Lyttelton was soon relieved of his unpleasant situation by promotion to another governorship and the ever-reliable Lieutenant Governor Bull succeeded to his place and inherited the evils of his blunders. He called upon the Commander-in-chief of the British forces for succor who since the fall of Quebec could spare Col. Montgomery for a brief expedition into upper South Carolina. In the meantime the savages were burning houses in the Ninety Six neighborhood, plundering, killing people and driving off the stock. In the latter part of April Col. Montgomery started northward, carrying only 350 of the rangers with him, the remainder being left to scour the country from Savannah to Catawba.

There was no opposition to the marching army before it reached 12 mile river; there after night about 200 men being left to guard the camp,[3] the main army proceeded in order to surprise the Indians. His expedition was not bloodless, but he was everywhere successful, the Indian tactics being now fully understood. Their villages were burnt, their supplies of provisions were destroyed and his soldiers exhausted in his expeditious warfare. Very few of the Indians were killed or captured, but their lower country was thoroughly devastated, Shermanized!

Col. Montgomery was under instructions to return, and in obeying orders he left the back settlers in great danger from the Indians who had been defeated but not subdued. The governor however kept rangers in the exposed places some of whom came in contact with the marauders. One of the captains whose activity and usefulness appeared above the horizon was John Dargan of St. Marks Parish; and it must be told in honor of those wonderful people, the Scotch Irish of Williamsburg, whose patriotism notwithstanding they were denied participation in the government, scintillated like red hot iron. The inhabitants of Williamsburg, natives of North Ireland, said a current newspaper, "are remarkably zealous and active in giving all possible assistance to the recruiting officers to raise men to act against the Cherokees; and that they have actually set on foot a subscription to add 5 pound to the bounty money allowed by the government to every man who shall enlist into the service from among them. Gov. Bull was indefatigable. He secured troops under Col. Grant to make the expedition in 1761 and tried at the same time to prevail on the governors of Virginia and North Carolina to make an irruption into the upper

---

[3]South Carolina Gazette, June 7, 1760.

Cherokees while Col. Grant was attacking on the hither side. About the middle of March, Col. Grant was at Monck's Corner waiting for suitable weather for advancing to the Congarees where some provincials had wintered and to Ninety Six the head quarters of the Rangers. The advance of the army met no obstacles from the enemy. Early in June, he set out from Fort Prince George on his punitive expedition. A battle was soon joined in which for several hours the braves on both sides stood their ground; but it was inevitable that the savages could not resist the forces of civilization, with their better equipment and superior forces. It is quite a travesty to speak of civilization even in contrast with Cherokee savages, when the towns reduced to ashes, the reservoir of grain burnt or charred beyond recovery and their beautiful valleys rendered desolate, were silent witnesses of the work of Col. Grant and his forces! It was as complete as that effected in the eastern part of the State in 1865 by a general under another Grant.

Col. Richard Richardson of St. Mark's received the thanks of his community and Capt. John Dargan, brother of the Rev. Timothy Dargan, and Col. George Gabriel Powell of Georgetown were men of note in this war. Capt. John Dargan's rangers were continued after peace in the upper parts. His company is found honored however, beyond others in having the full list, officers and privates, and their pay published in the Gazette. South Carolina, initiated into the war by the servile insurrection in 1739, saw the gates of Janus closed in 1761, in the north-western part of the colony. The peace then made with the fierce Cherokees was to last a few years only. Here the last hope of the French expired or was soon to expire in the struggle for supremacy in America. After France was now plainly vanquished on the sea also, Spain joined France against England in time to lose Havana and the Philippines both of which were afterwards restored to her, but Florida ceased to be a thorn in the side of Georgia and South Carolina after its annexation as an English possession. See S. C. Gazette, Sept. 3, 1763.

It was in the month of December 1762 that Georgetown had some lively times in hearing from the privateers plying along the coast. According to somewhat conflicting reports of the current Gazettes, the brig *Neptune* of Charles Town was captured on the 2nd and was relieved of two negroes, some sails and rigging by the captors. On the 4th the Schooner *Live Oak* was chased into Winyaw Bay and they surprised and plundered the pilot's house and took a long new boat. Joseph Du Bourdieu was carried off in his own sail boat but the negroes and Rev. Mr. Pearce, the parish rector who had been staying there some days for his health, were more resourceful and happy enough to escape. Their ultimate design was thought to be the surprise of Georgetown. On the 5th several boats were chased. On the 6th a ship and scow were chased off Winyaw, the latter escaped but on the 7th they captured ship *Black Prince* which was ransomed for $600.00. On the 8th the brig *Catherine* from Georgetown was captured with molasses. On the 9th, the long boat having gone from Winyaw to Raccoon bay, the crew landed and plundered one plantation, took 3 negroes, one of Mr. Richard Withers', the others from Isaac Mazyck. On the 10th, they took *Gen. Wolfe*, which had on board 50 valuable casks of French Indigo, 6 hogsheads of sugar, some coffee, mahogany, fruits and 250 pounds in cash, valued at 30,000 pounds. On the 11th the brig *Friendship* from Charles Town was taken by a French privateer. The long boat taken at North Island proved to be quite serviceable to the marauders in plundering and landing prisoners. The chasing was now generally unavailing off Winyaw and Cape Romaine. On the 21st two sloops engaged and took a brig off Shubrick's Island. Don Martin's *Santa Maria*, a privateer from St. Augustine, was one of the principal offenders in this crisis. It was said at the time that of their captures very few were carried into port.

Within these years 1739-1763 the dwellers on our streams, except those troubled by privateers, were dwelling in safety, screened from the Indian as well as from European enemies; but they went southward or westward as they were called upon in defence of the colony, and suffered financially, owing to the low prices of farm products. Were the South Carolinians grateful for the aid sent them against the Indians? Yes, but they had short memories!

CHAPTER IX

EDUCATION IN CRAVEN COUNTY BEFORE THE REVOLUTION

The period of peace (1763-1775) was not favorable to religion and education. On the latter subject there is little to be said in reference to this section north of the Santee. The one school which operated in the period 1755-1775 was at Georgetown opened and sustained by the Winyaw Indigo Society. No school elsewhere has been found referred to in the letters of the missionaries at Prince George Winyaw, Prince Frederick or St. Marks parish churches nor in the records of the Presbyterians as preserved by Dr. Howe, nor in McCrady's reply to McMaster nor in the History of Higher Education in South Carolina by Colyer Meriwether. The earliest small one was opened in Camden by Rev. Woodmason in 1766 as an aid to his missionary work. He found not a school nor a school teacher in a tour of above 500 miles. Another school comes to light in Rev. Jenkins' narrative. Born in 1764 he entered his first school near Port's Ferry in Marion County after his family had made two removals. It is not therefore to be inferred that there was no teaching done at home or in some thickly settled localities, in this vast region where so many of the white people of the whole province lived. That it was in a sadly neglected condition in respect even to primary education all the witnesses agree. Possibly this picture of the times found in the Remonstrance is overdrawn:

"Through the non-establishment of Public Schools a great multitude of children are now grown up (1767) in the greatest ignorance of everything: save vice in which they are adepts: consequently they lead idle and immoral lives: for they having no sort of education, naturally follow hunting, shooting, racing, drinking, gaming and every species of wickedness. Their lives are only one continual scene of depravity of manners, and reproach to the country, being more abandoned to sensuality, and more rude in manners than the poor savages around us."

No small hindrance was the difficulty in obtaining teachers. The scanty reward of the teacher included his board which had in some places as late as 1850 to be taken in succession at the various farms far and near from which the children came. Neither in the S. P. G. nor the state interested itself in this secular education in the outer parts. And in this practical indifference the Charles Town officials were walking in the footsteps of the mother country. In transporting so generously the poor and the poor Protestant to the new world, it had not entered into their thoughts that universal education was essential in transforming them into good citizens. This *laissez faire* policy in education included all the back country. There was a general belief that if any youth had gifts and a desire for an education, it was in his reach, and that whatever a man got by his own exertions stayed with him the longest. "What costs nothing is worth nothing." The plan of education in South Carolina up to 1865 is found in embryo in the school opened in 1720 in Charles Town by Rev. Thomas Morritt. He was a teacher sent out by S. P. G. and the second to locate in Charles Town. But Morritt built on his own foundation, or in other words, he opened the school and conducted it after the fashion in England. Those who were able paid tuition and free tuition was provided for a number of the poor. The ancient languages were not only a part of the schedule but an important part of it.

In aristocratic countries an instinct of preservation makes men see as Dr. Thomas Cooper did, when he affirmed that the progress and good influence of education is downward. Its progress could be in no other direction between parents and children, teachers and pupils, superiors in any line and inferiors; but he meant that such education was the best which reaches the strata of people one after another from the top downward. This theory put into active operation by the state up to the war furnished a stable government and many able men in every calling; but it also left untouched many illiterate people with a pedigree of illiteracy reaching back three to many generations.

The school in Georgetown was ready for work in May 1755. In that month the clerk Joseph DuBourdieu gave this notice to the public:

"Whereas the Winyaw Indigo Society, have established a fund for the endowment of a Free School at Georgetown, where 18 poor children are to be educated on the bounty of the Society, any person qualified for teaching the following branches of learning viz. reading, writing the English tongue, arithmetic and Latin and are inclinable to engage therein are desired to send their proposal to said Society, directed to their clerk in Georgetown."

The school owed its origin to a convivial club which had been in existence about 14 years. Its first president was that nobleman, Thomas Lynch, who acquired so much real estate on the Santee in and after 1732. The annual dues of the society being paid in Indigo, when its value rose, the question what to do with the accumulating funds became acute in 1753, at the annual meeting of which year, the president of the club, at the close of the banquet,[1] called on the members to fill their glasses, he wished to close the debate by a definite proposition; if it met their approbation each member would signify it by emptying his glass. "There may be intellectual food", said he, "which the present state of society is not fit to partake of; to lay such before it would be as absurd as to give a quadrant to an Indian; but knowledge is indeed as necessary as light, and ought to be as common as water and free as air. It has been wisely ordained that light should have no color, water no taste and air no odor; so indeed knowledge should be equally pure and without admixture of creed or cant. I move therefore that the surplus funds in the treasury be devoted to the establishment of an independent charity school for the poor." The speech met with unanimous approval. The meeting rose to its feet and every cup was drained and every vote was cast for the establishing of the school. Its growth in numbers was rapid. In June 1756, an usher was needed and notice was given the public that any person recommended to the president or the committee of the said Society, by Mr. William Henderson, master of the Free School in Charles Town, shall be accepted of; and shall be allowed 400 pounds currency per annum. The usher thus recommended introduced military training in 1757, carrying out said Henderson's ideas.

In 1761 the clerk was again in search of a Master for the Free School, particularly to teach reading in the English tongue, writing and arithmetic. How many students were annually enrolled and how many were drawn down the four rivers as boarding students to enjoy the benefits of the only known school in Craven County, it would be interesting to know. An average of 25 has

---

[1]History of Higher Education in S. C. by Colyer Meriwether, p. 19.

been named as the probable number. The names of teachers and of pupils have been mostly forgotten.

Interest in the school abated in the decade preceding hostilities and the school appears to have been suspended in 1772. The clerk, J. Skrine, gave notice in August of this year that a meeting of the Winyaw Indigo Society was appointed to be held at the house of Mr. William Flinn. And this was added: "The members are hereby earnestly desired to give due and regular attendance in order to examine into the state of the Society and to put their affairs (which have long been dormant) on a proper footing."[2]

One feature about the origin of this school is creditable to its founders, it sprung up out of rich soil and flourished. It was spontaneous and unselfish. Several schools were started in the late seventies as defensive measures just as it was the encouragement of local manufactures, in order to make the people independent of Great Britain. The people of the state went through a similar experience in 1830-60.

One of these later efforts began about 1764 when a committee of the assembly was appointed to consider of ways and means of endowing a public college in this province for the education of youth. In March following an article in the Gazette assumed as easy of proof "that no less than 50,000 pounds sterling had been sent out of the province in the last 30 years for the purpose of education and that there is more now annually spent in Great Britain for that purpose than 2000 pounds sterling. The greatest part of this sum, if we had a well established college, might be annually saved to the province and very probably, our youth much the better likewise." Several years elapsed before the subject

---

[2]S. C. Gazette, Aug. 2, 1772. Advertisements have to serve in the place of minutes of the trustees.

was sufficiently ventilated to insure action in the Assembly.

In 1770, the inhabitants of Charles Town petitioned the General Assembly that a college might be instituted in this province and like petitions were being signed in other places.[3] Within one week a bill was ordered to be brought into the Commons House for establishing the said college. The bill after having passed its second reading in both houses was lost by the sudden prorogation of the General Assembly. An observer thus commented:

"If the plan for founding, erecting and endowing a college in this province still should be carried into execution, which is scarce to be doubted there will remain only to fix on the most proper spot whereon to erect it ... if the most airy and healthy situation should be chosen, where youths may be least incommoded in their studies during the hot months and most free from danger of contagion, well removed from temptations to debauchery and where they have good water."

Two matters were left unsettled, said Charles Woodmason, whether the child shall be obliged to be brought up Conformist or not and what shall be the qualifications of the professors at the college. Only the Master is to be of the Church established.

Why the well thought out project of a college in Charles Town collapsed so suddenly and completely is hidden in the sudden prorogation of the body. In the light of subsequent events, the wiser course seems to have been followed. The subject was dropped until it was revived by an Act passed Aug. 12, 1783, appointing trustees of the 180 acres at Ninety Six, taken from a Tory for a Seminary of learning.

---

[3] S. C. Gazette, Feb. 8, 1770.

CHAPTER X

THE PARISH CHURCHES IN CRAVEN COUNTY 1721-1780

Prince George Winyaw Parish was a part of St. James Parish, south of the Santee until March 10, 1721 when it was enacted that its bounds should be "to the southwest on Santee River, and to the north-east on Cape Fear River, to the eastward on the ocean, and the west as far as it shall be inhabited by His Majesty's subjects." This fact was officially communicated to the S. P. G.[1] by the President of the Council and speaker of the House and by the clergy assembled in Charles Town.

Right Honble

. . . .

        We have likewise passed a Law for erecting a new Parish at Winean and have Ordered a sum of money for the building of a Church there; His Excellency our Governour, to forward so good a work, has given One Hundred Pounds, and we hope the hon^{ble} Society will send a person over to officiate as one of their Missionaries, and he pleased to supply the rest of our vacant Parishes as soon as possible.—

Charles City & Port
In South Carolina   Your Honour's most obed^t
July 3^d 1722   and most humble Serv^{ts}
    Ja:Moore Speaker   ArthurMiddleton:P:

                                S° Carolina Charles City
                                   July 12th 1722

Sir

    The Clergy being here met to return their United Thanks to his Excellency Governour Nicholson for the many Signal Services done to the Church in general, & to the Clergy in particular, we think it our Duty to

---

[1]Society for the Propagation of the Gospel in Foreign Parts.

lay before (the society) . . . a particular account . . . of the flourishing state of the Church here under the Patronage of so Religious a Governour . . . (after mentioning the act of the General Assembly for improvement and repair of several churches and parsonages) the letter continues:

And a new Parish by y^t name of King George's settled to the Northwards of the Province, at a place called Winean, for ye more speedy erecting of which parish Church, his Excellency hath very generously contributed nine Hundred Pounds. By his happy Influence, in his earnest & pathetick Speech to both Houses of Assembly at their last Sessions in the month of June a Law was passed with great Alacrity and Unanimity for the Augmenting ye Salaryes of the Clergy . . .

> Signed by Dr. Bull, Thos. Hasell, John Lapierre, William Guy, Albert Ponderous & A Garden.

Meredith Hughes, John Lane and John Hays were appointed commissioners to build the church and parsonage at a cost not exceeding 5,000 pounds. The letters sent from Winyaw for a clergyman have not been preserved, but their substance is doubtless found in the words of the Secretary of the Society: "This is a frontier place so far distant from any church, as the inhabitants have wrote to the Society that they have lived many years without seeing any divine service performed, without having their children baptized or the dead buried in any Christian order." This church was of spontaneous growth. Church of England families had been settling in the parish for 20 years. They corresponded with their friends and invited their former pastors and ministers to visit them. The earliest baptism of children was in 1713 in the family of John Lane.

The site for the church was about 13 miles from Georgetown on the right bank of the Black river, in a beautiful situation but as it proved later, not in a strategic position after Georgetown became a port. Rev. Mr. Pownel visited the flock in Christmas 1725, and in 1726 the church was built. The next is a letter from the vestry and warden to Gov. Nicholson, dated Nov. 12, 1726:

May it Please Your Excellency

It is the greatest Satisfaction Imaginable that We hear Your Excellency Intends very soon to return to Your Government, being persuaded that under Your Administration this province must prosper. We doubt not the General Assembly have thought it their duty in the most Grateful as well as publick manner to return your Excellency their Sincere and hearty thanks for your Constant and Assiduous application in Great Britain for the Service of this province, and particularly in the Care you are pleased to take that We should be Continued under his Maj^{ts} immediate protection a Peculiar happiness which this province had long wished for and at last with Difficulty Obtained.

As Your Excellency's Concern is the same for all parts of this his Maj^{ts} province but more Immediately for the inhabitants of Such parts as Labour under any Grievances or misfortunes We take leave to beg that Your Excellency will be pleased to Interceed with the Society to send Us a Missionary, and as partly by Your Bounty, and by Your Excellency's Encouragement, Our Church is now finished fit to perform Divine service in, We hope Your Excellency will be pleased to Cause it to be Supplied with an Orthodox Minister as soon as Possible who may bring over to the Church of England many People who are Waving in their opinion and are forced to ride many Miles to Communicate with the Dissenters for want of Such a Divine.

Your Excellency having Consented that Instructions should be given to Messenger Yonge and Lloyd when they went to Great Britain, Agents to Sollicit that a Port of Entry might be made in our parish it being so highly reasonable, We pray that when Your Excellencys thoughts are employed in the Service of this Country That You will be so good to remember so Importa^t an Affair. You will be pleased to remember that We are at least one hundred miles by watter from Charles Town, whereto We are obliged to Carry all our Goods to Market and to Cross severall large and dangerous Sounds which Subjects our Industry to many Great Hazards & Occasions Us to pay great & Unreasonable prices for freight which abates greatly of the proffit of Our Labor and Pains. And We presume there is as much if not more Reason that We should have a Port than Port Royall on this Acc^t. That Our Inhabitants are more numerous there now being Setled upon the several rivers in Prince Georges parish, at least one hundred families many of which are Good Settlers and have large Gangs of Negroes and make large Quantities of our produce, And that it likewise will prevent the Desertions from Us to Cape Fair which now is much occasioned by the Rigid Usage of the Merchants and lawyers to the Infinite prejudice and weakening of this his Maj^{ts} province.

We shall always hold Our Selves Extremely oblig'd to Your Excellency for the Services You have been pleased already to render Us, And We Entreat Your Excellency to Continue Your good Offices to Us in two Circumstances of So Great Consequence to Us We are

May it Please Your Excellency

SOUTH CAROLINA

Your Excellencys Most obed^t: &
most humble Servants

Prince Georges
    Parish
So Carolina Winyaw
November 12, 1726

Richd Smith Jas. Nichol	Representatives
Merrid: Hughs John Bell	Church Wardens
Jms Browne Jno Hayes Anth: White Rd Smith	Vestry Men

Prince Georges Parish Letter, Addressed to his Excellency ffra: Nicholson, Coffe house.

Rev. Mr. Morritt's letters are now next in order:

Charles Town S° Carl^{na} Feb. 3, 1726-7

Revrd S^r (Rev. Mr. Humphreys, Secretary of the Society)
... In the Northern parts of this Province here has been abour a Years ago a new parish Establish'd by Act of Assembly, tho' there has been for many Years a number of People settled in those parts, yet they have not had the benefit of a minist^r. among them 'till the Revrd Mr Pownel went about 12 Months ago, but stayed there only a Week. These People have sent to me, 3 times, to invite me among y^m, but by reason of ye dis-

tance of y° place from Charles Town y° confinem^t of my school, I could not have any earlier opportunity to go till Christmas, where I was receivd wth a great deal of civility & good nature. I preach'd there 3 Sundys & had every time an Audience of at least 100 people. They are, for the generality, a People very well dispos'd, & have by application to ye Public, got so much money advanc's as to enable y^m to build a Church, & in some small time, they will accomplish a Parsonage house for y° entertainment of a missionary. There are a great many Anabaptists & dissenters in y^t Parish, & the lett^r have got a Meeting house erected; but I am perswaded if a Missionary was once fix'd, those sectarists would be less numerous & the Church Comminion would encrease: provided they had a Gent: y^t was so happy as to give content. As the poor and illiterate are most liable to be seduc'd, & as these People chiefly dwell in ye out settlem^{ts} & lie straggl'd about, so y° dissenting & oth^r Teach^{rs} are allways hunting after 'em to pick up these scatter'd sheep, for wch reason it is, there is scarce a Parish in this Province y^t has not a meeting House or two in it, wch have been set up by those means, & some of their Congregations of late are become very numerous. There are but five Teachers In y^t Province wch supply these Meeting Houses wch they do w^{tb} so much indefatigable pains y^t they still make a shift to retain a number of followrs, they spare no Pains & grudge no labour provided they can gain over Proselytes to their Perswasion, as they are paid pr Sermon they make a shift to dispence 2 or 3 pr Week at different places from 20 to 40 or 50 miles asunder. Insomuch they seem to gain ground sensibly of the Church & I see no readier means whereby these growing encroachments may be remedied but by alike industry & diligence us'd on the other side.

South Carolina

When I was at Winnian ye Yestry of ye Parish were pleas'd to express a desire t'have me among ym, & since my coming down, have made me ye like offer, t'whom I answer'd it was not consistent with me to Comply wth any such proposal, but yt as every Minister had a stipend allowed by ye Society & yt their Parish deserv'd such an encouragement above any in the Province, so if I was appointed their Missionary I would cheerfully embrace their offer & serve ym. This Parish lies about 85 miles or upwards from Charles Town & is the largest Parish in ye Province for extent, there are about 90 Families in it & in all probability will, of white People, be a numerous settlement, but their interest at present is but small, they are dispers'd about & settled chiefly along ye sides of 3 rivers, wch renders it commodious for their coming to Church but very inconvenient for a Ministr to visit ym wch would be highly necessary for him to do as oft as possible especially as they are but ill grounded in their Principles, as they are not able to give their Ministr Negros, as many Parishes have done, so whoever is ministr thereof will meet wth some difficulty at first, for there is no place suitable to be boarded at othr wise it might suit best with a single Gent. He must be a House keeper or he cannot propose to live tolerably comfortable. Insomuch for ye first 3 or 4 Years it is my humble opinion a Missionary yt lives there justly merits a more bountiful encouragmt yn any yet in ye Province. It is now in its very Infancy, but in process of time 'twill become more comfortable & commodious, it lies 3 days journey from Charles Town & a very unpleasant road there is a Ferry to pass wch is 5 miles over, wch renders the journey very irksome & chargable, if any business demands their coming down to Charles Town.

As this Country is situated, Port Royal, St. James, & Christ Church & that parish of Winnian should of necessity be allway provided wth Residentiary Missionaries, because they lie very inconvenient to be serv'd by any neighboring ministr and as it is some expense to travel & difficulty to cross the Rivers, & that as the Country now, by the Church Act makes no allowance to a Ministr yt serves any vacant Parish, so as it is both a fateague & charge those Parishes wh they are vacant are entirely neglected . . . insomuch since Mr. Pownel left Christ Church the Dissentrs have gain'd ground to yt degree that they talk of Erecting forthwth anothr Meeting House not above 100 Yards from the Parsonage House I still endeavour to serve ym every 3d or 4th Sunday but it might be heartily wish'd that Parish was better attended then wt lies in the power of

        Revrd Sr
      Yr most Obed: H" Srt
        Tho: Morritt

    So Carolina Winneyaw Septr. 1st 1729

Revrd Sr

The favour of ye Lettr by Order of ye Honble Society, i did not receive 'till ye Latter end of Feby wch was wth some othrs detained as it sometimes happens, by Mastrs of Vessels knowing our names, who keep our Lettrs thinking thereby they do us a greater favour rather yn deliver ym into ye Post-Office. But as I had earlier notice of ye Honble Society's kind intentions of providing for me so I happen'd to be in those parts, a while, for my health wn ye Rev. Mr. Lambert arriv'd to wch end after I resigned up my school & ye Books wch were left in my hands, I return'd again to Prince George's Parish wth ye outmost dispatch, & have since, as far as health permitted, done my endeavours to use such care & diligence, requisite to make ym a united People, wch is a great pity, this place was not earlier provided for, because ye dissenters begin to distinguish ymselves fro ye church & have obtained a Teacher to settle amongst ym whom they sent for from Bermudas. This settlemt increases every day & by ye nearest computation, wch I am capable of making at present, we have no less yn 700 white people Young & Old & as many Negro's besides two or 300 Native Indians scatter'd about ye settlemts.

The Parish is of great extent near 130 miles in Breadth along ye Sea Coast & settled wth in Land upwards of 80 miles, variously dispersed & according to ye nature of these Country settlemts upon 3 large navigable Rivers more considerable for navigation yn any in ye Province. Which as ye People are scatter'd about at Present for commodiousness of settlemt so I have a Parish of such extent, as will and must be In a few Years divided into 3 Parishes, in ye mean time I have almost an insupportable charge upon my hands, & at present am obliged to settle a Chappel of Ease about 14 miles from ye Parish Church for ye conveniency of about 15 families, wch cannot wth out ye outmost fateague both by Land & by Water, othrwise obtain any benefit of a Ministr, & in a short time I must be forced to attend at another place, if not at two more, at all suitable intervals.

I am not yet provided wth horses & othr conveniences for such journeys otherwise I should have visited, befor this, all ye parts of my Parish; But I hope shortly I shall be able to accomplish these necessary assistances, in order I may be capable of giving ye Honble Society a more complete acct of ye due extent situation & nature of my Parish.

Since my last I have Baptiz'd 26 children besides two young Ladies One about 13 and anothr about 11 Years Old, who gave an incomparable acc't of their Faith,' allso one Adult ye husband of ye Gentlewoman mantion'd in my last ye Fath'r of a numerous Family, there are two or 3 Families more yt are unbaptiz'd wch I find are inclinable to joyn in communion wth ye Church. As soon as I can provide myself wth conveniences for passing and repassing I shall be more frequent in my Visits in order to regain more to ye Church, I cannot yet be able to give a perfect Acc't wth number of Churchpeople, Dissenters, & AnaBaptists respectively we have in our Parish, because I am not thoroughly, or perhaps not rightly inform'd of their principles, but generally I have a numerous audience, sometimes near 200, often 150 & seldom less than 100. At Michaelmas I had nine communicants & at Eastr & Whitsuntide 19 & upwards, some othrs were sick wch diminish'd ye expected number, but in general I doubt not but I shall have 30 or 33 constant Communicants besides othrs wch are othrwise well dispos'd but cannot attend so constantly.

The church is a Wooden Fabric, but very decently raid'd 45 foot long & 25 wide & is very commodiously situated on ye side of a River, where it branches and makes it convenient for about 120 Families wch are not above 12 or 14 miles at farthest distant from ye Church, where most can & do frequently come by Water. The Parsonage-house lies about half a mile from ye Church wch is likewise a wooden building but palister'd within, a story & half high & 25 foot Square, it stands upon ye same river, agreeably situated, wth a pretty Glebe contiguous of about 200 Acres, the House is not yet finish'd neith'r can I tell wn it will be, because it depends upon ye pleasure of ye Assembly, who about three years ago voted a supply of £300 for ye finishing of ye church & (torn) But ye Assembly was dissolved before ye Estimate or Taxbill was agreed to, & ever since wh have had no Assembly yt has entr'd upon any business, insomuch yt this affair as well as othr concerns of ye Public are entirely at a stand; In ye meantime I make a very sorry shift wth accomodations as I can get elsewhere, wch as I was in hopes ere this, would have been bettr'd, so I have accordingly sent for my Family over, wch if they arrive speedily I fear I must be forc'd to finish ye house at my own expence, these othr inconveniences we must dispence with if we want to live in peace & tranquility wch I shall alway make it my endeavour to seek yt I may not interrupt ye pious ends of my Mission   I am wth due respects Revrd Sr Yr most Obedt. Yr Humble Srt

         Tho: Morritt

     So Carolina Jan. 10th 1731-2

Revrd Sr

I gave you an acct in my last how apprehensive I was lest ye Books wch ye Honble Society provided for ye benefit of my Parish were lost wch came not by Capt. Paine but by Capt. Homer who lost his ship bur preserv'd the Books wth very little damage & convey'd ym to hand I advid's wm Tryon Esqr of ye receipt thereof & have since had deliver'd to me 50 of my Lord of London's Pastoral Lettrs wch are very acceptable in these remote parts.

Since my last we have had eight settlers more come amongst us; insomuch yt my Parish now begins to exceed in number any Country Parish in ye Province—

I am in hopes we shall in some short time get two Chappels of Ease serected for ye conveniency of several Inhabitants wch are so inconveniently settled, by being intercepted by Rivers, yt they cannot possibly without ye outmost fateague, frequent ye Parish church. I endeavor to give attendance, at those places, every Seventh Sunday alternately; & as I find those places grow more populous shall endeavour to allow ym an equal share of my time, tho' ye Parish Church is generally frequented by a numerous Congregation. I was in hopes this great resort of People into these parts, would have inducd ye Public t'have taken it into Consideration to have some thoughts of dividing ye parish, but I find little appearance of any such provision. As my Constittution will not dispence wth ye like fateague as it could have done, so as I intimated in my Letters heretofore yt ye Parsonage house was not finish'd, & now yt my Family is com'd over above as twelve-month ago so by such, unsuitable accomodations I cannot forbear complaining of my misfortune how I have been baffled 4 years in Charles Town & now as many here wch makes time so irksome to me yt if I am not favourd wth a more conversible & convenient Parish yt is provided wth bettr accomodations I must be Oblig'd to leave ye Country, for a Sollicitrs Office is but a sorry Employ in these parts. I did not take this Parish out of inclination but as it was ye only one vacant & my affairs confin'd me to ye Country, but if my Employ has been thought agreeable to the Honble Societys approbation I hope I shall merit a share of their Honrs favour to prefer me to a more commodious Parish for this wch I now have is far from giving content to

 Revrd Sr Yr most Obedt Humble Srt

         T. Morritt

South Carolina

So Carolina May 3d 1731

Revrd Sr

... We have now a Town laid out & are under a prospect of obtaining a Port of Entry, wch if effected 'twill make ye place very populous by reason we have such commodious Rivers fit for Settlemts, as I mention'd in my formr Lettrs not inferior to those about Charles Town wch branch into ye adjacent Parishes

... My Family arriv'd here Octobr last, where as I, all along intimated, was but endeaferently provided to receive ym by reason ye house was not finished etc. ... ye Numbr of Communicants Xtmas & Eastr last, have not exceeded above one I gave an acct of in my last, But those Families I mention'd above are most of ym well disposed & I do not question but I shall find ym constant Communicants as soon as they can wth conveniency be provided wth a place & opportunity. Since Eastr 1730 I have Baptiz'd 23 Children & endeavour myself agreeable to ye Honble Society's late instructions to instruct my Negro's, I have 4 Children wch I propose God Willing to teach & Baptize ym as soon as my Family is settled & I have 3 Men & two Women more yt give some proof of a steady application wch attend ye Evening Prayrs & on Sundays I constantly read ym something of ye fundamentals of ye Xtian Religion wch gives me hopes will prove to good effect, I constantly continue as usual to read Catechistical Lectures in ye mothod I observed before in my formr Lettrs I am wth due respects
Revrd Sr Yr most Obedt Humble Srt

T. Morritt

So Carolina Augt 24th 1731

Revrd Sr

I receiv'd ye favour of Yr Lettr by Captn John Payne intimating ye Books wch ye Honble Society was pleasd to provide for the Service of our Parish. We live at such a distance from Charles Town yt our Lettrs often meet wth great delay, for Capt. Payne was ready to sail before yr Lettr came to hand, & having therewth no orders to demand ye Box I could do no more yn enquire of him about it, I have sent you this advice yt at his return He may be intercepted in London: yt farthr enquiry, if needful may be made about it.

It is incredible to relate how People daily resort from all parts of this Province, & elsewhere, to settle in my Parish; on ye prospect of having a Port of Entry establish'd here, insomuch yt I cannot possibly render a just acct wt number of Inhabitants we have. I preach now at two places, besides ye Parish church, Where there will be Chappels immediately Erected, & where of necessity books will be wanting, being hard to be Obtain'd & generally ye last things provided.

The Vestry & Ch Wardens gratefully acknowledge ye favour of ye Books & request their thanks may be given to ye society for ye same hopeing not but they will come in safely to ye hands of

  Revrd Sr Yr most Obedt Humble Srt

        T. Morritt

   So Carolina Prince Georges Parish
     Feb: 3d 1734-5

Mt Lord (Bishop of London)

I have intimated to yr Lordship that this Settlemt by appointmt of ye Genl Assembly is Divided into two Parishes ye one part distinguished by ye name of Prince Georges & ye othr of Prince Fredericks Parish

In ye Upper as well as lower districts of this Parish there is a considerable increase of People wth this few Years, insomuch yt ye remotest parts are now become ye best settled, for Wackamaw Neck according to ye plan I sent yr Lordship think ymselves hardly dealt wth in yt they are not provided for as a separate Parish but are appendage still of Prince Georges, wch I must own they labour under great hardships because they can attend divine service no othr way yn come by watr wch sometimes is very hazardous in blowing weathr . . .

Georgetown is already become more populous yn Port Royal & exceeds in number of People, tho' not in riches, any Congregation in this Province, Except Charles Town, but 'twill in time become a flourishing Place & be behind wth none in a due encouragemt of any generous design . . .

T. Morritt

Rev. Mr. Morritt was a misfit as a missionary either in regard to his parishioners or to Commissary Garden. He relieved the situation in 1736 by making room for his successor, who arrived in September following. In the Register Book for the parish is found a list of baptisms, marriages and burials but no names of communicants. They were few while the adherents were reported as high as 800. The names of the vestrymen and church wardens are given in full. In Rev. Mr. Morritt's incumbency the vestrymen were John Hayes, John Bell, John Lane, Peter Sanders, Robert Stewart, Elias Horry, Richard Smith and Josias Garnier Dupre. Those who served successively as wardens or vestrymen were Meredith Hughes, Anthony White, Anthony Atkinson, Francis Avant, Arthur Foster, Eduard Henlyr, John White, Daniel Shaw and John Barton were only church wardens.

This church of which Mr. Morritt had been rector fell into Prince Frederick parish, which was created in 1734-5. It began at the Southtermost part of the plantation of John DuBose, on Santee River, from thence on a line to the head of John Green's Creek and down the said creek to Black river to the plantation of John Bogg and from the said plantation of John Bogg, to be included in the town parish, in a due north line to Pee Dee River, and that part of the said parish whereon the parish church now is, shall and is hereby declared to be a district parish by itself." Rev. John Fordyce was the second rector of this church and extracts from his letters must tell their own story.

. . . Feb. 1, 1739. I would have wrote the Hon. Society long before this time, with the state of my parish but have been prevented by a long and severe sickness of the fever and ague from the 4th of August to the latter end of December last, that none expected I could live, but I thank God am now upon recovery and officiate in church every Sabbath day. My auditory of the parish as well as communicants, still increase, notwithstanding the great number of Dissenters, with whom I'm surrounded as appears in the present state of my parish, yet many of them attend service at our church. I have hitherto done duty at George Town once in a few weeks, where there is a congregation of about 100 people and eight communicants; and I generally preach at the Chapel of Wackamaw once per annum, being a part of George Town parish at a Distance and inconvenient for Travelling where I had a Large Congregation of Religious people and about 15 Communicants, upon the first Day of Lent 1737-8 having given notice of my attendance upon that occasion.

At the Request of some Gentlemen at Cape fear N. Carolina, as well as the Rev. Mr. Garden, (Having obtained leave from my parish) I went and preached at Brunswick on Trinity Sunday last, to a large Congregation of people, well affected by the Church of England and gave notice of the Holy Sacrament the Sunday following which administered to 20 Commts and Baptised five infants ... Here they are at a great loss for want of a minister being a lot of good Religious people and ready to contribute to the Building of a Church and the maintainance of a Minister. They have yet greater need of a missionary towards Eden-Town, where as I was credibly informed when at Cape fear, that those who ought to be promoters of Religion and virtue are Rather abandoned to Atheism and Infidelity and Ignorant of their Duty to God; their Neighbor, and Loyalty to their Prince or those in authority under him. In so much that they have oppos'd and prevented those Religious people that are among them from Building a Church or Chapel for the publick worship of Almighty God: So regardless are they & Irreligious.

John Fordyce.

No. of Christian Inhabitants about	1200
No. of Actual Commts of Church of England	35
No. of those who profess ymselves of the Ch. of England	400
No. of Dissenters of all sorts (papists none) about	800
No. of Heathens and Infidels about	1400
No. of Infants Baptis'd in this parish since the 25th July 1737 and of George Town parish, including Wackamaw and pedee Rivers	46
Adults Bap. White Women	2
Niger Wom: Married, who gave acct. of her Faith and read several portions of Scripture...	1

The church was looking up under the guidance of Mr. Fordyce, growing in the number of its congregation and respected by the dissenters whose church was two miles up stream. His life and conversation and the diligent attention to his ministerial functions for three years had gained for the minister the love and esteem of this parish as well as that of George Town where he officiated once in five weeks.

Jan. 1, 1740. The state of the parish continued in a flourishing condition. Writes for Bishop King's Discourse Concerning the Inventions of Men in the Worship of God, and other books on Schism. A Confutation of Quakerism was thought necessary for many people on the Pee Dee, who some time since came from Philadelphia and settled on that river and were in his parish. As there were many Anabaptists here, Wall upon Infant Baptism and tracts preservative from their errors were requested . . .

"On the 24th of June last, I preached at Williamsburg about thirty miles distant from hence to the West, where I Baptized five children, having proper God Fathers etc. According to the Rubrick of the Church. Likewise the 2nd Dec. Last, I gave my Attendance at Wackamaw Chapel where I had a Large Congregation and Baptized two children.

The people of George Town parish are preparing to Build a Large Brick Church there this Spring, having some of the Bricks already in the Town for that purpose, but are not come to Resolution about the Dimensions of the Church.

Several Gentlemen have Subscribed largely to that work, besides the Duty of Rum Imported in George Town for three years obtain'd by Act of Assembly some time Since.

May 16, 1742. The 19th of July Last, I preached at Wackamaw Chapel, a Distant part of Prince Georges Parish having given notice of my attendance & Design a Month before. I administer'd the Holy Sacrament of the Lord's Supper, at which time I had 20 Communicants, Religious and Devout People, most of them were formerly Inhabitants of St. John's Parish.

As for the vestry of George Town and the Gentlemen that are appointed Commissioners for Building a Church there; I can write little in their favour, because they will do nothing unless the Government do it for them. They are more zealous about the affairs of this world, than that of Religion, or Building a Church for the Service of Worship of God; will scarce spare a mite out of their Talent for that Purpose. In my Last I wrote the Honble Society that they had got some of the Bricks ready for that design, but there is not so much as one Laid in the Foundation as yet.

Dec. 2, 1742. The 13th of June, I preached at Williamsburg, about 30 miles West from hence, where I had a large Congregation of Church people, & several of the Irish Dissenters, & Baptis'd 10 children & 5 negro do with their proper God-Fathers etc. From thence I proceeded to English Santee, above 50 miles farther and preached twice there the 19th to a Congregation of above one hundred people and Baptis'd 11 children, two adults, one of which of Anabaptist Parents, and two Mullato Children. Being informed by some people there that an Anabaptist Teacher was propagating his Heterodox principles in a corner among the ignorant, I immediately distributed some of Walls Conference about Infant Baptism which I doubt not through God's Blessing, will prevent the ill consequence of that pernicious Doctrine.

I intended this Fall to have gone about one hundred miles up peedee River, in the Execution of my Duty, but have been prevented by a Severe fit of sickness of the Ague and Fever from the 4th of Octr. which have reduc'd me to a very Low and weak State of Health & rendered me incapable of Attending Divine Service till now, as well as occasion'd my delay in writing the Society Sooner. I purpose (God willing) to undertake the journey to Pedee in the Spring; in the meantime I have also sent them some of the Walls Tracts, which I know will be Serviceable.

I thank God the Labours of my ministry have been hitherto attended with success, that *some are daily added to the Church.*

Other letters written by Rev. Fordyce to Dr. Bearcroft of the S. P. G. are epitomized:

Oct. 24, 1743: (Mr. F.) Has returned from visiting the Cheraws settlement. Mentions people from Pennsylvania whom he found in his travels who are very ignorant set of Anabaptists.

Oct. 3rd 1744: His parish is extensive and is not bounded on the W., where are many new settlements. In it the dissenters—Presbyterians and Baptists—are very numerous. Begs to come home for his health. The summer has been "exceeding hot." Much sickness. Cattle distemper—Sends number of Baptisms, etc.

Nov. 4, 1745. Has been at the great Cheraw on Pee Dee River for near three weeks. The Anabaptists are so possessed of the spirit of Enthusiasm that there are about as many ignorant preachers as there were in Oliver's Camp. An itinerant missionary might do great good. Preached on Trinity Sunday at a new church on the lower parts of Pee Dee River in Prince Georges Parish. (Britton's Neck, evidently a church noticed by Bishop Gregg but not by Dalcho).

April 2, 1746. Many members lost to his church by death.

South Carolina

Oct. 6, 1747. Has preached at Williamsburg, 30 miles distant. Many deaths have reduced his congregation. Begs for Common Prayer Book for the poor, Keith's Presbyterian and Independent churches brought to the test, etc.

April 18, 1748: His congregation is regular and orderly and if health and weather permit, come a long distance to church. He always studies to keep a friendly familiarity with the dissenters and their ministers. His wife died of consumption the 1st ult.

Mr. Fordyce continued to supply both places until or near 1746 when he was relieved of the work at Georgetown and from that time till his death in 1751 devoted himself to his own regular missionary work.

The vestrymen in Rev. Fordyce's day, not already mentioned, were John Thompson, Peter Tamplet, Abraham Staples, William Brown, John Barton, John Pyatt, William Gardner, Joseph King, Leonard Outerbridge, Richard Walker, John Bassett, James Boyd, William Forbes, John Naylor, Alex Brown, Leonard White, William Hughes, George Atkinson, John King, James Lane.

The Church Wardens who were not also at times Vestrymen were Crafton Karwon and J. Walker.

Two years later, Rev. Michael Smith was sent out to the Black as missionary and arrived Dec. 24th, 1752.

A letter that he wrote upon his arrival is presented, dated, South Carolina,

May 13, 1753:

My Lord,

I am fixed 73 miles from the Capitol where I am put to the greatest difficulties to get the common necessities of life for so large a family; and not being able as yet to purchase a Negro or two and there being no white servants to be got we were in the utmost distress during our indisposition For the adherents of the Church of England in this Parish are so few and those so very poor that they could not give me any assistance. This obliged me, My Lord, to remove out of my parish to a small town about 13 miles distant from the church, where I can not only have a Doctor but other necessary assistance. The Church of England, my Lord, (by the accounts given me of it) was in the beginning of my Predecessor's time in a flourishing condition in this Parish, but by the death of some and the instability of Principles in others, it is now reduced to a very low ebb; so low that out of about a thousand families there are but, eleven of the Church of England. There are 5 dissenting Teachers who all preach to a numerous congregation the least of which amounts to three hundred souls, whilst I have the mortification to preach to eighteen or twenty . . .

Michl Smith.

In the next year he reported more cheerfully "that his hearers increased every Sunday and at his best he claimed that his income amounted to £1500 annually. His immorality, however, soon shut the doors of the churches against him, while the Winyaw Indigo Society refused to countenance him as a chaplain.

With the close of 1766, the Society withdrew its aid from churches in South Carolina. In these ten years prior to that time the Rector was paid 107 pounds sterling, furnished a parsonage, a glebe of 200 acres and a stock of cattle valued at 35 pounds; but notwithstanding these advantages and other perquisites it was not possible to keep the church open. Charles Woodmason, lay reader, Rev. Charles Fenner Warren, Mr. Fayerweather, an occasional supply, Rev. Mr. Dormer and Rev. George Skene, served the church in the order named. The last serving from 1762-66 died at his post. Rev. Paul Turquam and Rev. James Cosgrive supplied until Rev. George Spencer, sent by the Bishop of London, arrived in November 1767 and died in June 1769. The next two years appear to have been marked only by the activity of the Vestrymen and Church Wardens. Rev. Mr. Villette remained in the cure about six months and returned to England. Mr. Miller was soon dispensed with and a more worthy man, Rev. James Stewart supplied at intervals from 1773 to 1776 who seems to have been the last supply before the capture of Charles Town. The Vestrymen of this period not previously named were Robert Stewart, John Handlen, John Glen, William Walker, Joseph White, James McPherson, William Green, William Wilson, Charles Woodmason, James Crocket, John Connor, James McDowell, Daniel DuPre, Isaac Carr, John Godfrey, John McDole, Francis Lesesne, Anthony Martin White, Daniel McGinney, Barkley Clarke, Jehu Walker, John Wagenfield, Henry Bossard, Charles Baxter, Alexander Tweed, William Pawley, Jno. Angus Finke, John Burns, William Inerr, Elias McPherson, Thomas Wood, William Grace, Thomas North, William Sheppard, James Snow. The Church Wardens not also Vestrymen were John Glen, Peter Lessesne, John McDonald, Moses Miller, James Merrell & Thomas Scott. As has been stated Rev. John Fordyce succeeded Mr. Morritt and besides his regular duties visited the Chapel of Waccamaw once a year and found there 20 communicants. Once in five weeks he held services in Georgetown. It was in his first year that a subscription of more than 1000 pounds[2] was made by the leading men of Georgetown and vicinity, to which was added £100 by the will of Meredith Hughes, who must be accorded the honor also of being the first in Craven County who devised a sum of money for educational purposes.

The first bricks were collected for the church edifice at Georgetown during his supply at the close of 1739. On April 14, 1741, the following was written at Georgetown, Winyaw, South Carolina:

Rev. Sir,

This part of the Province of South Carolina called Winyaw being of late years greatly increased and the number of inhabitants widely settled, the General Assembly of the Province thought fitt to divide the same into two distinct Parishes, one of which called Prince Frederick Parish has been for some years past supplied by a missionary from the Honorable Society but the other called Prince George's Parish (of which we the under written are the church wardens and vestry) has not hitherto been supplied with any settled minister and as the inhabitants of this Parish are the least able to contribute towards the support of a minister of any in the whole Province, we therefore beg leave to apply ourselves to the Honorable Society Humbly praying they would be pleased to take our destitute condition into con-

---

[2]Of this amount Daniel Laroche & Co. subscribed £200 John Clecland do. or 100 acres of glebe land, Anthony White £100, Wm. Whiteside, James Gordon, William Waties, Maurice Lewis and George Pawley gave each £50, William Colt, Wm. Allston, Col. Wm. Bull, Thomas Blein, each £40. Daniel Shaw, Wm. Fleming, Jos. LaBruce, Wm. Poole, 30£, Geo. Dick, Thos. Paget, Charles Hose, Wm. Anderson, Robt. Stewart, Wm. Ramsay £20, John Brown, £15, Wm. Hinchy, Henry Bossard, George Threadcraft, Jonathan Skrine, Joseph Allen £10, John Paris 800 bushels of lime, Rev. Thomas Morritt the Communion plate, Henry Laubus a carpet and cloth, Capt. John Paris 800 bushels of lime cleland £200 or 100 acres near Georgetown for a glebe, & John Pollixen, a bell. Dalcho p. 305.

sideration and to appoint us a missionary . . . With our duty to the Bishop of London and the Society we are Reverend Sir, Your most Obedient and Humble Serts

                Church Wardens
                John Dexter
                Wm. Shackleford

                Vestry
                John Cleland
                Wm. Whiteside
                Arthur Foster
                Elias Foisine
                John Ouldfield
                Daniel Laroche

An Act March 8, 1741-2 was passed to enable George Pawley, Daniel LaRoche and Wm. Whitesides to build the church and parsonage house in Georgetown to carry on and complete the same. This act appropriated "all cash moneys as should be paid into the public treasury, by virtue of the general duty act, for duties or goods imported into the port of Georgetown, negroes excepted, for five years, to be applied toward defraying the charges of building a church and parsonage house in and for the parish of Prince George Winyaw." The building committee did not prove to be as forward as the rector anticipated; for on February 6th, 1745, Gov. Glen who had visited Georgetown said, "They are building a handsome brick church, the walls of which are a good way raised.[3] In May 1755 proposals were solicited through the South Carolina Gazette from workmen "who are inclinable to undertake the joining, carpentry, plaistering, glazine and painting." The commissioners in charge being George Pawley, Thomas Mitchel and Thomas

---

[3]Public Records, Vol. XXII, 134.

Hasell. But the date of its completion for service or of these final touches has not been found. It was 60 ft. by 50, had three aisles but no galleries in 1766.[4]

One of the first if not the first rector of Prince George Winyaw was the Rev. Alexander Keith whose term of service expired in December 1749. For about eight years it appeared that the church was dependent on occasional supplies from neighboring churches until Mr. Fayerweather arrived in 1757 and entered upon the duties of the church. He was a New Englander and so homesick by June 1760 that he was anxious "to bid an everlasting adieu to this worst of all places on the whole Terraqueous Globe." Mr. Fayerweather got a letter of recommendation from Prince Frederick Church which bore testimony to his worth and conduct. He had probably been drawn southward by the better provision made for the clergy, as may be inferred from a statement made to the Society: "In about a fortnight or three weeks at furthest I shall bid a final adieu to this Dismal Country: to go to the land of my forefathers' nativity; the land of my desires; a land in which dwells every good thing . . . Narragansett is agreeably situated in a healthy clime; and even with its poverty (in point of the small emoluments from the inhabitants thereof, as parishioners) is a Paradise to Carolina" . . . He had been a Presbyterian clergyman.

Rev. Offspring Pearce was elected Rector in 1763 and continued here till 1767. Rev. James Stuart was the Officiating minister 1772-1777. He was, according to Sabine, Rector of All Saints also and a loyalist. His widow Anne died in England in 1805.

Prince Frederick's Parish suffered another diminution in 1757 by an Act of the Assembly which formed St. Mark's Parish, by continuing the North-westernmost

[4] Woodmason's Account.

line of Williamsburg Township to Pee Dee and to Santee Rivers; and all the lands situated to the Northward of the said line. The letter below though unsigned is none the less interesting:

Parish of St. Mark in
S° Carolina April 20, 1767.

May it please your Lordship

We the Vestry Men and Church Wardens of the Parish of St. Mark in the Province of South Carolina beg leave to acquaint your Lordship that this parish is now (and has for two years past been) destitute of a minister, thro' the Removal of the Rev. Mr. Evans to the Parish of St. Paul. We therefore make humble suit to your Lordship for the favour of another Pastor, for whose reception, we shall make all necessary Provision. This our Parish, lyes on the North side of the Santee River, above the Parishes of Prince George and Prince Frederick, and is the largest in the Province. Our Parish Church is 80 miles distant from the metropolis Charles Town. But the duty to an incumbent will be very easy, as the laborious Part is executed by an Itinerant Minister placed about fifty miles above us by the church Commissioners . . . Nor can our Parish be deemed the poorest in the Province, but it may be asserted to be the healthiest, an article which may influence some worthy gentleman disposed to come this way in our favor . . . As to accommodations and situation for our Minister, we have all that are necessary, and we may add, desirable and inviting—a new built house just finished, 36 ft. front, with four good rooms, lobby and staircase—a good kitchen, garden, orchard, stables and necessary out houses where a gentleman may lead an easy and comfortable, contemplative life. The River is near, abounding with fish and wild-fowl. So that a gentleman with a small family may (with a little industry) live comfortably. And this Place, in particular, would suit an Englishman as would a pious, good, moderate English Gentleman us, who are with greatest deference and Respect"

The itinerant minister placed about 50 miles above the St. Mark's Parish Church was Charles Woodmason. Dalcho, followed by others makes this minister, not Mr. Evans, the first rector of St. Mark's, 1766-1770, who at the expiration of that period, left the province. He was rather the first itinerant minister in the parish who was still in this mission in 1771. His letter to the Bishop of London opens up a vivid view of the situation.

Charlestown, Oct. 19, 1766.

My Lord

It is my duty to acquaint your Lordship that I arrived here Aug. 12, last—after a passage of nine weeks. I found the season hotter than ever known, and both town and country exceedingly sickly, owing to a most inclement spring and summer more rain having fallen March to August last than in 7 preceding. Since which it has been exceeding hot and dry and likely to continue—. Sept. 5, the Church Commissioners met and gave me Induction to my settlement—. The next day I set off and (after officiating at St. Andrews, St. James and St. Marks) arrived at my Station of Fredericksburg the 16th. The people instantly framed a Petition to the Assembly for a church and house to be built which will be granted. And I have carried the Liturgy and the Bible, 50 miles further than ever yet read in these parts. Not a house could I set foot in but found some sick, some dead so that have had a melancholy progress. I've baptized numbers of children. Have been among the sectaries called *New Lights* and rode above 500 miles around thro the hot burning sun and sands; I bless God without injury to my health, but with much fatigue and expense...

As most of my flock are Sectaries of various Denominations and countries, and a mixed multitude, and not a school or school master among them, I have undertaken to educate gratis in writing, Arithmetic, Psalmody, and the Principles of Religion and things—. These I make attend Divine Service regularly, and through their aides (?) I hope to make impression on their relatives. But I have a wide field before me! My District is 150 miles in breadth and 300 in length: And as this country ever was the grave of the clergy, it has been bitterly so this summer." The remainder of this letter naming eight or ten ministers who were cut off this year in the great epidemic fever, will appear in another connection. It may be noted in passing that Mr. Woodmason was the first Church of England minister at his station of Fredericksburg or Camden and he may mean the first minister. He also mentioned an item not found in "Historic Camden"—"a tract of rich land of 640 acres, a mile square, originally laid out for the Town of Fredericksburg, but abandoned as too low for a settlement, the people have petitioned for it as a Glebe and to be settled on the church." It is now worth 500 guineas."

The next original communication brings us back to St. Marks Church. It is without a date, but is probably in 1767 or 1768 not much later than the letter given above, written by the Vestrymen of St. Marks. Rev. Mr. James Harrison of Goose Creek is the author and is explaining at great length the reasons for giving up that parish and accepting a call to St. Marks:

"I received an invitation from the Parish of St. Marks to be their minister; a parish but lately established; and which being inhabited by a prodigious number of emigrants from the northern colonies (for there are 5000 gunmen in it) afforded a pleasing prospect of being serviceable in my Ministry; which being situated in the remote hilly parts of the country promised me the enjoyment of a greater share of Health than I had been accustomed to in these lower settlements. I promised to move thither after Easter following, provided they had the Parsonage and other necessary houses, for the building of which the Publick had already granted them money, finished by that time. I promised with this proviso, because some jealousies and animosities but too common among people much upon a level, had already greatly retarded the erecting of them . . . When Easter arrived, no advances had been made in the Buildings at St. Marks; and there was no possibility of procuring accomodations for myself and family without them; the people in these parts living in Hovels formed of rough unhewn logs which seldom contain more than two rooms." He therefore deferred leaving Goose Creek til Whitsuntide when on his return he found everything in the same state as before. He was however persuaded to remain by the importunities of the parishioners and in his letter continued: "The very improper situation of the Parsonage has ever been productive of great interruption of my necessary studies and of great addition to my expenses. It is built within 40 yards of the grand road, which branching out afterwards, leads from the N. E. to the Northwest parts of the Province, to the Cherokee and Catawba nations and to the northern colonies. Neither is there any public house or place of refreshment nearer to it than seven miles on each side: so that it is thereby rendered but too convenient a retreat from extreme heat and rains and from the profession of its possessor is too much incumbered with the poor, the sick and the weary. Such an opportunity indeed of being serviceable to mankind would be an inexpressible happiness to a mind actuated by the Principles of Christianity were the means equivalent to it; but the misfortune is, that the income of the clergy in general of this province is insufficient, for the necessary purposes of life, mine most remarkably so."

The names of several governors of South Carolina might be mentioned in whose veins flowed the blood of some of the men and women in this congregation which appeared to the missionary to be on one common level and all living in two room cabins built of unhewn logs. Character whether in a castle or log cabin eventually distinguishes one family from another in whatever walk of life it is exhibited.

The letter, descriptive of this period dated March 20, 1771 in the "Parish of St. Marks, S. C." was written, very probably, at Fredericksburg and was directed to the Bishop of London, in reference to the state of religion in "these parts." In an earlier letter, Mr. Woodmason had described the "endemic sickness" in such vivid colors that it brought him sharp criticism in the churches because it prevented other ministers coming over:

"It was urged to his Lordship," said Mr. Woodmason, "that I spoke an untruth when I said that there was never a clergyman save myself on the north side of Santee River, from that River to the line, and from the sea to the Mountains. It was very true. It is true still. Where is there or now is? Can any dare contradict this?

Yet this space contains the best half of this province, and more than two thirds of the white inhabitants. And I here assert again and again that there is not one Episcopal gentleman save myself, in all this vast District, which contains the parishes of Prince George, Prince Frederick, St. David's and St. Mark. Indeed a gentleman came out for St. Mark and lived a fortnight . . . So far from having new parishes, we have two that were made, annull'd from home. A Bill is in the house for making 6 new ones out of this large one I now am in, but it cannot pass . . . Meanwhile Religion and the Church lye bleeding—wounded every day—overrun with Sectaries, especially the New Light Baptists, who have broke up every congregation I have founded. All the whole Back country is now lost to the Church thro' want of ministers and churches . . .

Where I am is neither beef nor mutton. Nor beer, cyder, or anything better than water, people eat twice a day only. Their Bread of Indian Corn, Pork in Winter and Bacon in Summer. If any beef they jerk it and dry it in the sun. So that you may as well eat a deal board. And yet it costs me for this hard living, at least 50p. sterling per annum. The intrinsic worth of which is not so many shillings . . . Unhappily for my poor Back country people, their interest and those of the inhabitants of Charles Town have been incompatible tho demonstrably otherwise. They are quite connected . . . The Dissenting Influence entirely prevails . . . We have but 4 or 5 gentlemen at Council Board, 3 of whom are Dissenters, and the majority of our House of Assembly are such as well as most of the Acting Magistrates."

This brief survey of the activities of the Church of England in this period prior to the Revolution leaves an impression that circumstances beyond man's control were not favorable to its rapid expansion. It was impossible to secure and retain ministers because the supply in England which could be induced to cross the Atlantic was insufficient and as the impression spread abroad that South Carolina was the grave of the ministry the difficulty was not diminished. Outside of the parish church and minister there was also some friction in reference to encroachments by dissenters upon the functions and perquisites of the parish minister. Complaints about this were made continually to the Bishop of London, who was an ex-officio member of the Board of Trade and to him were referred "the laws relating to religion and religious questions as legal knots were handed over to crown attorneys. The Board did not always approve of the way in which the Bishop exercised his jurisdiction and informed him when complaints came against unfit ministers that "persons of piety, principles and exemplary conduct should be sent to America." Had the Board been composed of ecclesiastics it could hardly have withstood the pressure from the missionaries, the commissioners and such men as Rev. Gideon Johnson, Rev. Tredwell Bull, Gov. Nicholson and Charles Woodmason who advocated the enforcement or the creation of such laws as would protect the parish minister in his legal rights; but the Board of Trade was not friendly to any legislation that would endanger the main business for which it existed. The dissenters were too alert not to profit by these halfway measures, and being more energetic, partly by necessity and partly by an evangelistic spirit in the midst of great destitution, were correspondingly encouraged. The dissenting influence in the government circles was also strong enough to be felt in an obstructive way. But the lack of ministers was more hurtful than all other causes.

"Not a minister in 50 miles of Georgetown," "one minister of the Church of England north of the Santee where two thirds of the white population lived," are statements made by writers to the Religious Society. It is to be noted in this connection that the laymen in the parish churches of the Prince Frederick and Prince George Winyaw harrassed by unworthy clergymen, accomplished two things: They helped to elevate the standard in the pulpit, below which an unworthy minister shut himself out of consideration, and like all the earliest churches which lived through several generations, they dominated their neighborhoods and moulded the prevailing religious sentiments.

In April 1768 the Assembly authorized the erection of another parish out of the upper parts of St. Mark's, Prince Frederick and Prince George Winyaw parishes. It was to be bounded "by a north-west line to be run from the northwardmost corner of Williamsburg township to Lynche's creek and from thence by that Creek to the provincial line; and that the line dividing St. Mark from Prince Frederick's parish, be carried on in the same course from the great Pee Dee where it now ends to the provincial line aforesaid, and Lynche's Creek, the new parish shall be bounded, and that the said Parish shall hereafter be called and known by the name of St. David." Of the fourteen commissioners appointed for the building of the church and parsonage, Thomas Port, Robert Weaver, Thomas Crawford and James Thompson lived nearer the lower extremity of the parish. Clauding Pegues, Philip Pledger, George Hicks, Thomas Lide, Charles Bedingfield and Thomas Ellerbe lived in the upper parts. Alexander McIntosh, Robert Allison, James James and Benjamin Rogers were more centrally situated. If there were any aspirants in the church at Sandy Bluff to become the parish church, the presence of Robert Weaver, its nearest commissioner with his unpopularity among the Regulators, would have operated adversely to its wishes. At the very time Weaver was in the midst of his troubles as a magistrate these commissioners met at the house of Charles Bedingfield not far from Cheraw and received the declination of James James, Robert Allison and Alexander McIntosh to serve as commissioners. The commissioners or those by whom they were appointed named the parish St. David in honor of the Welsh people, an influential part of the inhabitants, who had not been active or concerned about the parish, as they had been about the establishment of Courts, to hold in check the evil disposed part of the population. They made a contract for building a church with Thomas Bingham on a lot on the old Cheraws presented by Ely Kershaw,[5] to be finished in a specified time. Its erection was at a slow pace, extending over more than four years after the money was voted. Claudius Pegues, Philip Pledger, William Godfrey, Charles Bedingfield, Thomas Lide, Thomas Ellerbe and Thomas Bingham were the vestrymen, and Alexander Gordon, Benjamin Rogers, the wardens and Durham Hitt the clerk first appointed. They failed to find a minister for the church in the period 1768-1818, owing to the dearth of missionaries who were willing to immure themselves in the American frontier. Overseers of the poor, however, were appointed, who collected funds and helped the indigent, buried the friendless and put out orphan boys and girls; but no Register of the births and deaths and marriages were kept.

---

[5] W. R. Godfrey's Old St. David, p. 4.

CHAPTER XI

PRESBYTERIAN CHURCH IN CRAVEN COUNTY
(1726-1780)

In Craven County, the churches of all the dissenting congregations were called meeting houses and so marked in the maps and alluded to in the letters to the Society. The one earliest built was on the neck of land between the Black Mingo and the Black. It was, it seems, a mixed congregation of Congregationalists and Presbyterians whose building was finished in 1726, six years before the Scotch Irish Presbyterians landed at Williamsburg. This fact is learned from the rector of Prince Frederick. A statement is made in a church history[1] which corroborates the above date, but the author being in doubt asks the question, Was there a Presbyterian community and congregation so early as this in Georgetown district? and inclines to a negative answer. But in this he was leaning in the wrong direction. Rev. Mr. Morritt visited the Prince Frederick Church in the Christmas of 1726 and at that time stated that the dissenters had a building finished. A later minister said it was within two miles of the parsonage. Its successor, probably the one built in 1741 was about six. Besides this direct testimony, a deed passed over to William Swinton in 1733 on Black Mingo mentioned that it was bounded on one side by the meeting house land. As to whether it was of large or small area, the brief allusion to it leaves no clue; but it was afterwards known as "the Brick Church." Swinton in his will recorded in 1742 left 100 pounds to this church. It was regarded by some as the original Church of the Scotch Irish Presbyterians who arrived in 1732-3. In point

---
[1] Howe's Presbyterian Church in South Carolina, pp. 589, 282.

of time it is the original meeting house in Craven County and was ready for use in 1726 if not earlier. The evidence at hand points to the Circular Church of Charles Town as the source whence emigrants went to the Black River neighborhood and carried their religion with them. It also appears to have been more Congregational than Presbyterian and it is probable that the same division which occurred in the Circular Church in 1731 was extended through the scattered sheep of the same persuasions on the Black. This church was not in the South Carolina Presbytery. The polity of the Congregationalists was so much like that of two other denominations that insufficient footing was left for it as a third and it was destined to make little headway in the coming struggle for existence and supremacy. They prevailed in New England, the Presbyterians in S. C. The evidence referred to is found in the names of the men who owned plantations above and below the Black Mingo. Samuel Eveleigh, a wealthy merchant, who died in 1733, had 1000 acres here and left in his will a mention of his uncle, Rev. Nathan Basset and a bequest of 500 pounds for the Circular Church, of which he was pastor. The second landgrave, Thomas Smith, owned a larger amount of land about which he is supposed to have put the following in his will: "Whereas William Swinton has in a triumphant manner writ me word that he was before me in getting the King's grant for 2000 acres of my land, beginning on the east side of Mr. Commander's also Black river which was surveyed and platted first of all by Mr. Legrand who could not finish it, he having a misfortune of falling into a pitch hole. I got Mr. Robinson, one of Mr. St. John's deputies to resurvey and return the same as a sworn officer in part of my landgrave patent. All this was done before

Swinton's undermining Title of which I complained in Gov. Broughton's time, who sent me such an answer as Mr. Swinton's friends won't care to see. I was also informed by Maj. Pawley that Capt. Akeings had also run out several hundred acres of my land that was returned me by virtue of my patent by the late Gov. Broughton when Surveyor General above 26 years ago and some since returned by Mr. Young when Surveyor General and taxes and rent always paid for so that I trust and hope the succeeding government will not let my poor family suffer contrary to all law and equity."[2]

Others who were either dissenters or anabaptists, or "prophane" persons were the Commanders, Elisha Screven, Dougal McKitchen, Edward Vanvelson, William Brockinton, Miles Sweeney, Isaac Durant, William Swinton and many others. Josias Smith, pastor and co-pastor, of the Circular Church, or his son of the same name, appeared in the Gazette as one interested in the Commander estate. He was the grandson of the first landgrave and consequently a close relative of the second, who had his troubles in retaining his vast estate intact.

"In 1727, these dissenters had five teachers in the whole province who supplied these meeting houses which they do", said Mr. Morritt, "with so much indefatigable pains that they still make a shift to retain a number of followers, they spare no pains nor grudge no labor provided they can gain over proselytes to their persuasion, as they are paid per sermon, they make shift to dispense two or three per week at different places from 20 to 40 or 50 miles asunder." The connection between the S. P. G. and the missionaries in South Carolina has been preserved in the British Museum, but the not less effec-

---

[2]Landgrave Thomas Smith made his cross mark, but it was due to his hand, not to illiteracy.

tive connection, in the shape of sympathy, money and missionaries between the Presbyterians in Scotland and in Craven County, has been allowed to drop out of sight.

In 1729, this Black Mingo Congregation is credited by Rev. Mr. Morritt with having a teacher from Bermudas, but he has not been identified in this field either as a minister or pedagogue. Job How who got grants on the Black and Lynch's Lake was one of the Society's teachers engaged below the Santee. It was probably 1734-5 before a minister was with the congregation; for in that year, Rev. Samuel Hunter came into the Province and was the minister here at least from 1744 to 1754. He was succeeded after an interval by Rev. William Knox whose piety and usefulness in this congregation and another small one near Lynch's Lake, till about 1800, deserved to be lodged more fully in the memories of men.

The fourth decade of the 18th century witnessed the planting of the first Presbyterian church in Williamsburg County by the Scotch emigrants who reached the township early in 1733. It was the mother church which sent out colony after colony from itself and its offshoots to become separate seats of worship. The township of Williamsburg was laid off for Irish Presbyterians but it was not a parish, nor was the land held in reserve for the Scotch immigrants. Keen eyed investors from below had the best lands surveyed for themselves and some of the immigrants lost the lands they had improved. Kingstree of today or Williamsburg Town, laid out in 1735, had a vacant space near the centre marked "Parade" and west of it was the "Church Yard." The authorities at Charles Town did not give the church acre, but it did grant a glebe of 100 acres. In 1733 and 1734 these Scotch Irish emigrants in goodly numbers took possession of their forest homes and began in a few years to talk about getting a minister from Home. A little more than three years elapsed, August 1736, before the Williamsburg Church was formally organized and served by their pastor, Rev. Robert Heron. It greatly prospered in his pastorate which lasted about five years.

A church brought from the old country with a minister from the same place, could be nothing else than a duplicate of the churches in the homeland, in respect to doctrine and discipline. Rev. John Rae was the successor in 1743 and had as elders chosen as the seven were in the church at Jerusalem David Allan, William James, David Wilson and Rodger Gibson. Here was a church in the woods which transacted its business "with all the strictness of the Scotch discipline in its purest form." But the colony and the church were in a few years (1749-1750) decimated by a "great mortality" which carried off eighty from the township and among them John Fleming, William James and David Witherspoon, original elders of the church. The leading men in 1752 in the church are brought out in their signing the Confession of Faith, approved by the General Assembly of the Church of Scotland: John James, James McClelland, James Witherspoon, John Liviston, Robert Witherspoon, Samuel Fulton, Robert Wilson, Robert Paisley, Gavin Witherspoon and William Dobien. A fuller list is given in chapter IV. Mr. Rae married in this decade and continued to perform his clerical duties with diligence and faithfulness, until his life was cut short in 1761. On July 8, 1761, his wife Rachel put up for sale "some black cattle, horses, household furniture and a choice library of books," which her husband had acquired. A pastorate of 18 years is not long for a shepherd who had the confidence of the sheep of the community. Rev. David McKee succeeded Mr. Rae who soon after accepted the call to Salem. He was soon followed by Rev. Hector Alison, who had in his care about 90 families, who appears to have been a missionary as well as a pastor, until he was cut off in the great "endemic sickness" of 1766. Some writers think he preceded Mr. McKee.

The antebellum period of this church's history was closed in the pastorate of Rev. Thomas Kennedy. For nearly forty years, the church at Williamsburg had increased in number and swarmed eastward and northward, not so much because of missionary activity, as by reason of the emigration of its members and their calls for ministers. About 1759, there began to be a church at Salem, up stream, with Capt. David Anderson, William Wilson, Roger Wilson, James Armstrong, Robert Carter, Moses Gordon, Samuel and James Bradley as leaders and ruling elders. Indian Town on Cedar Creek started on its road of service about 1760 with such leaders as Robert and David Wilson, William Cooper, Robert McCottry, Robert Dick, John Gordon, James Daniel, Roger McGill, George McCutcheon, George Barr, Thomas McCrea, Maj. John James of Lynch's Lake and Robert Witherspoon of Lynch's Creek. It soon embraced 50 families. Revs. Mr. Knox, Edward and Thomas Reese being pastors. Aimwell on the Pee Dee either originated from the Williamsburg and Indian Town Churches or their members reinforced others who had settled between the Lynch and the Pee Dee. Hugh and John Ervin, Gavin and John Witherspoon were in this congregation.

Some distance up the Pee Dee was the Hopewell Church opposite the mouth of the Catfish stream. The Greggs father and four sons and a son-in-law from Indian Town Church were the leaders who nourished the enterprise, strengthened later by William Wilson from Salem, an elder, Waccamaw had a congregation in 1756 of Presbyterians, but nothing further is known of it before 1795, when Bishop Asbury said he preached in "an old Presbyterian meeting house, now repaired for the Methodists."[3]

The Presbyterians in Craven County had a distinct advantage over all comers and competitors. They did not have the pecuniary assistance of the establishment, but they enjoyed a greater general respect than the independent bodies, because of their connection with and assistance by the Church of Scotland. They had come as a compact colony and in a few years they had built a church and reaped the advantages of a settled pastorate; but their greatest gains came by constant emigration from the old country. As late as 1770, large numbers of Protestants from Ireland were arriving and being sent up to the inland townships. Their reinforcements came also in such numbers from the northern states that there is a tendency to claim that the Independence of the state was gained by Scotch Presbyterians from Virginia, Tennessee, North and South Carolina. An observant critic, Rev. Charles Woodmason, who observed the religious skies with the keenness of a Palinurus said in 1766 that "7 ministers from Scotland were in the Province who had formed a Presbytery and governed their members after the plan of the Scotch Kirk. Most of these congregations are in decay though strongly supported from home." A year later the same observant writer in his Comments on "the Remonstrance," the subject of a chapter to follow, declared that the Sectaries were very alert to settle themselves in every hole and corner where they could raise a congregation. "Having built upwards of 20 meeting houses . . . not less than 20 itinerant

---
[3] Dr. Howe is followed as of the first importance.

Presbyterian, Baptist, and Independent preachers are maintained by the synods of Pennsylvania and New England to traverse this country." The establishment below the Santee tended to disintegrate dissenting churches, but the trend above that river was in the opposite direction. The numerous congregations of Presbyterians at Waxhaws and further south and west of it are not within the compass of present inquiries.

CHAPTER XII

THE EARLY BAPTIST CHURCHES, 1726-1780

The early history of the people north of the Santee called Anabaptists by the writers of the day, is less consecutive than that of the Church of England with its system of minutes and parish records and that of the Presbyterian churches, which largely dominated Craven County. The Baptist Churches were entirely independent and isolated until 1751 when the Charles Town Association was formed of three churches the Welsh Neck, the Charles Town and Ashley River churches. When formed it claimed no jurisdiction over the churches and was careful to restrict itself to matters which the churches separately could not manage for themselves. It sent out the first missionary in 1755, on hearing of the great destitution up the Pee Dee in Anson County. The minutes of the Association for the first twenty-five years, if printed, were suffered to be lost. Other sources of information have to be relied on and when all that can be marshalled is collected, there is room for error in fitting the broken parts together. There were Baptists on all the streams but no church can be named before the Welsh Neck was founded in 1738. It is said to have been the first Baptist Church in the Pee Dee Basin. One writer who had an old Welsh history in his possession is responsible for the statement that a church of 33 members was formed in 1737 on the Catfish and that 30 of these migrated and constituted the Welsh Neck Church the following January.[1] It is certain that these men from Pennsylvania began to settle on the Catfish in 1737 and that a church known as Catfish existed in Marion County. The exact location is not known, but

---

[1] E. David in a letter to Dr. Furman. Furman Library.

it was probably near the mouth of that stream and not far below Mars Bluff. It dismissed members to other churches and became extinct after 1783. John Alvan went up stream and became prominent as a Justice of the Peace, a Regulator and as one of the Committeemen of Observation in the Revolution.

The Welsh Neck Church existed about five years before it had an ordained minister and he arose out of the congregation. Rev. Philip James was the fittest, it may be assumed, to fill the place of leader in the church. It so happens that the only additional light thrown upon this period is found in the record in England. Rev. J. Fordyce was minister of the Prince Frederick Church and also it appears, a supply for the church at Georgetown, the Prince George Winyaw. His duties as parish priest carried him up to the North Carolina line, to Cheraw and Long Bluff in 1743 and 1745. In his first letter to the S. P. G. he represented the people up there from Pennsylvania to be "a very ignorant set of Anabaptists." In his next years' letter he added that his parish was extensive and not bounded on the west, where are many new settlements. In it the dissenters, Presbyterians and Baptists are very numerous. On his last tour to Cheraw in 1745, he tarried about three weeks and found the "Anabaptists so possessed of the spirit of enthusiasm that there are almost as many ignorant preachers as there were in Oliver's Camp."

The land for the building and a log house for the church were also provided. The "Meeting House" is not a full translation of "synagogue" which was a part of the civil government; its equivalent may be found more nearly in Acts I, 15 in the three words translated "together." Next in the evolution of the dissenting churches was the making of sheds on the sides of the building;

and as the congregation multiplied in number and increased in ability, a plain weatherboarded house went up, with gallery for the slaves when needed and finally up to date edifices. Rev. Philip James was the minister of the log house and puncheon seats and the tradition yet extant makes him none the less a saint in his humble place of worship.

It was apparently necessary before this time for couples to go down to the Prince Frederick parsonage to be married. Rev. Mr. Fordyce married Joab Edwards and Mary Wild in 1737 before their ascent to the Upper Pee Dee. Tinman (Tillman) Kolb and Beersheba Watkins, Widow, William Smith and Elenor James, John Goodwin and Lydia Wilds, Samuel Wilds and Elizabeth James. One of these marriages may have been performed when Rev. Fordyce made his journey in 1743 to the North Carolina line and preached in four places. Rev. John Brown and Rev. Robert Williams, both ordained in the congregations, served the church till 1759. Rev. Nicholas Bedgegood succeeded to the pastoral office. He seems to have shaken up things and had a catalogue of the members of the church made. The list given below is taken from the Church Minutes, but some of the dates of death or dismissal are later additions. It is worth while to know the names of the few who were thus associated:

Philip Douglass, died Oct. 17, 1706
Elizabeth James
Hannah Evans, died Jan. 9, 1761
Martha Rogers, died Jan. 26, 1761
William Terrel
Anne Terrel, died April 2, 1743
Barbury Monochan, died June 9, '61.
Samuel Wilds

South Carolina

John Evans
Thomas Evans, died Jan. 28, 1785
Daniel Monochan, died April 30, 1785
Sarah James, wife of Wm. James, died Jan. 28, '61
Sarah Bowdry
Elizabeth Wilds
William James, died Jan. 26, 1761
Griffith John, died Aug. 1765
Abel Evans, died June 4th
Philip Evans, died Dec. 5, 1771
Margaret John
James James, died Nov. 21, 1769
William Jones, died July 2
John Perkins, dismissed 1778
David Evans
Voluntine Hollinsworth, died Mar. 26, '60
Elizabeth Powers, died Oct. 1st
Sarah McDaniel, died May 12, 1744
Eleanor Harry (Mrs. Jones), died April 20, '45
Abel Wilds, died May 15, 1781
Samuel Evans
Mary Jones, died Dec. 1751
Sarah Jones
——— Jones, now McIntosh, died Dec. 30, 1764
Martha Roach (now Evans)
James Harry, dismissed
Hannah Howell, died Dec. 24, 1761
Alice Lucas
Wm. Killingsworth, Nov. 1, 1760
Samuel Reredon
Edward Jones
Jenken David
Eleanor Evans, died Feb. 16, 1765
Margaret Evans

Anne Jones (Mrs. Douglass), died April '66
Sarah James
Mary Hollingsworth
Howell James
John Sutton
Mary Plethero, died Feb. 21, 1766
Jacob DeSarrency
Sarah James
Mary Cleary
Thomas James
Walter Downs
Rachel Downes
Sarah Booth (Mrs. Wilds)
Jane Polando, died Nov. 30, 1766
Naomi Harry (Mrs. Underwood)
Mary Edwards
Mary Wilds
Elizabeth Evans
James Rogers
Joshua Edwards
Charity Edwards
Thomas Edwards
Sarah Edwards
Anne Roblyn, died May 1, 1768

There were other names to this list, but so entirely defaced that they could not be "decyphered." Of which undeciphered number were:

Sarah Hollingsworth, died Dec. 14, 1759
Nicholas Rogers, Dec. 12, 1759
David Harry, Sr., Aug. 9, 1759
James Finlay, Jan. 4, 1760
William Killingsworth, Nov. 1, 1770
Rev. Robert Williams
Mrs. Anne Williams

The Records of Prince Frederick Church, beginning in 1726 and of the Presbyterian Church at Williamsburg and early Methodist histories of later date dealt more prominently with ministers or officers than with the members of the congregations, but among the Baptists much more attention was given by the church and its secretary to the people, to the preservation of the church roll, including private conduct, the amusements of the times and thus incidentally they threw light on the prevailing manners and morals when there was practically little civil government over them.

Members were suspended for absenting themselves, for disorderly conduct, for fighting, spending one's time in idleness, quarreling, profanity, drinking to excess, travelling up or down the Pee Dee on Sunday without an absolute necessity and horse racing with drinking. A couple engaged to be married was publicly suspended for improper conversation. Two incorrigible sisters were excluded and one was summoned for selling liquor at a horse race. In most cases the reproof of the church was heeded. Even those who were expelled eventually returned penitent and asked for reinstatement. A difference between two members was ordered to be settled by three arbitrators. A leading member informed the church one Sunday that he had been led into the use of angry and abusive language and stated the case so frankly and regretfully that he was promptly excused. Several of the leading sisters found themselves reported for unseemly gossip. There was no respect for rank or station all had to toe the mark. Rev. Joshua Edwards was suspended for awhile because of excessive drinking. When compared with the blue laws of New England, these Welsh Christians were far in advance in matters of personal liberty and conduct.

In 1760, an article was signed by all parents to bring up their children in the fear and admonition of the Lord. Rev. Elnathan Winchester was the last pre-revolutionary minister and he was the first to inaugurate a revival which existed for weeks and drew into its current many of the leading people within a radius of 25 miles and so many slaves that a colored church was formed. The official record of this meeting, one of the first and the only one found preserved in the records of the various churches is too long to be given as an important event of the time, not fully approved of by certain orthodox ministers.

Rev. Edmund Botsford, Chaplain in one of Gen. Williamson's regiments was pastor from November 1779 till the 1st of June 1780 when he went northward to escape capture. Rev. Joshua Lewis of Cheraw Hill preached occasionally in Rev. Botsford's absence.

Cashaway Church an offshoot of the Welsh Neck was constituted the 28th of September 1756. It was on the eastern side of the river near the Cashaway ferry. Its first pastor was Rev. Joshua Edwards. Rev. John Brown became a member in 1759 and preached for sometime as a supply. In 1763, Rev. Hezekiah Smith from New Jersey was the pastor. In 1764, Rev. Mr. Pugh divided his time between the two Churches, in 1766, the Welsh Neck claimed his entire services. After that year Mr. Pugh was to spend the remainder of his days with the Cashaway or its successors. "We," said the church committee, "the subscribers of the Church of Christ at Cashaway Neck being met together this 14th day of February, 1767 and having considered the necessity we have of a minister to break us the bread of life, have with one heart and one voice agreed to present you with this our call hoping it may be agreeable to you and for your support will pay unto the sum of 350 pounds current money of South Carolina, for one year and do all in our power as becomes a people to a minister. (Signed by) Martin Kolb, Joseph Allison, John Keith, Thomas Coker, William Owens, William Watkins, Robert Lide, James Webb, Thomas Burton, Benjamin James.

In the next two years, Mr. Pugh was wholly devoted to Cashaway preaching afterwards also at Keith's, Brown's, Roblyn's Neck; but in 1775 he was preaching also at the Welsh Neck and a place called Spiney's.

The earliest list of Cashaway members contained the following names:

Peter Kolb (dismissed)
Benjamin James
Jeremiah Rowell (d)
Joseph Alison
Thomas Burton
Wm. Owen
John Keith
John Whittenton
Nathaniel Cothran
James Webb
Wm. Watkins
Joseph Harry
Thomas Coker
Wm. Sweet
Robert Lide
Charles Lowther
Manuel Cox
John Brown
George Wilds
Anthony Pouncey
Thomas Wiggins
Samuel Russell

John Burk
Jordan Gibson
Ab McKinney
Arthur Hart
Jacob Bruce
Thomas Edwards
Rev. Evan Pugh
Lewis Malone
Phebe Malone
Margaret Sexton
Benjamin Kolb
Morris Murphy
Henry Kolb
Sarah Kolb
Xanney Keith
Ann Webb
Mary Knott
Hannah Kimbrough
Mary Hodge
Mary Whittington
Robert Hodges
Charles Jenkins

Jeremiah Jenkins
James McGee
Christopher Teale
C. Keith
Ann Peggy McGee
Ann Brown
Wm. Cherry
Sarah Cherry
Mrs. Pearson
Dorothy Peele

John Padgett
Deborah Sanders
Patience King
John Chambliss
Luse Chambliss
Henry and Peter Kolb,
Trustees of the land

Thomas Burton, Clerk
Joseph, Singing Clerk

In March 1775, Rev. Mr. Pugh took up a subscription and collection for Rhode Island College. Arthur Hart, Robert Lide, Emanuel Cox, Thomas Edwards, William Watkins, William Sweet, Benjamin James, Evan Pugh, Welwisher Vining and Span Sweeney responded in a manner that showed a willing spirit. In that squad of the contributors of that small church were two great grandfathers of Maj. J. L. Coker, the founder of Coker College.

From the northward came down about 1760 another stream into the upper parts of the state and penetrated to the central parts. By 1771 there were seven churches of the Separate or New Light Baptists—Congaree not far below Columbia, Fair Forest in Union County, Stephen's Creek in Edgefield, Burch River, Mine Creek, and two called Little River, one on the Saluda, the other on a branch of the Broad. It was no doubt from the Congaree Church the centre of the Congaree Association, that the New Lights, referred to by Rev. Charles Woodmason in 1766, as from a strategic point, extended their influence, by sending out such ministers as Joseph Reese, Timothy and Jeremiah Dargan and Richard Furman into the destitute fields. Richard Furman came up from Charles Town in May 1770 and fell immediately under the influence of Rev. Joseph Reese and became a boy preacher in 1774. He represented the maritime type of church people, steady, conservative and afraid of enthusiasm, but in coming under the influence of Joseph Reese he blended in his person and conduct the solid virtues of the Regulars with the fervor of the Separates and avoided both extremes of depending on erudition in the pulpit or of running into those forms of enthusiasm which have been likened unto clouds without water. In company with Rev. Timothy Dargan, he made numerous preaching expeditions between Charles Town, Georgetown and the Cheraws and from the Santee to the Little Pee Dee. These Separates like the Methodists after the Revolution, understood the New Testament propagandism—"As ye go, preach," and their unlearned discourses were backed by poverty, self-denial, and conduct which gave power to their preaching. The two divisions were planning to amalgamate but their union was deferred by the war.

CHAPTER XIII

Pre-Revolutionary Methodism

The name of a Methodist, as applied to a minister in the Church of England is found in Commissary Garden's letters as early as 1741. This species of Methodism was regarded by him as the ill effects of Whitefield's example. This early comer, named Thompson, preached several days at Winyaw before he came to Charles Town and appeared as an immoral man. The first man who may be called a Methodist minister was probably the one reported in February 1773: "There[1] lately arrived here from the northward, the Rev. Mr. Pillmoor, a Methodist divine, after the manner of Mr. Wesley, who preached at 6 o'c every evening at the old Baptist Meeting House." What ever success was attained at this time was probably dissipated by the war which soon followed. Ten years later Dr. Richard Furman mentions in a letter that the Methodists were holding forth in the same old meeting house and this was corroborated the next year by a man of less note. "There are several preachers here of the Methodist sect, who lecture almost every night at the old Baptist Meeting house." They remained in it till 1808.[2] It seems therefore an anachronism in "A Tradition of the Old Cheraw," by Crayon Rigmarole,[3] Esqr., in making a Methodist minister one of his characters during the Revolution. There is nevertheless a place for a Pre-Revolutionary Methodism as it was maturing in England; for religious bodies are subject to the laws of heredity as much as individuals. It

---

[1] S. C. Gazette, Feb. 3, 1773.
[2] See Mrs. Poyas' Our Forefathers and their homes and Churches, p. 90.
[3] The author was A. Dromgoole Sims, a lawyer of Darlington who died in Congress.

will serve by comparison with later times to show how common sense adapted the hard and fast original regulations to a more democratic society in the new world.

The Arminian Methodists formed a Conference, members of which were originally chosen by Mr. Wesley.

Every Society (now called church) was divided into bands of 5 to 10 persons who met to confess to one another, one of whom was leader. A class from 10 to 30 met weekly in which the leader told his experience and others were expected to follow. When the religious part of the meeting was closed with prayer and hymns the leader collected the contributions, one penny a week, and besides was one shilling per quarter. Members of bands and classes took out quarterly tickets, and to withhold one from a member was an inoffensive way of removing the disorderly. Preaching was to be the constant business. The helpers or ministers met the bands and societies weekly.

The helpers, about 5 in a circuit, went around it, spending one or two days in a place, except at their quarters in the principle towns and never more than two years in the same circuit. Itineracy was considered the main pillar of the Connexion. The attention was stimulated by new preachers as long pastorates might tend toward Independency and thus weaken or destroy the indivisibility of the Wesleyan republic. Four years trial preceded the admission of ministers. If he married in these four years, he was set aside . . . Wesley recommended celibacy to his ministers for manifest reasons, for cheapness and less expense in living as well as the reasons given by an Apostle.—16 pounds a year for himself, 16 pounds for his wife and an allowance for every child. If he had travelled ten years or had a single preacher boarding with him, 16 pounds additional. The circuits were to defray the expenses of housekeeping. Local preachers served gratuitously.

The business of the bishop or superintendent was to see that the other preachers behaved well and wanted nothing and reported all their defects to the Conference. He visited the classes quarterly in every place within the circuit, to regulate the bands and give out the band and class tickets, admitting or putting out members, to keep watch night and love feast, to hold quarterly meeting, to inquire into temporal and spiritual state of the societies, to take care that every society be supplied with books, sold in behalf of the Conference and that the money for them be constantly returned.

Quarterly meetings were composed of all ministers, leaders and stewards of the circuit and of such local preachers and members as may be invited. Circuits were formed into districts, three to eight circuits under a Chairman. He presided at district meetings, formed of all the preachers in full connection within his province. Here was lodged the authority to suspend preachers who were immoral, erroneous in doctrine or deficient in ability. The conference met annually and the whole business was arranged by 100 members. Inquiries were made about the ministers, each one being called out by name. The accounts were audited and the fields for the coming year appointed. Returns were made from all the churches and in the conference was a clear cut knowledge of its empire in all its parts. While Mr. Wesley lived the government was an absolute monarchy and the conference carried out his will. The minister was bound to recommend the books which the Conference had published and so intense was the society or clan feeling that their hopes and feelings were concentrated in the interests of the connexions rather than in those of the country.

"Never be unemployed for a moment," said Mr. Wesley to his helpers. "Never be triflingly employed. Never spend any more time at any place than is strictly necessary. Avoid all lightness, jesting and foolish talking. Converse sparingly and cautiously with women, especially young women. Take no steps toward marriage without first consulting with your brethren. Do not affect the gentleman. You have no more business with this character than with that of a dancing master. Be ashamed of nothing but sin; not of fetching wood[4] (if time permit) or drawing water; not of cleaning your own shoes or your neighbor's. Be punctual. Do everything exactly at the time and in general do not mind our rules but keep them. You have nothing to do but to save souls; therefore spend and be spent in this work. Above all, if you labor with us in the same vineyard it is needful that you do the part of the work we advise, at those times and places which we judge most for His glory."[5]

John Wesley and George Whitefield were the great preachers of England who stood forth in the first half of the 18th century. The cause of the rise of Methodism under the preaching of these young ministers is thus clearly and judiciously stated: "Methodism arose in the eighteenth century directly out of the bosom of the Church of England. Its founders were John and Charles Wesley and George Whitefield. The last half of the 17th and the first half of the 18th centuries constitute a period of scepticism and moral decay. England was never at a lower ebb religiously and morally than in

---

[4]Bishop Asbury used to join the Pegues family at night in picking lint from cotton seed.

[5]In an address before the Historical Society of the South Carolina Conference in 1912 on the March of Democracy in the Methodist Episcopal Church, South, Dr. J. L. Stokes said "It is only a simple matter of history that Wesley was as veritable an autocrat in Methodism as his Grace of Canterbury among the Anglicans or his holiness of Rome among the Catholics."

1725. Methodism arose as the chief means of saving the English nation from that condition. They immediately began to preach, delivering a warm, evangelical message, filled with fervor, movement and vocal expression. They were soon excluded from the churches and began work in the open air and in rented halls. As they gained converts here and there, they organized them into societies for the purpose of worship and of instruction. Gradually the preachers of these societies were organized in conferences and thus gradually the Methodist organization was built up. John Wesley was a great man and profoundly influenced the lives of multitudes of individuals and the national life itself. His movement was reassertion of the rights of the heart in religion. His effort meant to remain in the Episcopal Church but the character of his movement was incompatible with the older body, and after his death the Methodists separated and organized the various Wesleyan Societies of the English speaking world."[6]

Wesley, being Arminian in his theology, and having a genius for organization, became the founder of the Methodist Church, one of the most numerous bodies in the United States. Whitefield was Calvinistic and careless about the future, left the fruits of his labors to take care of themselves. The Church of England was unfriendly and his Calvinistic doctrines separated him from Wesley's adherents and a part of the Presbyterians were also out of harmony with his manner of procedure.[7]

---

[6]By Dr. W. J. McGlothlin of the Southern Baptist Theological Seminary, now President of Furman University.

[7]Rev. Alexander Hewatt, pastor of the First Presbyterian Church in Charleston wrote in 1779: Whitefield's great ambition was to be the founder of a new sect, regulated entirely by popular fancy and caprice, depending on the gifts of nature regardless of the improvements of education and all ecclesiastical laws and institutions. After him a servile race of ignorant and despicable imitators sprung up and wandered from place to place, spreading doctrines subversive of all public order and peace." Verily time tests all things!

Thus it happened that the fruits of his labors were more abundantly reaped by the Baptists. Whitefield did not, like Wesley, create a new denomination to meet a special need, but he revivified one and revived a more active evangelistic spirit in it. No one can understand the growth of the denominations in the south without harking back to the conditions of the century preceding 1750. There was a religious vacuum in the new world and these competitive forces were more zealous in filling it.

CHAPTER XIV

THE POOR AND THE POOR PROTESTANT

"The poor ye have always with you" is true in all lands. In South Carolina there were special reasons why their number was disproportionate. There were many poor who owned their homes, reared large families and without the aid of slaves laid up enough annually to subsist upon until another crop was made. When their children enjoyed even scant school and church privileges they sometimes surprised their neighbors by their unexpected success in life. To-day talent obscured by poverty and illiteracy of several generations is reappearing in mill villages as opportunity calls it into exercise. Their ancestors not so ambitious to be rich as to deserve a good name in the neighborhood, were the happy, care-free people of their day, with their minds stored with bits of rustic wisdom and experience. In their houses cheap New Testaments well thumbed were often found and Bunyan's Pilgrim's Progress. In the 18th century South Carolina was a paradise for the poor energetic man. Entitled to 50 acres of land and an additional acreage for each member of his household, he could build his house, clear his patch and fence it with no other tools than an axe, saw, hammer, hoe, wedge, auger, gimlet and pocket knife. An African negro caught the eye of Zamba as he was building his cabin 12 x 20 with nothing but wooden pegs, working at night by a fire kept up by his children who threw in chips, twigs and resinous pine burrs which made a bright light. And men still living remember how doors and gates were made and fastened without any iron and how scaffolds were secured by twisted hickory withes and how boards were laid to cover the house and kept in place either by pegs, hand-made nails or superimposed weights. Many of the conveniences of life found substitutes. The goose quill furnished tooth picks and pens while the balls on the oaks served as ink and inkstand. For buttons horns were made to serve and in the field thorns were used as skewers and strips of cloth for suspenders, the pair being often reduced to one gave rise to the epithet "The one gallus crowd." Ashes furnished soap, sedge the brooms and gourds the dippers, buckets and other receptacles. It was the ease of living in many cases in a debilitating summer that reconciled many families to food and fuel abundant and near at hand.

"I never saw there" (in South Carolina) said James Freeman[1] in 1712, any man, woman or child in the country beg an alms, neither do I know any family so poor and in want but that if a small gift of any kind of provisions was offered them because it was supposed that they could not subsist without such helps, they would refuse it and scorn acceptance thereof; for I truly affirm that a laborious man, being settled for himself, may by his own labor and industry, maintain a wife and ten children, sufficient with corn, peas, rice, fresh fish and fowl, without such assistance of Charity."

Another class has been stigmatized as "crackers," "poor whites" and "white trash" by negroes and writers who have lifted them up into unenviable reputation by descriptions in books of travel and even for the use of schools. One capable and judicious writer[2] attributes the existence of the sand-hillers and the poor to the economic system, the fruitage of slavery. How much of this allegation is true, it is not easy to ascertain. To

---

[1] Profitable Advice to Rich and Poor in a Dialogue or Discourse Between James Freeman, a Carolina Farmer and Simon Question a west county Farmer, containing a Description or True Relation of South Carolina, an English Plantation or Colony in America. London. 1712.

[2] Shaper's Sectionalism in South Carolina.

raise a suspicion that slavery is not a full and satisfactory explanation of the South Carolina anomaly, a look backward into the history of the poor in England, a subject handled ably and constantly by the Edinburgh and other reviews, will be sufficient. The poor in the province of South Carolina were sufficiently in evidence before 1700 to have some provision made for them and by 1712, the care of them was entrusted to the parishes, whose overseers levied taxes for their support. The slaves were about equal in number to the whites and were filling, it is true, the places allotted to the poor in free countries and making manual labor an unfit occupation for the freeman; but the source of the evil from which the poor kept coming to America was in England and it had never been touched by African slavery. The cupidity of the Spaniards in the 16th and 17th centuries had disturbed the economic world and they were now regarding the colony in Charles Town a dangerous intruder which they had unwittingly helped to bring into their own borders. The precious metals plundered from American mines and natives carried back in such quantities to Spain, so depreciated the purchasing value of the precious metals that in one hundred years after the discovery of America, it required two and a half times more labor to secure breadstuffs than it did in 1492. The capital engaged in manufacturing was so small in these early centuries that the price of labor remained stationary or declined. The laboring classes under the operation of economic laws and of unwise legislation, were deprived of the comforts of life and many of them reduced to beggary. They had no voice in the government but being numerous and feared, they were treated as sleeping Gulliver was by the Lilliputians. Other causes, such as the dissolution of the monasteries and the breaking up of the feudal system tended to increase rather than diminish the poverty which made a redundancy of population ripe for emigration and colonization. For more than two centuries England faced the task of regulating, employing and maintaining the poor, of diminishing their number and of elevating their morals.[3] It appealed to the benevolent and attracted the prolonged attention of statesmen, but notwithstanding, pauperism remained a spreading cancer in the body politic. The treatment of the disease began by voluntary gifts or contributions to the poor which were gathered and distributed by the minister of the parish or church warden, the collection still taken in communion occasions being a survival of the ancient custom. The legislation was intended to curb and regulate the evil, but it grew by 1562 to such an extent that it was thought necessary to levy weekly sums upon all persons and to take the power to levy from the justice of the peace and lodge it in the hands of respectable men in each parish. In 1601 the foundation of the legal system was laid and on many occasions during the century attempts were made to amend or improve the regulations; but notwithstanding, from the foundation of Charles Town in 1670 to 1725, it has been estimated by competent writers that the poor in England and Wales cost the government one million pounds annually. One of the arguments put forward by Sir Humphrey Gilbert in 1675 for explorations in the new world was "that homes might be provided for many needy people who troubled the commonwealth and through want here at home are forced to commit outrageous offences whereby they are daily consumed by the gallows." Another reason—so British-like—was that new industries might spring up at home to supply articles to these eastern people and thus provide employment for vagabonds and

---

[3]It was a subject frequently threshed out in the Quarterlies.

such-like people. This great field in America to the southward was opened in 1670 by the Lords Proprietors but it did not become an outlet of importance for this burdensome population before the colony became a royal province and both the king and the people combined business and philanthrophy in draining the mother country in some measure of this part of the population.

After South Carolina was brought under the control of the Board of Trade the day of the Poor in England and of the Poor Protestants of Western Europe dawned in brightness. The interest aroused in transporting them to the new world amounted to a crusade which appealed to philanthrophy, to economic considerations and to statesmanship. It was an effort to free their country from an evil which was growing faster than the political gumption needed to lessen it. South Carolina, which at this time included Georgia, was selected as the locality to which the poor were especially to be transported. It was an exposed outpost of the empire and every male carried over was to be strength added to the fighting force of the colony. The Colony of Georgia founded in 1732 was partly a charitable experiment as is evident from its Charter: "His Majesty having taken into consideration the miserable circumstances of many of his poor subjects ready to perish for want; as likewise the distresses of many poor foreigners who would take refuge from persecution; and having a princely regard to the great danger the east frontiers of South Carolina are exposed to by reason of the small number of white inhabitants there, hath out of his fatherly compassion toward his subjects been graciously pleased to grant a charter—The Trustees intend to relieve such unfortunate persons as cannot subsist here and establish them in an orderly manner—will defray the charge of their passage to Georgia; give them necessaries, cattle, land and subsistence, till such time as they can build their houses and clear their land. By such a colony many families who would otherwise starve, will be provided for, and made masters of houses and lands; the people in Great Britain, to whom these necessitous families were a burden, will be relieved—factories here will be employed in supplying them with clothes and working tools."

In Charles Town the Council was most liberal in helping the poor and indigent by transporting them to the new townships and in furnishing means for subsistence while they were building cabins, clearing land and making a crop. In writing to the Lords of Trade and Plantations in November, 1734, Governor Johnson exhibited his own and his successor's attitude toward the poor and poor Protestants:

"Mr. Purry (the leader of the Swiss Colony) is arrived with about 280 souls. I ordered provisions to be ready against their arrival, and I doubt not that the assembly to whom I recommended it will make good any deficiency that may happen in subsisting them for a year, having already subsisted those that arrived before, above a year and eight months, besides great assistance given to Georgia, and subsisting other new comers from Ireland and other places." This policy was continued to the Revolution. He also encouraged by proclamation private liberality and named an officer to whom contributions might be made. The grand jury in the same month presented it as a grievance that there was no workhouse[4] in the province in order to punish the idle and prevent the great increase of the poor.

---
[4] The first chapters of Oliver Twist and the modicum of truth in Manuel Pereira written in 1852 in Charleston, S. C. by an abolitionist, would be considered as utterly groundless were they not supported by some evidence.

Rambles in the Pee Dee Basin

The number of poor Protestants and poor Englishmen sent to South Carolina cannot be given. They came singly and in crowds and were dispatched to the various township at Purrysburgh, Kingston, Williamsburg, Amelia Township, Fredericksburg, Londonderry, New Bordeaux etc. with their expenses paid across the ocean in some cases, with their board while in town and costly transportation into the interior with provisions for a year and tools and animals to make a start in life, furnished free of cost. During the decade after the peace of 1763 the emigrants from Ireland and Germany were pushing north westerly in great numbers. The north of Ireland was greatly drained on account of crop failures and demands of landlords; and the exodus for many of them had Williamsburg township as the end of their journey. And so it happened that South Carolina as a colony was favored with a large population of the poor and of the poor Protestants included in its population. And never in the history of the race, were the poor treated so generously by the men in power nor let down into a more congenial environment. The state is still considered the most illiterate in the union and the most unpromising field for the Catholic missionary. Poverty is a fine subsoil out of which great men spring; but when poverty marries poverty and engenders poverty, the offspring becomes unambitious, hopeless and improvident. Such were some of the poor sent over from England, satisfied to pass their lives in indigence until they became a stratum of the race as sterile as the sandhills to which the poor, it is alleged, were driven by the energetic planters who got possession of the desirable lands and left the sterile lands to them as wrecks of an unfortunate industrial system. The foreseeing men did get the desirable lands, sometimes by grants, oftener as a result of greater thrift and industry. But it is an error of judgment to make the so-called sand-hillers and the poor generally a wreck of the slavery system only. The theory did not take into consideration that the industrial system which originally wrecked them was still wrecking them in England, so that with all the efforts of philanthropy and legislation the burden kept growing. "At the close of the war in 1783, the annual amount of the poor rate was 2,132,487 pounds. In half a century that is, in 1833, the amount had risen to 8,606,501 pounds. The population of England and Wales in the first period was 8 millions; in the second period almost 14 millions. The poor rate had increased 300 per cent; the population had increased about 75 per cent.[5] Despairing philosophers said twenty years later that the evil had struck its roots too deep and the masses infested by sloth, ignorance, drunkenness and filth, were too formidable to be raised."[6]

Any explanation of these unfortunate people in South Carolina as to their origin and deterioration ought at least to take some notice of their unusual physical environment. They were not duplicated in any other colony except Georgia. The retreating ocean, for centuries, beat upon that part of the state extending from Cheraw to Augusta and deposited the sand which presents a striking contrast in the growth of its forests. The oaks feed in the surface and do not reach their usual size and height, but remain small and dwarfed while the pine sends down deep its tap root for food and moisture and raises high in the air its stately trunk and branching crown. The parallel between the oak trees and the people who drew their sustenance from the same sandy surface is so patent that it suggests a

[5] Knight's Popular History of England.
[6] Mrs. Schoolcraft's "The Black Gauntlet."

similar reason for the deterioration in the minds and the bodies—a lack of sustenance.[7] If the unfortunate industrial system due to slavery was the cause of this collection of the poor on the sand hills, it did not produce a like effect in the Alleghany range in the northern part of the state and in western North Carolina where the redundant population or the late new comers took up lands with soil so thin that the difficulty of making a crop and in getting it to market, "made a dollar look as large as a cart wheel." The conclusion reached, to recapitulate, is that South Carolina was the receptacle for many of the poor of England and the paradise of the poor persecuted Protestant and that the so called "poor whites" were not a separate class but like the stunted oaks in the sand hills, they gradually fell behind and appeared to be a distinct race. Their day is in the future.

---

[7]That the dwarfed oak and the "poor whites" were due to the soil is corroborated by a satisfying explanation of their origin through Mr. D. R. Williams: They were at first "the same as the other settlers, but they were so handicapped by the poverty of their soil and environment that in time they became a distinct class."

CHAPTER XV

First Friction Between the Sections

In the midst of the stamp act excitement, occurrences in the backwoods, were demanding the serious attention of the authorities in Charles Town. The assembly had succeeded in transferring the centre of gravity from the Board of Trade to Charles Town, by encroaching upon the prerogatives of the Crown and now it was confronted with an inevitable struggle, both with the crown officials and with the multitude of people who were going inland, in order to keep the centre of gravity in Charles Town. The plan of defense, on account of the Establishment was made manifest when representation in the assembly was denied to the inhabitants of Williamsburg and Orangeburg Townships though clearly entitled to it by the King's Instructions to Gov. Johnson. A region extending one hundred and fifty to two hundred miles, situated further off, was thus also left to become more populous than the organized parishes and to shift as best it could with the ordinary machinery of government no nearer than Charles Town.

In September 1762, Charles Woodmason, a justice of the peace, offered a reward of 20 pounds for the capture of one William McKay, both in order to have him punished and to learn through him information about the gang of thieves whose hiding place was on the borders of the state. It was in this year and in Charles Woodmason's neighborhood—on the Pee Dee and Lynch's Creek—that the people being harassed by "Horse stealers and other felons from North Carolina and other parts," petitioned the Governor and the two houses to carve out of Craven County a new one on the Pee Dee and appoint 12 justices of the peace with powers to decide civil and criminal cases, subject only to appeal to the Superior Court in the metropolis. The assembly took the matter into consideration and adopted the adverse report of the committee which substituted Georgetown and Beaufort instead of Pee Dee as the place where courts should be established. To this the assembly agreed and went through the forms which were to make it an Act, only to let it end in smoke. Only justices of the peace with very limited powers were appointed.

This petition from the Pee Dee was on the side of good order and stability of government. The petitioners expected to tax themselves in order to erect the needed buildings, while the judicial machinery would have been engineered by the government. England was now claiming as an axiom that protection by her army and navy involved the right of taxation; but these tributary rustics had neither the right of representation in the assembly nor the happiness to be protected by it. They were thus to be thrown back upon the primitive principle of self-defense in the absence of constituted authority. Being deprived of the ordinary processes of the courts, they found it necessary in reference to confirmed evil doers to use the extraordinary methods known as Lynch law. According to the historian Ramsay the idleness enforced on those persons who fled from the Indians to the forts was the parent of the thieving in the states. Sallying out from the forts to the deserted plantations they took possession of the furniture and tools and drove off the horses and cattle left behind by families in their hurried flight. Detention at the forts may have led persons to engage in this sort of a life, but the horse thief was indigenous in the out skirts and, like the buffalo, went west in advance of organized government. There would be today the same reversion toward brutishness in any territory where there were no schools and churches and no laws to be feared, as was the case in these 18th Century outposts.

Another different kind of complaint came from an intelligent dissenter living in the forks of Broad and Saluda rivers, which in a few years was to be the abode of tories:

"It is no small satisfaction to us that we have a King whose love diffuseth itself to all his children—yet notwithstanding that favor, we apprehend that we labor under some hardships, in common with most, if not all the back settlers in the province in some things: particularly in paying our quota to the public tax, when the salaries of all the Clergy of the Church of England in the province are taken out of it, with parochial charges of each parish and frequently considerable sums given toward building and repairing of Churches and Chapels in the lower part of the province; whilst we in the back parts have neither Church nor parsonage and as many or most of the back settlers, we protestant dissenters from the Church of England; as Lutherans, Presbyterians, Independents, Quakers, Anabaptists, etc. who on their attachment and loyalty to the renowned King of England, the third, vie with the Church of England, think that in equity, they might expect to have money from the public fund assigned toward erecting places of worship for each sectary, as well as the Church of England, when their numbers are so many as to need it; and likewise to support their teachers, seeing the public tax is collected from their estates, in common with the lower settlement; therefore have as legal a property in it as they; to this it may be objected that the people in the back settlements pay but a small proportion of the tax as they are generally poor. The answer is easy—so much the harder to make them bear the burden of the rich. Though by the bye their estates in the back parts are chiefly lands and not fluctuating as personal estates are; and they are obliged to pay as much for an 100 acres as is paid per head for negroes, when in general people in the lower settlements would not give a slave for 500 or 1000 acres of our land, or even accept of it on gift; which makes us say, we think it hard the estates should be taxed to pay Clergy's salaries parochial expenses, building churches and chapels etc. in the lower settlements, while we have neither churches or places of worship in the back parts, at the charge of the public; and think no rational person can do otherwise than acknowledge that in the nature of things, it is equitable that those who contribute to any common stock are equally entitled to the benefits accruing or arising therefrom; and on the contrary, that to compel one part of a community to be at expense for the other without any advantage to themselves, is not equitable, whether it be just or lawful or not which will be, as the proverb has it, *might* overcomes *right* in such cases."

The complaint from this fork in the upper parts was not against the established church, but against taxation for it when the taxpayers were excluded from any share in the fund. It was also aimed at the inequality of taxation. When the wealthier half of the population in any state chooses the representatives, the taxes are made to bear on the masses. When Gov. Tryon of North Carolina persuaded the legislature to build his palace at New Berne, at the cost of about $80,000, it was to be paid by poll tax of 51,000 persons in three years. The people on the coast where the palace was, were comparatively few in number while the more populous inland counties whose inhabitants traded at Charles Town had to pay a very large part of the expense in building. On the other hand, when the lower half of the democracy are represented, the taxes already imposed are retained and others, like the income and inheritance taxes, are set so as to scoop out from the abundant treasures of the rich.

Another class of unrepresented citizens in these regions was thought to be more radical in its stand in ecclesiastical matters. "Not less than twenty itinerant Presbyterian, Baptist and Independent preachers are maintained by the synods of Pennsylvania and New England to traverse the country, poisoning the minds of the people, instilling democratical and commonwealth principles in their minds. Embittering them against the very name of Bishops and all episcopal government and laying deep their fatal republican notions and principles. Especially that they owe no subjection to Great Britain or the parliament, that they are a free people, that they are to pay allegiance to King George as the sovereign, but as to Great Britain or the Parliament or any there, that they have no more to think of or about them than the Turk or Pope."[1]

Another witness living in these times declared that Whitefield's followers in America were distinguished for unfriendliness to civil government and, for the most part, discovered "an aversion to our constitution of church and state. Toleration to men who remain peaceable subjects to the state is reasonable; but dissention when it grows lawless and headstrong is dangerous and summons men in general to take shelter under the Constitution, that the salutary laws of our country may be executed by its united strength."[2]

These two witnesses were royalists who abandoned the colony but their testimony as to the facts in their

---
[1] Rev. Woodmason's Note on Remonstrance.
[2] Hewatt.

allegations is credible and after personal equations and some allowance for exaggeration are made, may be regarded as a true picture in the pre-revolutionary times as seen from their point of view.

In 1762, the lawlessness in the country induced the legislature to pass an act to prevent stealing of horses and neat cattle and for the more effective discovery and punishment of such persons as shall unlawfully brand, mark or kill the same. In 1764, the band of robbers infested both states. Gov. Dobbs reported the capture of members of a confederated gang operating in several counties and one[3] of the historians states that in the same year Thomas Woodward, Joseph Kirkland, Barnaby Pope and others of the better class of settlers held a consultation over the situation and decided to draw up an instrument of writing which bound all who signed it to make a common cause in bringing horse thieves and other criminals to justice. Whenever caught and found guilty they were beaten and advised to leave the community. Hence arose the names "Regulators" and "Regulation." As the two elements were numerous, the evilly disposed entered also into a league in self-defense. Lt. Gov. Bull understood the situation so that in 1765 after he had made a tour to the north-westward said in his opening speech: "I recommend to you, seriously to consider of the distribution of justice in criminal and civil matters under the best regulations, in those remote parts, which may remove many of the great inconveniences these people are now liable to, and will tend to suppress in a great degree, the idlers and rogues who now infest and injure the industrious remote settlers too often with impunity."

---

[3]Ramsay's South Carolina, Vol. II, p. 312.

The speaker of the house, Othniel Beale, said in response that "the great increase of inhabitants in the interior parts of the province, rendered some regulations for that purpose in those places necessary."

Before this legislative session closed, the bill establishing courts, when it was about to undergo its final trial, created interest outside of the legislative walls. "Our city, too, it seems is averse to Circuit Courts, because it will in some little measure deprive them of customers whom they would otherwise seldom see and who by the bye have very little to spend."[4]

The strife had now reached that point in which the pen was brought in to supplement the sword. In the latter part of the year 1767, a Remonstrance was written and presented to the government, "In the Name, By Desire, And on Behalf of the Back Inhabitants, and signed in their presence, by us their Deputies." It was received by the three branches of the government whose appreciation of the document may be gauged by their failure to have it recorded in their proceedings.

This Remonstrance was searched for but not found by Bishop Gregg[5] and McCrady states that "it was objected to on account of improper and unbecoming expressions, which it may well have contained if he (Moses Kirkland) had a hand in its composition." One of these passages which gave offense was in the nature of a complaint that Lt. Gov. Bull, willing to close his applauded administration with an act of mercy, opened the prisons and let out the notorious evil doers who had been convicted at great cost and when they were again convicted and sentenced in 1766, Gov. Montagu willing to begin his administration as his predecessor

---

[4]S. C. Gazette, June 8, 1765.
[5]Gregg's History of the Old Cheraws, p. 135, footnote.

concluded it, with an act of clemency, pardoned the villains and set them at liberty again to rob and plunder. Another expression which gave offence was, "When the bands of society and government hang loose and ungirt about us, when no regular police is established, but every one left to do as seemeth him meet, there is not the least encouragement for any individual to be industrious," etc.

The Remonstrance being lengthy, scathing and at times not becomingly respectful, it was not preserved in the minutes or in the archives but about four years later, as the internal evidence indicates, Rev. Charles Woodmason sent a copy of it to some one connected with the S. P. G. and added some lengthy and caustic notes and comments of his own.

The back settlers had been under contribution to the bands of rogues for three years; and representations of their grievances and vexations having been often made to those in power without any redress, they set out in detail their grievances and drew up their petitions in 21 articles, covering courts, justices, lawyers, churches, ministers, lines of parishes, schools, etc.

It will also be observed that the Remonstrance could not have been intelligently signed by a great majority of the upper inhabitants. The four who signed the document did not escape the charge of being the sole authors, but it is not necessary in a critical time as this was to suppose that such a paper read to a promiscuous audience who found much in it to applaud would mar the harmony by open rupture or opposition. The four signatures were Benjamin Hart (who owned land on the eastern side of the Wateree), John Scott (who had recently bought some land laid out between Swift Creek and Rafting Creek) Moses Kirkland (of Amelia and of

SOUTH CAROLINA

Saxe Gotha township and Saluda, who figured conspicuously among the Regulators and unhappily in the Revolution) and Thomas Woodward who had lands on the north side of Broad River and proved himself to be a patriot as an officer in the same war. This petition had its birth apparently in the Camden section, but was adopted it seems by deputies generally.

Fulham MSS. N. C., S. C., Georgia, No. 72

Copy of a Remonstrance Presented to the Commons House of Assembly of South Carolina, by the Upper Inhabitants of the said Province Nov. 1767

To

His Excellency The Right Honorable Lord Charles Greville Montagu; Captain General &c And

To

The Honorable The Members of His Majesty's Council

And

To the Honorable Peter Manigault Speaker, and other the Members of the Commons House of Assembly
The Remonstrance and Petition of the Inhabitants of the Upper & Interior Parts of this Province on behalf of themselves, and all other the Settlers of the Back-Country.

Humbly Sheweth

That for many years past, the Back Parts of this province hath been infested with an infernal Gang of Villains, who have committed such horrid Depredations on our Properties and Estates—Such Insults on the Persons of many Settlers and perpetrated such shocking Outrages thro'out the Back Settlements, as is past description.

Our Large Stocks of Cattel are either stolen and destroyed—Our Cow pens are broke up and All our valuable Horses are carried off—Houses have been burned by these Rogues, & families stripp'd and turn'd naked into the Woods—Stores have been broken open & rifled by them (wherefrom several Traders are absolutely ruin'd) Private houses have been plundered and the Inhabitants wantonly tortured in the Indian Manner for to be made confess where they secreted their Effects from Plunder. Married Women have been Ravished—Virgins deflowered, and other unheard of Cruelties committed by these barbarous Ruffians—Who, by being let loose among Us (and conniv'd at) by the Acting Magistrates, have hereby reduc'd Numbers of Individuals to Poverty—and for these three Years last past have laid (in a Manner) this part of the province under Contribution.

No Trading Persons (or others) or with Money or Goods, No Responsible persons and Traders dare keep Cash, or any Valuable Articles by them—Nor can women stir abroad, but with a guard, or in Terror—The Chastity of many beauteous Maidens have been threatened by these Rogues, Merchants Stores are oblig'd for to be kept constantly guarded (which enhances the Price of Goods) And thus we live not as under a British Government (ev'ry Man sitting in peace and Security under his own Vine(& his own Fig Tree), But as if we were in *Hungary or Germany,* and in a State of War—continually exposed to the Incursions of *Hussars and Pandours;* Obliged to be constantly on the Watch, and on Our Guard against these Intruders, & having it not in our power to call what we possess our own, *not even for an Hour;* as being liable Daily and Hourly to be stripp'd of our Property.

Representations of these Grievances and Vexations have often been made by Us to those in Power—But without Redress—Our Cries must have pierc'd their Ears, tho' not enter'd into their Hearts—For, instead of Public Justice being executed on many of these Notorious Robbers (who have been taken by us at much Labour and Expence and Committed and on others (who with Great difficulty & Charge have been arraigned and Convicted) We have to lament that such have from Time to Time been pardon'd; and afresh set loose among Us, to repeat their Villainies, & strip Us of the few remaining Cattle Horses and Moveables which after their former Visits they had left us, Thus distressed; Thus situated & unreliev'd by Government, many among Us have been obliged to punish some of these Banditti & their Accomplices, in a proper Manner, —Necessity (that first principle) compelling them to Do, what was expected that the Executive Branch of the Legislature would *long ago* have done.

We are *Free-Men*—British Subjects—Not Born *Slaves* —We contribute our protection in all Public Taxations, and discharge our Duty to the Public, equally with our Fellow Provincials

Yet we do not participate with them in the Rights and Benefits which they Enjoy, tho' equally Entitled to them.

Property is of no Value, except it be secure: How Ours is secured, appears from the foremention'd Circumstances, and from our now being obliged to defend our Families, by *our own Strength*: As *Legal Methods* are beyond our Reach—or not as yet *extended* to Us.

Rambles in the Pee Dee Basin

We may be deemed too bold in saying *"That the present Constitution of this Province is very defective, & become a Burden, rather than being beneficial to the Back-Inhabitants"* For Instance—To have but One Place of Judicature in this Large and Growing Colony— And that seated *not Central,* but in *a Nook* by the Sea Side, The Back-Inhabitants to travel Two, three hundred Miles to carry down criminals, prosecute Offenders appear as Witnesses (tho secluded to serve as Jurors) attend the Courts & Suits of Law—The Governor and Court of Ordinary, all Land Matters, & on every Public Occasion are Great Grievances, and call loudly for *Redress* For 'tis not only Loss of Time which the poor Settlers sustain there from, but the *Toil of Travelling,* and *Heavy Expenses* therefrom arising. Poor Suitors are often driven to Great Distresses, Even to the spending their last Shilling or to sell their *Only* Horse for to defray their traveling and Town Costs; After which they are oblig'd to trudge home on foot, & beg for Subsistence by the Way: And after being Subpena'd and then attending Court as Witnesses or as Constables, they oft are never call'd for On Trials but are put off to next Court, & then the same Services must be repeated. These are Circumstances experienced by no Individuals under British Government, save those in South Carolina.

It is owing to these Burdens on our Shoulders, That the Gangs of Robbers who infest us, have so long reign'd without Repression: For if a Party hath Twenty Cattle or the best of his Stallions stollen from him, the Time and Charge consequent on a Prosecution of the Offenders, is equal too, or Greater than his loss—As, To Prosecute would make Him Doubly a Sufferer; And Poor Persons have not Money to answer the Cravings of Rapacious Lawyers—As proceedings at Law are *now* manag'd, it may cost a private person Fifty pounds to bring a Villain to Justice—And in Civil Cases, the Recovery of *Twenty* pounds, will frequently be attended with Seventy Pounds Costs—if not Treble that Sum.

When Cattle & Horses are Stollen, and the Thief is publickly known, (and they will committ their Robberies openly at Noon Day) Persons who see and know of these Evils, are backward in making Information, as they are certain to subject themselves to much Trouble and Expence, beside the Risque they run of being plunder'd themselves by the Rogues, in Revenge for Informing against them—And in Consequence of being subpena'd to attend the Courts of Charlestown, (under Great Disadvantages) they are often oblig'd to sell their Substance at half value, to defray Road Charges, the Public having made no Provision on this head—These long Journeys are often required too at some Critical Juncture, very detrimental to the Poor Planter; who therefrom, will endeavour to avoid appealing against Rogues, when they are brought to Trial. From which Circumstances, many Rogues have been acquitted at Court for want of Evidence—The Trials of Others delayed—The province (as well as Individuals) put to grievous Expence; And the Gangs of Robbers (here from Recruited and Spirited) have still reign'd without Controul, Ranging and Plundering the Country with Impunity. We can truly say, they Reign; as by their Menaces they intimidate many whom they have injur'd, from laying hold on, & bringing them to Justice—.

If we are thus insecure—If our Lives and properties are thus at Stake—If we cannot be protected—If these Villains are suffer'd to range the Country uncontroul'd & no Redress to be obtain'd for our Losses, All of Us, & our families must quit the province, & Retire where there are laws, Religion & Government: For as the Laws now stand, It is of no Import to bind lawless profligate Persons to the Good Behaviour: Recognizances are laugh'd at, because never put in Suit—Nor can be, but at the private Expence of the Suffering Party. Wherefrom, the Clergy, Magistracy, & all in public Authority (who ought to be protected in Execution of the Laws, and honour'd in their Public Stations) are Insulted and Abused by Licentious & Insolent Persons without Redress.

The Trial of Small & Mean Causes by a Single Magistrate (a Wise Institution in the Infancy of the Colony) is now become an Intolerable Grievance partly thro' the *Ignorance* of some Justices, and the *Bigotry and Partiality* of others. Individuals are rather Oppress'd than Reliev'd by their Decisions, for Persons are oft time saddled with Ten or Twelve Pounds Costs, on a Debt of as many Shillings, Thro' the Indolence, Connivance, or Corruption of several Justices, it is owing, that the Thieves have gain'd such Strength and risen to such a pitch of Audacity—They well know, that if Warrants are issued out against them, that they will be slowly pursu'd; Or that they shall have timely Notice given them for to avoid the officers: We could enumerate many flagrant Instances of this Sort But as ev'ry Complaint of this Nature from the Country have hitherto been disregarded, We can only close this Article with saying, That thro' the Venality of Mean Persons now in the Commission, *Contempt* instead of *Respect* is thrown on this so Honourable & Necessary Office.

By poor Persons being oblig'd to travel to Charlestown to obtain Patents for Small Tracts of Land, or to renew their Warrants, His Majestys Kindness to His Subjects is defeated—As it causes Land to come as dear, or prove as Expensive in Running Out, as if for to be purchas'd. The same fees being paid on a Grant of Ten, as on one of Ten thousand Acres. The like Grievance exists in Respect to the proving Wills, or taking out of Letters of Administration: the fees on which are treble to what is charg'd at home, even tho' clogg'd with Stamps, When Effects of a deceased party doth not exceed 40 or 50 pounds, half this Sum must be expended in Court fees no distinction being made—It being alike the same, if the Effects are fifty or fifty thousand pounds. There are great Hardships on the Poor—especially as the fee now claimed at the Public offices, are double to what were formerly demanded which merits the serious Attention of the Legislature

As the laws are now modell'd, any malicious, malevolent Party may arrest any Stranger any Innocent Person for any Sum Whatever without shewing Cause of Action, or making Oath of his Debt, or giving Security for joining Issue; Which often prevents Persons from getting Bail; for the years Debt or Ballance may not be Sixpence, yet the Sum alleged may be Six thousand Pounds. This intimidates Person from becoming Securities, & subjects many to wrongful & Injurious Imprisonment; Whereby their credit & Families are entirely ruined—Health impair'd—Lives sacrificed, by lying in a Close & Stinking Goal Crowded with Thieves and Vagabonds. No Separation, No Distinction made of Parties, not hardly even of Sexes—Who can boast of British Liberty, that is not safe One Hour from so dreadful an Oppression! A Stranger or Vagrant in this Province who can pay a lawyer Ten Pounds, may at his Pleasure, or for his Frolic, send to Prison (at 200 Miles distance) the best Person here among Us, without his knowing on what Account or for what Reason And this in so arbitrary a Manner, as in France, by a *Lettre de Cachet*—or in Spain, by Warrant from the *Inquisition*. Most sore are these evils! Especially too when a poor Wretch who has inadvertantly broke the Peace, (for which in Britain, he would be order'd a few lashes or a small Fine, & be dismissed) Must lye five or six Months in this loathsome Goal amidst Thieves and Robbers, in the Heat of Summer, & then afterward be discharged by Proclamation. Punishments ought to bear some Proportion to Tresspasses—Nor should Small and Great offences, be treated with equal Severity. To be confin'd six Months in Charlestown Goal at 2 or 300 miles distance from Friends or Family, & to live in this hot Clime on bread & Water is a far heavier punishment, than for to be in the French King's Gallies, or a slave in *Barbary*: And for persons to lye there Session after Session for small Sums, or Petty Offences, is contrary to All Humanity. And more so (as We Observed) When Persons of ev'ry Class, & each Sex are promiscuously confin'd together in a Space where they have not Room to lye; and no Distinction made between Offenders—but Thieves and Murderers—Debtors to the King— Offenders in Penal Laws, Vagrants & idle Persons are closely huddled in one mixt Crowd—

When Persons are unwarrantably arrested by vexatious Pettifoggers, or Litigious Miscreants (as such will infest every Society) and Bail is given In this Case, should the Plaintiff discontinue, and refuse joining the Issue, & drop the Suit, We apprehend (from the Sufferings of many) that no Remedy at present lies for relief of any innocent Person who is so treated, consistent with the Liberty of the Subject—But the Defendant must submit to sus-(tain?) 40 or 50 pounds Charge & Loss—Or if he sue for Damages or Costs expended or for false Imprisonment after being Ruin'd & Undone, What Satisfaction is to be obtain'd against Insolvent Prosecutors?

By our Birth-Right as *Britons,* We ought for to be try'd by a Jury of our Peers. This is the glorious Liberty of Free born Subjects—The darling Privilege that distinguishes Britain from all other Nations. But We Poor distress'd Settlers, enjoy only the Shadow, Not the Substance of this Happiness. For can We truly be said to be try'd by our Peers when few or No Persons on this North Side of Santee River (containing half the province) are on the Jury List? The Juries of ev'ry Court are generally composed of the Inhabitants of Charlestown or its Environs: Persons who never perhaps travell'd beyond Charlestown Neck: who know not even the Geography, much less the Persons and concerns of the Back Country. These determine Boundaries of our Lands, *without a View,* & decide on Matters of which they have no proper Conception. We think these proceedings as absurd as if Affairs of Shipping & Trade were to be settled by twelve Residents in our Woods, who never saw a Town, the Sea, or a Ship in their Lives.

Heretofore, the Lives and Properties of Us Back Settlers, may accidentally be affected thro' the Judge or Jurors having no Personal Knowledge[6] of Parties who

---

[6]The Gross Ignorance of the Carolinian Gentry (indeed all in General in the Lower Settlements) of the Upper Country is so Great & Astonishing, as if related, would not admit of Belief. Few among them ever travelled 50 Miles beyond Charlestown—and those who have only went the Rout of the Armies to the several Forts—knowing nothing of the Lands Settlements or people of the Interior parts—The very Council, & Clerks, & those in office, know not one County from another—Grants of Lands in Craven County (the most Northwardly) have been made out for Granville Settlers) the most Southerly County, next Georgia—In the public Proclamations, one place has been set down for another—Justices of the peace dead for years, continued in Rolls of the Commission—They knew not even one parish from another—and the writer of this avers, that a Gentleman (now one of the Assistant Judges) being chosen Member for p. Frederick parish (only 60 Miles from Charlestown was taken aside by said Gentleman and privately asked, Where the parish lay? Their Extreme Ignorance was so Great, so acknowledged by themselves,

depose in Court—or of their Quality, Estate or Character they bear where they dwell—All persons, without Exception, are now admitted to give Evidence, according to the Mode of their Profession and stand *Recta in Curia*. Now, as we are a mix'd People, & many conceal'd Papists among Us, especially in the Disguise of Quakers) and as such are often admitted as Witnesses & Jurors A Wrong Verdict may often pass thro' this General Admission of Persons of all Countries & Characters being suffer'd to be on Juries, and so give Evidence without Distinction or Restriction.

Nor can we be said to possess our Legal Rights as Freeholders, when We are so unequally represented in Assembly,—The South Side of Santee River, electing 44 Members, & the North Side, with these upper Parts of the Province (containing 2/3s of the White Inhabitants returning but Six—. It is to this Great Disproportion of Representatives on our Part that our Interests have been so long neglected, and the Back country disregarded. But it is the Number of *Free Men*, not *Black Slaves*, that constitute the Strength and Riches of a State.

---

that One of the principal Lawyers in the House moved, 'That before any Bill for Courts, Goals, etc. be made, a Survey of the province be made, that they might know their Route, etc. etc. This was instantly agreed to—And 3000 pounds Sterling voted for that purpose—The Execution of this, was intrusted to a Member of the House (deeply indebted to Mr. Speaker) and has been superficially executed However it will serve as a Base for a more correct Edifice to be rais'd upon—

The Lawyers (We ought to say the Spur Gallers, & Riders of this Country) made Motion, That wherever a Court House was to be, or should be built, there an House of Entertainment to be built likewise at the public Expence for their Reception— Which evidently shews, Of what Influence they have in the House, and how great their Ascendance over individuals, otherwise they never would have dared made so arrogant a demand.

However they took Care in the Bill for Courts &c not to suffer—The Attorney General was allowed 200 pounds Sterling p Ann, travelling Charges. This He thought insufficient (tho' he makes 700 pounds Sterling p an by his post) And he retarded

South Carolina

The not laying out the Back Country into Parishes, is another most sensible Grievance. This Evil We apprehend to arise from the Selfish Views of those, whose Fortunes & Estates, are in or near *Charlestown*—which makes them endeavor, That all Matters & Things shall center there, however detrimental to the Body Politic, hence it arises That Assemblies are kept sitting for six months, when the Business brought before them might be dispatched in six Weeks— to oblige Us (against Inclination) to chuse such Persons for Representatives. who live in or contiguous to *Charlestown;* and to render a Seat in the Assembly too heavy a Burden, for any Country planter, of a small Estate, for to bear. From this our Non-Representation in the House, We Conceive it is; That Sixty thousand Pounds Public Money, (of which we must pay the Greater Part, as being levy'd on the Consumer) hath lately been voted, for to build an Exchange to the Merchants, & Ball-Room for the Ladies of Charlestown; while near Sixty thousand of us Back Settlers, have not a minister, or a place of Worship to repair to As if We were not worth even the Thought of, or deem'd as Savages & not *Christians!*

---

the Bill in the privy Council of Britain till 'twas made 300 pounds Sterling p ann which now is fix'd—The Assistant Judges 300 pounds Sterling per annum who never before had a Shilling & was an Honorary post—The Clerke of the Crown secur'd to himself 300 pounds Sterling p ann for Life—and gave up his patent. The provost Marshal compounded for 6000 Sterling & Surrender of his patent (tho' 7 years before he offer'd it for 2000) And his Deputy secured the sheriffship of Charlestown for Life-Equal to 500 pounds Sterling p Ann—But this is spoken partly on Information, tho (I believe) strictly true—

Meanwhile the Chief Aim of the people was not attended to— For many Evils still remain—In all Suits as to Lands, they must still repair to Charlestown and how Should Charlestown Merchants know ought about lands or their Boundaries? Thus the very material Articles which they wanted to be decided on the Spot is to be heard in France or Spain—For to contest about 50 Acres of Land and carry the suit to Charlestown (where only it can be decided) is more Cost than the Land is worth.—And the Justices of the peace have no power to hear any Complaints

Rambles in the Pee Dee Basin

To leave our Native Countries, Friends, & Relations—the Service of God—the Enjoyment of our Civil and Religious Rights for to breathe here (as we (hop'd) a Purer Air of Freedom, & possess the *utmost Enjoyment of Liberty & Independency*—And instead to be set adrift in the Wild Woods among *Indians & Out Casts* To live in a State of Heathenism—without Law or Government or even the *Appearance of Religion*—Expos'd to the Insults of Lawless & Impudent Persons—To the Depredations of *Thieves* & Robbers and to be treated by our Fellow Provincials who hold the reign of Things, as Persons hardly worthy the public Atttention, Not so much as their Negroes; These Sufferings have broken the Hearts of Hundreds of our New Settlers Made others quit the Province, some return to *Europe,* (& therefrom prevent others coming this Way) and deterr'd Numbers of Persons of Fortune & Character (both at Home & in America) from taking up Lands here & settling this, our Back Country, as Otherwise they would have done.

But whatever Regulations—whatever Emoluments are offer'd for the Embellishment or Benefit of the Metropolis such are readily admitted (and if they could they would make us Hewers of Wood, and Drawers of Water, for Service of the Town: Who treat us not as Brethren of the same Kindred—United in the same Interests—& Subjects of the same Prince, not as if we were of a different Species from themselves; Reproaching us for our Ignorance and Unpoliteness, while they themselves contribute to it, and would chain us to these Oars, as unwillingly, that neither Us or Our Posterity,

---

as to Assaults, or Breach of the peace—Where-from, if a fellow should give another only a Simple Box on the Ear—He is sent to Goal, there to remain 5 or 6 Months, besides paying all Charges as if One Months Imprisonment were not adequate to the Nature, or Repration of the Fault.—Rev. Charles Woodmason.

should emerge from Darkness to Light, & from the power of Satan unto God. Their very Follies and extravagances would afford Us Means of Knowledge & Refinement—What they Waste and throw away would lay for us the foundation of Good Things. The Sums trifled away in a Play House there would have rais'd Us Fifty New Churches; And the heavy annual charges which the public is saddled with, attending and conveying Prisoners to Town—Summoning Juries & Other Incident Expenses, together with Mr. Provost Marshall & Mr. Attorney Generals Bills, would if thrown together for these last Seven Years have defrayed the Expense of building Goals Court Houses in ev'ry parish of the province, & all other Public Edifices. But this is not comparable to the Damage done the Mother Country & the West Indian Trade, by the Thieves stealing of all our best Horses, & then selling of them to Dutch Agents, for to be transported to the French Islands to work their Sugar Mills. Add to this, The Depression of Lands in Value—Prevention of their Sale and Culture; Of any Improvements in Planting or Public Works, thro' the Insecurity of all Property, by Incursions of the Thieves.—The Bad Character which the Back Settlements hath gain'd hereby (both in Britain & America) The Rise of Provisions thro' Loss of our Stocks of Neat Cattle—The Length of Time & Great Expence it will cost us to raise again a fine Breed of Horses—the Dread which Persons of Condition & Character entertain, even of their Persons should they travel among Us (which deterrs them from sending of any Slaves for to improve their Lands in the Back Country, thro' fear of their being Stollen) Prevents their paying Us any Attention or Regard, or attempting any New Branches of Commerce, tho' excited thereto by the Society of Arts at Home: In short, the Dread impress's on all Travellers, & which prevents Itinerants from visiting Us (and thereby making Cash to Circulate:) The Damp put on our Spirits thro' the disregards shown by the Legislature (which had prevented, as beforesaid many thousands from settling among Us, & lessening thereby the Weight of Taxes, & adding to the Increase of Provisions & Commodities for the Market—The drawing of Merchants and Mechanics among Us, thereby lowering the present Exhorbitant Prices of Goods & Labour, and opening New Channels of Trade) All these, & other striking Circumstances, have been little thought of or consider'd in *Charlestown*, 'midst scenes of Luxury & Dissipation.

Oppression will make *Wise Men Mad*: And many sober persons among us are become almost desperate in seeing the Non-Attention given to these and other Matters of Serious Concern, and which so nearly affects the foundation of Things. They seem weary of living (as they have done for Years past) without Exercise of their Civil and Religious Rights, which, they ought to share in Common with the Lower Settlements, and being deem'd and treated as if not Members of the same Body Politic—For, can We vote for Members of Assembly, Or chuse Vestrymen, or elect Parish Officers when We have no Churches to repair to or they are scituated, One, two hundred Miles from Us? Can our Poor be taken Charge Of, when there hath been neither Minister, Church Wardens, or Vestry in St. Marks, or St. Matthews Parish for these three Years past? Nor either a Church built, or Parish laid out in any of the Upper parts of the Province? Does not hereby a Great & heavy Incumbrance fall on the Generous & Humane? On all who have feelings for the Sufferings of others? For the Poor, the Sick, the Aged & Infirm must be relieved and Supported in some Manner, & not left to Perish. What care is or can be taken of Poor Orphans and their Effects (No proper Laws or Provisions being yet made on this Head?) Are they not liable to become the prey of ev'ry Invader? Nor is Here any Security to the Merchant or Trader who may Credit out their Goods, as Knaves and Villains may remove with their Substance unmolested into the neighboring Provinces, & there bid Defiance to their Creditors. Herefrom, no Credit can be given among Us—for no Writ can be obtain'd without going to *Charlestown*—No Attachment can be su'd out, but in *Charlestown*—and while are preparing your Debtor has taken flight, and is quite out of Reach. And no Marriage License can be obtain'd but in Charlestown—And there ev'ry Person must repair to get Married, that would marry judiciously and according to Law —for We have not Churches wherein to publish Banns, or Ministers to Marry Persons, Wherefore the Generality marry each other, which cause the vilest Abominations, & that Whoredom & Adultery overspreads our Land. Thus we live and have liv'd for Years past as if without God in the World, destitute of the Means of Knowledge, without Law or Gospel, Esteem or Credit. For We know not even the Laws of this Country We inhabit for where are they to be found but in the Secretary's Office in Charlestown? The printing a Code of the Laws, hath been long petitioned for, often recommended by the *Crown* & delineated in the *presentments of Grand Juries,* as a Matter long wanting, and of the utmost Consequence: But like all other of their Presentments, it lyes *totally unregarded.* Of what Service have been—Of what Use are the parish Churches of Prince George, Prince Frederic & St. Mark, to the Inhabitants of Williamsburg Great and Little Pedee, Lynch's Creek, Waccamaw, the Congarees, Waxaws, Waterees, Saluda, Long Canes, Ninety Six or Broad River! Places and

Settlements Containing Fifty thousand Souls? These Fabrics were placed where they are, to serve some Local Occasion, or Particular Person or Purposes; But are not (at least at present) of the least Benefit to the Back Country: What Church can We repair to for Divine Service, nearer than Dorchester or Charlestown? Several Parishes being now destitute of Ministers, and no effectual Plan settled for their being properly supplied—

It is notorious, That thro' Want of Churches & Ministers, New Sects have arisen, and now greatly prevail, especially those called *New Lights* (Separate Baptists). Prophaneness & Infidelity abound—Ignorance, Vice, Idleness prevail—And to the Great Indifference shown by all Ranks to promote the Interests of Religion & Virtue, it is in Great Measure owing that such few Checks have been given to the Villains & Outlaws, who have devour'd Us. For, the Common People hardly know the first Principles of Religion; And so Corrupt are their Morals that a reformation of Manners among them *in our* Time is more to be wish'd for than expected.

Thro' want of Churches & Ministers, many Persons go into the *North* Province, there to be Married by Magistrates; Which hath encouraged many of our Magistrates (so venal are they) for to take on them also to solemnize Marriages—And this, without any previous publication of Banns or any Sett Form, but each after his own Fancy, which occasions much Confusion, as they ask no Questions, but couple persons of all Ages, & ev'ry Complexion, to the Ruin, & Grief of many families. Their Example have been followed by the Low Lay Teachers of ev'ry petty Sect, and also copied by *Itinerant* and Stragling preachers of various Denominations, who traverse the Back Country, (sent this Way from *Pennsylvania* & *New England* to poison the Minds of the People).

From these irregular Practices, the sacred Bond of Marriage is so greatly slighted, as to be productive of many Great and innumerable Evils. For many loose Wretches are fond of such Marriages; On Supposition that they are only *Temporary*, or *Durante Placito*: Dissoluble, whenever their Interests or Passions incite them to Separate. Thus they live *Ad Libitum*: quitting each other at Pleasure, Inter-Marrying Year after Year with others; Changing from Hand to Hand as they remove from Place to Place, & swapping away their Wives and Children, as they would Horses or Cattle. Great Scandal arises herefrom to the Back Country, & Loss to the Community; For the Issue of such are too often expos'd deserted, & disowned: Beggars are hereby multiplied—Concubinage established (as it were) *by Law*: The most sacred Obligations are hereby trampled on, and Bastardy, Adultery, & other heinous Vices become so Common, so openly practic'd & avow'd as to lose the Stigma annex'd to their Commission: These are some of the Main Roots from whence the reigning Gangs of Horse Thieves have sprung from.

Through the Non-Establishment of Public Schools, A Great Multitude of Children are now grown up in the Greatest Ignorance, of every thing save Vice—in which they are adepts: Consequently they lead idle and Immoral Lives: For, they having no sort of Education, naturally follow Hunting—Shooting—Racing—Drinking—Gaming—& ev'ry Species of Wickedness Their Lives are only one continual scene of Depravity of Manners, and Reproach to the Country; being more abandoned to Sensuality, and more Rude in Manners, than the poor Savages around Us: They will learn no Trade, or Mechanic Arts whereby to obtain an honest Livlihood, or practice any Means of Industry; or if they *Know*, they will not

Practice them. But range the Country with their Horse & Gun, without Home or Habitation: All Persons, All Places, All Women being alike to them: These are other deep Roots from which the Hords of Mullatoes & Villains we are pester'd with, have shot up: Whereas, had We Churches & Ministers, Schools & Catechists, Children would be early taught the Principles of Religion and Goodness and their Heads and Hands, be employed in Exercises of the Manual and Useful Arts: Tradesmen would increase—Manufactures be followed up—Agriculture be improv'd—The Country wear a New Face, and Peace and Plenty smile around Us.

But in our present unsettled Situation— When the Bands of Society & Government hang Loose and Ungirt about Us When no regular Police is establish'd, but ev'ry one left to Do as seemeth Him Meet, there is not the least Encouragement for any Individual to be Industrious—Emulous in Well Doing—or Enterprising in any Attempt that is Laudable or public Spirited. Cunning, Rapine, Fraud, & Violence, are now the Studies & persuits of the Vulgar: If We save a little Money for to bring down to Town wherewith to purchase Slaves— Should it be known, Our Houses are beset and Robbers plunder Us, even of our Cloath & Beds: If we buy Liquor for to Retail, or for Hospitality, they will break into our dwellings, and consume it. If We purchase Bedding, Linen or Decent Furniture, they have early Notice, and we are certain for to be stripp'd of it. Should We raise Fat Cattle, or Prime Horses for the Market, they are constantly carried off tho' well Guarded—(A small Force is insufficient for their Security). Or if we collect Gangs of Hogs for to kill, and to barrel up for Sale: Or plant Orchards or Gardens—the Rogues, & other Idle, worthless vagrant People, with whom We are overrun, are continually destroying of them, and subsisting on the Stocks and Labours of the Industrious Planter. If we are in any wise injur'd in our Persons, Fame, or Fortune, What Remedy Have We? What Redress can be obtain'd, without travelling Two Hundred Miles to Charlestown? Where (thro' the Chicanery of Lawyers—Slowness of Law Proceedings and Expences thence arising), We are Greater Sufferers than before, and only thereby add Evil to Evil; Nay, We have had, and daily do see, those very Horses & Creatures which have been stollen from Us (and for which we have endeavour'd to bring Villains to Justice) We have seen these Creatures sold before our Faces, for to raise Money to fee Lawyers to plead against us, and to save Rogues from the Halter.

And what defence are the Laws (as they now are dispens'd) to Us, against such as are *Below the Law?* For in many Cases (as in branding and killing of Cattle) Fines only being impos'd, and no Provision made for the Sufferer should the Injurer be a Vagrant, or Insolvent incapable of paying the Fine—What Redress lies in this Case? The confining of the Transgressor for six Months (at the private expense of the Sufferer beside his Charges of Prosecution) in the Common Goal of *Charlestown*: Where it is as agreeable to Him to live an Idle Life, In, as Out of it; Work being the Article he would avoid at any Rate, And We have not a Bridewell, Whipping Post, or pair of Stocks in the Province—And the Workhouse of Charlestown is only so in Name.

As the Back Country is now daily increasing by Imports of People from *Ireland*, and elsewhere (most of whom are very Poor) the Number of the Idle & Worthless must also increase, if our Settlements long remain in their present neglected State. Many of these *New Settlers*, greatly repent their coming here, to languish away Life in a Country that falls so very short of their Expectations; And the sober part of them, would more willingly return than remain here They have indeed, Land, given them. And may, with Industry, raise a bare Subsistence; But they are discourag'd from any bold Pursuits, or exerting their laudable Endeavours to make Improvements, thro' the Uncertainty, that attends Us all, i. e. Whether in the End, they may reap the fruits of their Labour—for such Number of Idle and Vagrant Persons from the Northern Colonies traverse & infest this province, that if a Spot of Ground be planted (Especially with fruit Trees for Cyder &c) the Proprietor cannot be certain of gathering the produce, but may see it carried off before his face without controul. So great is the weakness of the Government in these parts, that our Magistrates are weary of committing Persons to *Charlestown* for Petit Offences—And they have no Authority to inflict Punishments. It is therefore invain for Us to attempt the laying out of Vineyards Sheepwalks, or Bleaching Grounds, as it would only be working for these Indolent, unsettled, roving Wretches.

Property being this Insecure, No Improvements are attempted No New Plans can take Place—Nothing Out of the Common Road can be executed, till Legislation is extended to Us. A Damp is now put on all spirited Endeavours to make Matters run in their proper Channel—And (shameful to say) our Lands (some of the finest in *America*) lye useless & unclear'd, being render'd of small Value from the many licentious Persons intermix'd among Us, whom we cannot drive off without Force or Violence—But these our Lands would be of infinite Value and (in Time) the most desirable in the Province, were proper Regulations to take place, and

Good Manners and Order be introduc'd among Us. Our Soil is not only fruitful, but capable of producing any Grain whatever: Our Vales and Woods are delightful Our Hills Healthful & Pleasant: This single Consideration merits the public Attention:—For, was the Country to be once clear'd of Lawless & Idle People (or were they only for to be put under proper Restraint) were Courts of Justice once establish'd—The Roads repair'd & Improv'd—Bridges built in Proper Places and Travelling render'd safe & Commodious. We should no longer be pester'd with insolent & licentious Persons from the Neighboring Governments: Nor would this Province be the *Sink* (as now it is) of the refuse of other Colonies. Such abandon'd Wretches would no longer seek Shelter or find Protection here: Not set bad Examples to our Rising Progeny We should chase them away as *Beasts of Prey*. And was the Country once clear'd of such Vermin, it would induce Genteel persons to *make the Tour of their Native Country* and not embark annually for *Rhode Island* or *New York* for the Benefit of *Cool Air* & They may breathe equal as salubrious on our Hills, And the Specie which is now carried out of the province by our travelling Gentry (*never to return!*) would circulate among the Poor Back Inhabitants, & quickly find its way down to *Charlestown*.

We may be despised, or slighted for our Poverty, but Poor the Country ever will be, if it long remains in its present disorder'd State; as the few Persons of property among us, must be oblig'd to quit their Farms, instead of engaging of New Adventurers to sit down among Us. Were our Interests (which is the Interest of the Community) but properly attended to, and the Laws duly administer'd among Us, Our Industry & Application to raise Staple Articles for the Foreign Market would render this Province in a few years a most valuable Country, and one of the brightest Jewels in the Crown of *Great Britain*.

By our urging of these Particulars and thus bringing them home to the Attention of the Legislature, We do not presume to reflect on or to censure the Conduct, much less to prescribe or Dictate to those in Authority; But we humbly submit our Selves Dutiful & Loyal Subjects to His Majesty King *George*. True Lovers of our Country—Zealous for its true Interests, the Rights & Liberties of the Subject, & the Stability of our present happy Constitution in Church and State: We only enumerate *Plain* and *Glaring Facts*

And all We crave is—The Enjoyment of these *Native Rights*, which as Freeborn Subjects We are entitled unto, but at present are debarr'd of; And also the proper Establishment of Religion[7] & Dispensation of the Laws on the Upper Part of the Country. All which our Petitions, We humbly beg leave (with the greatest Deference and Submission) to Sum up in the following Articles, humbly Praying that the Legislature would be pleas'd to grant us a such Relief as may be conducive to the Public Welfare—the Honour of the Crown—The Good of the Church, and the peace and Prosperity of all His Majesty's Leige People in this His province.

---

[7] The Indifference of these people as to Religion is very Glaring—The Wateree has been without a Minister, these thirteen Years—tho a Salary fix'd—& no House or Habitation provided. Not a Chapel or House provided at the Congarees, tho a Salary fix'd—So that a Minister has not where to lay his Head at these places—All Saints & St. Luke have been laid out 3 Years—No Minister—St. Davids 4 years. No Minister Georgetown, but one (& that for few months) in 15 Years—Purrysburgh not one these 12 years. Christ Church not these 10 Years—& so of others—St. Johns Church was burnt down 12 Years past, & not yet rebuilt, St. Matthews begun on 5 Years past—the Shell up—St. Marks 12 Years past—Neither Church or Parsonage finished or habitable—& so of many others. (Woodmason)

South Carolina

With all due Respect, We humbly request First) That Circuit or County Courts for the Due and speedy Administration of Justice be established in this, as in the Neighboring Provinces

2nd) That some subordinate Courts (to consist of Justices & Freeholders be erected in each parish for the Trial of Slaves—Small & Mean Causes, & other Local Matters—And that (under the Governor) they may grant Probate of Wills, & Letters of Administration for all Effects under 100 pounds.—Also to pass small Grants of Lands—Renew Warrants &c (paying the Common fees—To prevent poor persons from travelling down to *Charlestown,* on account of these & other such petty Matters.

3d) That these Circuit or County Courts, May decide all Suits exceeding 10 pounds Currency without Appeal And that no *Noli Prosequi's,* or Traverses, be fil'd against Informations made against Transgressors of the Local, or Penal Laws.

4th) That the Clerk of the Circuit or County Court, may issue Writs, or Attachments for any Sum—All above 100 pounds Currency to be made returnable to the Supreme Court in *Charlestown,* and all under that Sum, returnable by the Sheriff of each County to His Particular Court—And that Justices of the peace, or Clerk of the Court, may issue Attachments (as now they do Executions) for Sums under 20 pounds Currency.

5th) That the poor Laws be amended, & some better provision made for the care of the Poor Orphans & their Estates—Also of the Effects of Strangers Travellers & transient persons dying within the province—

6th) That Court Houses, Goals and Bridewells, be built in proper Places, and Coercive Laws fram'd for the punishment of Idleness and Vice, and for the lessening of the Number of Vagrants & Indolent persons, who now prey on the Industrious—And that none such be allow'd to traverse the province without proper *Licences or passes.*

7th) That the Laws respecting public Houses & Taverns be amended—& the prices of Articles vended by them, for to be ascertain'd as to *Quality and Quantity** And that none be permitted for to retail Liquors on the public Roads, but such as can Lodge Travellers, & provide Entertainment for Man and Horse—

8th) That the laws concerning the Stealing and branding of Cattle—Tolling of Horses—Taking up of Strays &c to be amended; That Hunters be put under some Restrictions, & Oblig'd not to leave Carcasses unburied in the Woods; And that some few Regulations be made in Respect to Swine.

9th) That the provincial Laws be Digested into a Regular Code, and be printed as soon as possible.[8]

10th) That the Interior and Upper parts of the province, & all beyond Black River, be laid out into Parishes, or Chapels, Churches, & parsonages be founded among them.

11th) That Gentlemen, who may be Elected as Members of Assembly Commissioners of the Roads, & into other public Offices, be oblig'd to Serve, or Fine.

12th) That Ministers be provided for these *New,* as well as Vacant Old Parishes—And that some Method

---

[8]This has strongly been press'd on the Assembly from home but never taken under Consideration till this Remonstrance awaken'd them—for it was not the Interest of the Lawyers, for the Laws ever to be publish'd—They are still a Blank to ev'ry one—The House Voted One Thousand pounds Sterling for a Compilment of the Laws which was undertaken by John R———e, Esq—but not yet printed—The Sum he demands for the Copies when printed, is beyond the Abilities of any to comply with. (Woodmason)

be devis'd for an immediate Supply of Parishes with Ministers on the Death or Cession of Incumbents—Also for the better Care (than at present) of Vacant Churches and parsonages.

13th) That the Salaries of the Country Clergy be augmented and some provision made for their Widows, thereby, that Learned & Goodly Men may be excited to come over to us, & not profligates.

14th) That all Magistrates, Lay persons, & Itinerant preachers & Teachers, be inhibited from Marrying and the Mode & Authenticity of Marriages be settled; And that Dissenting Teachers be oblig'd to register their Meeting Houses, & to take the State Oaths, agreeable to the Statute (William & Mary) And that none but such settled pastors be allowed to teach or preach among the people.

15th) That some Expedient be devis'd for His Majestys Attorneys general to put Recognizances in Suit & that he may be empower'd for to prosecute all Recognizances given for the Observance of the provincial Laws.

16th) That a proper Table of Fees be fram'd for all Ministers Ecclesiastical and civil, to govern themselves by; And that the Length & enormous Expense of Law Suits be Moderated. This province being harder rode at present by Lawyers, than Spain or Italy by Priests.

17th) That Juries be impanelled from, & all Offences try'd in that County, wherein Crimes, Trespasses & Damages have been committed, or Sustain'd—Agreeable to *Magna Charta.*

18) That no Attorney be put into Commission of the peace And that their Number be limited in the Commons House of Assembly.

19th) That some public schools be founded in the Back Settlements for training up of the Rising generation in the true principles of Things—that so they may become useful, & not pernicious Members of Society.

20th) That proper premiums be annually distributed, for promoting Agriculture, the raising of Articles for Exportation, & establishing Useful Arts, on the plan of the Dublin Society, & that of Arts of Commerce in London.

21st) That the Statute for Limitation of Actions, & that for preventing frivolous & vexatious Suits, be enforc'd & Elucidated; And that the Liberty of the Subject, as to Arrests, & Wrongful Imprisonments be better secur'd—

22nd) That the lines of the several Counties be run out from the Sea to the Cherokee Boundary—Also that the Lines of Each Old & New parish be ascertain'd and known, that we may no longer wander in the Mases of Supposition.

23rd) Lastly We earnestly pray That the Legislature would import a Quantity of Bibles, Common Prayers & Devotional Tracts, to be distributed by the Ministers among the poor, which will be far greater Utility to the province, than erecting the Statute of Mr. Pitt.

The above particulars are with the greatest Deference & Respect submitted to the Wisdom of the Legislature:

> In the Name, By Desire, And on Behalf of the
> Back Inhabitants, And Sign'd in their presence,
> By us their Deputies
>
> BENJAMIN HART
> JOHN SCOTT
> MOSES KIRKLAND
> THOMAS WOODWARD

South Carolina

The war of words did not cease with the Remonstrance. The newspapers being closed to the Regulators they posted in public places whatever they wished to reach the public. Letters also were written to influential persons in town, but no replies were received. One of these was addressed to Henry Laurens "by Insurgents who call themselves Regulators," whose excuse for so doing was their being denied the liberty of the press, they had to send to Virginia to have their pieces printed, especially "The Groans of the Back Settlers." Petitions were disregarded by the House and the governor and Lt. governor were so pestered with them as to be out of all patience. Some who came down with petitions were imprisoned as disturbers of the public peace, which caused a loss in trade. Persons refused to draw petitions lest they should incur the resentment of the House, wherefore the people had to go into N. C. to get their writing in proper shape.[9]

"If we could be but calmly and tenderly heard", said the Insurgents to Col. Laurens, "we would quickly disperse the mists that now seem to cloud the eyes of our lower settlers in respect to us. We could draw the curtain and disclose many scenes of oppression not yet laid open to public view, which if they had been duly attended to, the word Regulator would never have been heard." The word "mists" in the above connection appears to have suggested the following

Advertisement.

Whereas a terrible fogg has arisen within these four years from the Rice plantations which greatly affect the visual nerves of the Proprietors so that they cannot discern the pleasant hills, rising grounds, and beautiful

---

[9]Charles Woodmason's Notes.

prospects of the Back Country, nor can (thro' the weakness of their sight) find the Roads that would lead them to as fine Air and as sweet water as is in America; and as thro' defect of this Organ, many Gentlemen and ladies annually embark for Rhode Island and New York, in order to enjoy these Blessings.

Whereas would they move westwardly they might not only partake of them but from these hills view the turrets of Charlestown. These are to offer a Post Chariott and Sett of Horses, to any ingenious oculist who can touch the eyes of such weak sighted mortals, or to any skilful Naturalist who can dispel this mist, so as to render the Back Country perceptible to the Gentry below."

Another paper was drawn up and posted at the Exchange. It gave offence to the senators but it interested others in behalf of the inland people. It was an effort to effect by satire what reasoning had failed in. A bill for courts had been passed and sent home for the royal assent, yet it was held up, the Regulators claimed, more than 12 months, till the salary of the Attorney General and others were settled to their satisfaction. The paper imitated the advertisements which preceded the sale of negroes:

Advertisement

To be disposed off

On the Congaree, Saludy, Savannah, Wateree & Broad Rivers

A Cargo

of

Fifty Thousand

Prime Slaves

South Carolina

(Remarkably healthy and free from the Small Pox)
Lately imported from Great Britain, Ireland and the Northern Colonies

In the Good Ship
Carolina
George Rex, Master.

In a short passage of Ten Years—The sale will begin on Monday of the 17th day of Aprill next—Credit will be given till Public Good be preferred to Private Interest N. B. The Above slaves are sold for no fault—But they being stript of their property by Thieves and Vagabonds, &c., you (J. R.) say it is very impertinent and invidious for the back inhabitants to call themselves slaves when no people on earth are in so great a state of freedom and that they turn their liberty into Licentiousness. And you ask with what Consistence or Propriety they presume to use the word slavery in the advertisement posted up at the Exchange.

You also say That our Legislature and Executive Powers have done for us all services which we merit, or require, even beyond our deserts—and shewn us every possible mark of Kindness and goodness, but that we take too much upon us. Whatever you in town may fix on as the Criterion of things, we who know and feel where the shoe pinches, can best determine. We think ourselves in a state of servitude and those who are so, what other can they be denominated than slaves?

You say that a great deal hath been done for us, and much more than we merit. If so, then much remains undone to bring us on the same level (which you want not) the same foot with yourselves. Pray are we not all Subjects of the same King? Fellow Protestants? Fellow Christians? Fellow Britons? Of the same blood and origin? Are any of your Descent greater, nobler, ancienter, more reputable than ours? Many of you (tho' you abound in riches) Far ignobler: Have you more virtue, more religion, more goodness than us? Many, far less; Indeed you may be said to have more Learning, Politeness, Wealth, Slaves and Lands, but we speak of intrinsic Worth—You call us a pack of beggars. Pray sir, look back to your own origin. Draw the Curtain up but for one twenty years only, and view persons then and now. It is a strange succession of fortuitous Causes that has lifted up many of your heads.

Not your own wisdom or virtue: quite the reverse—but step back only to the beginning of the Century—What then was Carolina? What Charlestown? What the then settlers (your ancestors)—even such as we now are.

The letter was closed with 24 reasons why the back settlers were in a state of slavery, the last sentence of which was: "If any peasant in Russia, Poland, or Germany are in a worse state of servitude than this, then sir we will join you in that pious wish you made in the House That the Back Country was at bottom of the sea."

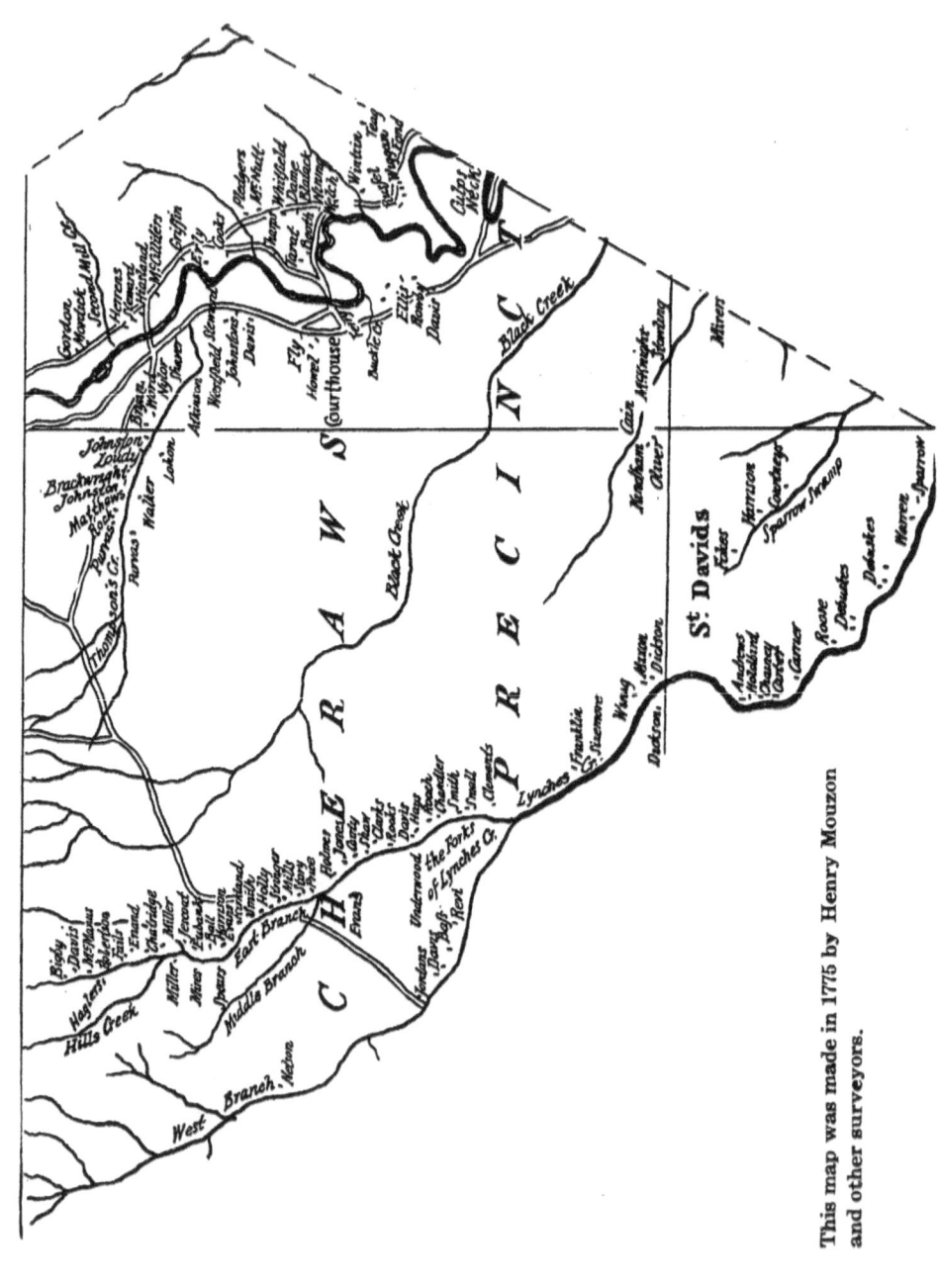

This map was made in 1775 by Henry Mouzon and other surveyors.

CHAPTER XVI

Friction Continued and Brought to a Conclusion

The Remonstrance having made no favorable impression upon the Assembly and Council, another paper was prepared and presented early in 1768 asking for the establishment of County Courts. This was not thought worthy of consideration; but a knowledge of the facts which caused the stand of the petitioners soon brought about a complete change of purpose. On the first of April the Circuit Court Bill was passed and on the 17th St. David's parish was authorized to be laid out and two roads opened, leading to it, one eastwardly and the other up and down the country. In July of this year certain petitions[1] reached the Assembly, among which was one from the Calhoun settlement, enumerating the privations to which they were subjected, at a distance of many miles and asked for what as British subjects they were fairly entitled to—the division into parishes, the right to vote which had been refused them after travelling a great distance to the polling precinct in Prince William's parish, also Commissioners of roads, ministers of the gospel, school teachers and bounty on flour. They protested against the Assembly's insisting upon the tenure of the judges during good behavior which would be deferring the passage of the Act forever, as the King had issued orders to have the judges elected during pleasure. These petitions were favorably reported on two occasions but the Assembly was not prepared for such long strides in the direction of democracy.

This failure to divide the country into parishes Mr. McCrady attributed to the turmoil of the Revolution but Bishop Gregg saw it in a clearer light: "The Provin-

---

[1] McCrady's History of South Carolina 1719-1776, p. 640.

cial government, reflecting the wishes of the mother country, was unwilling, as will be found in the sequel, to establish courts in the interior. These once secured, other privileges it was thought, would be demanded, gradual encroachments be made on the established order of things, the influence of the government in Charles Town lessened, and by degrees the way prepared for the spirit of liberty and the assertion of their rights by the people of South Carolina. It was a short sighted and fatal policy. For the people who were thus aggrieved began to feel at length, that those who ought to have been most deeply alive to their sufferings and who had the power to give redress, were willing to sacrifice them, if need be, to the interests of the Crown."

There were practical difficulties in the way also. The convenience and gainfulness in having all litigants come to Charles Town made the influential legal fraternity averse to a change. There was in North and South Carolina too much evidence that the people at this time were sheep to be sheared on every occasion. As early as 1726 there was a complaint by the Representatives and church officers at Winyaw against "the Rigid Usage of the merchants and lawyers to the infinite prejudice and weakening of this his Majesty's province" and one of the grievances put forth by the most intelligent of the Regulators was "the Exhorbitant Expense of the Law, as it now stands." Gov. Montagu had not been indifferent to the up country troubles. He had recommended the legislature to "fall upon some method that would relieve the distresses of their fellow subjects and if possible prevent such illegal insurrections in the future." Capt. Kirkland had succeeded in capturing and carrying to Wilmington the three most noted robbers who infested the borders of the two Carolinas—two Seymours and Noel Williams who were thought to be connected with the robbery on Waccamaw; and the North Carolinians had driven a gang of robbers into South Carolina and created fresh uneasiness.

According to a letter in the Gazette[2] the Regulators adopted a plan of Regulation which was vigorously put in operation, viz.: to purge the country of all persons who had no visible means of support or were suspected of malpractices and to prevent and resist the service of any writ or warrant from Charles Town." The month was not to pass before some of the evil doers were punished and the writs from the Provost Marshal had been resisted. A lawful deputy named Wood went up with a writ of *Capias ad referendum vs. Moses Kirkland, Thomas Sumter* and about ten others, among whom William Scott[3] was arrested and was being escorted to town with eight of his negroes when five men overtook the officer, treated him roughly and carried him as a prisoner to a house on Broad river. Thence he was led in succession to the houses of Barnaby Pope and Thomas Woodward where he overheard that he and others were to be tried Saturday. While on his journey to the place of trial he escaped from his guard and by riding through the woods and swimming Saluda and Broad Rivers at the risk of his life got back to town after a two weeks' journey and sojourn in the interior. His report was disquieting but the Governor strongly recommended the enforcement of the law. Within the month an effort was made to arrest Thomas Woodward whose life was saved by the barrel of his gun which intercepted the bullet aimed at him by one of the deputies who was immediately shot down.

The year 1769 was to bring increased solicitude about the back country. Guided by the advice of Gov. Mon-

---
[2]S. C. Gazette, Sept. 2, 1768.
[3]Ramsay's account.

tagu the Assembly passed another Act establishing Circuit Courts, so worded that it was ratified in England on the 25th of November 1769. This yielding in reference to the tenure of the judge's office was called by Bancroft "trusting to the honor of the king," but McCrady rightly perceived that the lower representatives yielded that they might afford immediate relief to the upper parts. This was a true reason but not the only one. The Assembly was steering between Scylla and Charybdis and it showed its usual sagacity in granting the least possible in order to have the bill ratified by the king and just the same amount of concession that would pacify the greatly disturbed people above. And this was done with mathematical precision. Nothing was yielded with reference to the division of territory into parishes, building churches, erecting a school system and least of all granting equal representation. It would have been a wild measure to have laid off parishes and built churches all over the country unless there had been some way provided for ministers. It took ten years to find a minister for Camden section and the St. David's parish had no missionary in the whole century. Besides parishes laid off in North Carolina had commissioners of dissenting persuasions who simply neglected their duties with the tacit approval of the community. There was no chance for the establishment of a school system; and if there had been, the wiser heads knew better the state of the finances and that the struggle near at hand demanded sacrifices of another kind. The very mention of the Stamp Act caused the increase of the salaries of the ministers to be dropped after the second reading and there is reason to think the tax on tea had something to do with the abandonment of the College scheme for Charles Town.

South Carolina

One must go back to Locke's Constitution to find the key to these eddies of legislation or failures to keep step with the progress of the times and to do at least gradually something kin to justice to a majority of the inhabitants. "That the government of this province may be made most agreeable to the monarchy under which we live, and of which this province is a part; and that we may avoid erecting a numerous democracy." Coupled with this aversion to democracy must be noticed in Article 91, "the building of churches and the public maintenance of divines, to be employed in the exercise of religion, according to the Church of England; which being the only true and orthodox and the national religion of all the king's dominions, is so also of Carolina." These articles and regulations were with fairness published before the colony was planted. About 30 years passed before the Assembly took steps to establish the Church of England and this first step made it necessary to be forever on guard against "a numerous democracy." A generation passed before representation in the Assembly was denied to the Presbyterians on the Black, and well nigh another before a petition for a parish and county courts on Pee Dee and Lynch's rivers was rejected. In 1768, when St. Matthews parish was laid out and also St. David's, each was allowed one representative, but there was no increase in the members of the Assembly. One representative was taken from St. Mark's and given to St. David's and one from St. James' Goose Creek and given to St. Matthews'. All the devices known to statesmen were resorted to, to keep the system established in equipoise. The refusal to pay expenses of the legislators, the allowing residents in the city to represent distant parishes, the appointment of select men to office, the restriction of the number of Assembly men and the greater representation of the town, all conspired to the same end. It was nothing unusual or particularly selfish except in the tenacity of its purpose. The very heart of politics is selfishness and of the two great parties in all free countries the Charles Town regime ably represented the conservative vs. the progressive, the centripetal vs. the centrifugal.

The relation of the Regulators and of the government at Charles Town were to become more strained. The former were active in suppressing the banditti and chastising individual offenders and in some cases had resisted the constable and his posse. While this conflict between the officers of the law and the Regulators was going on in one part, up on Thompson Creek a gang of villains successfully raided the neighborhood. As an answer to this men assembled on Lynch's Creek and determined to order out of the country the persons who were known or supposed to be bad characters. This clearing out process was about the time that the troubles at Mars Bluff, the most serious in the whole history of the Regulators, began to attract the government's attention. A constable and a posse who had seized the chattels of a Regulator were met, captured and maltreated by Gideon Gibson and his company, after several had been killed or wounded in the skirmish. Information from the magistrate Robert Weaver and an affidavit signed by some of his neighbors at Mars Bluff were sent to the Governor, who laid it before the council and took steps to still the tumult and bring the 'atrocious' offenders to punishment. A proclamation was issued by Gov. Bull requiring and commending all the officers of the province to use their utmost endeavors to prevent and suppress the tumult, and unlawful assemblies, promising all who obeyed the proclamation the protection and support of the law. This was followed immediately by another which took into consideration the repeated injuries done by gangs of robbers and Banditti and preferring to prevent rather than to inflict punishment, ordered the unlawful assemblies to disperse and repair peaceably to their homes, promising at the same time pardon to all persons for former misdemeanors except those with Gideon Gibson who committed violence against a lawful constable in the execution of a legal warrant. The Gazette had at last exhibited as much interest in the people of the back woods as in what was transpiring northward and in Europe. It was reporting the state of the insurrection on the Pee Dee week after week, coloring what was reported against those who were offenders in the eyes of the government. George Gabriel Powell, who lived in Georgetown, Colonel of the Pee Dee regiment, was sent to the spot with Provost Marshal who used to no purpose their eloquence and threats upon the assembled Regulators. What happened can best be told by Col. Powell, whose letter was first brought to light by Bishop Gregg who wrote the fullest account of these times:

"To the Hon. Wm Bull, &c.

"Hon Sir,

"On the 9th instant I set out with Mr. Pinckney for Mars-Bluff, and reached Lynch's Creek—distance 42 miles, that night where we were joined by about 25 of the Posse Comitatus; and the following evening arrived at Mars-bluff, distance 30 miles; at which place we found 15 men of Capt. Weaver's company, and were the day following reinforced by 20 men of Capt. Thomson's company. It appeared to us, by all accounts, that Gibson was guarded by a large body of men, and could in an hour raise 300 more. Mr. Pinckney and myself thought it prudent that I should send orders to the Captains Pledger, Hicks, M'intosh, and to the Lieutenants Clary and Michael, to join us with 20 men of each of their companys, at Mars-Bluff, the 15th inst., under the hopeful expectation of being able to prevail on these gentlemen to assist us readily in taking Gibson, Lance, &c. Mr. Pinckney being informed that Gibson would surrender himself, and desirous of accomplishing his purpose in the most prudent manner, nor willing to risk the lives of those of the King's subjects he had with him by opposing them against such unequal numbers, agreed with me in opinion, that my inviting Gibson to meet me in a certain place in the woods, where he and I might be alone, and there talking the matter calmly over with him, might perhaps have a good effect. I wrote to Mr. Gibson, and met him accordingly, on Sunday, the 14th, where, after an hour and an half's conversation, he solemnly promised to deliver himself up to Mr. Pinckney the following Monday, 8 o'clock in the forenoon; and, indeed, I had not the least doubt but that the man would have fulfilled his promise. However, when the time came about, I found myself egregiously mistaken; for, instead of coming, he wrote me a letter signifying that he had altered his resolution and would not surrender himself. About 10 o'clock, that day, Monday the 15th, Mr. Claudius Pegues came to Mars-bluff and assured me he would render all the service in his power, seemed to know nothing of Gibson's measures, nor the intentions of Captains Pledger, Hicks and M'Intosh, and Lieutenants Clary and Michael, who arrived about noon; drawing up their company in the woods at half a mile's distance from Weaver's house. Mr. Pegues then told us, they did not intend to advance any further. Whereupon, Mr. Pinckney and myself, together with Pegues, went to meet them; where, to our surprise we found, instead of 100, 300 men and upwards. I acquainted the officers with the occasion of my calling upon them and the service expected from them.

"Mr. Pinckney also acquainted them with his errand in these parts, read to them his authority, and your Honor's Proclamation, and demanded their aid accordingly. Which, instead of paying any regard to, they absolutely refused, as Gibson, they said, was one of them (Regulators) and had applied to them for protection.

"They said much about certain grievances which they conceived themselves laboring under, for the want of county courts, and the exhorbitant expense of the Law, as it now stands. It was with the greatest difficulty we could persuade them to march to Weaver's against whom they express much resentment. However, as victuals were provided for them there, and I was in hopes of bringing them into better temper, by taking opportunity of conversing with the leading men singly, I put myself at the head as their Colonel, and marched them to Weaver's house, where both Mr. Pinckney and myself took great pains to point out to them the mistakes they were running into, prompted, as it appears evidently to us they were, by some turbulent, designing persons. Mr. Pegues seemed to be an active man among them, and is a person pitched upon to represent them in the next General Assembly; for which purpose, a subscription is already set on foot to bear his expenses. To enter into a detail of their unprecedented behavior, would be drawing this letter to too great a length, and I must beg leave to refer your Honor to Mr. Pinckney.

"Only I would observe that, notwithstanding I had heard much of the notorious behaviour of the Regulators in general, yet, as several of them are men of good property, I flattered myself they might be open to conviction, and induced to admit that the method they were pursuing was not the proper mode to bring about their wished for purpose; but, to my astonishment, I found all arguments lost upon them, and I am ashamed to tell your Honor, that if there had not been left amongst them some faint regard for their Colonel, the Provost Marshal would have been grossly abused, a scheme having been laid for that purpose.

"These people proposed to Alran, his releasement; and it was only owing to himself, the Provost Marshal could bring him to town.

"Upon the whole, Sir, these disturbances seem to have so dismal a tendency, that I am at a loss to guess where they may terminate, and I think I may now say with safety, that unless some speedy measures are fallen upon to put a stop to them, the consequence will be very shocking. I cannot, with any propriety, continue to be Colonel of a Regiment of Militia, amongst whom I have the mortification to find myself of so little weight as not to have been able to persuade them to do the duty they owe to their king and country. I must therefore beg leave to resign my commission, and I would have enclosed it to your Honor, but that I lost it on my return from Keeowee, in fording Broad River. In consequence of my promise, I enclose to your Honor a letter from the Officers of the Regiment respecting Captain Weaver.

> I am, with great respect,
> Honorable Sir,
> Your most obedient, humble Servant,
> "G. G. Powell.

"Weymouth, 19th August, 1768."

The proclamation issued by the governor and the conferences at Mars Bluff did not bring about a cessation of hostilities on the part of the Regulators. Reports of further punishments inflicted on the offenders continued to be brought down. There was also a disquieting rumor that the Regulators were coming down in September in great numbers to the several County parishes where it appeared they had a right to vote. Instead of the great disorder feared, the Gazette reported that they behaved with decency and propriety. Woodmason, who writes as one who participated in the election, thought that the ill behavior was on the other side:

"In one parish, a gang of negroes, he said, was armed and kept in the bushes to aid and assist their owners, in case of emergency, while they by noise and uproar strove to intimidate the people from voting. In another parish the wrong day was advertised and even put into the Gazette—In another parish great tumult and consternation arose, Bench Warrants against 25 persons were issued for those persons (gentlemen of the back country) to be taken as they came downward to vote at the election. These warrants were given to a most abject and atrocious villain to serve. He had private instructions what to do while the inhabitants were departed from their homes and gone down to vote. He assembled a gang of horse-thieves to aid and assist him to secure honest men, for actually endeavoring to secure these thieves, and bringing them to justice. This gang of rogues under pretext of being armed with authority, entered into the plantations and plundered all the dwellings of these inhabitants who were gone down to the election, seized on their wives, daughters, cattle, horses, meal, provisions, and everything they could carry off.

News of this flew downward which obliged 300 men to return back to secure their families from insult of the rogues, and therefrom the election of a County member in that parish was lost. And the lawyers gained their ends. But this only served to aggravate their sorrows, and caused a general rising in the country, 6 or 700 men armed turned out and marched immediately after the rogues, who hearing of their coming collected their whole strength and drew up in their defence. About 600 on each side—2 or 3 lives only were lost. The inhabitants were resolute, well disciplined and marched in battalia to the camp of the insurgents, who stood ready to receive them. Nothing was wanting but the word of command for to fire. The pieces of each company were leveled and bloody work would have ensued, had not some capital gentlemen thrown themselves in between the two armies and kept them at bay. A parley was brought on, when some of the principal rogues were delivered up to justice. The rest fled. Many of whom since have been taken and executed. And this put an end to the reign of the Banditti who never since have annoyed the people openly, and all are now pretty well subdued and the peace of the country settled."

The Conference at Mars Bluff between the Regulators and the government as represented by the Provost Marshal and Col. Powell appears to have ended in a tacit armistice on the Pee Dee until courts could be established, in which period the Regulators did not abate their determination to deal out justice to the unrestrained part of their neighbors and visitors and to resist all the writs with force served from below.

It was well for the colony that Gov. Bull and not Gov. Tryon was at the head of the government at Charles Town, or the battle of Almanance would have been duplicated in South Carolina. "Above three thousand men well armed, said Woodmason, held themselves in readiness in North Carolina to march into this province to assist the Regulators had there been any troops sent against them." Officers of the Regular forces offered their services to Gov. Bull but the Governor wisely declined them—and effected that by mildness which severity would not have compassed. The laws slept awhile and then awoke with undiminished force. The following letter, written at this juncture before Courts were established in the interior shows that feeling was still running high and in what way some of the Regulators were to ripen into tories:

Congarees March 16, 1769.

Mr. Crouch.

I desire through the Channel of your paper to state a political problem and shall be obliged to any of your ingenious readers for a solution

PROBLEM

The Colonists deny that any power rests with, or is inherent in the British Parliament, for to levy taxes, or impose Duties on them, without or against their consent, and for these reasons

1—That they are not, nor cannot be represented in the British Parliament.

2—That no British Subject whatever, ought to pay taxes, or duties of any nature, to which he has not given consent, by his representatives in Parliament.

The colonists have also exploded the doctrine of *Virtual Representation*, and the above reasoning have been adopted by the two last General Assemblies of the Province

Query 1. As the back inhabitants were debarred from giving their votes for members of the Parishes in which they reside (being deemed extra-parochial) How or in what manner are they, or can they be said to be represented in General Assembly And if not there Represented, with what propriety can they be taxed. or subjected to payment of inland duties imposed on goods which they consume?

Query 2. Is it not paradoxical, That the Frontier and Interior Inhabitants should pay duties and taxes imposed on them by their fellow Provincials, to which they have not given, or had their assent required? And with what Consistency can our Assembly exercise such powers, whence do they derive it? When they deny such authority over themselves to be vested in the British Parliament?

Query 3. How can such procedure be reconciled with the above Reasonings, and declarations of the Americans in their Disputes with Great Britain or the votes of our own Assembly?"

Mr. Gadsden (the Scriblerus of the Libertines) returned a vague answer (Woodmason said) granted certain facts, but did not enter into the merits of the case. A snare was laid for him in which his own artillery was to be turned on him; but it was spread in vain before so alert a bird. He merely "flourished off a little declamation, to desire people to guard against Incendiaries—that this was a subtle Scheme or Bait thrown out to divide them and make them take Umbrage at this Terrible crisis when their Lives, Liberties, Fortunes, and all was at stake ready to be swallowed up by Placemen, Ministers, Pensioners, Commissioners."

"Lo!" was the reply, "such are the men who bounce and make such a noise about Liberty! Freedom! Property! Rights! Privileges! and what not; and at the same time keep half their fellow subjects in a state of slavery; all that they set down under the head of Apprehension from the Ministry—they now realize and execute over others. What they pretend for to fear, they make others feel—What they paint in Idea, the people experience in reality And these very Scribblers, and Assembly Orators, who raise such an outcry against Statesmen and Government, who ride, oppress, distress and keep under the lowest subjection half the inhabitants of the Province. Not caring who may starve so they can but eat—who sink so they swim—who labors and are heavy laden so they can keep their equipages. Their throats bellow one thing but their hands would execute the reverse— These are the sons of Liberty. On Paper and in Print. But we will never believe them such, while they admit not their fellow subjects to be represented, to give away their own Money, to consent to the Laws of government, to partake of civil and religious Rights and to have justice—the Laws—the Gospel and sacred ordinances administered to others as well as to themselves."

CHAPTER XVII

THE STAMP ACT

The colony of South Carolina was nearly 100 years old when the peace of 1763 was signed. Peace and war, health and sickness, prosperity and adversity, and all the vicissitudes of life, hastened maturity in its corporate growth. It emerged victorious from the conflict with the neighboring savages and felt a refreshing security from the vanquished French and Spaniards. It was proven to be a worthy part of so great and so liberal an empire where freedom dwelt under its protecting wings. Henceforth America was to be English. The colony had spent 89,000 pounds in the wars of 1701-16 and 95,000 pounds in the following year. Now they could look back with a feeling of relief at these past struggles in which their very existence was at stake and amid the general rejoicing over the deliverance from inveterate enemies, assume the heavier burden left by the Cherokee war. England had come out of the same struggle glowing with the pride of victory and elated by the prospect of enlarged empire on sea and land and a consequent augmentation of her commerce; but she was sobered by a burdensome debt of 140,000,000 pounds to the bearers of which it seemed just and right for the colonies, for whom so many lives had been sacrificed and so much treasure expended, to share in relieving the burden. Commerce was the vital stream in this serious situation and it was the commerce of the colonies that had contributed to the general growth of England in all her parts. Along with this growth an impression had been gaining ground that it was necessary in the interest of the empire to curb the Assemblies and tighten the reins before it was too late. In South Carolina the Assembly which had encroached upon the prerogative of the governor and the council under the Lords Proprietors in 1719, had been succeeded by men who walked the same road which led eventually to independence of the crown also. Instead of following the Instructions of the King to the first Governor Johnson and of preserving the equilibrium intended, "The people," said Gov. Glen in 1748, "have got the whole administration in their hands; the election of members of the Assembly is by ballot; not civil posts only but all ecclesiastical preferment are in the disposal or election of the people." The people in Gov. Glen's mouth meant the lower house as well as the people they represented, as opposed to the governor and council who stood for the crown. They stood for a will 3000 miles distant while the Assembly on the ground and deeply interested illustrated a law scarcely less invariable than that of gravity, that in a government composed of monarchical or aristocratic elements along with that of the people, the democratic part or their representatives gradually encroach upon the functions of the less popular branches, modifying if not undermining and subverting them. And this when it is gradual means progress. The great mass of the people as they rise in the scale of being should increase in influence also. This encroachment was steady and gradual in most of the colonies upon the perogatives of the crown as represented by the governor and his council. "The Assemblies through their assumed power over what they chose to call a money bill, were able to usurp the chief legislative powers of the council by denying to that body the right to amend proposed financial measures, thus rendering it powerless to assist the governor. With the council eliminated and with the full control of the purse in their hands, the assemblies proceeded to force the governors to sign forbidden legislation and to strip them of their executive functions by designating officers by name in the appropriation bills, the governor to appoint such persons to office as was pleasing to itself, extraordinary and ordinary executive duties were delegated to committees of the lower House, and finally the control of the military was assumed so that governors were reduced to little more than figureheads. Instead of being dependent on the Board of Trade in England, they had become dependent on the assemblies, whose speakers had acquired almost the powers of a prime minister. As he was backed by a majority of the assembly, the governor had to consult him upon nearly all measures and take his advice if he wished things to go ahead smoothly in his administration."[1] Such was the predominance of the Assembly in reference to internal regulations and taxation, before the accession of George III in 1760 and the necessities of the British Empire in 1765. When the Stamp Act discussion began the Assembly was refusing to appropriate money as requested by the Board of Trade for continuing the line between North and South Carolina, unless it should be allowed to come out of the Quit rents. It also declined to provide for Gov. Boone's salary during his last two and a half years. His term, 1761-4, was an unpopular one because of his invasion of the privileges of the House or his efforts to regain the lost power of his office. The royalists in America foreseeing the evil that was brewing had become more and more insistent upon a general strengthening of the hands of the mother country by a stricter enforcement of the Navigation Laws, the suppression of smuggling, raising by taxation a fund to make the crown officials independent of the assemblies

---

[1] Dickerson's American Colonial Government, p. 361.

and the keeping of a standing army in the colonies. It was in a mood of this sort, of incipient alienation from the mother country, due to the new policy of George III, that the Stamp Act was proposed and referred to the colonial assemblies through their respective agents with the alternative of naming some other method of raising the needed revenue; but no colony favored the measure or suggested a substitute. It drew forth from a committee appointed by the assembly in Charles Town the first remonstrance from the colony.[2] They charged their agent Mr. Garth, to make all possible opposition in conjunction with other colonies against the laying of a stamp duty or any other tax on the colonies, basing their advice upon the inherent right of every British subject not to be taxed but by his own consent or that of his representative. Other reasons of a financial nature being given against the said act, the committee was not prepared to believe that the British parliament would endeavor to augment instead of alleviate the many hardships and difficulties peculiar to her sons in this hot climate, to a degree that would reduce them almost to despair by carrying into execution so baneful an expedient as that of laying an internal tax upon the provinces.

The committee who penned the remonstrance was composed of such men as Rawlins Lowndes, Thomas Lynch, Charles Pinckney, Christopher Gadsden and John Rutledge, who in political capacity compared not unfavorably with any cabinet of George III. They were loyal to the mother country and had no desire at the time for a separation. The tax was in itself a trifle which could not have disturbed the equanimity of such men. It was their knowledge of the past that made them fear

---

[2]Gibbes Documentary History 1764-76.

the stamp act as an entering wedge to be driven deeper by successive blows. They knew that the taxing and the sovereign power was one and the same.

The history of the colony up to this time flowed in one channel, as it were, now the stream is to divide for a few years, one connected with the domestic troubles already related, the other with foreign entanglements and then they were to unite again in a few years.

On the 27th of May the Stamp Act became a law to become effective on the first of November following. When tidings reached Virginia "there[3] was a solemn feeling in the legislature, then in session, that something ought to be done in protest, yet that nothing radical or revolutionary should be done. No one seemed willing to take the lead, the older members restrained by their loyal devotion to the mother country and her traditions, the younger members held back by modesty and diffidence. At length a young member not yet thirty years old, a man of plain appearance and manner, tearing a blank leaf from a law book wrote a series of resolutions practically committing Virginia to resistance; and presenting them he supported them with such fiery eloquence, such cogency of argument, such splendor of language, such warmth of patriotic devotion to liberty that he swept the majority along with him. The older conservative leaders were not ready for such action; and when the orator cried out, "Caesar had his Brutus, Charles I his Cromwell, and George III" (a cry of treason! treason! treason! he continued) "may profit by their example. If that be treason make the most of it." One of a series of resolutions passed by a small majority asserted that the general Assembly had the only sole and

---

[3]From a forgotten author.

exclusive right and power to lay taxes on the inhabitants of the colony.

From the Assembly in Massachusetts came the proposition through Otis that all the colonies should send representatives to a Convention in New York early in October. This was one of the early steps leading to the union of the states, proposed by Massachusetts; it was saved from failure by South Carolina by sending delegates to the proposed Convention, after several colonies had refused or neglected to do so. Christopher Gadsden, Thomas Lynch and John Rutledge were chosen to represent the Colony and it was the verdict of a leading historian that South Carolina saved the Union with its consequent blessings by her warm heartedness.[4]

One of these delegates, Thomas Lynch, owned a house in Charles Town and a large plantation on both sides of Santee, and being a parishioner of prince George Winyaw, was a representative of the people north of the Santee.

North and South Carolina behaved very much alike and as well as could have been expected under the circumstances—the common people taking the lead. On the last week day before the Stamp Act was to be in force, "in the middle of Broad Street and Church Street in Charleston near Mr. Dilon's (being the most central and public part of town) appeared suspended on a gallows 20 feet high, an effigy designed to represent a distributor of stamp paper, with the figure of the devil on his right and on his left boot with a head stuck on it distinguished by a blue bonnet, to each of which were affixed labels expressive of the sense of the people, unshaken in their loyalty but tenacious of their liberty. On the gallows, in very conspicuous characters were writ-

---

[4]Bancroft, Vol. V, Chap. XIV, 185.

ten, Liberty and no Stamp Act, and on the back of the principal figures these words: Whoever shall dare attempt to pull down these effigies had better been born with a millstone about his neck and cast into the sea."[5]

The persons appointed to receive and distribute the stamps were all treated harshly. Some of them being of the highest integrity. They were made to affirm on oath that they would not accept the office or they were ordered out of the country. Trade with the mother country was broken off and business was at a stand still. Petitions from London merchants for the repeal of the Stamp Act, Burke's opinion that Parliament had the right to manipulate the Navigation laws in the interests of Great Britain and to do any other thing than take money out of their pockets and Franklin's illuminating testimony caused the Stamp Act to be repealed, Feb. 21st, 1766, to the great relief of the merchants and great joy of the colonies. It was the opinion of Secretary Conway that the kind testimony of those persons whom the outrage of the populace had driven from America, had great weight in repealing the distasteful Act. Twenty bales of Stamp paper imported in 1765 were returned in 1769 in the *Brig Grant*.

The conduct of Parliament in passing and repealing this act is explicable on the supposition that that august body was in a state of ignorance about the political capacity and ardor of the people in America for self-government. The tenderness exhibited by the Chancellor of the Exchequer was not hesitation in regard to the legality of the Act but a feeling in the dark for some way to avoid the rupture of friendly relations subsisting between—the parent and the progeny. The outcome of the

---

[5] S. C. Gazette & McCrady's Vol. II, p. 565. The Stamp Act and the Tea disclosed a superfluity of naughtiness in the colonies.

colonial experiment in America had been often discussed. Forty years earlier than this crisis, "Cato, reasoning from the common course of human affairs, foreshadowed that it would be to the advantage of the colonies to wean themselves just as it was of every other creature, when better food could be found elsewhere. As it was advantageous for the mother to keep them in dependence, it was wise policy to keep the desire of being weaned out of their will, by using them well. For the sum of 16,000 pounds, the British government would not have jeopardized the unity of the empire by acts which tended to unite in opposition rather than isolate the colonies. So it must be imputed to unfamiliarity with the people in the outskirts of the empire, whose inherited love of personal liberty had been deepened by their hardships and struggles in the new world, rather than laid at the door of a proud sense of sovereignty, which engineered parliament into a position from which it was dangerous to advance and humiliating to retreat. "It is certain," said the historian Graham, that till a very late period, these territories in America were generally regarded in England as wild inhospitable deserts infested with Savages and wild beasts."[6]

A resident in Charles Town during these troubles declared that the most sanguine of the inhabitants expected to be compelled in the end to submit. A very small force in the province at that time would have been sufficient to quell the tumults and insurrections of the people and enforce obedience to legal authority. But to the imprudence of ministers, the faction in parliament, and the weakness of civil power in America, the resistance of the colonies may be ascribed."[7]

---

[6] A lady in New York inquired in the present generation whether any bears were near Greenville, the textile centre.
[7] Hewatt, p. 528.

The excitement caused by the Stamp Act and the rejoicing over its repeal extended into the back provinces. The Chief Justice Hasell in North Carolina did not meet in a large circuit a man in favor of the Act and in South Carolina where there were no circuits one has to fall back on the veracious Charles Woodmason who went over to England during the excitement and was sent back as a missionary in 1766 and after travelling over a field extending many miles north of the Santee thus unburdened himself: "I really find not the people the same as formerly. The Stamp Act has introduced so much party rage, faction and debate that the ancient hospitality, generosity and urbanity for which the people were celebrated is destroyed and at an end. Malicious minds greatly injured me in my absence, by insinuating that I corresponded with and was a spy of the ministry and went home, not for orders, but with information and Anecdotes."

Every other country clergyman of the Church of England also felt the shock occasioned by the proposed Stamp Act. The Commons house of Assembly, having been convinced of the general insufficiency of the income of the country clergy had twice read a bill for the augmentation of their salaries when the news of the unhappy Stamp Act arrived; which giving rise to apprehensions, either real or pretended, of ensuing poverty to the province occasioned its being thrown out at its third reading.[8]

In 1767, the parish of All Saints and in 1768, St. Matthews, embracing Orangeburg and Amelia townships, and St. David's parish were laid out. By a northwest line to be run from the northward-most Corner of Williamsburg Township to Lynch's creek and from thence by that Creek to the provincial line; and that the line divid-

---
[8]Rev. Jas. Harrison S. P. G.

ing St. Mark's from Prince Frederick's parish, be carried on in the same course from the great Pee Dee where it now ends to the provincial line, aforesaid, and by which, together with lines aforesaid Lynch's Creek, the new parish shall be bounded, and that the said Parish shall hereafter be called and known by the name of St. David." Of the fourteen commissioners appointed for the building of the church and parsonage, Thomas Port, Robert Weaver, Thomas Crawford and James Thompson lived nearer the lower extremity of the parish. Claudius Pegues, Philip Pledger, George Hicks, Thomas Lide, Charles Bedingfield and Thomas Ellerbe, Benjamin Rogers lived in the upper parts. Alexander McIntosh, Robert Allison and James James were more centrally situated. If there were any aspirations in the church at Sandy Bluff to become the parish church, the presence of Robert Weaver, its nearest commissioner with his unpopularity among the Regulators, would have operated adversely to its wishes. It is probable that the Sandy Bluff church was extinct, as it was one of the grievances of the first juries that there was no chapel of ease in the lower part. At the very time Weaver was in the midst of his troubles as a magistrate these commissioners met at the house of Charles Bedingfield not far from Cheraw and received the declination of James James, Robert Allison and Alexander McIntosh to serve as commissioners. The commissioners or those by whom they were appointed named the parish St. David in honor of the Welsh people, an influential part of the inhabitants, who had not been active or concerned about the parish as they had been about the establishment of Courts, to hold in check the evil disposed part of the population. The Commissioners made a contract for building a church with Thomas Bingham on a lot on the old Cheraws presented by Ely Kershaw,[9] to be finished in a specified time. Its erection was at a slow pace, extending over more than four years after the money was voted. Claudius Pegues, Philip Pledger, William Godfrey, Charles Bedingfield, Thomas Lide, Thomas Ellerbe and Thomas Bingham were the vestrymen, and Alexander Gordon, Benjamin Rogers, the wardens and Durham Hitt the clerk first appointed. They failed to find a minister for the church in the period 1768-1818, owing to the dearth of missionaries who were willing to immure themselves in the American frontier. Overseers of the Poor, however, were appointed, who collected funds, helped the indigent, buried the friendless and put out orphan boys and girls.

On August the 1st 1768 the commissioners met, elected their officers and set up the machinery for the election of one member of the Assembly. That honor fell to Claudius Pegues whose expenses had been previously provided by private subscription. He served the parish for one year and had little to see or do in the short time before the Assembly was dissolved by the governor. He was succeeded in 1769 by George Gabriel Powell, who served as Colonel of the Pee Dee regiment. It was in this capacity that he tried but without loss of popularity to command that regiment when acting as Regulators at Mars Bluff. He was evidently a man of some magnetism as appears from the rank he obtained in the favor of his fellow assemblymen and citizens of the metropolis. The next assemblyman was Charles Augustus Steward, son-in-law of Mr. Powell whose one term was a mere interruption of that of Mr. Powell who was the last under the Royal government. He died in 1779.

A church was now in sight, a beginning of representation was secured and circuit courts were voted all in

---

[9]W. R. Godfrey's Old St. David, p. 4.

1768; but owing to a disagreement between the king who demanded judges whose tenure of office was during pleasure, and the Assembly who preferred an independent judiciary, it was not till the latter part of 1769 that the Courts were ratified. Seven judicial districts were formed, seven sheriffs were appointed in place of the Provost Marshal. The Act was loaded with the proviso that Court Houses and jails must first be built. The choice of sites for churches and Court Houses was not left to the people. At this time George Gabriel Powell represented the parish and it was his official right to have a word in naming the commissioners. As in the naming of the Church commissioners he had selected a majority dwelling at Cheraw so in the building of the jail a majority dwelt there or in the neighborhood. They were George Hicks, Thomas Lide, Jonathan Wise, Benjamin Rogers, Ely Kershaw. Bishop Gregg has the honor of giving a full account of the struggle between the Commissioners at Cheraw and the body of the people in the middle and lower parts over the site of the Court House and his account is unique, the only one known to be in existence of the local rivalries to secure public institutions. His opinion was decidedly against the commissioners" the struggle was between the interests of a few and the convenience of many. "And not less reprehensible, under this same sentence, must be the conduct of their representatives who wrote the commissioners that a bill for removing the Court House to Long Bluff had been framed but had not passed; that, therefore, the Commissioners were at liberty to have the said buildings carried on with all possible dispatch; at any place they thought proper." After learning that the General Assembly thought proper to have the buildings at Long Bluff, the Commissioners halted their work and waited for positive orders.

CHAPTER XVIII

THE LAST DAYS OF THE COLONY OF SOUTH CAROLINA

The good will of the people of South Carolina for the people and government of England survived the indiscreet administration of Gov. Boone and revived in the rejoicings over the repeal of the obnoxious, stamp act, though it was tinged with regret that so generous an action was coupled with the assertion of the right to bind the Americans in all cases whatsoever.

William Bull was acting governor in the time of this excitement. He gave way to Gov. Charles Greville Montagu on the 17th of June 1766, who arrived in the lull after the general rejoicings and was kindly received. In the next year, duties on glass, lead, papers, paint and tea were laid and commissioners were appointed to enforce the Navigation Laws and collect the customs at Boston. These restrictions on the trade did not disturb the South Carolinians as they did the merchants of Boston who had built up an extensive foreign trade, much of it illicit, and accumulated considerable wealth by commerce. It threw men out of employment, paralyzed business and aroused a determined spirit of resistance. All other devices having failed, the last resort was to boycott all English articles of commerce, by not importing manufactures.

The mind of the public in South Carolina turned away from these external happenings long enough to hear and redress grievances at home. Several parishes were laid out and representation granted, 3500 pounds were given to George Veitch for an improved machine for pounding rice, and the Irish potato was being grown in so great plenty that its exportation was begun. William Bull in the absence of Lord Montagu presided 1769, 1770 and a part of 1771, and under his administration were the developments known as the non-importation agreements. After much controversy in the papers, a mass meeting was held in the city and an agreement reached to enter into the said agreement and to appoint a committee of 39 to carry out the public will. There was unanimity in the meeting but not in the town. William Wragg and William Henry Drayton opposed the methods to be used in carrying out the resolutions of the meeting but to no avail. Public opinion, that capricious tyrant, was in the saddle and the integrity of William Wragg and the ability of William Henry Drayton were counted for nought. The former retired to his country seat, the latter went into voluntary exile and after basking awhile in the Royal favor, came back to enter the King's Council.

These non-importing agreements gave rise to much talk about economy, industry, home manufactures, in order to encourage provincial labor and keep as much money as possible at home. Even the summer visitors of cooler climates estimated that in 1769 they carried 3500 guineas out of the province and three families in the next year were said to have carried away no less a sum. "A noble spirit is diffusing itself, said the South Carolina Gazette in June 1769, in entering into protective associations, to discountenance every kind of luxury, to promote and improve the present and establish new manufactures and to form any new beneficial arrangements." In December a bill was before the House, "to encourage the making of flax, linen and thread in the province, by allowing 12s. proclamation money on 100 weight of flax and 30 per cent on the value of linens and thread."

The grievances of these years as presented by the juries related to the want of a hospital for the reception of the poor who were flocking to Charles Town, the place assigned them being insufficient and an improper receptacle among criminals, vagrants, sailors and negroes, the want of schools, a law to hinder unqualified persons from acting as ministers, roads in bad condition, exhorbitant charges attending law suits and lack of legislation to establish more reasonable fees.

Wrangling between the Assembly and the governor and the Council was the order of the day. The Assembly exceeded its legitimate authority by disposing of the public funds without the concurrence of the governor and council. The appropriation of 10,000 pounds to the Wilkes fund was insulting to the king and of course it lined up the governor and council in direct antagonism. The king sent over "Additional Instructions," commanding the governor not to give his assent to any bill passed by the lower house appropriating money for defraying any expense, not immediately connected with the province. The assembly, as a deaf man, heard not, nor cared for the king's approval of the course of the governor. They proceeded on previous lines of conduct and even reasserted their right to control and dispose of the people's money. "The consequence of the disagreement was that all tax bills from August 1770 were rejected by the council and not a public debt was provided for from the commencement of the dispute on the 8th of June 1769, until just before the breaking out of the Revolution in 1774, when certificates were issued by the commons without the consent of either governor or Council."[1]

Gov. Montagu returned to Charles Town in Sept. 1771 and was received in a cordial manner; but he was in no wise to find the Assembly tractable or ready to relinquish the complete control of the taxes. Even the treasurer whose duty had been sharply defined in the addi-

---

[1] McCrady's South Carolina Under the Royal Government 1719-1776, p. 692.

tional Instructions did not escape imprisonment for contempt of the assembly. Of course nothing could be accomplished with such opposition one to the other. The assembly was therefore dissolved and with the vain hope of bettering the situation, Gov. Montagu decided to call the Assembly to meet at Beaufort, on the 8th of October, out from under the baleful influence of the city. But whatever were his motives his hopes failed to be realized, and his blunder added another grievance against the governor who heeded not the better advice of his friends. The remainder of his administration tended to solidify the opposition, just as the successive events around Boston were unifying the sentiment in America in favor of Boston.

Having exhausted his resources in the efforts to govern the assembly, he left the colony on the 8th of March 1773, and turned the steering of the ship of state over to Lt. Gov. Bull, who was soon to need all of his equanimity and self control in the temptestuous times within the Council and in those caused by the persistent stand of the assembly against the representatives of the king. He had scarcely taken up the reins of government, before a new issue was sprung by an arrangement to sell tea in America, not untaxed but cheaper than it could be shipped in. The duty on all the articles enumerated except on tea were repealed; and in order to make the tea palatable, draw backs were allowed on May 10, 1773, so that the East India Company could sell more cheaply in America. This device broke up the non-importation agreement and led straight to the Revolution. Two hundred and fifty chests of tea were sent to Charles Town and reached that port about December the 1st, 1773. As the tea belonged to private owners, there was doubt about how it ought to be handled. After several meetings of the people, it was thought best not to allow the tea to be landed; but it was and stored in a cellar hired for that purpose where it remained until it was sold by the state. Tea had also been sent to Boston at an earlier day and after fruitless counsels, a company of men, dressed as Indians seized the tea and threw it into the ocean. It was an act much lauded in after times, but it appeared indefensible to Benjamin Franklin who advised payment to be made for it. The conduct of the South Carolinians in disposing of the tea on several occasions might be summed up as "much ado about nothing."

The destruction of the tea in Boston harbor was a slap in the face which the patient but resolute John Bull met with the closing of the port and by upholding British authority with a fleet and an army. Gen. Gage soon appeared in the double capacity of governor of the Colony and commander of the army. The town meetings held in consequence of what their conduct had drawn upon themselves, showed alarm and in their extremity asked the other colonies to unite in stopping all trading with Great Britain until the city should be freed from blockade and restored to her rightful place in the trading world. At Charles Town a meeting of the Citizens was called, but the magnitude of the business suggested the necessity of a broader base of action than a town meeting. Accordingly they called a general meeting of the inhabitants of the colony "to consider of the papers, letters, and resolutions transmitted to the Committee, from the northern colonies; and, also, of such steps as are necessary to be pursued, in union with all the inhabitants of all our sister colonies, in this continent, to avert the dangers impending over American liberties in general, by the late hostile acts of parliament against Boston, and other arbitrary measures of the British ministry." On the day appointed—6th of July 1774—one hundred and four delegates answered the summons. They considered the rights of Americans, the grievances to which the people of Boston were subjected, and in what way the grievances could be removed. The non-importation agreement was deferred for the consideration of the General Congress, to which they elected Henry Middleton, John Rutledge, Thomas Lynch, Christopher Gadsden and Edward Rutledge. On the 8th, a committee of 99 men was selected as an executive committee with full powers to act in any emergency that might arise until the next General meeting.

Five full years were frittered away in preparing for the opening of the Courts. In the fall 1773, the people saw the long expected courts open, judges presiding and juries composed of the best men sitting in judgment over the criminals of the time, lynch law having yielded to legal proceedings. By a glance at the appendix of McCrady's second volume, it will be seen that Charles Skinner and Thomas Knox Gordon were the chief justices in the years preceding the revolution and that Edward Savage, John Murray, John Feutrell, Matthews Cosslett, William Henry Drayton (in 1774) and William Gregory, were the Assistant justices. At the death of John Murray, there was no one to fill his place, the salary being small and the assistant judges being in ill odor, William Henry Drayton volunteered to act as assistant until Murray's successor should be appointed. As Councilman he was not in accord with everything done or proposed and it was doubtless here in this company of imported judges appointed over natives of superior qualifications that Mr. Drayton's revulsion began. He was the author of a pamphlet addressed to the deputies assembled in Congress in 1774 under the assumed name of "Freeman" in which he dwelt upon the fact that instead of men of property established in the colony, "we see more strangers from England than men of rank in the colony—councellors, because they are sent to fill offices of 200 or 300 pounds per annum, as their only subsistence in life. Thus strangers not to be supposed very solicitous about the prosperity of the colony, in which they have no interest but their commissions, are, as legislators, to determine upon the *res ardua* of the State; and ignorant of our law, and too often unexpectedly so of the English law, they are, as chancellors to decree in suits relating to the most valuable property of the subject." This of course brought him into trouble in the council; but the more serious behavior as Judge at Camden and at the Cheraws brought him to the unfavorable notice of the king. "In order", said he in a long and able charge to the Grand Jury, "to stimulate your exertions in favor of your civil liberties, which protect your religious rights—allow me to tell you what your civil liberties are, and to charge you, which I do in the most solemn manner, to hold them dearer than your lives; a lesson and charge at all times proper from a judge, but particularly so at this crisis, when America is one in one general and generous commotion touching this truly important point—. English people cannot be taxed, nay, they cannot be bound by any law, unless by their consent, expressed by themselves, or their representatives of their own election. This colony was settled by English subjects; by a people from England herself; a people who brought over with them, who planted this colony and who transmitted to posterity the invaluable rights of Englishmen—rights which no time, no contract, no climate, can diminish . . . Hence by the all the ties which mankind hold dear and sacred; your reverence to your ancestors; your love to your own interests; your tenderness to your posterity; by the lawful obligations of your oath; I charge you to do your duty; to maintain the laws, the rights, the constitution of your country, even at the hazard of your lives and fortunes."

These noble utterances of Judge Drayton were supported by these words: "But", referring to courtly judges who styled themselves servants of the king, "for my part, in my judicial character, I know no master but the law. I am a servant, not to the King, but to the Constitution; and in my estimation, I shall best discharge my duty as a good subject to the king, and a trusty officer under the constitution, when I boldly declare the law to the people, and instruct them in their civil rights."

This stirring address was made in November 1774 about the time of the election of members to the first Provincial Congress which was convened on the 11th of January 1775, mentioned more fully elsewhere. Mr. Drayton as "Freeman" influenced the General Congress by his pamphlet addressed to the deputies and before the year closed he was instructing the grand juries in their rights as citizens and preparing them for the shock that was to come. He had burnt the bridges behind him and, as he no doubt anticipated, was in consequence supplanted in the judgeship and removed from the council. The proceedings for and against him resulted in the loss of standing among the king's friends and a corresponding rise in the esteem of the people.

Rev. Charles Woodmason, often quoted as a prolific writer of this period, who has the commendation of the historian McCrady, left this picture of the imported judges whose bread depended on the favor of the crown:

"An old broken merchant who is totally ignorant of common sense. A quondam doctor of physic, who was originally a Scotch Presbyterian parson. Rejected for F———n turned philosopher, then practitioner in physic, then planter—and is now a judge. His looks rather denote him of the tribe of Issacher. Our fourth is a gentleman formerly governor of the Island of St. Helena. A shrewd, subtle, cunning fox, a professed deist—The greatest mimic in nature. He'd take off Foot himself, a proteus—can transform himself into any shape or color—can be anything—laughs at all things civil and sacred—Is a ridicule himself and ridicules all mankind. These gentlemen make about 500 guineas of their places, amazing that the crown do not send over some friends of its own. The chief justiceship is worth about 1000 pounds sterling per annum. Is now vacant The gentleman is offered to (who is very able lawyer and bright genius) is a friend of the crown, but will not accept the place, while such assistants as the above are on the Bench." William Wragg is supposed to have been the bright genius.

In the mean while during the waning hours of the Royal government which was carried on in its usual forms at Charles Town, the General Committees, seeing the preparations in England of a hostile character and the need of union and energetic action, decided to grant to the inland people what they could not obtain by petitions and demonstrances—representation in the assembly. On the 9th of November (1774) the General Committee set up the machinery for an election of representatives throughout the whole state. By this allotment 30 were for Charles Town, ten for each of the four large upper divisions and six each for the parishes. By this regulation 184 members met at Charles Town on Jan. 11, 1775, for the purpose of receiving an account of the doings in the General Congress, to elect a General Committee and delegates to the next Congress. They now proceeded to form a government as it was needed and not as one should be, after the manner of Locke's experiment:—General Committee, Committee of Inspection, Local Committees in each parish and district aided by Committees of inspection. Here was for a while a government by committees a central one articulated with many local ones scattered over the whole province, and it answered its purpose because the men in charge of the General Committee imparted confidence and energy to the whole system. Its defects led to better plans.

In the latter part of the year the Continental Congress adopted "The Association" consisting of 14 articles, a non-importation, non-consumption and non-exportation agreement, in order to redress in a peaceful way the grievances of the colonies. It was to be operative from the first day of December next. The 8th article encouraged frugality, economy and industry, the promotion of agriculture, arts, and manufactures; it also discouraged horse racing,[2] cock-fighting and other expensive diversions and entertainments. The delegates solemnly bound their constituents to observe these agreements, until relief is found.

On the 20th of April 1775 Charles Pinckney the President of the Provincial Congress of South Carolina, appointed a Secret Committee and nominated William

---

[2]During the talk about economy and home manufacture, a "Pee Dee Economist" rashly commended the spinning wheel and the distaff to the women. Margery Distaff silenced such writers by her reply: "There is not one night in the week, in which the men are not engaged in some club or other at the Tavern, where they injure their fortunes by gaming and impair their health by intemperate use of spirituous liquors. Another sort of gaming prevails to the greatest excess which is what they call horse-racing. By which inconceivably large sums are lost. Nay, further, the men will risk large sums on the chance stroke of a cock's heel; so addicted are they to extravagant dissipations."—S. C. Gazette, Oct. 5, 1769.

Henry Drayton who was asked to name four others, viz. Arthur Middleton, Charles Cotesworth Pinckney, William Gibbes and Edward Weyman. This Committee was appointed "to procure and distribute such articles as the present insecure state of the interior parts of this colony renders necessary, for the better defence and security of these parts, and other necessary purposes." Among the necessary purposes was the seizure at once of the public store of arms and ammunition and to put the town in a position of defence. On the 5th of May, the General Committee thought it wise to appoint a special committee to form such plans as would be best "for the security of the good people of this colony." It was composed of William Henry Drayton, Barnard Elliott, George Gabriel Powell, William Tennent, Arthur Middleton, Charles C. Pinckney, William Gibbes, John Huger, Edward Weyman, Thomas Lynch, Jr. and Thomas Bee. Three days later the battle of Lexington was reported and on that same day, the General Committee summoned Provincial Congress to meet on June 1st. In the mean time the special Committee was active in preparing measures for the consideration of Congress when convened. Henry Laurens was elected president and gave four reasons for the calling together the second Provincial Congress: The civil war in Massachusetts begun by British troops, the necessity of preparations against any immediate attacks of the British, the fear of an insurrection of the slaves and the formidable preparation in England of military and naval forces. A Committee of Ways and Means was appointed to act at once in placing the colony in a posture of defence. An Association to be entered into by all the inhabitants of the colony, designed to draw a line between friends and domestic enemies was stoutly opposed and was finally passed and signed; and it was resolved that "any person having violated or refused to obey the authority of the Provincial Congress shall by the Committee of the District or parish be questioned relative thereto; and upon due conviction of either offences aforesaid, and continuing contumacious, such persons shall by such committee be declared and advertised as enemy of the liberties of America, etc."

It was determined to raise two regiments of infantry and one of horse. A million of money was voted, Commissioners of the Treasury were appointed and a council of Safety elected. On the 1st of March William Henry Drayton was suspended by Gov. Bull from the King's Council. He was now at the same time a member of the General Committee, Chairman of the Special Committee and of the Secret Committee and was to be the most useful member of the Council of Safety along with Henry Laurens, president, Charles Pinckney, Rawlins Lowndes, Thomas Ferguson, Miles Brewton, Arthur Middleton, Thomas Heyward, Jr., Thomas Bee, John Huger, James Parsons, Benjamin Elliott and William Williamson. This famous body met June 16th and proceeded to have the money issued and military officers appointed. The council of Safety was now the executive department of the government and the history enacted was little more than an account of the doings of that virile man, William Henry Drayton, aided by his associates. He was the leading spirit in intercepting the letters from the Earl of Dartmouth and two from Gen. Wright of Georgia, one of which was to Gen. Gage and the other to Admiral Graves. Being not overscrupulous in a serious crisis, he drew out the letters to Gage and Graves and replaced clever forgeries and forwarded them; the information thus gained was promptly sent to officials who could profit by the information in advance. Over 20,000 pounds of powder were secured for use from the public stores and from ships bringing it for Gen. Wright of Georgia and the Indians, and to St. Augustine. In August he and Rev. Mr. Tennent passed back and forth in the upper parts trying to save the back settlers from the snares of Gov. Campbell and the disaffected Colonels Kirkland, Fletchall, Brown and Cunningham. About the middle of September after a remarkable campaign of persuasion, threats, proclamations and with armed militia, a treaty was signed by which a temporary pacification was made. Cunningham only excepted. Kirkland had fled. It was Drayton who persisted in October in having some steps taken to defend the city and when several captains declined to take charge of an armed ship, William Henry Drayton undertook its management. According to his own account Arthur Middleton, C. C. Pinckney, Thomas Ferguson and himself were for progressive and aggressive action, five were conservatives and the remainder independent in their voting. This was the world of politics in miniature. When the convention met on Nov. 1st the moderate men put him in the chair in order to muzzle him in the discussion but after hearing the debates he would leave the chair and as a representative speak for or against, with the weight of his office reinforcing his arguments. It was as the standard bearer of the colony and of its organizations that he went on board the *Defence* and supervised the sinking of four vessels to obstruct the Hog Island channel with the hope of tempting the enemy to act on the offensive; and having succeeded in this, he at the same time warmed up the conservatives who witnessed the interchange of shots and inspired them with a patriotic spirit.

In 1775, old things were passing away. In September the General Assembly ceased as the blowing wind ceases in a calm and the Royal Government already an empty name vanished from sight. In December the General Committee also had performed its duty and died a natural death. The Council of Safety with large and more clearly defined powers was to live and act several months longer and give way to a constitutional form of government. "Nine moons roll by ere infants see the light, ten years the elephant that beast of might, bears in its vasty womb its embryo freight;" but ten times ten years, a century great, brought into being the Palmetto State.

In the closing chapter of McCrady's invaluable volume, 1719-1776, he concluded with a summary showing that the revolutionary movements had been confined to Charles Town and the low country and in a great measure to the town where the Liberty Tree cast its shadow. The Germans at Orangeburg, Saxe Gotha and the Dutch Fork were looking on with stolid indifference, the Scotch-Irish in the upper and western parts were little disposed to follow the churchmen below, the Huguenots in Abbeville and the Londonderry colony were too busy settling in their new homes. "The Irish at Williamsburg", he said, "were ultimately to furnish splendid partisan soldiers for Marion's brigade; but as yet they do not appear to have been more interested than consulted about the proceedings in town. The Welsh in the Pee Dee, with few exceptions, were alike indifferent. The Scotch refugees from Culloden had had enough of rebellion in 1746 to last them for a while.—All these people were at last to be roused, when the tide of war rolled back upon them. But it required British bayonets, not to conquer, but to drive them into rebellion."

The dwellers on the streams should not have been included in the last statements. That they did not wait till the fall of Charles Town and the invasion of the state to enter into rebellion, the evidence is super abounding. George Gabriel Powell, the representative of St. David's parish was a leader in the revolutionary movements in Charles Town. In Georgetown, a chest of tea was thrown into the river and a trader found no market there because he came from Rhode Island the one state which had not adopted the non-importation resolutions. In 1774, a collection was taken up in St. David's parish for the poor in Boston, one paper showing a subscription of 51.15 pounds. Judge Drayton's charge found ears of leading men at Georgetown, Camden and Cheraw ready to receive and back it at the peril of their lives and fortunes. Of this collection for the poor in Boston, Bishop Gregg said in 1868 that it was "the saddest commentary furnished by the history of that period, on the changes that have since taken place." In 1921 the question may be asked, Has a crumb of the bread then cast upon the waters returned to South Carolina, after 53,296 days?

It was decided to raise two regiments of infantry; the men in the neighborhood of Cheraw met and chose Samuel Wise, Captain, John Donaldson, 1st lieutenant, Joseph Pledger 2nd Lieutenant, Tristam Thomas 1st Sergeant and Benjamin Hicks 2nd. The privates were:

Burgess Williams	Dixon Pearce
Thomas Dean	Isham Hodge
Thomas Cochran	Thomas Conner
Isham Gardner	Silvanus Cooper
Edmund Hodge	Samuel DeSarrency
Alexander Jernigan	David McDonald
Bently Pearson	Moses Mace
John Heard	Isaac Lockhart
Benjamin Fathern	John Jones
John Booth	Henry Wyley

South Carolina

William Covington
Jesse Smith
Thomas Pearce
Daniel Young
Daniel Welsh
Peter Hubbard
John Stubs
Lewis Conner
William Norris

These were in the service in September 1775. On the 9th of October (1775) a petition was sent to the Council of Safety by sixty men who lived between Brown and Three Creeks, in St. David's parish, praying for commissions for their captain, Robert Lide, and Lieutenants Thomas Powe and William Watkins. The signers were:

Philip Perry
Solomon Sturdevant
Willis Sturdevant
Owen Whittington
Francis Whittington
Jeremiah Rowell
Joseph Alison
Josiah Cox
Joseph Coleman
Manuel Cox
Andrew DuBose
William Jones
Levi Jones
Cornelius Atwood
Josiah Clement
John Courtney, Jr.
James Courtney
James Chandler
James Curtis
James Marler
John Warren
Nathaniel Pigott
Benjamin Curtis
Aaron Benton
John Pigott, Sr.
Benjamin Sowl
Abraham Alquin
James DuBose
Abraham Brown
Isaac DuBose
William Prescott
Richard Mims
John Evans
John Jones
Thomas Rows
Elisha DuBose
John Pigott, Jr.
John Norwood
John Hardee
William Sims
Thomas Harrison
Robert Courtney, Sr.
Samuel Courtney
Robert Courtney, Jr.

Soon after Mr. Drayton's election to the presidency of the Provincial Congress, Robert Cunningham was brought to town and put in the jail. He had been hunted and finally caught, but it was a costly prize. His brother Patrick Cunningham raised a company and followed in order to release him, but failing to overtake his escort he fell in by chance with some wagons conveying 1000 pounds of powder, which the Council of Safety at the advice of Mr. Drayton, were sending the Cherokee Indians. This powder he seized and carried away. Col. Richard Richardson was appointed to command the expedition to subdue these insurgents.

On the 21st of November, President Drayton was ordered to write to the several colonels that they do forthwith proceed to draft one third of their respective regiments and hold them in readiness; and on the 25th Colonels Powell and Rothmaker were ordered to detach 600 men to rendezvous at Congarees and 150 at Cherokee Ponds. Nearly one month later Major Hicks of Cheraw was halted on his way to join Gen. Richardson's army which had increased to about 5000. He drew from the treasury in February following 9568 pounds for the pay and rations of these men.

From Nov. 30th to Feb. 26, 1776, the following Commissions were issued by the Council of Safety: Daniel Britton, 1st Lieutenant, Richard Reynolds 2nd Lieutenant, John Witherspoon Ensign of Capt. Port's Volunteer Company. These men were from the present Marion County.

Thomas Jenkins, Robert Hargrave, Robert Sutton, Captains, Joseph Jenkins, Samuel Hargrave and Jonathan Jordan, Lieutenants. 300 pounds of powder in the same month were ordered to be sent to St. David's parish by the Georgetown Committee. Abel Kolb, John Dozier, Luke Prior, James Ford, Luke Whitefield, William Davis,

South Carolina

George King, Thomas Hardyman, Thomas Lide, Charles Evans, Jr., Thomas Williamson and Maurice Murphy were commissioned Captains in Col. Powell's regiment.

General Richardson succeeded beyond expectation. When he reached the limit of the roads, he detached Col. Thomson with a sufficient force to scatter the tories in the Indian land, camped at the Cane Brakes 16 miles south-east of Greenville. This he accomplished, capturing a large number of prisoners, but failing to get hold of Patrick Cunningham, who entailed in later years of the war much misery by his inhuman conduct. General Richardson was already a man of acknowledged ability and probity, but the genuineness of the man is seen and felt in a paragraph of a letter written to the President of the Council of Safety on Jan. 2, 1776, at the close of the campaign.

"I am sure (if not interrupted by designing men) that country, which I had it in my power to lay waste, (and which the people expected) will be happy and peace and tranquility take place of ruin and discord. On the rivers, had I burnt, plundered and destroyed, ten thousand women and children must have been left to perish; a thought shocking to humanity." A commentary on later history in 1865.

With this auspicious close of the campaign which cost £460,366.5.5, President Laurens felt that the tories and the Indians in the rear were no longer to be dreaded, while the attention of all was focussed on the coming struggle near the city by the sea.

At this point the historian Ramsay[1] looked back on the colony 1763-1776 as a modern Elysian fields where reigned peace, plenty and contentment with the form of government and ecclesiastical relations. Mr. McCrady

---

[1] He was acquainted mostly with the city and its environs.

who had to look back upon that time through two intervening campaigns conducted by Cornwallis and Sherman was more sober in his description of the past and less enthusiastic over the wisdom of the wise men who led the colony in the path of resistance and rebellion. From an economic standpoint the Revolution in South Carolina was a blunder of the first magnitude for which the people have had to pay dearly for and are yet paying; but in the complex moral, religious and political aspect of the case, a philosopher has to suspend judgment, for there are events yet in the womb of the future which may more than repay for the property swept away by the besom of destruction, once by its mother and once by its elder brothers.

South Carolina might have been born a larger state, if the South Carolina Government had been better informed about and more interested in the people in the back parts and the nature of the country. At first the governors of North Carolina were equally ignorant. One of them wanted the Pee Dee to be the boundary which would have caused a loss to South Carolina of all that fine farming section east of that stream. The same governor failing in this proposition, then wanted the Waccamaw to be the boundary, which would have stripped the state of some sea front and added many more valuable acres west of the stream as far as Lake Waccamaw. In 1744, the governor of North Carolina stated that a section hitherto thought to be in South Carolina was now in North Carolina. The trend of population southward made the North Carolina government alert in trying to push the limits of the colony southward while the general indifference to the back parts of the state was not lessened on the South Carolina side by the type of back settlers who would be unassimilable to the genius of the government. It must be remembered, however, that this subject has not been duly investigated and set in order, the decision of the question being in the hands of the Board of Trade. A letter from a resident west of the Yadkin printed in the Boston Chronicle, Nov. 7-14, 1768 shows how a large section of North Carolina west of the Yadkin felt chagrined at their being cut off from the state at whose metropolis they found a natural outlet for their products:

"General dissatisfaction in Anson, Rowan, Mecklenburg and Dobbs Counties has been much heightened by the course which Mr. Cook has continued the bounding line between the two provinces, the people of these counties have always expected to fall to fourth (the south) province; as Pee Dee runs to its source (being a good natural boundary) would have left each about an equal quantity of back country. Whereas now the line of North Carolina joins Georgia not a great way above Ninety Six. That the loss of this fine tract to this province must be owing to the inattention of its agents at home to this great point who perhaps were even uninstructed, whilst the agent of North Carolina was sedulously laboring to get it included within the line of that province."

The writer goes on lamenting that the gentlemen of this province, who travel much into other countries, have taken little pains to acquire a useful knowledge of their own; as to be almost totally ignorant of its most important interests, and to have so long neglected a proper attention to its internal policy. To that inattention and neglect, he ascribes (as a primary cause) all the late disturbances. "These people," he concludes, "deserve the more of your attention, as they will always be your best barrier against foreign and domestic enemies." That last prediction was verified when (and before) the tide of war rolled back on South Carolina.

CHAPTER XIX
1776-1780

The pacification of the up-country permitted the Council of Saftey to concentrate its attention upon the defences of Charles Town on land and sea. It was planned to fit out an infant navy and to plant batteries on Sullivan's Island, Haddrell's Point and at places in the city. On the first of February the Provincial Congress met and had among the subjects to be considered a recommendation from the Continental Congress, "Resolved that if the Convention of South Carolina shall find it necessary to establish a form of government in that colony, it be recommended to said convention, to call a full and free representation of the people; and, that the said representatives, if they think it necessary, establish such form of government, as, in their judgment, will best produce the happiness of the people and most effectually secure peace and good order in the colony, during the continuance of the present dispute between Great Britain and the Colonies."[1]

The Council of Safety together with William Henry Drayton, G. G. Powell and C. C. Pinckney were appointed to consider the said recommendation. It was developed in the committee and in Congress by their report that there was no intention six months before the Declaration of Independence to separate from the mother coun-

---

[1] President Lincoln interpreted this recommendation to mean that the States stood to Congress as counties do to the state. The Assembly in South Carolina did not so regard it. It did not call a representation of the people; out of its own free and full sovereignty it made a constitution based upon its past experience with the Crown officers and circumscribed it so as to be well guarded against a democratic freshet from the up-country by holding the county officers subject to their appointment and control. Not long after this the same continental congress advised the same body to raise 3000 negro soldiers in South Carolina and Georgia, which advice they did not heed!

try; but the unwise legislation against the people in all the colonies put a damper on the friends of the Royal government and in the Continental Congress the representatives of South Carolina were borne along in the stronger currents of the northern colonies, moving toward an independent government. And thus without any intention to do more than stand for their rights within the British empire, the Provincial Congress was drawn step by step into the conflict between Massachusetts and Great Britain. It was in the first burst of this opposition to extreme measures that Christopher Gadsden's declaration[2] that he favored complete independence as well as the new form of government, produced a sensation among the conservatives kin to that made by Patrick Henry before the House of Burgesses which brought out from the audience the exclamation "Treason! Treason!" But wise counsels prevailed. It was known too well that the Council of Safety was inadequate to the proper government of the people, far and near, for the intelligence of this Congress not to devise better regulations. On the 11th of March, therefore, a Committee was elected to bring in a plan of government which would best promote the happiness of the people, viz.: Charles Cotesworth Pinckney, John Rutledge, Charles Pinckney, Henry Laurens, Christopher Gadsden, Rawlins Lowndes, Arthur Middleton, Henry Middleton, Thomas Bee, Thomas Lynch, Jr., Thomas Heywood, Jr. They proposed in this new form to change the name of Provincial Congress to the General Assembly of South Carolina, the King's Privy Council to the Legislative Council composed of 13 men chosen from the members in the Assembly, and the title Governor, to President and Lieutenant Governor to Vice-

---

[2]Drayton's Memoirs, Chapter XIII.

President. When brought in before Congress there were motions to strike out, to reduce representation in the Assembly and to make the President ineligible for a third term in succession. The progress made was slow and safe with a small majority favoring forward movement. The opposition was gradually silenced, not by arguments but by the high handed treatment of Americans and their property under the approval of Parliament. Much other business was transacted in these days spent in originating a constitution, among which was the resolution that delegates to the Continental Congress were empowered to concert, agree to and execute every measure which Congress shall judge necessary for the welfare of the Colonies. "On Tuesday the 26th day of March 1776, the engrossed copy of the Constitution was read and it was ordered, that the President of the Congress do sign the same and also the Secretary."[3]

The first president chosen was John Rutledge, Vice-president Henry Laurens, chief justice William Henry Drayton. "When this new constitution was promulgated and when the new government and Council and Assembly walked out in procession attended by the guards, cadets, light horse, etc. they were beheld by the people with transport of tears and joy. The people gazed at them with a kind of rapture. The thought that these gentlemen whom they all loved, esteemed and revered, gentlemen of their own choice, whom they could trust and whom they could displace, if any should behave amiss, affected them so that they could not help crying.[4]

All other offices were filled down to sheriff of the country districts, Edward Martin, John Wylley and Wil-

---

[3] March 26, 1776 established a new form of government upon a free & generous plan our rulers being chosen from among ourselves. Diary of Rev. Oliver Hart.

[4] A conversation with two lads from Charles Town held with John Adams in Philadelphia and reported by him.

liam Henry Harrington being chosen sheriff respectively for Georgetown, Camden and the Cheraws. There were 34 articles in this first constitution. One of them dealt with the Privy Council, a sort of fifth wheel, to be of aid as an advisory committee to the governor, to be chosen by the two houses, three each, and be presided over by the vice-president. Profiting by past experience, the Assembly kept in its own power the right to adjourn, prorogue or to dissolve itself. It was Aaron's rod. The court of chancery, the justices of the peace and other judicial officers, the sheriffs, the commissioners of the Treasury, the secretary of the Colony, Register of Mesne Conveyance, Attorney General, Powder Receiver, all field military officers and captains of the navy were all appointed by the general Assembly and the Legislative Council. The governor was further stripped of his power by depriving him of the right to make peace or war independently of the Assembly as Governor Lyttelton did with heavy cost to the colony in 1759. There was little that was new in the instrument. Like the Confederate Constitution in 1861, it was simply the former plan of government with its objectional features removed, with necessary alterations added. It was hammered out and beaten into shape by the needs and demands of the hour.

It was claimed by the opposition that the provincial Congress was not a full and free representation of the people and affirmed by the spokesmen of the majority. The question was soon answered by proof positive, that it was not. Outside of Provincial Congress a majority of the people felt that the new form of government was too close a corporation for a colony fighting for self-government.

An account of what followed makes the Congregationalist minister, Rev. Mr. Tennent, responsible for the agitation for disestablishment—(the White Meetners also having begun to clamor for disestablishment)—and also for the memorial printed on the subject and scattered broadcast throughout the province. But this was not all that happened.[5] "After the establishment of the Provisional government in 1776, much uneasiness was excited among Christians not connected with the establishment by the fact that it was retained with all its wealth and power. They felt the necessity of making vigorous efforts for the establishment of religious as well as of civil liberty. In order that proper and united exertions should be made for this purpose an invitation was given to the clergy and churches of the different denominations but particularly to the Baptist among whom the business originated, to meet at the High Hills church for the purpose of discussing this important subject and forming such resolutions as would after reflection appear best calculated to obtain the object they had in view. In accordance with this invitation, a large number of ministers of all denominations assembled early in the year 1776 at the place of appointment and formed plans for securing an equality in religious privileges which were afterwards carried into operation.[6] The date of the meeting is fixed in the minutes of the Welsh Neck Church as the 24th of April 1776. Thomas Evans and Abel Wilds, relatives if not ancestors, of Judges Evans and Wilds of 19th century, were appointed delegates, to this "continental Association" which had been called "in order to obtain our liberties and freedom from religious tyranny and ecclesiastical oppression." It will

---

[5]McCrady's South Carolina in the Revolution 1776-80, pp. 208-213.
[6]Biography of Richard Furman, p. 54.

be noticed that from the 8th of February till the 26th of March the Provincial Congress were betimes forging into shape the new form of government and that before another month had passed the dissenting ministers and delegates were in session at the High Hills. It is distinctly stated that the plans formed were afterwards carried into operation. A general propagandism on the subject, a pressure to bear upon representatives and a large audience when it came before the Assembly were probably a part of the order agreed upon. Rev. Mr. Tennent being the representative of the largest number of dissenters, a very able man and a member of the Assembly, was rightly the spokesman of the petitioners. As their protagonist, furnished with statistics of all shades of dissenters and of the established church, he made a speech[7] before the Assembly which brought out Messrs. Rawlins Lowndes and Charles Pinckney in defence of the establishment. They proposed that there should be an amendment by striking out "that there never shall be an establishment of any one denomination or sect of Protestants, by way of preference to another." It was lost by a vote of 70 to 60. The names were not reported, but it was Christopher Gadsden who introduced the petition of the dissenters and gave it the weight of his hearty approbation. In the time of candidacy for the presidency of the United States, Charles Cotesworth Pinckney was mentioned as one who had favored this change in the constitution; and when William Henry Drayton died in September 1779, the South Carolina Gazette said of him: Though his active zeal in support of equal impartial religious liberty amongst ourselves, may have procured him opposition and obloquy; yet the candid and impartial freely acknowledged

---

[7]Howe's Presbyterian Church in South Carolina, V. I, p. 370.

that his name deserves to be remembered with gratitude by every hearty friend of the Independence of America, and the civil and religious rights of mankind."

On the 5th of March 1777, the Constitution as amended was not passed at that session but printed and circulated before the vote upon it in 1778. When it was passed March 5, 1778, it was halted by a veto from President Rutledge. He had been one of the framers of the first constitution adopted in March 1776, in which the people was the source of power only on the election days, when they were choosing their deputies. As a lawyer he placed his veto on a technicality but as a statesman he was not yet ready to unroll so far in the direction of democracy. He therefore along with his veto, sent in his resignation. Rawlins Lowndes was made his successor on the 19th of March 1778. A letter[8] dated March 14, 1779, in Charles Town, by a visitor, John Cannon, to Hon. George Bryan of Pennsylvania, refers to this interesting occasion:

"Dear Sir,

I was greatly surprised when I arrived here to find, notwithstanding we were told so confidently by the opposers of our constitution that the people of South Carolina had reformed their constitution and were happy under it, but had reasons to fear it would not pass. It lately passed the Council with great difficulty as they made a bold effort to continue the choosing of their legislative council in the assembly, because then Charleston would have governed the state. However they were obliged to give that up. They then tried two other ways, one by reducing the legislature one half their present number, the other to have the members of the senate

---

[8]Johnson's Traditions. Notice wrong date—1779, one year in advance.

chosen anywhere in the state. In either of these cases, Charleston must have ruled the State. The consequence was that after the council, who were thought to be in the interest of the Rutledge family failed, the Constitution was then presented to the President, R. Lowndes for his confirmation. But at the very time everybody expected to have a constitution in a few hours, he called the Council and Assembly into the Council chamber, and, in a formal speech, gave the constitution a negative. This produced great consternation for a day or two but the assembly resolved to choose another president, and passed the constitution, and it is expected to have the new president's sanction in a day or two. Several propositions were made by the party opposed to the Constitution, to have it set aside, but those for it prevailed, having determined to pass no tax bill, nor do any other business of consequence until the constitution was established.[9] The church—I mean the church clergy—seem by their sermons very much displeased that their establishment is likely to be abolished. One of them told me that a state could not subsist without an established church; that an establishment was the support of the state and the state of an establishment was inseparable. I told him we had in America two happy instances to the contrary, viz.: one where all religions were established and one where none were established; and these two were the most populous and flourishing in the continent. He made no reply. There is, however, great nervousness on the religious head in the South Carolina Constitution."

[9] Mar. 19, 1778, "This day the new constitution of South Carolina was signed by his excellency, Rawlins Lowndes, Governor, &c of the state, by which our privileges and religion are secured to us upon the most liberal and permanent foundation."—Oliver Hart's Diary.

It was President Rutledge and not Rawlins Lowndes, who vetoed the reformed constitution, because he thought it, "neither politic expedient nor justifiable to change this form for another, especially as I think the one proposed will not be better than or so good as what we now enjoy; and whether it would or would not is a speculative point which time only can determine." Upon his consequent resignation, Rawlins Lowndes was made his successor and approved of the constitution on the 19th. To return to 1776. Other important and pressing matters were not neglected during the intermittent discussion of the new Constitution. President Rutledge and his Privy Council were in charge and instead of the divided counsels of the Council of Safety, the benefit of a clear judgment, prompt action and an inspiring presence was felt in every department. Judge Drayton set in motion the judicial machinery and the people as well as the military and naval officers were not slack, each in his own sphere, in their labors in behalf of the common safety. Friends and foes about the first of June, converging by sea and land, were meeting around Charles Town. Gen. Lee with 1400 North Carolinians and 500 Virginians arrived early in June and about the same time Sir Peter Parker and General Clinton arrived off the harbor with more than 50 ships of war and transports carrying about 3000 soldiers who were soon encamped in Long Island in order to attack Col. Moultrie in the rear, while he and his garrison were returning the fire from the ships. Fort Sullivan was the outer defence, hastily thrown up of Palmetto logs in parallel lines 16 feet apart, the interspace being filled with sand. It was manned with 413 men under Col. Moultrie aided by 22 artillery men. On the 28th of June the attack on the fort began from the ships, the *Active*,

Bristol, Experiment and *Solesbay* with a larger number drawn up at a greater distance in the rear, having an armament of 262 guns. Col. Moultrie with scant ammunition replied to the broadsides leisurely but very effectively while Gen. Clinton was kept in check by the gallant Col. Thomson and Col. Marion. The other soldiers and the citizens in the town were looking on with tense interest and anxiety. Gen. Charles Lee, the Commander-in-chief, was in the way with his greater knowledge of war and its operations. He was evidently expecting nothing less than a retreat or surrender of the garrison and his great concern was to prevent a catastrophe by evacuating or of having a safe means of retreat. He failed in not taking into his account the spirit of the garrison, the accuracy of the gunners and the quiet confidence of Col. Moultrie in their ability to hold the fort and in the foresight that Providence would be the ally of the besieged.

When the smoke of battle was cleared away the fort was found to have lost 37 in killed and wounded, the vessels about 200. Little damage was done the fort, but several of the largest ships in the squadron were badly battered though not sunk. From the close of the battle about 9 o'clock at night of June 28th till August 2nd, the British vessels were preparing to leave the place which they had so confidently expected to capture. Their departure meant a three years surcease from the presence of a British enemy and the baleful effects of war within the borders of the colony. This day's work by Carolinians as Mr. McCrady so well sums up, was one of the decisive events of the war; and coming to pass within one week of the Declaration of Independence it served to inspirit all the colonies with hopes of final success.

Lord William Campbell, the exiled governor was in the number of the wounded and among those humiliated by defeat were Lord Cornwallis and Gen. Clinton who were to return with better success later. One woe was past and another connected with it came quickly—the belated attack of the Indians upon the rear of several Southern states, in concert with Sir Peter Parker's attack on Charles Town. Fortunately the leaders of the tories and of the Indians, were either lacking in sagacity or in ability to control and direct and coordinate their movements so that their efforts might be successful. In this instance, the British had been decisively beaten several days before the Indians began their inroads, influenced by Stuart, the superintendent of Indian Affairs and his deputy Cameron. The tidings that a British fleet was off Charles Town, was the signal for the descent upon the frontiers, in order to divide and distract the forces and the people of the colony. Major Andrew Williamson, who seemed to be a tower of defence in that section, gathered slowly a band of 40 and by the eighth, 222 men and encamped near De-Witt's corner.[10] In another week his forces had more than doubled. At this juncture, the tide turned in favor of the Carolinians. Nearly 100 Indians and over 100 white men attacked an old fort near Rabun's Creek into which the inhabitants had fled. By the aid of 150 men under Major Downes, who happened to be spending the night there on his journey to join Major Williamson, this body of Indians and white profligates were completely defeated; and to make it more effective the victory over them and that over the fleet circulated together and made those inclined toward England change sides or become quiescent. Fourteen days elapsed before

---

[10] Drayton's Memoirs, Vol. II, Chapter XVII.

President Rutledge could reinforce Major Williamson, with rangers, ammunition and wagons. The expedition against the Indians began on the 25th of July and on the 29th, 1151 men were under arms. From his camp at 23 mile creek, spies were sent out and the intelligence brought back led him into an ambuscade which cost him the loss of several men among whom was the lamented ensign Patrick Calhoun and Francis Salvador. Failing in the main object Williamson retreated to his camp where he began to march upon the enemy's country. A skirmish at the ford of Tugaloo River halted his line of march and on the 12th a more severe skirmish ensued with the usual issue. The course of Major Williamson was marked by burnt towns and 2000 acres of growing corn destroyed. After unavoidable delays, Major Williamson crossed over toward the middle settlement and walked into an ambush laid by 1200 Indians, at a cost of 14 lives and 34 wounded men. Thence he continued burning villages and fields, in which business were also forces from North Carolina, until all of any importance had been laid waste and thence returned to Fort Rutledge which he had built and from which the over hill expedition set out; 22 had been killed, 11 mortally wounded and 63 wounded.

The battle of Fort Moultrie was fought on June 28th and the Declaration of Independence made on the 4th of July. Six militia regiments were made continental. The most successful of all the Indian campaigns was completed and valuable additions made to the territory of the state. With the exception of Nathanael Greene, the generals sent southward by Gen. Washington or by Congress, were not so fit and competent as natives on the spot. The expedition under Gen. Lee could not have been seriously considered by a southerner in the months of August and September and both South Carolina and

Georgia were to suffer generally and egregiously at the hands of incompetent general officers. Within this year the outlook became dark in Washington's campaigns, New York having fallen, but the battle of Trenton on Christmas Eve was a light at evening time.

On the 20th of May 1777, a treaty was made with the Indians at DeWitt's corner, with the cession of territory now included in Greenville, Anderson and Oconee Counties. LaFayette on the 14th of June arrived on the coast of South Carolina and landed on North Island where he was hospitably entertained by Major Huger and conveyed after a day's rest to Charles Town. In September, George Washington was defeated at Brandywine and Philadelphia fell to Lord Cornwallis. At Saratoga, Burgoyne surrendered 5791 men on the 17th of October. On the 15th of November, the Articles of Confederation were adopted by Congress. In the beginning of President Lowndes presidency, March 20, 1778, the General Assembly of South Carolina resolved itself into a committee of the whole to consider whether these articles of confederation should be adopted. William Henry Drayton, a member of congress, was one of the chief speakers before this assembly and his words as an architect of the new government show that he was a clear eyed statesman, anticipating the evils which caused nullification and secession, as may be observed in part of his discourse:

"I cannot but be displeased with the prospect that the most important transactions in Congress may be done contrary to the united opposition of Virginia and the two Carolinas and Georgia, states possessing more than one half of the whole confederacy; and forming, I may say the body of Southern interests. If things of such transcendant weight may be done notwithstanding such opposition; the honor, the interest and sovereignty of the south are in effect delivered up to the north. Do we intend to make such a surrender? I hope not, there is no occasion for it. Nor would I have it understood that I fear the north would abuse the confidence of the south. But common prudence, sir, admonishes me that confidence should not wantonly be placed anywhere. It is but the other day that we thought our liberties secure in the care of Britain. I am assisting to form a confederacy of the United States; it is my duty to speak plainly. I engage in the great work with a determined purpose, to endeavor as far as my slender abilities enable me, to render it equal, just and binding.

I therefore hope I shall not be thought unreasonable because I object to the 9 voices in Congress; and wish the 11 may be substituted to enable that body to transact their most important business. The States General of Holland must be unanimous; their government is accounted a wise one; and although it causes their proceedings to be slow, yet it secures the freedom and interest of its respective states. (This is Calhoun's Disquisition on government, *multum in parvo*.)

Is not this our great aim? I cannot admit of any confederacy, that gives Congress any power that can, with propriety, be exercised by the several states, or any power, but what is clearly defined beyond a doubt. Nor can I think of entering into any agreements which are not as equal as may be between the states,—engagements of compelling nature, and the whole to be understood according to the letter."[11] (Here was State rights and justice.)

President Lowndes' administration was brief and yet not free from petty annoyances or grave anxiety about the present and immediate future of the commonwealth.

---

[11] He was needed as Rawlin Lowndes' ally in 1788.

His coming into office under the revised social compact which was objectionable to many of the good people of the town and the unpopularity of the alliance with France, the ancient enemy of the colony, the rapid depreciation of the currency, and the general drift from bad to worse, formed a heritage that did not lighten his gubernatorial labors. The militia decreased in number and in the matter of discipline it had not passed in efficiency the proverbial broken stick or foot out of joint, as the first expedition of the year glaringly disclosed.

What part the Pee Dee soldiers took in the expeditions against the Indians in the north-west and against the tories and British in Georgia and Florida cannot be told; but such soldiers were present under Gen. Alexander McIntosh after the fall of Savannah and the battle of Brier Creek. Gen. Lincoln had assumed command, and with a view to break the communication of the British with the tories and Indians rashly went up toward Augusta, leaving Gen. Moultrie and Col. Alexander McIntosh in command of the 1000 left between Provost and Charles Town. By the advance of Provost, with a superior force, Gen. Moultrie and Col. McIntosh were pushed back toward Charles Town. Before the union of their forces at Tulifinny, Col. McIntosh wrote a letter to Gen. Moultrie which shows the situation at the beginning of their retreat:

Coosahatchie,
April 30th, 1779.

Dear General:

Last night two deserters from the enemy came to Bee's Creek; they were the light infantry. They say Col. Maitland commanded yesterday, that he had the light infantry and the 2nd battalion of the 71st regiment, amounting to eight or nine hundred men; that they were to send for three field pieces and three six-pounders with a reinforcement to make them up 1500 men; that they did not know the Colonel's plan, but that they heard it said that he intended to proceed to Charlestown and that he had thirty or forty Indians with him. I have given Gen. Bull and Col. Skirving information of these particulars; the men are so lame that I cannot be up before tomorrow night. We are all safe. I am &c

ALEXANDER MCINTOSH.

Brig. Gen. Moultrie

Prevost met no serious check in his advance towards Charles Town. He crossed the Ashley river without opposition and began the siege of the town after reinforcements had been received under Gov. Rutledge and others and would have been rewarded with its voluntary surrender, had he been willing to accept it on the terms of strict neutrality during the remainder of the war.

In the correspondence between Gen. Moultrie and Gen. Prevost about the terms of surrender, Gen. Moultrie found some difficulty in securing suitable persons who knew its import, to carry the message. Col. Alexander McIntosh was requested to accompany Col. Roger Smith, both of whom preferred that the General would find other messengers; but he pressed them into a compliance. This appears to have been the last service of Col. Alexander McIntosh, who is liable to confusion with Gen. Lachlan McIntosh of Georgia who was prominent at this time. It is probable that his health caused his retirement; for his death occurred in the following year, on the 18th of November. In Mr. Pugh's Diary is this entry: "Sunday, 19th November, preached General McIntosh's funeral, at Welsh Neck."

Great was the surprise in Charles Town on the morning after Cols. Rogers and McIntosh performed their unwilling service to find that Prevost had decamped and retired to John's Island to avoid complications with Gen. Lincoln's advancing army. On the 6th of June the battle of Stono was fought. It was well designed, but on account of the failure in carrying out the concerted plan it was illy executed. The enemy afterwards retired, at his leisure, to Savannah, leaving a garrison at Beaufort, and carrying away a rich spoil. July and August passed without further campaigning and fighting but October witnessed a great disaster—the siege and assault on the 9th upon Savannah by Count D'Estaing and Gen. Lincoln and their bloody repulse.

One officer from the upper part of Pee Dee, Maj. Samuel Wise, was killed, and how many of the militia from the eastern parts of the state were killed and wounded failed to be recorded. The loss of Carolinians in this battle ranged according to various estimates from 240 to over 450. Stevens of Georgia allots 469 as the casualties of all the Americans and places it next to Bunker Hill in the relative number of killed and wounded. "We lost many a youth" said Mr. Pugh in his journal, for whom a funeral sermon was preached in November.

Thereupon followed another pause during November, December and January. The new year, 1780, had still greater disasters in store for the brave but unfortunate state. The offers of peace to the authorities at Charles Town gave place to a powerful fleet to cooperate with a valiant army which was not far from the gates of the town. By the first of April, Charles Town Neck was occupied by Sir Henry Clinton who commanded the land forces, assisted by Admiral Arbuthnot and his blockading squadron. Lincoln was nominally in charge of the American forces and Gov. Rutledge was clothed by the expiring assembly with power to do everything necessary for the public good, except taking away the life of a citizen without a legal trial.

Extreme necessity drove the assembly to the dictatorship like that of ancient Rome but limited it by the ancient hard earned right of everyman, when life was in jeopardy, of a legal trial, separate and not in a body, established by Athenian democracy.

On the 10th of April, the summons to surrender was courteously declined. On the 13th Gov. Rutledge soon to be the embodiment of the government of South Carolina, was sent out so that in case of surrender, there might not be a total paralysis as there would be in case of his capture. On the same night, Tarleton surprised Gen. Huger at Monck's Corner and captured valuable and much needed supplies. Gov. Rutledge was actively engaged in collecting forces at Lenud's ferry in the vain hope of raising the seige, a hope that was soon cast down by the fall of Fort Moultrie and the dispersion of the cavalry at Lenud's ferry by Tarleton.

On the 21st, Gen. Lincoln proposed to surrender on terms which Sir Henry Clinton declined to accept, being fully aware that capitulation on his own terms would be inevitable in the near future. The 12th of May, 1780, was the fateful day in which the bitter cup was passed to the lips of the proud city and of the state which was as prostrate as the city before the feet of the invaders. Generals Mountrie, Richardson, Williamson, William Henry Drayton, Christopher Gadsden and many others prominent in the councils of the state were now dead or imprisoned or on parole as prisoners of war. Out of the dense gloom which settled upon the cause of liberty there came forth new leaders and men who made the prostrate state immortal by their sufferings and the brilliancy of their deeds. And it will appear at the close of the conflict that no state was more impoverished in resources or more magnanimous in their treatment of their misguided fellow-citizens, the tories.

CHAPTER XX
1780

By the capitulation of Charles Town an effective blockade was established, a garrison of 5683 men, British count, were lost to the American cause, as active officers and men and a not less serious loss, most of the leading men in Charles Town were rendered valueless either in the field or in the councils of state. Charles Town had been politically the state and when it fell the machinery of government was involved in the same ruin. Every German settlement was either neutral or not unfriendly to the king's forces and every parish was as thoroughly paralyzed as the metropolis and at the mercy of the invader. Indeed it was said that the majority of the people preferred submission to resistance but it is more probable that "the Carolinians felt that they were a swarm of rice birds with a hand full of British hawks among them and rather than be plucked to the pin feathers or picked to the bone, they and their little ones, they were fain to flatter these furious falcons and ofttimes to chirp and sing when they were much in the humor to hate and curse."[1]

But all was not lost. An exasperated regulator had said in his haste that Charles Town had not produced one unselfish statesman who thought and planned for the benefit of the whole people; but that reproach, if it had any foundation, was to be abundantly wiped away by many. Gov. John Rutledge, the peripatetic governor, was at Kensington, near Georgetown, at the home of Mrs. Kinloch and Mrs. Huger, just before the fall of Charles Town and thence he went to Camden where he wrote to the South Carolina delegates in Congress an

---
[1] Weem's Life of Marion, p. 82.

account of the affairs twelve days after the surrender. His correspondence, found in the South Carolina Historical and Genealogical Magazines, furnishes information about these critical times second in reliability and trustworthiness to no literature of the time: "On Saturday last", said Gov. Rutledge, "on the 24th of May, 1780, the enemy took post with a considerable force at Dupree's ferry on Santee river which they began to cross, that day on their march to Georgetown, which was not defensible. Gen. Caswell who lay a little below Dupree's ferry with the North Carolina Brigades and the Virginia Continentals, under Col. Buford, had luckily retreated this way before the enemy got to that ferry and thereby prevented their cutting off his retreat, which was probably their first scheme. These troops now under the command of Gen. Huger are about 15 miles below this place (Camden) and will be here today. Huger's motions will be directed by the corresponding force of the enemy. The enemy according to advices received last night, were the evening before at Black Mingo—but whether with intention to take a circuit by way of Hanging Rock road, in order to get into the rear of our troops, or proceed for North Carolina, is as yet uncertain. The next movement they make will demonstrate which of these points is their object . . . We have no certain account of what the above mentioned force is, or, by whom commanded, but it is said, and I believe it, to be considerable and under Lord Cornwallis. It is evident that the conquest of North and South Carolina is the enemy's plan. The time for which they endeavor to enlist men is until these countries are conquered; and a juncture with the disaffected by the body above mentioned, who have with them a large Highland regiment . . . I cannot account for the backwardness of the troops ordered hither by Congress and Virginia and for our want of intelligence respecting them. We know not where any of them are. I still hope, however, that a combination of force and better fortune than our last, will soon oblige the enemy to tread back their steps, and though, I have no hope of regaining Charles Town, except by treaty, that the country will be preserved and North and South Carolina and even Georgia retained in the union . . . Whether the enemy will make any attempt on our back settlement, except by Tories and Indians, is still uncertain. If they send us up a regular force, I am convinced they will be joined by numbers and many men will fall a sacrifice to the resentment of our domestic or internal enemies. But if regular troops are not sent up, I think our people will manage the disaffected and keep them from doing any considerable mischief; however, I expect no other service from the militia. They are so apprehensive of their families being killed and their property destroyed (by the Tories and Indians who daily threaten hostilities) while they are absent from their districts, that I believe it will be impracticable to keep any number worth mentioning on duty, with the army or at any distance from their own homes. If I can get them to embody in their own districts and keep the country quiet, it is really as much as I expect they will do at present and until troops arrive from the northward—but even this depends on the enemy's not sending up regular forces to take posts on the back parts of the state, for, if they do, the disaffected will either abscond, if they can, or (which is more probable) be taken prisoners without arms, in which case they will expect to be treated as those who have been taken under similar circumstances, viz. put on parole— a piece of policy which the enemy have adopted, with respect to our militia, for obvious reasons. This is a melancholy, but a faithful account of our affairs, at this time. However, we must not despair; I will still hope for great and speedy succor from our brethren, to animate and support our people and for a reverse of our late bad fortune. But immediate and the greatest exertions of the northern states and of Congress are (be assured) indispensable, to prevent the desolation and ruin of this state and Georgia and the enemy's obtaining (what they flatter themselves with shortly securing) the three southernmost states[2]—too valuable a prize ever to be given up to them. I request the favor of hearing, fully and of knowing what aid we may expect from you and when we may be assured of it."

In a postscript two days later there was a rumor "that Great Britain will offer America the independence of all the states except North and South Carolina and Georgia and perhaps even of North Carolina—and that such a proposition will be accepted—I think it impossible that Congress will leave us in the lurch—but, pray inform me candidly and fully what may be expected on that head. If they never will give up the independence of any one state (which I trust they will not) it would be best to declare it immediately in the most pointed terms to satisfy the wavering and defeat the schemes of our enemies. Such a declaration[3] generally made known with a good number of troops would revive the spirits of many of our credulous and dejected, the well meaning people."

While Gov. Rutledge was so clearly analyzing the factors in the situation of affairs so that Congress

---

[2] If Gov. Rutledge could have foreseen the ravaging of the state in 1780-82 and in 1865, would he have been willing for the 3 states to have become a Southern Canada?

[3] Congress accordingly made the declaration June 25th.

through the congressmen from the state might understand and act promptly, the enemy was not slow in his movements and in disclosing his policy of treating with the whig element in the state. A proclamation[4] issued by Sir Henry Clinton on the 22nd of May, showed that there were some wicked and desperate men who were still supporting the flame of rebellion and attempting by enormous fines, grievous imprisonments and sanguinary punishments, to compel his Majesty's faithful and unwilling subjects to take up arms against his authority and government. Such persons were of course to feel in person and in estate the heavy hand of the invader; but the faithful and peaceable subjects were to meet with effectual countenance, protection and support and as soon as the situation would permit, be restored to the full possession of that liberty in their persons and property which they had before experienced. Another proclamation on June 1st reiterated the offer of mercy and forgiveness to his Majesty's deluded subjects and promised reinstatement into the rights and immunities heretofore enjoyed, if they immediately returned to their allegiance and due obedience to those laws and that government which they formerly boasted was their birthright and noblest inheritance. Exemption from taxation except by their own legislature, which had been the bone of contention and a proximate cause of the war, was also promised. This was too good to be true for on the 3rd of June another proclamation was forthcoming declaring that all the inhabitants of the province who are now prisoners upon parole and were not in military line, that from and after the 20th day of June instant, they are freed and exempted from all such paroles and may hold themselves as restored to all the

---

[4]The proclamations referred to are found in Ramsay's Revolution in South Carolina, beginning at Note X.

rights and duties belonging to citizens and inhabitants. And all persons under the description before mentioned who shall afterwards neglect to return to their allegiance and to his Majesty's government, will be considered as enemies and rebels to the same and be treated accordingly."

In Lord Cornwallis' Papers, Vol. III, is found a response to his efforts to bring about a cessation of the rebellion: "We inhabitants in and about Georgetown Winyah, beg leave to represent to Major Wemyss that as the original cause of the disputes between Great Britain and her Colonies, was our being taxed without being represented—And as by a proclamation of the 1st of June last issued by his excellency Sir Henry Clinton, Knight of the Bath, General and Commander in Chief of his Majesty's forces in America and Mariot Arbuthnot, Esquire, Vice Admiral of the Blue and commander-in-chief of his majesty's ships. We are assured that we shall not be taxed but by our representatives in General Assembly, we are therefore desirous of becoming British subjects in which capacity we promise to behave ourselves with all becoming fidelity and loyalty." Signed Thomas Mitchell, Francis Marshall, Peter Lesesne and 30 others.

This last proclamation was truly called a Pandora's box of evils. It was a bomb in the camp of the rebel sympathizers and proved in the end a boomerang to its author and to his royal master. The uncertainty in which Gov. Rutledge was in was of short duration. Col. Brown was sent to Augusta with a detachment, Col. Balfour to Ninety Six, Major Wemyss to Georgetown, Maj. McArthur to Cheraw and Lord Cornwallis to Camden, a point from which he could advance into North Carolina, retreat to the seaboard or succor any endangered garrison. The British commanders thought, planned and executed with marked celerity and efficiency, but they were to be out thought and out planned in the end. Gov. Rutledge, after narrowly escaping capture by Tarleton on the night of May 27th, made his way into North Carolina, preceded or followed by such ministers as Thomas Reese of Salem, Black River, Richard Furman of Stateburg, Oliver Hart of Charles Town, Timothy Dargan of Jeffries Creek and Edmund Botsford of the Welsh Neck, an Englishman who had been acting as chaplain to Col. Williamson's regiment. There were also in the same exile Gen. Isaac Huger, Col. Sumter, Col. Marion, Major Peter Horry and others. With the governor driven out of the state, the soldiers gone into North Carolina and so many parts of the state securely garrisoned, the little commonwealth was so prostrate that Sir Henry Clinton wrote on June 3rd: "There are few men in South Carolina who are not either our prisoners or in arms with us." While the people were in this quiet submissive mood, Col. Tarleton overtook Buford and his detachment on their retreat and butchered five out of six of those who surrendered. This was on the 29th of May at Waxhaws in the neighborhood of people who had not been assimilated to the parish system. A revulsion of feeling set in which may be reckoned in a small way as the beginning of the end of British rule in the state. Tarleton's triumph showed what sort of clemency rebels might expect in the day of Clinton and Cornwallis. Tarleton returned to receive an ovation at Camden and pass a month of sickness contracted in his exposure to the climate. A widespread terror preceded the advancing barbarians. On May 22nd, Rev. Evan Pugh was the mouthpiece of the whigs on the Pee Dee: "At home—much terrified about the English Light Horse coming;" and on the next day "our men came up"—dates that show that Wemyss was at his dread work a week before Tarleton's massacre at Waxhaws. They indeed proved to be a source of terror. Wemyss went up the Pee Dee burning houses, pillaging right and left, living upon the people and even hanging men when it suited his purpose or inclination. Nathan Savage, on Lynch's Creek, Moses Murphy and Jordan Gibson at Wiggins landing were among the 200 or more who lost their dwellings, some of them being destroyed because of their owner's leadership in repressing the revived banditti and tories who were now emboldened and anxious to retaliate. Adam Cusack was one of the unfortunate rebels whose path was crossed by Wemyss and who came into his power. Being tried and convicted of several alleged misdemeanors of trifling import, he was sentenced to be hung. Those who interceded in his behalf, including his prostrate wife and children and his benevolent physician, taught the community how dangerous it was to mention pity and pardon for a stiff necked rebel, however valuable a citizen he might be.

On his return to Georgetown and the Santee, the true inwardness of Major Wemyss became manifest. Having collected several hundred of the citizens, he amused them with a harangue to show how the British were present to rescue the people from oppression, while on the outskirts his men were stealing their horses. Murrel, the great leader of the last organized band of robbers in this and other states farther west, used to pose as a passing parson and preach to the people while his confederates were selecting from the horses in the grove and escaping with the best. In June there were no battles; but July witnessed startling audacity on the part of Whigs here and there in the north western parts. On July 12th, skirmishes were fought at Williamson's Plantation, at Brandon's camp and at Stallions; on the 13th, at Cedar Springs; on the 14th at Gowen's old Fort and the 15th at

McDowell's Camp; on the 20th at Flat Rock and on the 30th at Thickety Ford. The total casualties in killed and wounded were greatly in favor of the aggressive partisan forces 44 being killed and wounded and 267 on the side of the British.[4]

On the 11th of July, Mr. Pugh went to Cheraw where Major McArthur held sway and on the next day signed parole as a prisoner of war and after a brief interval returned and tried in vain to give it back. He was in touch with the leading whigs but it cannot now be decided what cause produced the vacillation in him or others at this time, as within a few days he took the oath of allegiance. Major McArthur's stay at Cheraw, with headquarters in the old St. David's Church, lasted perhaps six weeks and in that time many soldiers were buried in the St. David's churchyard and the number of the sick was 106, who had to be removed in a boat when Cheraw was abandoned as an outpost.

Being reinforced by a militia regiment from North Carolina under Col. Bryan, Maj. McArthur, still at Cheraws made extensive forays into the region round about, pillaging, burning houses, driving off cattle and horses and abducting slaves, giving special treatment to active whigs. Gen. Harrington, just above the state line, who was absent in service and Thomas Ayer, were the most noted cases which held McArthur's attention. He found no obstruction to his will in the destruction of the former's property—it was war upon a defenceless woman; but the latter who lived below Hunt's Bluff was found equal to the watchful tories and the vigilant Major who offered a reward for his capture. Thomas Ayer, it was said, had earned the fear of the tories and their friends, by his leadership in bringing them to punishment.

---

[4]McCrady's South Carolina in the Revolution 1776-1780, p. 616.

Under the guidance of George Manderson, Thomas Ayer was watched and captured and carried up to Hunt's Bluff where they were unexpectedly compelled to spend the night. In the meantime, Hartwell Ayer, his son, with several Georgians pursued and surprised the tories and left but one of them not killed or wounded. McArthur in consequence of this exploit, destroyed the property of Thomas Ayer and redoubled his efforts to capture him; but the advancing army from North Carolina broke up his encampment and saved a crib of corn on Ayer's plantation—the crib to be the dwelling and the corn to be the food of the family. Exposure in the swamps in midsummer and scanty food and anxiety for his family and his country may have brought about in the next 12 months what McArthur's soldiers and the tories failed in accomplishing—the death of Thomas Ayer.[5] The short respite he enjoyed was due to McArthur's precipitate retreat; "I have just received intelligence from Lord Rawdon," wrote Lord Cornwallis on the 15th of July, "that DeKalb has certainly joined Caswell at Coxe's plantation on Deep River; his lordship in consequence had withdrawn McArthur's detachment over the Black river (creek)" When Wemyss and McArthur reached Cheraw, they found the inhabitants ready to yield to pressure like a rubber ball; but the treatment received at their hands made men who had preferred submission to resistance, ready for resistance; and the approach of the continental army kindled the desire to resist into open rebellion. As soon as McArthur got out of sight the rubber ball freed from pressure sprang back into its normal shape. On the day of McArthur's retreat, he also sent down the river, a boatload

---

[5] For a full account of the Ayer episode see Gregg's History of the Old Cheraws, pp. 307-311. Hartwell Ayer was his son, not elder brother.

of the sick soldiers under Lord Nairne and a detachment of militia under Col. William Henry Mills. A number of men who had returned to their allegiance to the crown, got together and made an ambuscade at Hunt's Bluff to intercept and capture the boat, men and all. On August the first the enterprise was entirely successful and at the command or signal of Maj. Tristam Thomas, the militia on board delivered all the men prisoners, except Col. William Henry Mills who was allowed to escape and make his way to Charles Town. The prisoners were marched off to North Carolina and another boat coming up the river with stores and supplies was captured the same day.[6] Lord Cornwallis knew the effect of such a victory when an army from the northward was inciting to a general revolt and Tarleton, who knew how to put a good face on his own conduct in the war, did not when he turned historian fail to point out the folly of trusting the American loyalists, when not mixed with seasoned troops; but he overlooked a greater evil of exercising his own power outside of the rules of civilized warfare. One error lost the victory at Hunt's Bluff; the other lost the state by a systematic disregard of these primal rights which even animals die in defense of. On the same day two other skirmishes at Rocky Mount and Hanging Rock were fought and on the 8th at Old Iron Works. The casualties were 135 to 262 in favor of the Americans. The retreat of McArthur and the crossing of the state line by Gates with his continental soldiers and North Carolina militia revived the hopes of the whigs but did not induce any to join his army. Gov. Rutledge had foreseen that there were tories enough everywhere in the state and in the parts of North Carolina east of the state to make the whigs apprehensive

---

[6]Ramsay's Revolution, Vol. II, p. 139.

and unwilling to go far from home. On the 4th of August, Gates issued a proclamation to the citizens of the state and on the 7th in Chesterfield County, 45 miles from Camden, his forces were joined by the militia of North Carolina under Gen. Caswell and on the 14th by Gen. Stephens and the Virginians. Gen. Gates was in a great hurry to get in sight of Cornwallis and his army, as if nothing else was wanting to enable him, after the manner of Medusa, to turn them into stone. His vision of victory was not to be realized. Gen. Sumter on the 15th succeeded in intercepting at Wateree ferry vehicles with clothing, arms, and stores for the British at Camden and having cut Cornwallis' communication with Charles Town, made it advisable for the British general to fight or retreat. He chose to fight and on the next morning it was his good fortune to gain a complete victory and to rout Gen. Gates' army; and what seemed even worse, Gen. Sumter in his retreat with his booty and not a few prisoners were overtaken by that dashing Light Horse Commander, Tarleton, and routed so thoroughly at Fishing Creek that he barely escaped capture without hat, coat or saddle. Col. Tarleton was heard remarking prematurely that he was satisfied that the game cock of South Carolina was dead as he had secured his plume from a tory which the general had lost in crossing a ferry. Not a South Carolina private was in the battle of Camden. It was commanded by a continental officer and in the ranks were Virginians and North Carolinians. It was the first of the unsuccessful battles thus manned and officered by Continental Congress. There was scarcely a circumstance connected with it that was not disheartening and even heart rending and not one more so than the sacrifice of that brave spirit Baron DeKalb. The British lost 324 killed, wounded and missing; the Americans, British count, 2070.

South Carolina

The reader is indebted to Rev. Mr. Pugh for the little that is known about the happenings in Cheraw District in the time of suspense after Gates' defeat, the news of which reached the upper Pee Dee on the third day. There was great trouble on the 19th, and moving of goods on Sunday. On the 3rd of September men were scouting after tories and on the 17th the minister was severely plundered. Next week was full of trouble, but on the 27th the British left Long Bluff and stock hidden from the plunderers were looked after and on October 10th Whigs were flying from here. Lord Cornwallis in the hour of victory decided upon very harsh and vindictive measures. His well-known letter sent to the Commandant of the garrison at Ninety Six divided the offending population into three classes and defined the punishment to be meted out to each: Those who had subscribed and took part in the revolt were to be punished with the greatest rigor; those who would not turn out, were to be imprisoned and their property confiscated; and his last pressing order was that "every militiaman who had borne arms in the British army and afterwards joined the enemy shall be immediately hanged." And he set the example by hanging at least 7 men in Camden: Samuel Andrews, Richard Tucker, John Miles, Josiah Gayle, Eleazer Smith, being the only ones whose names were preserved. This autocratic exercise of power made Gov. Rutledge think of retaliation by confiscating the property of those who were avowedly Cornwallis' friends, but he more wisely decided that their property in time could be put to a better use.

Col. Marion has been mentioned among the first refugees from the state who awaited the advance of DeKalb and Gates into South Carolina. Early in August Gates received a request from several companies collected from the men who lived between the Santee and Pee Dee for a commanding officer to be sent them. This by chance was hit upon, the plan of warfare that kept the whigs in heart and the enemy in fear of his line of communications. The choice fell upon Col. Marion who was recommended by Gov. Rutledge. He at once made his way to Lynch's Creek and reached it on the 10th with orders to destroy all the boats on the river so as to cut off the retreat of the British from Camden; no other issue to this campaign than a victory ever occurred to Gen. Gates, if concurrent testimony of the time is reliable. At any rate, Gen. Gates was wiser in the appointment than he himself believed; for matters were being shaped, as it were, by an unseen hand, for the reception of Marion and for his initiation into that partisan warfare which merited from his great adversary the name of Swamp Fox and brought out distinctly those higher qualities which, never possessed by a fox, were to shine at a later time in Gen. R. E. Lee. The Pee Dee was soon to become his theatre of war and he, the hero of our story. About two months before Col. Marion's arrival, a proclamation was issued from Georgetown, by a British Captain inviting the people to come in and renew their allegiance to King George. Many of the inhabitants of Georgetown who had no grievance and no wish to disturb their former relations with the crown, swore allegiance and took protection; but up in Williamsburg County and part of Marion district, there was little disposition to be in a hurry to renew their allegiance. In this section therefore, a public meeting was called and after full discussion, Maj. John James was sent as a deputy to ascertain upon what terms they would be allowed to submit. Maj. James accordingly fulfilled his mission and was informed by the officer, Captain Ardesoif, "that their submission must be unconditional." To his inquiry, "whether they would be allowed to stay at home upon their plantations in peace and quiet?" came the response, "You must take up arms in his cause." And when Major James intimated that the people whom he represented would not submit on such terms, Capt. Ardesoif lost his self control and Maj. James, with chair uplifted before him, or brandished in the direction of the captain, passed out of a back door and went home.[7] The simple story he had to tell his compatriots caused them to take up arms in behalf of their adopted land. Companies were formed under their revolutionary captains, William McCottry, Henry Mouzon and John James, Jr. These 400 men were consciously drawing down upon themselves the weight of the foremost nation in the world. Thornly's and Witherspoon's companies under Giles were added to these. Tarleton undertook to surprise them but retreated without a battle. It was at this point that the request for a commanding officer reached Gen. Gates and about the 10th of August, Col. Marion arrived and found Col. Hugh Horry with a small company, the senior officer. Not long after his arrival, he led his men across the Pee Dee to attack Major Gainey who was in command of a body of tories on Britton's Neck. In this first effort, in which secrecy and celerity played an important part, he was successful in scattering the enemy and driving them from the swamps. Capt. Barfield was the next tory commander who fell into a snare and suffered a complete defeat. Marion then threw up a redoubt at Port's ferry on the eastern bank to restrain the tories. While at this place and in this work there was brought to him in some private channel the tidings of Gates' defeat at Camden. With the secret shut up in his own breast, he went at once to Nelson's ferry where a party of 16 under Col. Horry took a British guard of 32 men and released 150

---

[7]See Howe's Presbyterian Church in South Carolina.

continental soldiers with only one man wounded and one killed.

Here of course the whole band under Marion learned of Gates' disaster which eclipsed the brilliancy of their present success. On his way back Col. Marion's band was constantly lessened by the returning home of his soldiers and the desertion of the released continentals, except two or three. He and his little band were the remnant in the state and Cornwallis wrote to Tarleton, "I sincerely hope you will get at Mr. Marion." Near the end of August, Marion heard of the approach of Major Wemyss from Kingstree with two regiments, one of them being Harrison's band of tories. When it was found out through Major James that the enemy was twice as strong as Marion's force, the line of march was turned again toward Lynch's Creek. Rather than leave their property and families at the mercy of a ruthless enemy, one half of Marion's men is said to have dropped out of ranks. Less than 70 men and officers were now under him (Col. Marion) and among these were Cols. Peter and Hugh Horry, John Ervin, John Baxter and Majors John Vanderhorst, John James and Benson.

After appointing Captain James with a squad of men to succor the distressed and convey intelligence, Col. Marion set out for his redoubt on the Pee Dee and on the same day turned his horse toward North Carolina and went to Drowning Creek. Here Maj. James with a few volunteers, went back to Williamsburg. He soon returned with the tidings that Wemyss was desolating their homes and reducing Marion's soldiers from easy circumstances to poverty and want. The fortunes of the state were now at its lowest ebb. The little band under Marion, serving without pay and in want of everything, the ultimate hope of the state, was now scattered and the leader in exile. But a few days' rest recuperated the discouraged but irrepressible Marion and sent him by forced marches toward South Carolina, to get on track of the tories, now at the zenith of wanton power. They were found at Black Mingo, Sept. 14th, at Shepherd's ferry on the South side a circumstance which turned out favorable to the tories; for in having to cross a bridge in order to attack them, the horses feet gave the signal to the enemy who had time to prepare a surprise for a part of Marion's men. The battle lasted some time in close quarters and the wounded on both sides were numerous, before a loud misleading command issued by Marion sent the tories scampering into Black Mingo swamp. Some of Marion's former soldiers were among the wounded tories, but he was too good and too wise a man to treat them according to the laws of war.

The wisdom of this course was verified in a concrete way. Peter Gaillard who had espoused the British cause and was second in command over the tories at this battle, afterwards approached Marion through DuBose and signified his wish to serve in Marion's band, if it could be done without humiliating his feelings. He was met with evident good will and showed himself afterwards a brave, faithful valiant soldier.[8]

In this battle so bravely fought on both sides, the advantage lay with Marion's men, though the loss of the gallant officers, Mouzon and Scott, for the remainder of the war and other wounded men, was keenly felt. Marion learned by this night's experience to prefer fords for crossing streams.

Being reinforced from men in this neighborhood, Col. Marion decided to let the tories who had assisted Wemyss feel the weight of his rebel force. He learned that Col. Tynes was collecting a large body of tories in the fork

---

[8]DuBose's History of the Huguenot's, p. 17.

of Black River, distant about 30 miles. Having crossed the north branch of Black River, he surprised and defeated him without the loss of a man, and fortunately captured much needed supplies and ammunition. Among the tories killed was Captain Gaskins, one of Weymss' plundering companies, with a card in his hand. Soon after this routing of the tories, Col. Marion made his camp in Snow's Island, at the conflux of Lynch's Creek and Pee Dee River. It was about this time, September 20th, one month and four days after the battle of Camden, that Gov. Rutledge wrote the delegates in Congress:

"On the 15th inst. Col. Sumter lay, with about 200 men, to the westward of Catawba, General Davison was with about 400 militia, below Charlotte and Gen. Sumner with about 800 more, that day reached Salisbury where he halted and this is all our force that I can find to be actually embodied and in the field, except the little party under Marion and a few at Cross Creek, North Carolina under Col. Harrington."

On the day it was written Col. Davis gained a victory at Wahub's Plantation in Mecklenburg County and on the 25th Lord Cornwallis occupied Charlotte. In the meantime Col. Fergusen, a British officer of the 71st Regiment had been spending the months after the fall of Charles Town in the tory settlements where he engaged 6 battalions of militia for service in the reduction of North and South Carolina. The battle of Musgrove's mill gave him a taste of the mountaineer's ability to fight and led to the indiscretion of sending to the overmountain men a message that if they did not behave themselves he would come over and hang their leaders and devastate their country. This threat brought them over the mountains to anticipate such an event by attacking Ferguson on his own ground. Several Colonels, Campbell, Shelby, Sevier, Cleveland, McDowell, Williams,

Lacey, and others collected their forces together and on October the 7th fought the battle of King's Mountain in which Ferguson was killed and his army captured.

Tidings of this battle and victory went throughout the United States, carrying as much encouragement to the friends of liberty as it alarmed and humiliated Lord Cornwallis who was at Charlotte.

It was about this time that Capt. Wade and Capt. Abel Kolb who had fled to North Carolina decided to come back to their homes. Capt. Kolb lived in the Welsh Neck. The story of their return and what it led to is told by Caruther, a historian of North Carolina, who related it evidently as told and colored by the tories in the neighborhood and no doubt with some errors and with too much truth after all discounts are made. Two thirds of the men, sometimes one half had to remain at home to guard against the violence of the tories whose barbarity invited similar treatment in turn. The struggle on the Pee Dees, Lynch's and Drowning Creeks, whig and tory, surpassed in fierceness anything known in other states.

The battle of King's Mountain deranged the plans of the enemy and caused Lord Cornwallis to consult for his own safety, by beginning after a week's delay his retreat from Charlotte and, after his army had suffered great hardships, rested on the 29th at Winnsboro, his new encampment. From this place he found it necessary to dispatch Tarleton in pursuit of Marion, who was soon discovered near the High Hills of Santee. On the 10th Marion saw the fires of Tarleton's men near General Richardson's house and prepared to attack him; but desisted when he learned the strength of Tarleton's army. Accordingly he employed the darkness of the night to put a safe distance between him and his more powerful pursuer. Using one of Marion's best guides, who had deserted, Tarleton chased Marion and his men seven hours and ceased by an order of Cornwallis who requested him to return. This was fortunate for Tarleton for whom Marion had set a snare. Up the Broad River at Fishdam, Nov. 9, Wemyss had overtaken Sumter and in the skirmish which he provoked, was defeated, captured and put out of harness by his wounds. This defeat of Wemyss occurred at the time that Tarleton and Marion were about to engage in battle near the High Hills; and Cornwallis in his uneasiness sent for Tarleton to checkmate other moves Sumter was about to make. Tarleton is reported to have said, "Come, my boys, let us go back and we will find the Game Cock (Sumter); but as for this d——d old fox, the devil himself could not catch him." On the 20th, Tarleton overtook the Game Cock at Blackstock and had to retreat after heavy losses. Sumter and two others were wounded and one killed. By the recall of Tarleton, the situation was eased for Marion, though he was still to be harassed by other parties sent out in pursuit of him. In his moving around between the Santee and the Pee Dee, his friends ever ready to keep him posted in reference to the tories or the British, made him not less formidable to the British than the larger rebel armies were in the upper parts where the tories kept the British in touch with whatever was undertaken. Even Charles Town became interested in Marion's overthrow or capture; for Capt. Maxwell with 204 regulars was sent up to Lenud's ferry and Kingstree, ten miles above which place Tarleton had left the Swamp Fox.

Gen. Green arrived at Charlotte in December and relieved Gates of his command. On the 4th Col. Washington with his log cannon captured Rugely and 112 men. On the 8th Gov. Rutledge made the following estimate of the opposing forces: The British had 300 at

Augusta and the same number at Ninety Six. At Stephenson's Creek under Kirkland, there were 50, Little River 200 under Gen. Robert Cunningham, on Broad river 200 regulars under McArthur, about 300 under Tarleton, at Winnsboro under Lord Cornwallis 900 regulars and 100 militia, at Congaree 60; 500 regulars at Charles Town, 200 at Nelson's ferry, 500 at Camden under Lord Rawdon, 80 regulars at Georgetown.

On the American side were about 1000 regulars from Maryland, Delaware and Virginia, 150 cavalry andd 250 militia with Smallwood, the time of the latter to expire in a few days. Under Gen. Stephens 600 Virginians a great part of their time already expired, under Col. Marion on the Pee Dee 154, under Gen. Harrington 194, nearly ready to disband, lately under Gen. Sumter who was wounded, four or five hundred South Carolina and Georgia militia, 150 under Gen. Butler guarding prisoners and 200 regulars on the march from Hillsboro.

His position as governor and dictator over the state and its mouthpiece in North Carolina, Virginia and Congress, put him in possession of information that tried his patience; and a visit to York county supplemented by trustworthy letters from other parts of the state, describing the cruelty of the enemy, burdened him beyond words to express it. The visit was to consult with General Sumter who had been removed into York County while he was recovering from his wound. There he saw Col. Hill's fine iron works, mills, dwellings, houses and buildings of every kind reduced to ashes and his wife and children living in a little log hut. He was shocked at the sight of soldiers clothed in rags who had taken arms, with halters around their necks in order to serve their downtrodden state. "Tarleton has," he continued, "since the action at Blackstock, hung a magistrate of respectable character. They have burnt a prodigious number of houses and turned a vast number of women, formerly of affluent or easy fortune, with their children almost naked, into the woods. Tarleton at General Richardson's widow's exceeded his usual barbarity, for having dined in her house, he not only burnt it after plundering everything it contained, but having driven into a barn a number of cattle, hogs & poultry, he consumed them, together with the barn and the corn in it, in one general blaze——this because he pretended to believe that the poor old general was with the rebel army." As Gov. Rutledge turned away from this harrowing sight within the state, he saw the enemy's reinforcements coming to Charles Town, while the main army and the French troops remained in winter quarters in the eastern states where they had nothing to do. In this gloomy outlook, his own men being few and in rags, the governor failed to see the great asset on the side of the state, viz. "a self supporting institution" as the soldier was called in North Carolina, or "the unpaid gentleman" in South Carolina. In one of his letters, he enclosed an account of General Sumter's engagement with Wemyss and Tarleton, of Col. Marion's with the tories and of Col. Washington's success against Rugely, "but", said he, "what do all these things avail, toward the great point of regg. our country, the distresses of which I want words to describe?" This thought was amplified in a few days by the inquiry, "but when shall we retake the town? not unless our allies exert themselves very powerfully for that purpose—until that event takes place and we can open the trade of the country I shall think everything else poor trifling business." Had he known how dejected Lord Cornwallis was, he would have seen the situation in a juster light. On the 27th of September after Sumter's wound was reported, he declared in a communication to Tarleton that

Sumter "certainly has been our greatest plague in this country," and ten days later he reported to Sir Henry Clinton, "Bad as the state of our affairs was in the northern frontier the eastern part was much worse. Col. Tynes, who commanded the militia of the high hills of Santee, who was posted on Black River, was surprised and taken, and his men lost all their arms. Col. Marion had so wrought on the minds of the people, partly by the terror of his threats and cruelty of his punishments, and partly by promise of plunder, that there was scarce an inhabitant between the Santee and Pee Dee that was not in arms."[9] From the first skirmish on the 12th of July to the last one at Long Cane, five full months of 1780, the partisan soldiers fought 26 battles with a loss of 497 killed and wounded and 320 prisoners. The British loss was 1200 in killed and wounded, 1286 prisoners, a total of 2486.[10]

An intelligent loyalist in London at this very time when the fortunes of South Carolina were so desperate, denied the practicability of the reduction of the colonies, saying, "We have beaten the rebel army and expelled that army out of Carolina with half their number; have riveted the inhabitants to our interests; they are become loyalists and have sworn allegiance and that they will always do whilst you can command their estates and persons.

> 'Tis he that breaks an oath who makes it;
> Not he who for convenience takes it.

. . . While under British power they are loyal, that power removed, they as naturally return to their former conditions as any elastic body returns to its natural form when the force is removed."

---
[9] S. Curwen. Journal & Letters, p. 284.
[10] McCrady's S. C. in the Revolution, p. 854.

Rambles in the Pee Dee Basin

It was the hope of Governor Rutledge that General Greene would collect the scattered forces to a good tenable position and detach strong parties to oppose the enemy's light troops who did the most mischief, to harass the enemy, circumscribe their limits, and in time oblige them to retire to Charles Town and give an opportunity of reestablishing civil government, in some parts of the country, of electing and convening a legislature and of making and enforcing laws. In this attitude of mind, he anticipated Washington in the noble example of putting constitutional government, based upon the will of the people, above any possible personal preferment. His oath of office also demanded it.

On the 20th, Gen. Greene set out for Haly's ferry on the Pee Dee and from thence he went by the advice of his engineer to Hick's creek, a short distance above Cheraw on the left bank of the river. Gen. Morgan was sent down the west side of the Catawba and was placed in command of all militia to the west of that stream, while General Sumter was recovering from the wound received at Blackstock. On the 25th Morgan reached Union County and the theatre of skirmishes was again in the western part of the state around and west of Ninety Six; where the advantage remained with the rebel forces, in the gaining of forage, grain and other supplies. Col. Washington gained victories at Hammonds store, Abbeville County on the 30th and at Hard Labor on the 31st. On the 27th Marion left Santee river. Major Mcleroth had taken post at Great Savannah with about 300 men. Leslie's troops, lately arrived in Charles Town, were advancing toward Nelson's ferry. Colonel Kolb succeeded Colonel George Hicks who was still in Virginia, as the head of the upper Pee Dee regiment was engaged in warding off the plundering expeditions from the neighboring hiding places and from North

Carolina. Morgan on Pacolet stream reinforced by 70 men led by Bowie and Col. Pickens, who had scrupulously observed his parole as long as patience was a virtue. Gov. Rutledge and Gen. Greene were sojourning near Cheraw, the one at Thomas' Plantation, collecting and reporting the events occurring on Hick's Creek. Thus closed the year 1780. It was yet a dark hour. Wemyss who had laid waste a tract 15 x 70 miles had been rendered a cripple for life and the fortunes of Tarleton had passed the zenith. The invincible native spirit was rising under the leadership of Marion, Sumter, Pickens, Williams, Davie; and even Gov. Rutledge, to whom Charles Town, fast in the hands of the British, appeared as Jerusalem did to the exiles in Babylon, was soon to feel the glow of assurance that better days were coming.

CHAPTER XXI
1781

General Greene entered the new year apprized of the dangers confronting his scattered troops and of the straits in reference to arms, ammunition and clothing to which his men were reduced. He was disposed to lean on Gen. Marion to whom he was going to send Gen. Lee and his legion to reduce Georgetown and Fort Watson, ordering him in the meantime to collect horses, scour the Black and the Pee Dee for boats suitable for transportation and procure provision for his own and the continental army. Gen. Greene was not unsuited for the double task of check-mating the wily Cornwallis and Tarleton and the not less difficult task of commanding and keeping in harmony the brave independent leaders under him—Sumter, Marion, Lee, Horry and others. All the suavity of language at his command, bordering at times on insincerity, was needed to supplement his authority as commander-in-chief. The coolness between Sumter and Morgan arising from orders issued by the latter to officers under Gen. Sumter while recovering from his wound, was the first incident to disclose this capacity for mediation. Morgan had his camp on the Pacolet at Christmas time and like a hawk on a distant limb, Lord Cornwallis was preparing to swoop down upon him. Col. Washington had made in December Hammond's Store in Abbeville and Williams' Plantation in Newberry memorable as places struck by whig lightning. Tarleton was selected to pursue Morgan and give battle and Cornwallis was to move up stream and help corner whatever was left of Morgan's forces. Morgan was indeed overtaken and forced to give battle, but on ground of his own choosing and in such battle array as to be the most formidable; for Tarleton's tactics were well known. Before noon Tarleton was routed,[1] and out of 1200 all told, 150 killed 200 wounded and more than 500 made prisoners; 35 wagons and 70 negroes were taken in the camp. Out of Morgan's 900, 72 were killed and wounded. This was a great day in which the mountaineer fighting for his home and fireside was superior to the best soldiers in Lord Cornwallis' army. It stirred up congress to honor the brave leaders who had achieved a victory over the far-famed and much feared Tarleton. Morgan was to add fame to his laurels by the success with which he moved with his prisoners to a place of safety. After the battle was announced to Gen. Greene, he performed another feat which broke the rules of orthodox strategists. Putting his army under Huger to retreat to Guilford Court House, he with a handful of men and a guide crossed near Cornwallis' army to Morgan's no doubt to help extricate him from the army in between Morgan's and his own. There are occasions which make a genius rise above ordinary precautions, as Caesar did, when he said to his oarsman in a violent tempest, "Why do you fear? You are carrying Caesar." The race that ensued was disappointing to Cornwallis, while the success in making a junction at Guilford Court House and in removing the prisoners out of danger did not place the patriot army on a level with Cornwallis' forces.

South Carolina was now free from Cornwallis' main army, but less than 1000 militia in the state was all that could be mustered to hold in check and annoy the 4000 British left in it as garrisons. Gov. Rutledge being re-

---

[1] Mr. Thomas Littlejohn of Union County, born near 1800 lived in a hundred yards of Tarleton's camp on the night before the battle and could point out a narrow lane along which Tarleton came galloping after his defeat on a charger which leaped without effort the tongue of an ox-cart turned across the road and raised upon the fence to impede his retreat.

duced to a nullity in South Carolina and in North Carolina by the presence of armies, left early in March with Philadelphia in view. The state was therefore left up to April 1st to Sumter and Marion, the former in command of all the militia west of the Catawba, Wateree and Santee and Marion east of it.*

In December, 1780, Col. Marion was made Brigadier General and his promotion was forwarded from the governor's stopping place near Cheraw. Marion's command embraced the Pee Dee section, including Col. Kolb's, Murphy's and Major Benton's men who were in arms to protect the whigs from the raids of the tories. At some time not made definite in Weem's narrative, probably Christmas week, Gen. Marion led his famished band into Waccamaw section and there revelled among the Hugers, Trapiers and Allstons who threw open as if to brothers, the gates of their elegant yards for the cavalry and hurried them up their princely steps, notwithstanding their dirt and rags, ushered them into their grand saloons and dining rooms, where the famous mahogany sideboards were quickly covered with the pitchers of amber colored brandy and sugar dishes of double refined with honey for drams of julips; and their horses were up to their ears and eyes in corn and sweet scented fodder, while nothing that air, land or water could furnish was too good for the men.

Marion had obeyed as far as possible General Greene's order to collect horses for his army, to take every possible measure for obtaining intelligence, to collect boats as low down as Georgetown and to send a return of his strength and the condition of his troops. From January 1st to April 1st there were 24 collisions between the British and the Carolinians, 12 of which were under the direction of Marion. In March especially was

Marion's genius taxed. On the 18th of January Capt. Postell was sent by Marion to capture a squad of the enemy posted at his father's house in St. Mark's parish. The owner of the house was a prisoner at Georgetown while his mansion was occupied by Capt. James De Peyster as a fortification, it being as convenient to obtain supplies for the army. Here they were as snugly situated as if they had been the owners of the palace and the lords of creation. But Marion hearing of their comfortable quarters, resolved to disturb their repose and break up their nest; nor could he be at a loss what officers to send; here was young Postell himself well acquainted with every nook and corner about the place. He was already nettled at his father's treatment and begrudged them his former home, while he had to lie in the swamps, with the leaves as his covering. His fingers were itching to get hold of them; so off he starts with 14 men to rout these intruders from the home of his youth; and in order to conceal his numbers, formed them in a line four deep and charged up behind the kitchen. He immediately sent in a flag and ordered them to surrender. The officer asked for a short time to make up his mind; Postell said he would not give him five minutes and ordered his men to bring straw and set fire to the kitchen from which the dwelling might take fire. But the officer seeing what they were up to, made his men stack their arms and march out into the yard. When he presented his sword to Postell he asked, "Where are your men?" and on being told these 14 were all, he was the most angry man, said the narrator, he ever saw. But this being now British ground, they put off for camp, Postell's men mounted, these on foot and by the time they reached camp, the poor fellows on foot were mortified more than ever, having soiled their pretty trousers; for, being in a hurry, Postell had made them plunge every creek and mud hole on the way.[2] Col. Horry was now dispatched with Capt. Baxter, Lieut. Postell, Sergeant McDonald and 30 men to march toward Georgetown and engage the enemy wherever found.[3] Leaving camp near midnight, they reached the outposts of the enemy by dawn and halted for refreshment; but the firing of the sentinels called to arms and in the chase of the enemy 24 out of 25 were killed or captured. A brave officer named Mariott glided into the swamps and in the morning reached Georgetown as "gray as a badger." On the next morning Colonel Horry with Capt. Snipes and 30 men went down the Sampit road in quest of the enemy. Near the town they saw a body of horsemen getting into line. Whereupon Col. Horry ordered a charge and dashed upon them and caused a genuine flight; but in the confusion of a battle in the woods, Col. Horry when about to be shot by one Capt. Lewis, was saved by a sprightly lad named Gwinn who brought down Lewis, though in falling he discharged his gun and killed Horry's horse. This day became somewhat noted for a race between Sergeant McDonald and the tory, Col. Gainey on a level road about two or three miles from Georgetown, beginning near White's bridge, the pursued and pursuer made their horses' feet clatter as they stretched every nerve to speed on their way. As they were about to turn a corner McDonald thrust his bayonet into the back of Gainey and by some chance McDonald kept the musket and Gainey rode into town with the bayonet in his back. The day's work was, however, costly. Some men had been taken prisoners and others killed. A captain had also been dispatched to surprise a squad of tories at the Pens, a plantation of Col-

[2]James Jenkins' version of the episode.
[3]McCrady, South Carolina in the Revolution 1780-1783, p. 83.

onel Allston. Samuel Jenkins and perhaps Gabriel Marion were on picket guard when the tories rode up and being identified as the King's friend the guard fired and wheeled to escape, "but," said Jenkins, "several were thrown from their horses and taken; Samuel Jenkins fell also, but mounted again before they could seize him. The enemy pursued and so close was the chase, they ran immediately into Marion's camp; and wheeling to retreat they fell by our marksmen like fruit to the ground. It was a sad day for the tories; several old neighbors (among them Jenkins' blacksmith) were killed. But Marion suffered also; for they not only made prisoners of the men they took, but killed them in cold blood, particularly, young Marion, it was believed by one Sweat who was overtaken by justice the same day and shared a similar fate." The spot of ground where Gabriel Marion fell is still pointed out near the bridge on White's Creek.

On the 23rd of January General Lee with his Light horse arrived in Marion's camp and they set out at once to capture Georgetown by stealthy approaches down the river in boats and on the land side. Capt. Carnes and Capt. Rudulph were in command of the water squadron the other under Gen. Marion, though Gov. Rutledge reported it under Col. Lee. The militia was below par in their estimation. On the land side the forces lay in concealment until firing began and then they rushed into the town. The Commandant, Capt. Campbell with some others were captured and Major Irvine killed. There was no resistance and no loss by Marion who prudently declined to assault the fort at the risk of failure and of the loss of useful lives. On the same day of this partial victory, Gen. Marion and Gen. Lee set out for Nelson's ferry against Fort Watson but distant events broke up the operations in that quarter. Watson went to

Camden and Col. Lee was recalled to North Carolina, having had only a few days of actual service with Marion. His cavalry was at Gibson's mill, Marlboro County, February 3rd, near Mr. Pugh's. On the 29th Capt. John Postell was ordered by Marion to cross the Santee with a small detachment and proceed southward nearer Charles Town to Wadboo to destroy valuable stores of pork, flour, rice, salt, turpentine there collected and to come back by Monck's Corner where he burnt 14 wagons loaded with soldiers' clothes and baggage, destroyed 20 hogsheads of rum and retired with 40 prisoners. Major Postell on the same day was ordered to burn the enemy's stores at Thomson's but they had been removed. On his way back, he destroyed without the loss of a man, a great quantity of rum, sugar, salt, flour, pork, clothes, and baggage at Manigault's ferry. For which, General Greene sent the Postells from Guilford Court House his particular thanks. Gov. Rutledge in his letter of February 10th stated that young Conyers, a brother of the Captain, lately went with 16 militia and took 48 prisoners on the west side of Santee, with considerable number of wagons, horses, a large quantity of salt and other stores, while Marion when last heard from was at or near Dorchester destroying the enemy's stores and breaking up their quarters in different places. These last raids were nominally under General Greene's orders, but some of them were already planned or suggested by Marion and all of them were in accord with his general purpose of harrassing the enemy in the rear and of attacking him in any exposed situation. Gen. Greene showed his confidence in Marion by giving him large discretion. The further the enemy advanced from the base, the more costly and difficult was it to keep intact the line of communication. While Greene and Cornwallis were absent from the state, it required of the enemy perhaps two or three times as many men as Sumter and Marion had under arms, to guard those posts and convoy the wagons loaded with army stores. In like manner the scattered tories caused many more whigs than their own number to stay at home on guard. Gov. Rutledge who had regarded this partisan warfare relatively as "trifling business" now saw that Lord Cornwallis while gaining new territory in North Carolina might not consider that behind him entirely secure. About the middle of February, Major McLeroth of the 64th regiment, while conveying a train of wagons, was attacked by Marion at a place called half way swamp (in Clarendon County) and reduced to straits by Marion's equal number of men. In his pursuit of McLeroth, it is a tradition that when Marion stopped at the house of a well known mistress of a family, she said to him "I have always been glad to see you but am not glad to see you now." McLeroth had treated her kindly and justly, paid her in full for all that he had used or taken and had left a tent and a surgeon to attend to the wounded, with a promise like that made by the good Samaritan to the inn-keeper of his day. Whether the story is founded on fact or fiction, it was very much like the truth, when the woman pulled out of her pocket the handful of real money, given her with kind words added, and wished him not to be pursued by Marion. The state might easily have been recovered, if the British had had wise and magnanimous leaders. McLeroth was a diplomat in his dealings with Marion and with the inn-keeper, but lost his heavy baggage to save his men.

After recovering from his wound, Gen. Sumter had been engaging the full attention of Lord Rawdon at Camden, by his movements on the west side of the Broad, and as far down as Orangeburg; but on his return to northern parts after having been in four battles, Lord Rawdon decided to have a grand chase after the Swamp Fox whose headquarters were still at Snow Island. Col. Watson with about 500 men at Nelson's ferry, was to march down the Santee and cross the Black, Col. Doyle was to come down the Wateree and Jeffries' Creek and join with Watson. Marion being apprized of his double danger, set out in advance in the direction of Col. Watson. In doing so he exhibited in a small theatre generalship of a high order in meeting and defeating both armies before they united. In 1915, a correspondent of the Saturday Evening Post interviewed in succession Generals Robert, French and Joffre as to whom they regarded the greatest military genius of history. The unanimous answer was, "Stonewall Jackson" who crushed three armies, each larger than his own under Fremont, Banks and Shields. Marion met Watson on the 6th of March at Wiboo Swamp and engaged in a spirited skirmish in which Captains' McCauley and Conyers with their companies and private Gavin James were mentioned for their signal services in resisting or dispersing the enemy. Col. Watson after tarrying a day continued his march down the Santee, having to meet all the opposition that Marion could furnish and to remove all the obstructions put in his way, as well as build bridges broken to slacken the speed of his march. At Mount Hope he had to bring up his cannon to dislodge Marion's men whose rear guard resisted his crossing. After crossing the bridge and turning to the left, Col. Watson passed down the Black river road which led to the lower bridge, whither Marion, divining Watson's purpose had sent a detachment under Major James, who crossed and destroyed the bridge on the northern side of the river and prepared to dispute the passage of the stream. Marion was soon drawn up behind James and ready to meet Watson when he arrived at the crossing. Here the cannon brought up by Watson to clear away the enemy on the opposite bank, owing to the configuration of the southern or right side of the river, shot above them and when the cannon were drawn up on the elevation James' men on the low ground picked off the cannoneers before they could fire. Failing in this Col. Watson ordered a crossing at the ford which ended in loss and failure. Thence Col. Watson went upstream to the plantations of John Witherspoon and thence to Blakeley's, where for more than a week Marion's riflemen kept the soldiers in constant dread. When it became necessary to send out foraging parties Marion's men made Col. Watson hunt for safer quarters. McDonald, one of the men who joined Marion when he released the 150 continentals captured at the battle of Camden, shot at a distance of 300 yards and wounded a Lieutenant Torriano, whom Col. Watson received permission to send to Charles Town. Torriano had been billeted in a whig family in Charles Town and in that position he had defended them from insults (Weems), but it may have been due entirely to Marion's compassionate nature. Col. Watson was now in no condition to disturb Marion's nest at Snow Island. He was more interested in getting provisions for his army, burying his dead, caring for his wounded and in getting to a place of safety. Turning now to the right, he went through the woods to the Santee road and made his way towards Georgetown, being harassed along the whole journey till he reached the Sampit bridge, whence he was allowed to proceed to the town and get supplies for his famishing soldiers. In all this fighting and skirmishing Marion's loss was small, that of the enemy was concealed. His halt in the pursuit of Watson was caused by tidings from Col. Ervin who had been defeated by Col. Doyle and forced to destroy the stores of ammunition on Snow Island or let it fall into the enemy's hand. Marion at once set out in pursuit of Doyle who lay at Witherspoon's ferry with a swollen stream between him and Marion who had to march several miles, swim the stream and pursue Doyle for two days to the point where the latter had destroyed his heavy baggage, in order to expedite his retreat to Camden. Col. Watson was not willing to rest in safety in Georgetown but was soon on his march to Catfish Creek where he contemplated an addition to his forces from Gainey and his tories. At this point Jenkins' narrative is partly that of an eye-witness: "About this time, Watson started toward Lumberton, N. C. on a plundering expedition. He is supposed to have crossed at Britton's ferry and came up through the Neck and arrived at the Jenkins' house on the 7th of April early in the morning. James, the lad, went out in the swamp side and got on the fence to see the company pass. The horse in front galloped up to the house and prepared to camp. By this time John Jenkins rode up the hill, having been sent to reconnoitre by Col. Horry who was in the back swamp. But he was soon discovered and hither they came full tilt; but they did not pursue very far, thinking that Marion was near by. James jumped up behind John Jenkins and rode out of danger; but on returning home late that day, he found his mother's English peas devoured, seven beeves slaughtered and two likely negroes abducted. Watson himself during his stay had taken up quarters in the house; and being in the presence of Mrs. Jenkins, she asked if he did not find it difficult to get from the ferry to her house with the baggage, as the bridges had been torn up, to which he replied: "No, madam, I never find any difficulty when on British ground. Do you not believe, madam, the British will conquer the Americans?" "No, Sir, I wish I was as sure of heaven as I am that the Americans will gain their independence; and, I think, sir, you believe so too." "No, madam," he replied, "I do not believe it." "How many sons have you among the rebels, madam?" "None, sir, the King has rebelled against us, and not we against the King." "Well, madam, how many have you with Marion?" "I have three , sir, and I only wish they were 3000." "Send for them, madam, and let them take protection, marry wives and settle their plantations." "Will you stay and protect them?" "No, madam," quite enraged, "it is enough for me to pardon them." "Pardon them sir! they have not asked for it." Cooling down a little he asked her to take a glass of wine with him, to which through courtesy she consented. As he was in the act of taking the wine he said: "Health to King George." But it was her time next and she retaliated by saying, "Health to George Washington!" He made a wry face, but could not refuse. This over, Col. Watson resumed the conversation: "Well, madam, have you heard that General Marion has joined Lord Rawdon?" "No, sir, indeed I have not." "Well, madam, it is a matter of fact." "Sir, I do not believe it." This vexed him again, insomuch that he struck his tent and went a mile further, to John Ray's where he spent the night . . . The next day Watson proceeded toward North Carolina in great glee, blowing their bugles as they went, until they heard that Gen. Greene was coming: when they turned about and made for Georgetown in great haste and with all possible silence—" "The route to Lumberton" was, no doubt, promulgated to mislead the whigs; for Watson was on the Catfish with Gainey and a large force of tories, when the scampering to Georgetown began. Marion crossed the Pee Dee at Wahees Bluff with 500 men in five miles of Gainey and Watson, with but two rounds of ammunition and could not risk a battle. A second time reduced to such straits he was considering whether he should not retreat to North Carolina, but the same tidings which sent Watson and Doyle hurrying to a safe retreat, brought hope and courage to Marion and his men.

On the 17th of March, after retreating into Virginia, General Greene returned and fought with Lord Cornwallis the battle of Guilford Court House. He was forced to retire defeated but the victorious enemy marched off towards Wilmington, disappointed in not receiving the expected aid from the tories and in not crushing the American army. Gen. Greene returned to South Carolina—the news which disturbed Lord Rawdon and his officers. In this month Gen. Sumter raised three regiments of state troops and five light horse troops under Col. Peter Horry, Hezekiah Mayham, Henry Hampton, Wade Hampton and ——— Middleton. Gen. Sumter in command of all the militia of the state found Gen. Marion disposed to be self directing.

In the latter part of February, Gen. Greene was informed that the garrison at Camden being short of provisions would be forced to quit the post, if the mill at the place should be destroyed. He therefore expressed an earnest desire to Gen. Sumter that he should take every prudent measure in his power to effect its destruction. Marion's men were selected to accomplish the destruction of the mill, and the account of the unsucesful effort is graphically described in James Jenkins' biography:

"Marion sent a small company to make observations, when the British were in possession of Camden. The British had charge also of the mills, afterwards belonging to Col. Chesnut, where they got grinding done for their army, and had stationed a company of men to defend it. This Scouts of Marion approached in the night and young Jenkins and one or two others were in the act of setting fire to the building, when McPherson contrary to orders shot down their sentry. This roused the men in the house, who came swarming down like bees; and alarmed the horse in Camden whose feet roared like thunder as they came to their relief, as the scouts had to retreat. After they left Camden, they came upon a party of tories dancing, and ordered them to surrender, they did so but when Major Downes, their leader, came out, not knowing that there were more just behind, he ran back, shut the door and commanded his men to fire. Here the brave McDonald was shot down in the yard. By this time the balance of the squad came up, rushed in and killed every man. Downes was shot under the bed. His daughter was wounded and remained a cripple near Camden until she died in old age. After McDonald fell, he begged not to be left; but the Camden horse was pressing, hence they had to escape for their lives.

In April the battles of Four Holes, Waxhaws Church, Barton's Post, Pocitaligo Road, Fort Balfur, the siege of Fort Watson, Matthews' Bluff, Wiggins Hill, Horner's Corner and Hammond's Mill were engaged in by state troops or militia only. On the 25th of April the battle of Hobkirk's Hill was fought and lost by General Greene but Lord Rawdon's loss in killed, wounded and missing and especially the manoeuvres of Sumter and Marion and other militia officers, turned the defeat into a victory. Gen. Greene's casualties amounted to 268, the British a somewhat smaller number. In this month also Col. Kolb found it necessary to move against the tories down into Marion county to suppress a gang of Major Gainey's outlaws. Col. Kolb was not more able than Gen. Marion to suppress cruelty of his men when they caught tories who had destroyed their homes and insulted their families. It was after this expedition to Marion, that the tories who suffered and survived, planned to go up the Pee Dee hastily on the heels of Col. Kolb and catch him off his guard. And in this they were successful. Two or more traditions have come down respecting his murder. Bishop Gregg adopted the one which made Capt. Jones of Gainey's men the leader and Mike Goings, a private in the tory ranks, the murderer. Judge James in his life of Marion makes Gibson and his party responsible for the deed. Without any effort to decide between these eminent writers, this subject will be dismissed with some traditions which were handed down by members of the Kolb family. His daughter, Ann, a school girl at the time of his death at the hands of the tories, retained a vivid recollection of the event. She gave this version of her father's murder: "Colonel Kolb was at home from the army on some necessary business. Two young men, tailors by trade, had spent the night in the house. Quite unexpectedly to them all, a considerable squad of tories raided upon the house, murdered the two young men and threatened to burn the house of Mrs. Kolb, if she did not produce her husband, but promising not to hurt him if she did. She came down the stairs with her husband, but as soon as her foot touched the porch, with her arm around him, a large mulatto who stood at the end of the porch, raised his gun and put the load in her father's heart."

While Mrs. Ann Pouncey was giving this statement to her pastor Rev. Evander David, her aged husband, James Pouncey, mentioned that he went to mill the same day and saw the same squad of men near Brown's mill shoot and kill a man named Flowers who was trying to make his escape from them. The name of the mulatto murderer was Gibson who was excluded along with the notorious Fanning from amnesty when General Marion made his treaty with Gainey through Col. Horry.

Another tradition was handed down through Sarah Kolb, the sister of Abel who was present on that momentous night: "When Col. Abel Kolb was shot by the tories, he was sick and was standing between his sister Sarah and his wife who were helping him to get out of the house which was burned. Sarah Kolb (Mrs. Evander McIver) kept for many years the dress she wore with places where shot had passed through it."

The death of Col. Kolb made a profound impression which the battle of Hobkirk's Hill, three days previously, fought and lost by Gen. Greene, could not obliterate. And after the lapse of nearly a century and a half, it is still the best known and most tragic event of the times.

On the first of May the engagements at Friday's ferry and Bush River in Newberry occurred and these were followed by the evacuation of Camden by Lord Rawdon on the 10th, a step which meant the abandonment of inland forts and the breaking of the tendrils of the tories who were clinging to him for protection. On the 11th Sumter gained at Orangeburg a great victory; on the same day Fort Motte fell and on the 15th Fort Granby near Columbia capitulated to Gen. Lee. May was a disastrous month to the British. Lord Rawdon had ordered Col. Cruger to evacuate Ninety Six and retire to Augusta but Gen. Greene, ignorant of his intention, was at the forks of a road, one leading him to the siege of Ninety Six and of Augusta, the other to a combined attack upon Lord Rawdon to drive him below the Santee and cause a voluntary evacuation of these remote fortified posts. General Greene favored the siege, and Sumter the combined attack. Pickens sent to Augusta succeeded, but General Greene who arrived at Ninety Six on the 22nd of May pushed in vain the siege with vigor and without intermission. In the meantime reinforcements having arrived in Charles Town, Lord Rawdon turned about and made rapid marches toward the beleaguered garrison and arrived in time to render the lives lost in the siege a useless sacrifice and to cause Greene to retreat. Lord Rawdon, now in the ascendency again and having recovered the sites of his lost forts, recognized his inability to reconstruct and hold them in so hostile surroundings. He therefore retired to Orangeburg where he was joined by Cruger and the Ninety Six garrison. He was followed by tory families who were to suffer and die within the British lines.

Just before these developments and this purpose to rescue Ninety Six became apparent, General Marion at his own request was allowed to attack Georgetown and occupy that post, and open up a new source of supplies. On the 5th of June he found it evacuated by a retreating enemy. His next important success was the treaty made by Marion and Gainey the tory leader, by which they were to lay down arms, serve the state when called on, deliver stolen goods and demean themselves as quiet citizens. But Marion's absence was felt when there was need to harass Lord Rawdon's command on its way to Ninety Six. From this time to the battle of Eutaw on September the 9th, 13 skirmishes were fought in what is now Lexington, Colleton, Berkeley, Orangeburg and Edgefield counties.

South Carolina

With a war map of the state at this time with the garrisoned places and the fortified line of communication in view, one can easily apprehend the plan of the British officers to conquer these states. The line of march from South to North that led to Nelson's ferry and thence to Camden where the central army was kept and thence to Charlotte explains also why the numerous battles in the western and eastern parts of the state were mostly between the whigs and tories. The garrisons kept alive the tory interests and enlisted some of the inhabitants in the British army. On the eastern side of the state the whigs were amply able to manage the tories in pitched skirmishes but the tories were sufficiently numerous and organized to keep a large part of Marion's regiments at home to guard the citizens. On the western side the conditions were entirely different. Cruger was wiser in his treatment of the paroled Whigs, but he failed in not restraining the banditti part of his friends whose rapacity and cruelty drove Col. Pickens and his brave men into the rebel army. Only a few years prior to the war, a great many Germans had been located north of Augusta, toward Ninety Six, who had no reason to be dissatisfied with the rule of George III. Of these about 500, amounting in 1770 to 200 families, settled between Cuffeetown Creek and Hard Labor in Londonderry township, Edgefield County, had been personally favored by the King and being poor and scarcely comfortably situated in these upper woods when the war began, it is not at all probable that these Germans who had all the freedom they wanted were for fighting on either side. Moses Kirkland visited the election precinct at Cuffee Town to prevent them from electing delegates to congress but not a line has been found referring to the part these Londonderry men, excepting two or three tories, took in the war, but it may be taken for granted that a friendly communication existed between these industrious Germans and the German soldiers in the Ninety Six garrison, some of whom were Hessians.

The advance then of Cornwallis through the middle of the state elated the tories and his retreat encouraged the whigs; but until April 1781, there was no organic connection between the continental army and the South Carolina militia, one came and retired, the other stayed and rose and fell as the waves of defeat or success moved around them. They were all united in a common purpose of wearing out the enemy in every possible way, notwithstanding the cleavage between them. Even then the ties were too weak for prompt and united action. The collision between the British and the continentals from the northward had been at Camden, Guilford Court House, Hobkirk's Hill and Ninety Six, but in none of these was General Gates or General Greene victorious, nor were the enemy except at Camden; for anything less than a rout of the Americans was felt to be equal to a defeat to men who had followed after Buford or fought with Lord Cornwallis at Camden. Greene was defeated everywhere he was present in command and yet he was never routed or driven in disorder from the field. Victories fell to his opponents who always acted afterwards as if they had been defeated. Few generals have done better under so many extremely perplexing difficulties. He was sometimes despondent for a moment but never beaten.

Lord Rawdon returned toward Friday's ferry and thence he collected his forces at Orangeburg and awaited Greene's movements. The latter also collected his forces and tried to draw Lord Rawdon out of his fortifications, to try the issue of battle in the open; but when the challenge was not accepted, Gen. Greene withdrew into summer quarters on the High Hills of Santee and remained there from the 13th of July till early in September. On the 14th General Sumter with an excellent command, consisting of state troops, except Lee's cavalry, crossed the Santee, and through Lee captured Dorchester without a battle, with much plunder in the shape of horses, ammunition and wagons. Col. Wade Hampton also captured some prisoners and horses at a church. On the 15th he dashed down to the Quarter House in four miles of the city and captured prisoners. On the day following was fought the first skirmish at Wadboo bridge which discomfited the attacking parties but caused the retreat of the enemy under Col. Coates. The casualties in this battle fell largely to the command of Marion, which was down from the Pee Dee and Williamsburg sections.

General Sumter's raid sent alarm to the gates of Charles Town. Besides 150 prisoners, stores of much value, above what could be carried off, were destroyed. The raid was made while the main armies were unemployed in the heat of summer, and it was to be paralleled by another made by Marion beginning August 22nd and ending September 2nd just before Greene was breaking up at the High Hills with a view of attacking Col. Stuart who had succeeded Lord Rawdon in command of the British. His own condensed report gives an idea of how much toil and danger Gen. Marion could press into eleven days, travelling over 200 miles, planning battles, laying ambuscades, gaining a victory less complete on account of inefficient subordinates, while fasting 24 hours in the midst of danger and deaths.

Aug. 22. Started to Col. Hardin's.

Aug. 23. Arrived at Round O and found the Colonel very sick.

Aug. 24. Marched to Horse Shoe.

Aug. 26. Was joined at night by Col. Stafford with 150 men and Maj. Hardin with 80, which made our number about 400.

27th crossed the great swamp at the head of the Ashepoo and encamped in 3 miles of the enemy, who had 180 Hessians, 150 British, 80 of the Queen's Rangers, 130 tories.

The guard Marion placed at an important causeway abandoned it without firing a gun.

28th. followed the enemy who was found too strong to attack.

29th passed the Fish Ponds 3 miles above the enemy at Ashepoo.

30th. went below them and formed an ambuscade near Parker's ferry about 110 yards of the road the enemy must pass, 100 tories being at the ferry. Here they remained till sunset when the tories in passing saw the enemy and started the firing. The cavalry of the enemy came riding up pell mell only to be fired at by the whole line. The victory was spoiled by a wretch who shouted out they are fllanking us on the right and allowed the enemy to retire in order during the consequent confusion. Cols. Stafford, Ervin and Horry behaved well in battle, Maj. Hardin and Maj. Cooper did not obey orders. The enemy retreated toward Charles Town and a party sent out found over 40 dead and wounded horses. The enemy lost upwards of 80 men and several officers wounded.

31st. Started to give some orders to Col. Hardin and put that part of the country in a more regular way for doing their duty.

1st of Sept., at eleven o'clock left Round O and marched 42 miles that night.

South Carolina

2nd. Arrived at St. Stevens and found the enemy at Eutaw.

3rd. reported the above with a hint that he would try to annoy the enemy at Eutaw as soon as his horses were a little recovered."

Capt. Cooper left behind to cover his expedition to Edisto, routed tories, drove off cattle from Dorchester and brought prisoners to the camp where Marion was awaiting him.

This affair which saved Hardin drew the attention of Congress to Marion and his brave officers and men and elicited a tardy vote of thanks. On the 5th of September, Gen. Greene having waited for Marion's return, set out from the High Hills to attack the British main army at Eutaw, on the 8th of September. Gen. Greene had many reasons for counting on a complete victory with his continentals from Maryland, Virginia and North Carolina and the seasoned marksmen under Sumter, Marion and other South Carolina leaders. The victory would have been his, it is agreed, had his own men, hungry, thirsty and poorly clad, not passed through the British camp and had not a well built brick house served the British in their extremity for a fortress. It was a bloody battle in which the lives of men and horses were lavishly sacrificed. Of the 2092[4] men reported under Greene 340 were under Marion. Greene's casualties were reported to be 517, the enemy's 683. Both sides claimed the victory. The British retained the field, after their men had been routed, but in the end the Americans were thrown back and roughly handled by Major Majoribanks whose presence of mind and good generalship scattered the enemy and saved Stuart from a disastrous rout. The British took no prisoners and though reinforced, retired

---
[4]McCrady's S. C. in the Revolution 1780-1783, p. 463.

toward Charles Town leaving 70 sick or wounded, 1000 arms broken, 20 or 30 barrels of rum poured out and other stores abandoned.

Gen. Greene's cavalry was superior to that of the enemy and gave him the advantage in pursuing the retreating enemy and taking a part of the 500 prisoners rounded up on the occasion. The soldiers under Marion from Williamsburg County, not far from Eutaw, were well represented in this sanguinary struggle, who nearly overpowered by heat and thirst threw themselves flat pell mell over one another in and around the spring only to get a drop of the water to ease their parched tongues and exhausted bodies. John Clary, William Wilson and James Bradley were in this battle and years afterwards not being of one mind as Elders of the Church, Mr. Clary said: "How can we be on opposite sides when we fought side by side during the whole day, in different places on the battle ground, whether by our own charges or forced back by the enemy." "No, no," said Wilson, "and to add to that day's horrors" said Bradley we were so busy loading our guns and firing and defending ourselves in the hand to hand fight that we could not assist our comrades in the fight, who, wounded at our side, were falling at our feet.[5]

Six days after the battle Gov. Rutledge called it a glorious victory; by that time it was clearly seen that in spite of the repulse from the brick house that the enemy had been greatly weakened and dispirited. And it was after this final great battle that the governor bestirred himself in setting up civil government. William Richardson was sent out to get indigo, the reorganization of the militia was expedited, the suspension of continental and state currency as tender in law was

---

[5] McGill's Reminiscences of Williamsburg County, p. 282.

proclaimed and a proclamation offering pardon to the rank and file of tories, who would offer to serve six months in the ranks and on other specified conditions, certain classes of the preeminently wicked tories being expected. The naming of the ordinaries for the counties and the managers of election for members of the House and assembly was entrusted to the Brigadiers who had better opportunities to know the men that could be trusted.

One other unexpected development followed the battle and it grew out of happenings in North Carolina. The activity of the tories, notwithstanding the truce with Gainey who could not control individuals, was renewed on the Waccamaw, on Britton's Neck and Lynch's Creek and even at Indian Town, the home of John James, an alarm caused him to collect 40 men to defend the stores at that place. Gainey had agreed to the truce and was anxious to observe it, but he complained of Col. Murphy's violation of the terms and Murphy retorted that his own horses had been driven off. Skirmishes continued throughout the state from Greenville, upper Pee Dee, to Berkeley county during the closing months of this great year in the history of South Carolina and of the United States. Cornwallis had surrendered, the battle of Eutaw had reversed the situation of the two armies at the beginning of the year and that oneness of heart and purpose which had pressed together the continentals and the militia on voluntary principles, was giving way to estrangement caused by trying to economise by putting order, discipline and due submission in its place.

Gen. Greene was now facing difficulties kin to those which vexed Lord Cornwallis. In driving the enemy into the Charles Town Neck, he found the enemy in his front and the tories in his rear. This divided his attention and made him plan to break up the tory solidarity which harassed him more than the British, by granting humane terms of accommodation. The report that large reinforcement had arrived in Charles Town caused the proclamation calling the assembly to meet at Jacksonborough, a respectable village near Charles Town, to be deferred till the New Year, after the report was discredited. This little village with its several dozens of homes was saved from the oblivion which covered the early villages located by haphazard, by the fact that the legislature of 1781 met in it.

The last year of the war in South Carolina came gradually and slowly to a frazzled end. Gen. Sumter with his headquarters at Orangeburg, was not in the battle of Eutaw not being able to mount his horse. He was in a position to realize more fully than Gen. Greene the demoralization that was pervading the American side. The militia were trifling, consisting of the worst men and arms in the brigade and the state troops were below expectation and desertions were not uncommon. His small brigade was scattered here and there, making drives after tories, of whom it seemed the woods were full; but notwithstanding he was kept in touch by his men and spies with the development in and around Charles Town and was not slow to communicate to Gen. Greene and suggest possible moves to be made.

By the middle of December 1781, Gen. Sumter had reached a point where there had to be some bending or breaking. Gov. Rutledge had ordered the mounted militia to return on foot and leave their horses at home but this order was not enforced in all the brigades. Gen. Sumter complained of this partiality and got the cool reply that it was done at Greene's special request. Gen. Sumter also notified Gen. Greene that he was dismounting his infantry but it was disagreeable to him and to his men on account of the neglect of his brigade by the public. Gen. Greene noticed the remark and declared as an excuse that poverty and want stared them in the face every where and praised Gen. Sumter's service to the state at times when many men were hiding their heads. The commendation of his past services was not thrown away upon the judicious minded Sumter. He knew it was deserved; but it did not prevent his telling Gen. Greene that the treatment of his brigade was owing to design and not inability and begged not to be honored with farther commands before a proper inquiry made as to his worthiness to receive them. Why Gen. Greene demanded the horses should be left at home might be explained on the score of economy and after the surrender at Yorktown, a less need for them; but why Gen. Sumter felt that his brigade was designedly militated against Gen. Greene failed to elicit by instituting an investigation. Gov. Rutledge was at the close of his term greatly influenced by the success of Gen. Greene's strategy in driving the enemy into Charles Town Neck and Gen. Greene seeing the end in sight felt in the interest of a disciplined and subordinated army, able and willing to part with Gen. Sumter rather than to allow the few militia under Sumter to keep their horses. And thus, taking only a surface view of the matter, Gen. Greene was eliminating regretfully a man who had served his state in its darkest hour, in the interest of the same state at a later time, while Gen. Sumter resigned because he felt that he would be mean and pusillanimous if he bore in silence the ludicrous treatment of his brigade.

The year 1782 opened in the tented field inauspiciously. On the 2nd of January at Videau's bridge, the patriots were worsted and the 24th of February were two reverses one at Savannah River and one at Wambaw, and on the next day Gen. Marion was worsted; for in his absence the enemy wisely surmised that the officers left in charge while Marion was in the Assembly might be surprised and the soldiers scattered and demoralized. In this they were not mistaken. Marion was now the hope of the state. Sumter was on the shelf and Marion's men were part new recruits, new whigs, late tories who had come in under Gov. Rutledge's proclamation. Gen. Greene was still in command but becoming less and less essential to the situation. It was the genius of Marion only that glistened now and then and the cool determined bravery of Pickens that kept up the standard of the previous year. Early in the year, Gen. Pickens marched into Oconee county and destroyed Indian villages and in September he set out with about 400 men and in 14 days reduced the militant Cherokees to the ranks of suppliants for peace which some of them had interrupted by the advice of British emissaries. And in June, Gen. Marion found it necessary to glide noiselessly into the Pee Dee to quell another disturbance raised by an emissary of the British sent out for the purpose of recalling Marion from the front. Gainey with his 500 tories were suddenly faced by Marion and his men and Gainey was overcome by Marion's diplomacy rather than by his skill in battle. So rapid was his triumph that he was back unperceived by the enemy in time to turn the second skirmish at Wadboo into a victory.[6] We are told that Gen. Marion's career as an officer was closed at Wadboo, but not on what day, by the current histories. He had been a member of the recent Assembly and went home from the army penniless to find his plantation stripped of everything portable or that could be led or

---

[6]South Carolina Historical & Genealogical Magazine, V. 17, p. 176.

driven. In the Assembly of 1783, he was voted a gold medal for his services to the state. He was a man however whom gold could not decorate. His qualities shone out in the dark days as a light in midnight surroundings and was still shining by contrast when Sherman in 1865 was passing victoriously over his field of action. He was in the Assembly but silent when that body voted 10,000 guineas to Gen. Greene as "singular marks of their approbation and gratitude." There has been a general acquiescence in the justice of the gratuity; for Gen. Greene was in the service seven years without an hour's leave and could give no attention to his private affairs. That he had proven himself a capable general in 1781 there ought not to be a doubt and yet when one looks below the surface, he can hardly avoid the conclusion that the general who was willing in the great poverty of the state to accept such a gratuity was not born under a southern sun. Perhaps under the colonial government when the governor and council came from the east, South Carolinians were learning to overlook native virtue and genius in the enchantment lent by distance. So it appeared in 1784 when Gen. Marion reduced to poverty by the war was put in command of Fort Johnson at a salary of 500 pounds, but in a year or two complaints were made of the useless tax and it was reduced to $500 and then abolished.[7]

Gen. Greene presided over the evacuation of Charles Town and brought to a successful conclusion the devastating war. How it left the state can be conjectured from the 1400 widows and orphans left in Ninety Six district and the journeys of two men in the year of the evacuation. One was passing through Sumter and Darlington on horse back accompanied by a servant,

---
[7]Simms' Marion.

along the route ravaged by Wemyss and Tarleton. After riding till late at night, without refreshment, or place of rest for himself and his jaded horses, he stopped under a tree, tied the horses each to a bush that they might eat the leaves, while he and his servant laid down on the ground, without dinner or supper and slept soundly under the anodyne influence of fatigue. At the dawn of day he awoke and heard indistinctly the crowing of a cock. They mounted their horses and followed the welcome sound in that dreary waste. They soon found the log cabin from which issued the cock's friendly invitation and obtained the much needed food for man and beast. This rough habitation was the only one in many miles and it had been built off the road that it might be safer from discovery.

The other journey was made from Georgetown to Gen. Greene's army by Gen. Moultrie after his release from captivity. "It was the most dull, melancholy dreary ride," said the General, "that any one could possibly take, of about 100 miles through the woods of that country which I had been accustomed to see abound with live stock and wild fowl of every kind, was now destitute of all. It had been so completely chequered by the different parties that no part of it had been left unexplored; consequently not the vestiges of horses, cattle, hogs, or deer, etc. were to be found. The squirrels and birds of every kind were totally destroyed. The dragoons told me that on their scouts no living creature was to be seen except now and then a few camp scavengers picking the bones of some unfortunate fellows who had been shot or cut down and left in the woods above ground."

Gen. Moultrie was in the select number allowed to be in the company with Gen. Greene and his continentals who entered the city on the 18th of December

1782. As the years passed and events could be seen in their relative importance and true proportions, it was noticed with pain that the militia was not present at the evacuation. "The American regular army entered it in triumph, but our poor partisans were thought too irregular, too ragged of raiment, to share this triumph! They were not too ragged to fight, only too ragged for show."[8]

A northern author passed this judgment on Greene, the hero of the hour, and upon South Carolinians: "To the women of South Carolina and to Marion, Sumter and Pickens, who kept the field without the promise of men, money or supplies, it was owing that the spirit and name of liberty did not become utterly extinct."

The returning soldier and the exiles were at their old places of residence in time to spend their Christmas. Many of them were penniless and it was indeed waste which greeted their eyes. Besides the men lost by disease and in battle, estimated by Weems at 4000, and the slaves abducted, there were missing old men and women who had been turned adrift in want and weather and infants[9] who expired in the arms of their fleeing mothers. The tempest of war was over but the angry waves did not subside at once. Murders and robbery and revenge for past injuries were common. A country physician at Saltcatcher and a planter from Ninety Six in passing near Dorchester were murdered and the gov-

---

[8]Quoted by McCrady. Vol. 1780-1783, p. 674.

[9]A stone in the graveyard at Haley's ferry stands over "the remains of Harriet H. the daughter of Gen. H. W. Harrington who being exposed to the inclemency of the sickly season fell a sacrifice to the cruelty of a vindictive foe." Mrs. Botsford reached in her flight with her dead babe in her arms the house of a tory, who reluctantly allowed her to occupy the loom house, abused her for being the wife of a rebel and took her last two dollars in silver as compensation, for the room with a little water to drink. Memoir of Elder Botsford, p. 57.

ernor was offering rewards for ruffians operating in different localities and for incendiaries in town. Judge Burke with great fearlessness bearded the lion of lawlessness in June while addressing the jury. He likened the state to a ship needing repair after it had weathered the storm and descanted on the evil effects of war which begets contempt for law and a love for pleasure and dissipation and unhinges the mind from the principles of religion and morality. He regarded private revenge as the demon of civil discord, arising from the habit of putting their enemies to death and reconciling their minds to the killing of one another, an evidence that man may by custom become so brutalized as to relish human blood the more he has spilt of it. He referred to the assassinations in the country and the four murders in the city in the previous six months. It was a dishonor to the Revolution "if we should continue the butcher policy of worrying each other by mutual hatred and revenge and keep up the destruction of whig and tory when the cause of it was done away and worse than that nature herself would share in the reproach of it as we should then afford a clearer evidence of the wretchedness and depravity she has entailed upon us." Oblivion of past injuries and past errors and a disposition of benevolence going out through the law to connect our citizens in ties of harmony and common brotherhood, he commended, that it might be well with them and their children. Judge Burke was the South Carolina Thrasybulus who after the reign of the 30 tyrants and the 1500 estimated victims of their cruelty, caused an amnesty to be proclaimed and enforced. The judge at Cheraw after a few years noted with pleasure that benevolence and hospitality marked again the plantations and respect and piety the churches and remarked upon the need of the calm operation of judgment and temperate admonitions of reason to take the place of the dominion of passion and licentiousness which pervaded the state.

From many quarters came precept on precept in support of a virtuous citizenship in the freer atmosphere of a democracy. Justice Champion explained to the jury at Lancaster how much greater the evil of luxury was in a democracy than in a monarchy and a pastoral letter of a Presbyterian origin was called out by the decadence of morality attested by non-attendance at worship and non-observance of the Sabbath. In Monarchies, it said, sense of honor, subordination of rank in society, and the rigor of despotic government must supply in some measure the place of virtue in producing public order, but in free states where the power is ultimately lodged in the body of the people, if there is a general corruption of the mass, the government itself must speedily be dissolved.

Rev. Mr. Botsford, a refugee, returned to the Welsh Neck Church, made the observation, "The war has made sad havoc of friends and property; and religion was almost forgotten. The prospect of peace, however, cast a few rays of cheering light into the dismal gloom and amidst the wreck of property, the prostration of fond hopes and the weeping and lamentation for fathers, sons and brothers slain, caused the voice of joy and gladness once more to be heard."

CHAPTER XXII

LEGISLATIVE PROCEEDINGS

The first session of the Legislature after the fall of Charles Town was held at Jacksonborough beginning Jan. 8, 1782, and adjourning on Feb. 26 following. Gov. Rutledge had been looking forward to this gathering, that he might give an account of his stewardship, make recommendations and resign his dictatorship to his successor who should reestablish the laws. Among his recommendations in the address before the Assembly was a liberal appropriation to Gen. Greene, in response to which 10,000 guineas were appropriated for his benefit. In this and the ensuing session Tristam Thomas, William DeWitt, Philip Pledger, Lemuel Benton, William and Capt. Pegues, represented St. David's Parish. William Benison, Christopher Gadsden, Peter Horry and Thomas Mitchell represented Prince George Winyaw, John Baxter, Maj. John James, John McCauley, William McCottry and Thomas Potts represented Prince Frederick; William Allston and Timothy Dwight represented All Saints.

In August Gov. Matthews who succeeded Gov. Rutledge allowed certain British subjects to remain in town to dispose of their merchandise, a kindness that was approved by the Assembly and productive of doubtful legislation in a few years. Their presence and the credit they offered to the planters exhausted by the war, gave the authorities and the people much anxiety. The merchants sold out their slaves in great numbers at immense profit on credit; but when the day of reckoning came from one end of the state to the other, inability to meet obligations caused suits which exposed the estates to sale at a time when money was so scarce that property went far below its value.

The debtor class seeing the fate awaiting them, began to see what ought to have been visible before they went into debt, that they had rashly assumed obligations which were beyond their power to meet. It was too near the time when whig and tory struggled for the mastery for the multitude of them to sit quietly and see the courts deciding in favor of the tory or British money lender. The debtors in a fright began to revive the Regulation methods of defying law and resisting the sheriff. Col. Mayham, who had given Gen. Marion and Col. Horry trouble, surpassed the other debtors in giving reins to his passion by making the server of the sheriff's writ eat it in his presence. He was tried in Charles Town and sentenced to imprisonment of four months and a fine.

The judges in the meanwhile seeing the drift toward a government by the populace, consulted with the governor and the governor advised the legislature to consult the bench of judges and learn from them the ruin that was pendent over hundreds. If allowed to operate forcibly the laws would transfer the whole property of a large part of the citizens into the possession of aliens and this much under its real worth. Here again in the language of Judge Burke the situation can be set in a clear light: "A great number of suits had been brought against various persons for debts contracted in 1784 and 1785 as the crops had failed in every part of the state, it became impossible to satisfy such creditors as would persist in suing: added to this when property was seized by the sheriff and set up for sale, such was the scarcity of money that if one fourth of the actual value was offered for property, it was considered a wonder; this ruinous practice provided a combination amongst the people at Camden and they unanimously determined to stop the courts from proceeding until something effective could be agreed on by the legislature to avert the general ruin that threatened to fall on them. On a representation of this to the governor, he called a meeting of the legislature and in consequence of his recommendation a grand committee of the house met for three days, after that the business was carried before the house when it took up much time and every gentleman must remember what difficulties appeared and what embarrassments and perplexities stood in their way, how much debate ensued upon the best method to relieve such persons as were in debt and unable to pay, and yet to offer something to their creditors; at last this bill for regulating sheriffs' sales was brought forward and after mature consideration agreed on; as the best way of suspending the operation of the laws, a gentle manner of shutting up the courts, for that it absolutely shut them up he felt himself perfectly satisfied; it was however hoped that the crops of this year might introduce more specie amongst us and this bill would cease to be in effect about the time when money became more plenty; for our crops of this year had been as those of the preceding ones and public distress had rather increased than diminished. As much relief was expected from the paper medium until it could be issued, what good consequences could reasonably be looked for from permitting property to be seized from its present owners and set to sale? There was not at this time 50,000 pounds of specie in circulation; the debts due to individuals perhaps amounted to a million, now what monstrous injustice would be to expose so great a body of property to public sale at a time when the specie in this state bore so small a proportion of its value. But he could assure gentlemen that even if they as a legislative body were to resolve on allowing such an impolitic and ruinous mode of creditors harassing debtors, that the people would not suffer it; nor did he think

5,000 troops the best in America or Europe could enforce obedience to the Common Pleas: he wished to prevent mischief and because he well knew the high spirit of the people; perhaps this might hurt our credit, but for this he did not feel himself so anxious; he wished a fair and punctual discharge of debts, foreign and domestic and he did not doubt satisfaction would be made as soon as possible; but he thought our first care ought to be an attention to our internal improvement in preference to foreign credit; wise men will make generous allowance for our conduct when they consider our situation. The people are everywhere peaceable and well disposed; the only way to keep them so was by continuing the sheriffs' sale[1] act until the new paper medium had got into general circulation."

The sanity of Judge Burke's reasoning and conduct was fully established by a pursuit of the opposite course in Massachusetts where the law was allowed to operate as in normal times. A loyalist brought suit against a debtor, partly as a test case and found himself rewarded with principal and compound interest. Others followed and caused Shay's rebellion and by the lawlessness of the men whom he led, that state was in no little measure prepared to adopt a strong general government in preference to the confederation; and the same wish was fostered for a strong government by the money lenders in South Carolina who suffered by the pine barren act.

A different view is presented in Ford's[3] Journal of 1785-86: "Foreseeing the great demand there would

---

[1]The regulation of sheriff sales was called "the pine barren act" because it authorized the debtor in case of prosecution to tender any kind of land in payment (to be valued by persons chosen for that purpose) at 2/3 their value and if they excused the debt the creditor to give his bond and security for the remainder. Timothy Ford. Historical & Genealogical Magazine, Vol. XIII.

[3]Historical and Genealogical Magazine, Vol. XIII, p. 133.

be for slaves and being the only person possessed of capital, they early imported vast cargoes of negroes from Africa. The planters impelled by their necessities to procure slaves eagerly grasped at the first opportunities that offered; and unable to pay down the cash supplied themselves on credit, at whatever rate the British merchants were pleased to fix; and they failed not to take advantage of their necessities and advanced upon them from 50 to 75 per cent. In a short time they became the creditors of a great part of the state; and the infatuated debtors began to view the situation with a degree of regret and concern to the prospect of which they had been put too easily or voluntarily blinded by their necessities at this time of the contract. The time of payment began to draw nigh and they began to perceive (as they might or perhaps did foresee) how far they must fall short of their engagements. The merchants influenced by no particular feelings of generosity to their late enemies, or pressed by their credit to make remittances, or as likely as either, expecting to get into their possessions the plantations of their debtors for much less than their value, insisted rigidly upon the punctual fulfillment of their contracts. The crisis was important and melancholy for the planters and many of them were torn to pieces by legal process. An universal alarm took place—it became a common cause on both sides. The court of justice being the resort of one became the terror and hatred of the other. The sheriff and the officers were threatened in the execution of their duty; and at length the people in the district of Camden grew outrageous—planted out sentinals to intercept the sheriff and put the laws at defiance; and one Col. Mayham being served by the sheriff with a writ, obliged him to eat it on the spot.

"News of these transactions being brought, the governor immediately assembled the legislature, laid before them the proceedings in the language of a frightened man, and requested them to deliberate on the subject and strike out some mode either of restoring to the laws their wonted efficacy or of abating their vigor. They took into consideration the distresses of the people, the necessities of which first impelled them to forego the dictates of judgment and discretion, and the character of the persons who had thus taken advantage of them. On the one hand it was urged that no precedent is more dangerous to society or more destructive of public credit, than that of the legislatures interfering in private contracts fairly made; that it unsettled all confidence between man and man, renders property uncertain, breaks down the pillars of commerce and makes the people licentious and ungovernable. That the acts already passed with regard to old debts arose from a very singular and uncommon necessity, which alone could have justified them; as contracting parties before the war could not foresee the great depredations that were about to be committed on their property and that of war had so disabled them to pay their debts. Circumstances were now different. They had contracted their late debts with their eyes open and could make no such plea. If they were able to pay they ought to be compelled to do it—if not, they knew it beforehand, and therefore deserved to be distressed for their fraudulent contracts. In a word that the legislature could not afford them countenance or relief without flagrantly invading the rights of individuals who having already been treated like citizens (though they became so by sufferance) ought now to enjoy the privileges of such. On the other hand it was alleged that the people after several years suspension from business, after the loss of a great part of their property, and a consumption of their fortunes in exile, viewed their forlorn situation as the prelude of their speedy ruin unless they immediately availed themselves of their plantations; which having been stripped of their stock could get no relief unless they could fall on some mode of procuring negroes. That when the British merchant threw out the bait they took it as their only resource; and that it was no wonder their necessities got the better of their judgment. They represented them as harpies playing upon those distresses and using the word *tory* as a weapon, suggested that they had premeditated the design of getting into their hands extensive property thereby to infuse British influence into the government of this country and lastly that they might well afford to delay the recovery of their debts, seeing they sold at such exhorbitant prices, and that the debts were now at interest. These and like arguments applying to the prejudices, the passions, and the interest of the legislature, inclined them to interpose in behalf of the debtors; and being furnished with a plausible pretext for so doing from the recent meetings in the state, they easily brought themselves to pass an act for the regulation of sheriff sales commonly called the "pine barren act" because it authorized the debtor in case of prosecution to tender any kind of lands in payment (to be valued by persons chosen for that purpose) at 2/3 their value, and if they exceeded the debt the creditor to give his bond and security for the remainder payable in six months. Thus the legislature at one stroke put an end to all civil prosecutions by this most impolitic and iniquitous law. Such is the nature of a republican government . . .

"The person who had committed this daring abuse upon the sheriff was prosecuted and tried in Charles Town. The court sentenced him to four months imprisonment, a heavy fine and himself and two securities to be bound to the peace for six years. The governor suspended the sentence until the meeting of the legislature, who upon his submission entirely reversed the decree.

"On the 12th of October, in this same session, the legislature passed an act to establish a medium of circulation to the amount of 100,000 pounds. The failure of the crops and the exportation of specie had made the sheriff sale act a necessity and then the straits into which that act thrust the merchants made the legislators ready for this experiment for the public relief and to prevent the bankruptcy of the merchants and of the treasury to which they were indebted. Judge Pendleton thus discoursed on its origin: He had never desired to be understood as particularly sanguine for a paper emission, but at the last session several plans to relieve the national distresses by issuing paper money were then offered and all were rejected. Willing to contribute his mite, he had the honor to offer a plan which was received and passed into law. No person was to borrow more than 250 or less than 30 pounds, and every loan was to be secured by real estate of threefold value or by the deposition of twice the value in gold or silver plate. The whole to be repaid in five installments. The merchants were to be favored by placing one fifth of the whole amount in Charles Town. They were willing to receive it on a par with gold and silver and three merchants in England had signified their willingness to accept it. On May 1st, 1786 the committee of the Loan Office was ready for the disbursement of the funds. The merchants met soon after and formally agreed to accept it as currency equal to gold or silver and further agreed not to purchase the produce of a planter who refused it. The planters also adopted similar agreements. An editor in Jamaica found the paper currency to be received for debts, duties and taxes by the treasury and it appeared to him as unexceptional an Act and free from defects and as little liable to depreciation as any paper currency could well be formed." But not a few who had tenacious memories had great aversion to that species of currency. Mr. Bee, a legislator, when it served a good purpose of preventing another issue said in 1787, "Our paper medium grew better every day, answers all purposes of interior trade, being but a small discount and might soon be expected to pass at par if left to itself."[2]

The Sheriff Sale Act was *functus officio* practically null and void by January 1, 1787. The number of delinquents who had to be sued at the end of five years for paper money lent by the state was 38. Among those that were tardy on the Pee Dee were men mostly in good financial standing: Daniel Sparks, James Keith, Charles Evans, John O'Neill, Daniel DuBose, Enoch Evans, Benjamin Hicks, Drury Robertson, Alexander McIntosh, and David Graham on the Waccamaw. The interest collected from this loan was applied to the foreign debt, and in 1792 steps were taken to gradually call in and sink the paper medium. General Pinckney said in Congress that a majority of the people in South Carloina were notoriously for paper money. In 1791, a motion to issue 500,000 pounds in paper bills was negatived by a vote of 110 to 48 showing that a change had come over the people. The specie was kept in Pennsylvania by plugging the coin so as to lessen its worth abroad and yet be acceptable as a medium of exchange at home.

---

[2]Judge Brevard said that the paper medium "was the ruin of many and the public ultimately suffered by it. Judge Champion called it a wise and salutary measure. Vol. I, p. 435, Statutes or S. C.

CHAPTER XXIII

REVOLUTIONARY CLAIMS

Stub entries to Indents for Revolutionary Claims, now being edited,[1] bring to light a larger army than that commanded by Gen. Greene. One of its parts was in the field, another foraged for its subsistence and a third remained at home, some of them alternately, and produced food and provender for the soldiers, the foragers and for the men, women and children and slaves at home. The part of the work performed at home was the most essential for the final success of the contest. To the soldier who left his home to fight for his country, men everywhere ascribe honor, but to the old men and women and to the lowly slaves who in large numbers tilled the soil, little thought has been given, beyond the number of the latter abducted by the British and the consequent losses. It ought not to be forgotten that the rice upon which the army largely subsisted in 1781-2 was made by slaves and the indigo also which was converted into cash by Gov. Rutledge in this same period.

An army has been likened for milleniums to an animal organism with its commander as its head; but these stub entries deal with the individuals who composed the army, every one of whom who presented a claim against the state was at the same time presenting a brief history of himself during the long struggle. Unfortunately the men under Marion were paid at random, with no mention of their company and regiment and this indefiniteness is magnified by the duplication of names. John Smith would have answered to his name in 44 homes in the state as the head of a family and 26 John Browns and a multitude of others from ten to two times. The

---

[1] By A. S. Salley, Jr., Secretary Historical Commission of S. C.

phonetic spelling of the times which confused the names like Burquitt and Burket, Murphy and Murfee, Sanders and Saunders and interpreted Cris Hunt into Criswell Hunt or Christopher Hunt admonishes one that there is need of circumspection. In the Revolution as in 1865, South Carolina escaped a complete devastation. In an area of over 30,000 square miles the good providence of God reserved some farms from destruction, some of them estates of men who had died or been killed in the war, on which were raised for the quarter master year after year corn and wheat ground into meal and flour, rice, potatoes, beef, pork, cattle, swine, sheep, fruits or vegetables and other things edible, all or several of which are summed up in the receipts as "sundries." Horses and provender, wagons and teams, were also forced into service, but after it was all over, the bankrupt state called for all the claims against it, met its honest obligations, with sterling money and full interest. Some gleanings from the Stub Entries, LN, OQ, UW and RT, not intended to be exhaustive and from the first census (in this state in 1792) of All Saints, Prince George and Prince Frederick parishes and of the Cheraw district are presented in corroboration of the above mentioned statements:

All Saints parish lying on Waccamaw and the ocean contained one hundred and three heads of families, of whom 65 held one or more slaves. The six Allston families reported in their possession 877 of the 1795 slaves in the parish. Robert Heriot came next with 128, John Morrall with 60, Polly and John La Bruce with 55 and 43, Thomas Waring with 58 and Paul Michau with 38. According to the spelling of the census, Benjamin Allston, Sr. & Jr., John, Joseph and Thomas and William Allston were in All Saints parish, Elizabeth Allston in Prince George. Of the three "Alston" families given, two were near or in Charles Town and one, Samuel, in Fairfield whose name is retained in a station above Columbia. Josias Allston's estate is placed in Prince George under John Cogdell with 41 slaves. He and Francis Allston contributed jointly to the needs of the state.

Joseph Allston furnished in 1779, '80, '81, '82 provisions and forage valued at 982 pounds, 17 shillings, 4 pence sterling or over $1200 a year. Capt. John Allston in 1780 and 1782, supplied for continental and militia use, sundries amounting to £615. 10. 10.

Francis and Josias Allston for sundries in 1780 and 1781 received £44. 4. 7. The same names with one "l" received, one £25. 7. 6. for 1134 pounds indigo, the other £129. 14. 9. for 979 pounds, and in the same doubtful spelling was Peter Alston, for sundries in 1781 £1. 15. 10.

Georgetown fell in May 1780 and was recovered in 1781, and thus a short period and distance from military posts and roads and the absence of resident tories favored the parish which was predominantly for independence.

Prince George Winyaw, was doomed to British rule for a while, because of its port. As soon as it was occupied misleading proclamations from Gen. Clinton led 33 of its citizens to ask to be restored to citizenship. These no doubt when forced to choose between the belligerents, preferred to suffer with the state.

Cleland Kinloch left 300 slaves. Francis, his brother, had 212 and Archibald Taylor 166, Thomas Butler and Paul Trapier each 137. William Brailsford and John Pyatt 120 each, Joseph Wragg 119, Screven's Estate 115, Elizabeth Allston and James Hambleton 112 each, Thomas Whitfield 94, Edward Crock 87, John Wilson 79, Benjamin Smith 71, Peter Horry 66, Archibald Smith 65,

Hugh Horry 62, John Singleton 57, Matthew Irvine 55, Henry Lenud, George Skinner and Thomas Waties 50 each. The following entries condensed show the sort of activites for which claims were made:

Baxter, James and John, for beef in 1781-2. £210.

Bethea, Jesse—for corn beef in 1781-2. £25. 8. 8.

Bingham, Thomas for 500 pounds beef for continental army. £6. 8. 4.

Britton, Daniel, estate of for sundries 1778 & 1781. £48. 1. 9.

Burquett, Ephriam, for 75 days in militia in 1782. £5. 7. 1.

Cogdell, George, pork for Continentals & hire of negroes 5 days. £21. 3. 7.

Coker, Thomas—for sundries in 1781 & militia duty. £53. 12.10.

Dunnam, Ebenezer—for two hogs for militia use in 1782. £3. 5. 4.

Fleming, James, Jr. for 161 days in militia in 1780-2. £4. 14.

Foissin, Peter for services as Lieutenant in S. C. Continental regiment in 1779-82. £388. 10.

Ford, George for 15 barrels of rice in 1782 for the garrison at Georgetown and 10 barrels for Continental use in 1783. £96. 13. 7. Of the 41 Ford families in South Carolina at the first census, George, James, Joseph, Nathaniel, Preserved and one of the three Stephens were in Prince George parish.

Harvey, Jacob William. for sundries in 1780-1783. £194. 15.

Hume, Robert estate of for forage and provisions in 1780 & 1781. £69. 6.

Kinloch, Francis, estate of for sundries in 1782-3. £121. 8. 10.

LaBruce, Thomas—beef for continental use Jan. 1783. £3. 11. 10.

Lenud, Henry—for provisions and horses for militia use & for garrison of Georgetown 1781-3. £446. 19. 9.

Pawley, Anthony—for provisions for continental use. 1782. £46. 15.

Pawley, Percival, sundries for state troops 1779-1783. £13. 7. 9.

Postell, John, sr. for sundries furnished in 1780-83. £91. 14.

Pyatt, John for provisions for militia 1781-2. £61. 5.

Swinton, William for service as Quartermaster in 1780, 1781, 1782. £262. 18. 8.

Trapier, Benjamin for 147 days hire of wagon in 1782. £10. 10.

Rothmather, Col. Job. for 9, 982 rations for the use of the Continentals. £326. 8.

Shoemake, John for 34 days duty in militia in 1782. £2. 8. 6.

Shoemake, John for 250 bushels of corn, for apples for 20 barrels of cider and peaches for 32 gallons of brandy. £60. 11. The Shoemakes were restricted to Prince George in the census.

Prince Frederick parish had the misfortune of being in a central position which made it common ground for the conflict of British and Americans, tories and whigs. It presented the appearance of a more democratic neighborhood where inequalities of possessions were not conspicuous. Theodore Gourdin died within the Revolution and Theodore Jr. reported 150 slaves and next to him was Stephen Ford with 98. The respected actor in the last years of the Colony, Christopher Gadsden, with 90 slaves came third in number of dependents. Then came in succession Moses Murfee 87, John Baxter 83, Benjamin Porter 67, Alen McKnight 58, James Anderson 57, Hugh Montgomery 52, John Dickey 45, William Snow, estate of, 43, John Witherspoon 40 and many others with smaller numbers. Prince Frederick had in its bounds the Scotch-Irish colony as well as the patriotic yeomanry, of other lineage. Richard Green, a descendant of the Greens, the first settlers of Prince Frederick, was a valiant soldier under General Marion. He and four brothers volunteered after the fall of Charles Town and fought in almost all of Marion's engagements. Maj. Gainey with another tory visited his mother's house one night when Richard and James happened to be on furlough. They decamped at once with the boys in hot pursuit. This Maj. Gainey was the same man who carried the bayonet in his back into Georgetown. Being asked how it felt, replied it gave great pain but it was not half so bad as when Mr. Green's ball knocked nearly all his teeth down[2] his throat. Richard Green was a devout Methodist, too proud to accept a pension.

Barr, James. for provisions, forage for militia in 1781-1782. £5. 15. 1.

Baxter, John for 364 days duty as Captain & Major. £165. 19. 1.

Boone, Capers—for 458 pounds of indigo & 200 lbs beef in 1781. £51. 12. 3.

Boone, Thomas—for provisions and forage in 1782-3. £4. 19. 3.

Boyd, John for sundries for militia in 1780-1782. £35. 5. 8.

---

[2]Winyaw Intelligencer, Nov. 17, 1827.

South Carolina

Dobbin, John—for provisions and forage in 1779, 1780, 1781, 1782, 1783. £23. 12. 6.

Durant, Thomas for 40 days in militia service in 1783. £2. 3. 4.

Ervin, John for services as Major, Lieut. Col. and Col. of militia in 1780-1782. £312. 7. 1.

Fraser, William for 186 days in the militia in 1779, 1781. £22. 4. 3.

Frierson, William for sundries for continental and militia use in 1780 and 1782. £5. 17. 7.

Fryer, Drury for 94 days in the militia in 1782. £6. 14. 3.

Gourdin, Theodore for 400 lbs beef in 1781 & provisions and forage for continental use in 1781, 1782, 1783. £33. 1. 6.

Green, Richard for 40 days militia duty as captain. £7. 4. 10.

Green, Richard for provisions and forage in 1781 & 1782. £66. 12. 1.

Montgomery, Samuel for provisions in 1780 & 1781 and for boots and shoes for state troops. £134. 2. 9.

Montgomery, Nathaniel for 1250 lbs beef in 1781. £16.

Nesmith, Samuel for sundries in 1781, 1782. £3. 16.

Port, Benjamin for sundries for militia & state troops in 1779-1782. £5. 2. 8.

Snow, David, estate of, for beef & corn for continental army in 1781, 1782 and 1783. £20. 2. 8.

Witherspoon, Gavin, for sundries for continentals & militia in 1780, 1781, 1782. £42.

Witherspoon, John for militia duty as Captain in 1780 £25. 14. 3.; also for provisions and forage in 1780 and 1781. £144. 16. 10. He moved to the Pee Dee section.

Rambles in the Pee Dee Basin

His only daughter Elizabeth became the second wife of Gov. D. R. Williams.

The Cheraws District covered the counties of Chesterfield, Marlborough and Darlington. In this District, there were no great battles but many skirmishes between the whigs and tories. The British at Camden and the tories in North Carolina kept the people in alarm until Lord Rawdon retreated and Major Gainey came to terms with Gen. Marion. The large slave owners in this district were not so numerous, but they were friends of the cause. Had Gen. Alexander McIntosh not been cut off during the war, he would have been the largest slave owner. Of his three heirs, Alexander McIntosh, Jr. had 65 and Rev. Peter Bainbridge, his brother-in-law, 55. Nathaniel Saunders had 123 slaves, Claudius Pegues had 63, William Pegues 60, Malachi Murphy 52, John Kimbrough 46, Lemuel Benton 45, William Ellerbe 41, Thomas Powe 34, Benjamin Rogers 33, Robert Lide 32, Morgan Brown 30. The majority were non-slave holders, as many as 50 families in one neighborhood having no slaves. Yet there were twice as many slaves as there were heads of families. Space will not permit the insertion of the names of all the soldiers alternately planters, and of all who were visited by the quarter master in search of army supplies. The few given are selected rather as representatives of many in the same service.

Ayers, Francis for 1880 pounds beef for continentals in 1781. £25. 16. 1.

Blakeny, John 17 steers for Virginia militia in 1780 and for 43 days service in 1782. £71. 4. 3.

Blakney, Thomas Provisions, forage for militia and a mare impressed in 1781, also for duty in militia. £46. 4.

South Carolina

Brown, Morgan—sundries for State troops & militia in 1781 & 1782. £87. 17. 1.

Chance, Isaac. A horse impressed in 1780. £28. 8. 6.

Cherry, George. Provisions & forage in 1783. £19. 8.

Cox, Emanuel. Pork & fodder in 1780, 1781. £17. 15. 7.

Craig, Alexander a roan horse for militia in 1780. £5. 9. 2.

Crossland, Edward 2200 pounds beef in 1780 & 1781. £28. 4. 8.

Cusack, Adam, estate of. Ferriage, provisions and forage and a lot of steel for continental and militia use in 1779, 1780, 1781 & 1782. £18. 0. 8.

Dabbs, Joseph for provisions & forage for Continentals in 1781. £3. 19. 8.

DeWitt, Martin for forage for continental & militia use in 1780, 1781. £25. 9. 10.

DeWitt, William, ditto. £66. 13. 11.

Dial, John, for 63 days in militia in 1782. £4. 10.

Douglass, Jesse. for 110 days in militia in 1781. £7. 17. 1.

DuBose, Capt. Andrew 88 days and 625 lbs of pork for Continental use in 1782, £47. 18. 5. For Daniel DuBose's 1500 pounds fodder for the militia in 1781, £2. 6. 10. For Isaac DuBose's 240 lbs beef in 1782, £3. 1. 7. £4. 14. 3. for 66 days duty in militia in 1782. For John DuBose's provisions for Continental and militia in 1782. £11. 18. For Peter DuBose's 3 sheep for Continental use in 1782. £2. 2.

Easterling, Henry 100 bushels corn for militia in 1781. £17. 10.

Ellerbe, Thomas for forage & provender for Continentals and militia & 72 days as Captain in militia service. £325. 14. 1.

Ellerbe, William Sr., Sundries for Continental & militia use & 68 days in militia. £268. 9. 6.

Evans, Enoch, Jr. for 1210 weight of pork & horse impressed. £68. 15. 8.

Evans, Josiah. for provisions & forage and duty done in 1782, 1783. £8. 9. 6.

Evans, Thomas, Sr. Horses and sundries empressed for continental & militia use in 1779-1782. £219. 18.

Evans, Capt. Thomas. Services as captain in militia & 12 months due Lewis Roan for service in state troops and one hog. £90. 11. 5.

Fountain, William, provisions for continentals and militia in 1781 & 30 days in militia in 1783. £9. 5. 5.

Gibson, Gideon provisions for militia in 1780, 1781. £39. 15. 9.

Gillespie, James. Provisions and forage for Continentals and militia in 1780. £42. 8. 1.

Gregg, James. 1450 lbs. beef for Continentals and militia in 1781 & 1782. £18. 12. 2.

Jenkins, James. for 127 days duty as a lieutenant in 1782, 1783. £31. 15.

Keith, Mrs. Margaret for 250 pounds of beef in 1782. £3. 4. 3.

Kimbrough, John. Sundries in 1780-1782. £419. 18. 7.

Kolb, Abel estate of. Sundries for continentals & militia in 1780 & 1782. £126. 18. 6.

McIntosh, Alexander, estate of Sundries for continentals & militia 1780-82. £421. 8. 7.

McIntosh, Alexander, Jr. 2400 lbs beef & 69 days in militia in 1780-1781. £60. 6. 9.

McIver, Evander. Sundries for militia use & 35 days duty in militia. £36. 1. 3.

South Carolina

McMuldrough, John Sundries for continentals and militia in 1780-1782. £218. 2. 7.

McNatt, Joel. a hog & 40 days duty in militia in 1782. £3. 10. 1.

Moore, Gully pork, corn, and 32 days in militia in 1781. £25. 10.

Murphy, Malachi—beef, pork for continentals & militia in 1780-82. £486. 0. 4.

Murphy. Moses ditto. £471. 3. 4.

Norwood, Theophilus. Militia duty before and after the fall of Charles Town. £58. 14. 3.

Pouncey, Anthony—555 lbs pork for Continental use in 1781. £9. 1. 2.

Powe, Thomas, ferriage, wagon & wagon hire. £164. 5. 10.

Prestwood, William. Sundries for militia 1780 & 1781. £11. 4. 10.

Pugh, Rev. Evan. Provisions & forage for Continentals. £10. 17. 3.

Spencer, Calvin, as Quartermaster general, £548. 4. 6.

Thomas, William.—for wagon gear, horses impressed & provisions for continental use in 1780-1782. £38. 5. 2. also £13. 14. 3. for wagon and team.

Whittington, Lt. Ephraim. beef for militia & 68 days in service in 1782. £20. 17.

Wilds, Abel, estate of. Sundries in 1780-82. £54. 6. 3.

Wilds, Jesse. A horse, provisions & militia duty 1781, 1782. £75. 8. Samuel Wilds. £49. 1. 5.

Williams, David, estate of. Sundries for Continental use in 1781, 1782, 1783. £462. 7. 2.

Of the officers in command of the militia some not only fought continuously in the field but also had their fields cultivated. Gen. Marion received £700. 13.7. for sundries furnished Continentals and militia in 1780, 1781, 1782, and 1783. After his marriage with Miss Videau he had 194 slaves. The estate of his relative, Benjamin Marion, murdered at White's bridge near Georgetown in 1781 furnished 23,542 feet of boards for the state for £19. 18. 9.

Gen. Richard Richardson who died near the time of the capture of Charles Town left an estate which furnished £80. 18. 8. worth of sundries for the army; and his son Richard provided beef and provisions for Continental and militia use amounting to £339. 6. 7.

Col. Daniel Horry lost a negro man in the Continental service in 1779 and furnished 8 horses in 1781 and received therefor £370. Nathaniel Saunders, a private citizen who lived east of the Pee Dee not far below Cashaway ferry relieved the hunger of many a soldier with his 8090 pounds of pork and 37,575 pounds of beef in 1781 and 1782. To such men as the above abbreviated lists describe, is due the liberty we enjoy.

CHAPTER XXIV
JUDGE HENRY PENDLETON

The legislatures which met in the decade after peace was ratified were more democratic than the preceding and perhaps than the following ones. They were composed of forward looking men who were consciously laying the foundation of the commonwealth by assuming first of all that the restoring of the public credit, impaired by the poverty of the state, was a matter of the first consequence. The funds were so low in January 1783 when the first peace time legislature met that negroes on the confiscated list had to be sold to defray the expenses of the body and to pay the soldiers of Gov. Pickens who had made peace appear to the Cherokees preferable to war. Among the problems demanding prompt attention was the obliging every person who had negroes and property of any kind belonging to others to render an account of them. Petitions from persons whose estates had been listed for confiscation or amercement came in volumes and be it said to the credit of the legislators that they leaned decidedly toward clemency in their final actions. Petitions from Georgetown and Williamsburg came in, in favor of enforcing rigid punishment upon their late unscrupulous enemies, but notwithstanding the lawmakers treated the loyalist who had been neutral with consideration and even tories found an increasing tendency in the body, as the years passed, to restore forfeited property, to forgive and forget the past.

Provision was made by this first assembly after the evacuation of the city for the assistance of a few soldiers who had been rendered helpless by wounds received in battle. One widow had lost two husbands in the war and five children of Adam Cusack who had been wantonly sentenced to death and executed at Long Bluff by Wemyss were among the number who needed public aid. The latter reported that their father's house was burnt and everything pertaining to him destroyed on the complaint and false accusation of John Brockington.

General efforts were made to improve the judicial system which were partially successful in the end. A proper digest of the laws necessary for the good government of the state, reduced as far as practicable to as small a compass as possible, was thought to be required for the happiness and convenience of the people. The wish to have commissioners to do the work was common before and after the war and to all sections, but it was deferred to a later time.

A resolution That it would promote the interest and happiness of this state that the seat of government be fixed as near the centre as possible, "taking into consideration the benefits of water carriage, trade, health or situation and fertility of the adjacent country"— was offered but its consideration was postponed. It was more practical at that time to appoint a commissioner in each circuit court district to receive and adjust all accounts against the public, to arrange and number them in an orderly manner, prepare a schedule of the whole with remarks on each account and lay them with their vouchers before the General Assembly at the next session. The accounts due after January 1st, 1783 were not to be included. This legislation was carrying out Gen. Matthews' advice to preserve the public credit. Many little debts were thus canceled, much needed money was put in circulation and it saved an immense amount of fragmentary individual history of the men who fought the enemy and of the citizens who fed the soldiers in the Revolution.

The decade after the war was called "dark days" by an intelligent man who passed through them; but the darkness was not dense in the General Assembly. It was looking after the bridges broken down or destroyed in the war, opening new roads, reorganizing the militia, curbing thieves, examining the weights of gold and silver coins in circulation, distributing money in small quantities all over the state in payment of claims against the public, arranging to open colleges and to connect the city by the sea with the Santee by a costly canal to be made by private enterprise.

Improvement in the courts in the interior received early attention but several years elapsed before much progress was made. A commissioner in each district of the circuit court was to divide the same into counties of a convenient size not exceeding 40 miles square except where the territory or situation of the people required a deviation from instructions. In this way was begun in the legislature the plan of dividing the larger districts into counties more convenient for the people. Cheraws lost itself in Chesterfield, Marlboro and Darlington Districts and Liberty or Marion, Williamsburg and Georgetown Districts came into being with their new boundaries adjusted and fixed. The making of small counties out of large ones is a current running up stream and not along with the resistless consolidating volume rolling onward in mid-channel. But it is more apparent than actual, as the legislation looked largely to the convenience of the courts and of the part of the people whose litigious proclivities made them necessary. The small counties with their courts was a contribution from other states and an assimilation, to Virginia's judicial arrangements. It was accomplished at no cost of the state as each county was to pay for the Court House by a tax laid by the Courts. In 1785—that notable year in the annals of legislation—in which the counties were laid out, a Committee of three Judges, Henry Pendleton, Aedanus Burke and Judge Grimke, were empowered and directed to form "a complete and accurate digest of the state laws, with such additions, alterations and amendments" as they should see fit; and to require the production of such records and other public documents as should be necessary."[1] They were directed to make the establishment of county courts a part of their system. Their work was finished in 1789 and presented to the legislature. It was not adopted as a whole but the acts constituting circuit courts, courts of record, and giving them original and final jurisdiction and the abolition of the rights of primogeniture and some other parts were afterwards passed as separate acts by the General Assembly.[2] While other parts were rejected, notably a new system of punishing crimes in which banishment was prominent, another part of the digest providing for a uniformity of decision and practice was engrafted as an improvement in the Constitution adopted in the following year.[3]

The dominating spirit in the upcountry councils in this transition era was Henry Pendleton[4] who had been a soldier in the Revolution in Virginia and had moved to South Carolina.

Judge Pendleton at the time of his death in 1789 was living near Golden Grove, about 12 miles below Green-

---

[1] Statutes of South Carolina, Vol. I, p. 434.
[2] Statutes of South Carolina, Vol. I, p. 435.
[3] Statutes of South Carolina, Vol. I, p. 435.
[4] Judge O'Neall in his Bench and Bar, Vol. I, p. 33, says it is uncertain whether Henry Pendleton came to South Carolina before or after the Revolution. He confuses, on the authority of Dr. Joseph Johnson, Nathaniel Pendleton who was Aide-de-camp of Gen. Greene in his campaign in 1781-82 and was thanked by Congress for his gallant conduct at Eutaw Springs. National Encyclopaedia of American Biography, Vol. III, p. 273.

ville. One of the neighboring tracts was taken up by his colleague Justice Aedanus Burke and another by Nathaniel Pendleton who had acted as Aide-de-Camp to Gen. Greene in his campaign of 1781, and mistaken by one of Judge O'Neall's[5] authorities for Judge Henry Pendleton. When he came to South Carolina is not known nor is it certain where he lived or how he had become sufficiently prominent in 1776 to be appointed an associate justice. The tradition is that he was in the Virginia army of the Revolution but the records make him a representative of the people in the first year of peace. His services to the state were therefore confined to 7 years, 1783-1789, a period which no historian has investigated and added a volume to those left by the Historian McCrady. But enough is seen on the surface of the times to class him not only as 'tall, handsome and agreeable' but also as a level headed, judicious statesman who steered between the close corporation below and the licentious spirit above. He favored and expedited the division into counties, the erection of more convenient judicial machinery, the removal of the capital to a more central location and a fairer representation and a revised Constitution. He lived to see the digest of the laws made by himself, Burke and Grimke, the counties laid out, the courts in operation, the site of the capital chosen near Friday's ferry, but died before the state constitution was revised in 1790. Had his valuable life been spared, his wisdom would have contributed to the Constitution of the state and his prominence would have insured a seat in one of the houses of the general government. In the struggle between the upper and lower sections, Judge Pendleton is thought to have been the one person of 1783-1861 who was fitted and able to lead the

---

[5]O'Neall's Bench and Bar.

disjointed and independent forces from the upper parts. Not long after his death, his name was affixed to Pendleton District and when that territory gave birth to other counties, his name remained in the village of Pendleton. He was related to the celebrated Edmund Pendleton of Virginia and all that is known of him is indicative of clean morals, noble motives and high character. Had he lived in a state more fond of its own illustrious history, he would have ranked in our early history as one of the leading and most important statesman of his time.

CHAPTER XXV
REMOVING THE CAPITAL

The Revolution in South Carolina, begun by the government at Charles Town and concluded by the officers and people in the interior, inevitably led to a more democratic form of government. Sumter, Marion, Pickens, Hampton and other officers and the men they led, grew in the short space of two years out of rustic inhabitants into full grown citizens who had established their right to a full share in the government. Civil discord is favorable in the end to greater freedom for the good citizens who were numerous and greater licentiousness for the bad ones. The session of 1783, 84, and 85 were devoted to the most pressing objects left as a legacy of the war; but in 1786, the leaders of the inland people began to be felt in the Assembly. On the 3rd of February Judge Pendleton began to introduce for discussion some changes[1] in the machinery of government. He had given notice in the winter session of the previous year that at some future time he would offer a bill to revise the representation of the people. The present mode, he said, was inconvenient from the great number necessary to be returned, for it happened not unfrequently that gentlemen were not willing to serve, and some places of election so remote that electors could not attend. Since the time of framing our Constitution, very great alterations had taken place in the state, both with regard to actual property and number of inhabitants, the districts of Camden and Ninety Six in particular had become far more populous, owing to so much land being run out, yet their representation was the same.

---
[1]The Morning Post of February 4, 1786 freely used in this condensed report.

Another objection was the disproportion in point of numbers between that house and senate; it certainly being improper to throw an equal part of the government into the hands of so small a number of men. It would be better therefore to vary our representation so that it might approach nearer to equality: for which reason he wished to vary our representation in the following manner: This state to be divided into 35 counties, of 40 miles square each. He proposed that Charles Town should return two senators and six members to the house, and every other county one senator and three members; this arrangement would add nine to the senators and reduce their numbers to 180. General Pinckney replied that the bill "went in its tendency to sap the foundation of our present mode of representation, by throwing the election of Representatives into the hands of proprietors of barren acres, instead of persons possessed of real property."

To Gen. Pinckney's saying that previous notice ought to be given of such important business to prevent surprise, Judge Pendleton replied that it was impossible to take the House by surprise "when a distant day is fixed for the introduction of the bill and when it is maturely deliberated in the House."

Judge Burke thought such material alterations should be left to a Convention much talked of to be called. Dr. Budd declared he would oppose it at every stage—"our large representation the palladium of our liberty—if any man had art and influence enough to lessen our representation to one half, they could reduce it to what number they pleased, till our present happy free constitution would be succeeded by the worst form of government on earth—an autocratic government where the arbitrary will of a few men makes the laws and puts them in force, where the rulers are lords and the people slaves."

E. Rutledge could not account for fears entertained by gentlemen that by permitting a Committee to be named, an alteration of the Constitution would necessarily follow; all they could do was to report a bill, for such and such purposes and then if the House thought proper that bill might be published, and by this open manner of proceeding their constituents would have authentic information of a law intended to be passed for altering the Constitution. Besides a committee would wisely digest and methodize this business. They could call for information from those who were competent to give it, such as the state of taxable property, returns of militia etc. When all that had been done, then, perhaps, a bill would be reported, although he did not think there would be found ten members in that House who would vote for it, making such an alteration as had been proposed. Adverting to the question about notice, he thought the spirit if not the letter of that clause in our Constitution had been misconstrued; he was clearly of the opinion that when a bill even agreed on for the purpose above mentioned, it was necessary to give 90 days previous notice to the people before it ought to pass into a law.

Mr. Calhoun thought the notice regular; and that the House ought to institute an inquiry into the representation, though he wished it done by a committee who could investigate the matter and report a bill if judged necessary.

Judge Heyward called for the notice of 90 days referred to, and on being read, it appeared that the "next session" was inserted, now as no such bill had been offered last session, of course this notice fell to the ground. He submitted his opinion to the House.

Mr. Read observed that the Honorable member (Judge Pendleton) was a judge, now if he was seated on the bench in his official capacity, would he admit of this being good notice of trial. Surely not; and was that House to go into measures under an idea of being regular in their mode of proceedings upon a notice of such a kind as would be considered informal by the court below. Certainly not. Yet this was expected in this present instance. The Honorable gentleman had better amend his notice, take a longer time for bringing this business to an issue; and by this delay so necessary in matters of such high importance, his intention to alter the Constitution would go abroad and people without doors be possessed of the subject before it became law.

Judge Pendleton believed it would be found upon reviewing the accusation that there was no flaw in the indictment. He was justified in pressing forward his bill, upon the principle of justice; as he thought could be rendered obvious to even a common understanding. The last session was literally a special one; it had been called by the governor expressly to relieve the national exigencies and distress, and upon their meeting, resolutions were entered into, to take up some particular business and no other; how therefore could gentlemen think him compelled by forms to give notice of this intention to the legislature at the last sitting when they resolved to take up only particular business; but to leave this point, for he did not rely on it, he was regular and sanctioned in perseverance by the constitution itself; it was therefore expressly declared in a manner so clear as not to admit of objection, that every seven years such a plan as he proposed should be carried into effect. Seven years had already expired, and now this step became an indispensable duty; perhaps, even this plain definition might meet with objection but these objections could be only such as counsel would urge to amuse a jury and beguile their understanding from attending to the solid principles of law: for he was convinced that the legislature would not pass over this point; it was due in justice to themselves, it was due in justice to the citizens; they had a right to expect this from the House, because they had promised it by the Constitution. As to a gentleman's opinion relative to a Convention of the people, this subject had been discussed before and negatived; what sort of a convention could be expected if that House did appoint one, a sort of convention he never wished to see, a convention of the people. Every gentleman must anticipate the consequent horrors that must attend such an assembly, as another revolution might be expected to follow. He wished gentlemen to meet his proposition fairly and not shrink from it.

Mr. Read took fire from what had fallen from the honorable gentlemen, about that house being afraid to discuss his motion, but being called to order, appealed to the chair, and was ruled out of order.

Chancellor Rutledge observed the honorable judge had shielded himself with two points, the one was that he had given regular notice of his intention to bring in a bill for altering the Constitution and that seven years had expired since it was framed, that house was called on to revise or alter it in such manner as was pointed out by the Constitution. As the first had been given up, he should apply only to the second, and in order to meet every objection that had been offered should move that a committee be appointed to report a plan for proportioning the representation of the state, according to the comparative strength and taxable property of the white inhabitants, citizens thereof agreeable to the 15th article of the Constitution and this was agreed to. On the 3rd of February 1786, the calling of a Constitutional

Convention and the removal of the seat of government to a more central part of the state were brought before the house by a petition from inhabitants of York County. On the 22nd it was agreed to, to call the Convention, but the removal of the seat of government to a more convenient place met with decided opposition. Judge Pendleton was in favor of a change and the place he favored was near Friday's ferry where a liberal price could be paid the owners and lots could be sold at prices that would pay for the expenses of moving. General Pinckney preferred Charles Town, and if it must be moved, he moved that a place lower down the river be substituted. Mr. Izard declared it would give the country party the advantage in proportion of 4 to 1 and at present overshadowed that of the town. This estimate agreed with Mr. Hill's statement that it was a question whether there would be a compliance with the wishes of 200 rather than of 40 or 50 who disliked it. The opposition in the house appeared to be more ably led than in the Senate which saved the day. On March 6th Col. Gervais introduced a "bill for removing the seat of government from Charles Town and for other purposes therein mentioned." Then when it came to a vote a week later it stood 65 to 61 in favor of Friday's ferry. There were efforts to keep the seat of Government at Charles Town before and after the passing of the act and the appointment of a committee consisting of Commodore Gillon, Judge Pendleton, Gen. Wynn, Col. Richard Hampton and Col. Thomas Taylor to lay out Columbia for erecting a new town at Friday's ferry.

Gov. Charles Pinckney was made President of the Convention when it met on May 12, 1790. Mr. John Drayton made a motion to take advantage of several learned, respectable ministers to call on them for assistance in thanking the divine Being for his goodness in giving them an opportunity to assemble in peace and concord for the purpose of drawing up a form of government calculated to promote the happiness and welfare of the people of South Carolina, and also to solicit his gracious assistance in completing an important work by which they and their posterity were to be governed. This motion was successfully opposed by Col. Gervais, by deferring the subject to Sunday.

Mr. Carnes considered it a constitutional point to have a place for the citizens to resort and meet at, where the public offices should be kept, the courts of justice be held, whether they were to meet among the opulent at Charles Town, which to the upper country members was a different climate; or amongst those who were styled of Plebeian race, to fix permanently the seat of government now, would establish a basis for the committee to go upon and accelerate the business they were about at least three weeks, etc.

Gen. Pinckney thought Charles Town the proper place, but he did not want the Constitution to take notice of the seat of government at all, that would introduce feuds and animosities. Later also he argued strongly against the mention of the seat of government in the Constitution. Suppose, said he, a few daring men thought proper to seize the records, plunder the treasury, or commit any other act of violence against the government, what force was there to prevent them? None at all. To this Mr. Carnes replied against the idea of an itinerant legislature rambling up and down without a prospect of accomplishing their ends, for which they were sent by their constituents. He believed they were in more danger when in Charles Town, for he was informed that a little time ago at that place a rumor prevailed that the Algerians were coming. A panic ensued; they went to look for the means of defense and found two cannon buried in the sand, others with their touch holes plugged up, so that these fears of danger were imaginary and only thrown out to bewilder the understanding of those who were for Columbia. Without the means of defense, Charles Town might be ransacked, set on fire, and in a few minutes those who did this could be out of danger on the Atlantic Ocean.

The Court of Chancery was mentioned and on that point he begged leave to observe that an orphan who was entitled to £50, being denied it by those who held it, the remedy must be by giving £20 to an eminent attorney who would file a bill in Chancery, the other necessary expenses being £40 more; the orphan got the cause and was only out £10. Mr. Anderson was conciliatory and Mr. Gadsden also favored a two-thirds majority rule; others opposed the insertion of Columbia in the Constitution. The vote for Columbia was 109 to 105. The warmth engendered subsided when Gen. Pinckney moved that a compromise committee be appointed. The motion was lost, but was carried the next day. This committee was composed of Major Pinckney, Messrs. Pringle and E. Rutledge on one side; Gen. Pickens, Col. Anderson, Commodore Gillon and Mr. Calhoun on the other. They met on Sunday and agreed on two treasurers, a Secretary and his deputy; that judges after their circuits, should meet in Camden, Ninety Six and Columbia, to hear all matters respecting new trials, motions to arrest judgment etc., and then proceed to Charles Town and transact all business of a similar nature. All Courts as then established were to be retained. These points were unanimously agreed to and pledges passed on both sides that they would defend them, let the seat of government, or more properly the seat of the legislature, be ultimately fixed where it may. On the 31st the seat of government was fixed at Columbia, but subject to removal by two-thirds vote of each branch. Representatives were reduced to 125 in number, Senators to 36. The pay per diem was 7 shillings. Judges and ministers made ineligible.

This great real estate transaction was set on foot by the legislature on the 22nd of March, 1786. A tract of land two miles square, near Friday's Ferry, including the plain of the hill wherein John and Thomas Taylor resided was to be laid off into one half acre lots each facing streets not less than 60 feet, the two principal streets running through the centre of the town to be not less than 150 feet. Eight acres were reserved for the purpose of erecting such public buildings in such part as shall be most convenient and ornamental. The committee, Messrs. Gillon, T. Taylor, Judge Pendleton, Gen. Wynn, Richard Hampton and Col. Taylor, was ordered to sell one fifth of the lots remaining to the highest bidder, at a price not less than £20. When funds sufficient were in hand, they were to build a state house with rooms for the meeting of the General Assembly and other officers, on the most frugal plan the honor and interest of the state would permit.

Every purchaser of a lot was to build a house not less than 30 x 18 in the clear with brick or stone chimneys within the space of three years. This was to be the seat of government as soon as buildings were sufficient to accomodate the legislature. The Commissioners' compensation was to be 2½ per cent of sales of lots. (Statutes of S. C., Vol. IV, p. 753) Thus was to come into being the beautiful town of Columbia.

A Look Backward

In November 1750, the Governor called the attention of Assembly and Council to the sort of places the government had to use. Courts kept in a tavern and prisoners in private houses. In 1751 a state house was being built. In 1752, at the Court of General Sessions 2 were convicted of robbing on the highway, 2 of stealing and killing cattle, 1 each for wife murder, burglary, petty larceny and one woman for assaulting a constable in the execution of his office.

Agricola recommends Farmers' Clubs to meet once a month, like producers' arrangement now, caused by market fluctuations—45sh., 50sh., 40sh. for rice.

1765. The want of a general hospital or poor house for the reception of a number of poor objects who flock from all parts of the province to Charles Town; the places at present assigned to their accommodation being found insufficient, and is besides thought a very improper receptacle for the poor, being crowded with criminals, vagrants, sailors and negroes. Grievance of jury.

1773. This publishing of the laws has strongly been press'd on the Assembly from home but never taken under Consideration till this Remonstrance awaken'd them—for it was not the Interest of the Lawyers, for the Laws ever to be published. They are still a Blank to ev'ry one—The House voted One thousand pounds Sterling for a Compilement of the Laws which was undertaken by John R——e, Esq—but not yet printed—The Sum he demanded for the Copies when printed, is beyond the Abilities of any to comply with—Woodmason.

1774. A play house in Charles Town, being unfit for the present low estate of the province; for although there is a great want of money to procure conveniences and even the necessaries of life, yet large sums are weekly laid out for amusement there by persons who cannot afford it. A Grievance.

The present harvest, 1774, one of the most favorable ever known—crop of rice far in excess of previous ones.

Indigo not so good—no corn for export. Rice fell 55s. downward.

1775. The Commerce of America, the vital stream of this great empire. Earle of Shelburne.

1783. An ordinance to oblige males from 16 to 60 years of age to keep open Waccamaw river for navigation.

The state to be divided into counties not over 40 miles square.

1784. Assessors and tax collectors for the parish of St. David were Col. Geo. Hicks, Col. Thomas Lide, Edward Jones, Richard Brockington, Benjamin Jackson, Thomas Ellerby, Robert Lide, John McCall, Elias Dubose, David Perkins and Peter Allston.

For Parish of Prince Frederick, John Thomas Green, Samuel James, James Witherspoon, Jr.

For Prince George Winyaw, Peter Horry, John Skrine, Joseph Grier, John Baxter, James Johnson and James Ford, Jr.

For the parish of All Saints, Capt. William Allston and Robert Heriot. Men of high standing were selected.

Geo. Hicks, Sr., George Hicks, Thomas Powe, William Kershaw, William Pegues appointed to clear out great Pee Dee from the N. C. line, not to cost over £300.

The depreciation of the currency received the attention of the Solons.

Ware houses for inspection of tobacco erected, one at Georgetown, one at Cheraw.

For every negro imported from Africa the tax was £3 sterling. From any other port £5.

For the encouragement of inventiveness, a copy right of 14 years was granted.

In March the ordinance respecting suits for the recovery of debts. The legislature encouraged by legislation subjects of foreign countries to lend money at interest on real estate within the state.

The legislature showed its gratitude to the officers and soldiers of the Continental line and other officers and men by ordering lands to be run out free of cost to them.

1785. Official steps were taken to effect a revisal, digest and publication of the laws of the state—to relieve a long felt grievance. Also to lay off the several counties and erect public buildings.

The County Court Act was passed.

Charles Mason, Evander McIver, Thomas Powe and Wm. DeWitt set forth in their petition to the legislature that they had laid out the town at Long Bluff on Pee Dee, out of their own property, had given the streets, several lots of land, town house and market place.

An ordinance for the settlement of the public debt and five commissioners were appointed and instructed as to their duties.

In order to safeguard the reputation of the state abroad, rules for inspecting and exporting tobacco were to be put in force at Georgetown and other ports. At Cheraw, Benjamin Hicks, Sr., John Westfield and William Ellerby acted as inspectors.

Public lands hereafter were to be sold at $10 per hundred acres instead of £10.

The £100,000 issue of paper money were to be 4,000 ten pound bills, 10,000 two pound bills, 4,000 one pound bills, 12,000 five shillings and 24,000 two shillings.

This remarkable business legislature touched at many points the places that needed oiling, one of the last being a desire of a more speedy settlement of the accounts with the United States.

Ten shillings payable in taxes, offered for every panther or tiger, and five shillings for each wild cat—to extend over 5 years. One cat's premium paid more than the tax for most of the hunters. It was a bad day for most of the "varmints."

Without a certificate of good character from the Justice of the Peace, a traveller was deemed a vagrant.

1787. No negro or other slave be imported by land or water within 3 years. This veto lasted till the year 1803 approached.

Stringent laws against persons having no visible means of existence, against gambling, swapping horses or negroes, leading idle and disorderly lives, not producing certificate of good character signed by the Justices of the Peace.

1789. All public records not referring to Charles Town, Beaufort or Georgetown to be removed to Columbia.

1790. $5,000 appropriated for expenses of the Constitutional Convention.

CHAPTER XXVI

FORMING THE CONSTITUTION

The thirteen independent states—that is the language used by the Congress of the Confederation; and with these independent states peace was agreed upon in 1783. During this brief period of autonomy 1783-89, John Rutledge, Rawlins Lowndes, John Matthews, Benj. Guerard, Wm. Moultrie, Thomas Pinckney and Charles Pinckney were governors in succession. The state was making more progress than the confederation in recuperation and in paying debts. The great deficiency in the confederation was its inability to raise revenue to meet expenses and debts, and power to lay duties on imports. The opposition in the commercial states objected because it would bear hardest upon them. This was answered "that every duty on imports is incorporated with the price of the commodity, and ultimately paid for by the consumer, with a profit on the duty itself, as a compensation to the merchant for the advance of his money." As a consumer he pays a share of the duty, and that is his only burden. In Rhode Island, a small commercial state, the opposition was so strong that an argument had to be advanced in the interest of the Central government. Either loans must be made or the states must furnish revenue for the public needs. Thirteen different states which dealt with these matters were slow in deliberation and constant in revision, and therefore money lenders were cautious in lending to Congress under the circumstances.

England, too, was still the great adversary, vigilant and ready to seize every advantage over our necessities. The situation demanded some sort of legislation, that the fund should depend on a single will rather than that of thirteen. A debt had been contracted in Europe and in this country and on every principle of justice and policy, a fund for discharging this debt by degrees should be provided annually. To fail in doing this would stamp the national character with indellible disgrace. Impost duties was the most agreeable to the people; export duties by increasing the price of native commodities were injurious. The responsibility of Congress was greater than its power. Without any competent means, it had to conduct the war, but after full deliberation a committee proposed a measure to the states—the corner stone of the public safety—and yet after two years, it was partially complied with by some of the states, rejected by one, and consequently in danger of being frustrated, while the public embarrassment is every day increasing. This was the language in December, 1782, near the close of the war.

In April, 1783, Congress desired the several states to invest it with powers to raise revenue, to maintain public credit. This, said the Resolution, is necessary to render the fruits of the Revolution a full reward for the blood, the toils, the cares and the calamities which have purchased it. The contest had been for the rights of human nature which against all opposition have prevailed and form the basis of the thirteen independent states. The citizens of the United States, in the enjoyment of an unadulterated form of republican government, are responsible for the greatest trust ever confided to a people. "If justice, good faith, honor, gratitude, and all other qualities which ennoble the character of a nation and fulfill the ends of government, be the fruit of our establishments, the cause of liberty will acquire a dignity and lustre it has never yet enjoyed, and an example will be set which cannot but have the most favorable influence on mankind. If on the other side, our governments should be unfortunately blotted with the reverse of these cardinal and essential virtues, the great cause which we have engaged to vindicate will be dishonored and betrayed and the last and fairest experiment in favor of the rights of human nature will be turned against them." Mr. Madison headed the committee which brought in the above sentiments, too unearthly to last three generations. In 1784 the situation of commerce owing to the lack of one head to direct legislation, affected every citizen interested in its success. It was a set of circumstances which invited England to secure the trade of the colonies she had lost and had she been as wise politically as she was shrewd in forming commercial monopolies, the states could have been kept apart. Her navigation laws brought on the revolution and again after the war her commercial greed forced upon the disjointed states the necessity of having a stronger general government to preserve their commerce and that freedom which they had gained at so great cost. In order to establish a monopoly that would be lucrative to the British and destructive to their late enemies, the British colonies were not allowed to trade with the Americans except in British bottoms navigated by British mariners. It was openly avowed, so helpless the Americans appeared, that there was no material advantage the American States could give in return more than they already had. The restrictions placed upon their trading, however, bore heavily upon the sugar producing islands, by depriving them of a market for that part of the produce which was superfluous to England and Ireland; but some comfort was extracted from the belief that "the people of the United States would suffer more than any of the subjects of England and that their lumber and provisions must perish in their hands."

For the first time in her history, Massachusetts was at the end of her tether. She had come out of the war in better shape financially than the Southern States which were badly wasted by the conflict; but this restriction on American trade made that enterprising section as despondent as a hive of bees whose queen was missing. The fisheries had been rendered valueless by the bounties offered British fishermen, and the restrictions thrown around the British colonies curtailed the area of her commercial activities and laid up as useless a part of her ships. "It is to be hoped," said a sarcastic Englishman, "that these rebellious ingrates, who were the first to oppose the just authority of the mother country, will be last to receive at her hands any commercial boon whatever." Several American vessels having returned from Jamaica and other parts of the West Indies without being allowed to dispose of their cargoes or bring away produce of those islands, the Virginia legislature voted to retaliate; and this was interpreted by a British writer as equal to saying: "Concede to us a free trade to your West India possessions and the carrying of your sugar to European markets. Ship building is our trade. We can carry them cheaper than British built ships; grant this or we will retaliate." Virginia's effort acted as a boomerang, in that the lower rate of duties in sister states adjoining attracted the trade and made her pay tribute to them instead of receiving it from England. "Do you not perceive," said a Virginia editor, near the close of 1785, "that you are excluded (your own and your sister states) from every benefit of the trade—import and export—to the great injury of our own navy?"

In South Carolina there was indignation also seeing their commerce to be at the mercy of foreigners; but what was to be done? Despondency reigned throughout the states and minds of superior calibre were cogitating and planning to get out of the British meshes. Virginia, the largest state at the time was nourishing the Moses who was to lead them out of their servitude. James Madison who had served in Congress from 1780 to 1783 became thoroughly conversant with the defects of the central government and with the general indifference of the states to the need of the union. He was made a delegate to the House of Burgesses and there was begun the first legislation that was to bring relief.[1] The legislatures of Virginia and Maryland appointed commissioners "to form a compact relative to the navigation of the rivers Potomac and Pocomoke and part of the bay of the Chesapeake," which assembled at Alexandria in March 1785. This committee headed by Edmund Randolph visited Mount Vernon and there, no doubt with Washington's approval, decided to propose to their respective legislatures the appointment of other commissioners with power to make conjoint arrangement, to which the assent of Congress was to be solicited, for maintaining a naval force in the Chesapeake and establish a tariff of duties on imports to which the laws of both states should conform. The proposition met with approval and its original purpose was broadened by another resolution which impowered the committee "to take into consideration the trade of the United States, to examine the relative situation and trade of the said states, to consider how far a uniform system in their commercial relations may be necessary to their common interests and their permanent harmony and to report to the several states such an act relative to this great object, as when unanimously ratified by them will enable the United States in Congress Assembled effectually to provide for the same." Up to this time the aim was to come to some agreement which two or more states

---

[1]Madison's Papers 113. Sparks Life of Washington, V. II, p. 205.

might adopt with the consent of Congress and it brought to light a conciliatory spirit. Congress would have been satisfied with a duty of 5 per cent *ad valorem* on imports, but the delegates from five states at Annapolis, led by Hamilton and Madison, decided to accelerate the slow process of strengthening the confederation, by recommending in a strong paper to all the legislatures the election of delegates with more extensive powers to meet at Philadelphia in May 1787. This communication from the Annapolis delegates was held for months under consideration by Congress until 10 states had elected delegates. They finally acceded to the wishes of the delegates and called the convention. To Madison's Papers we are indebted for much that is known about this pivotal part of our history.

All the members of Congress thought the present government inefficient. The members of the southern and the middle states wanted an efficient organization which would preserve the Union. Only one member, Mr. Bingham, wanted several confederacies, while the eastern men, except those from Connecticut, were thought after Shay's rebellion, not so ardent in their desire for republican insitutions! In the meantime discussions in the newspapers favoring a change to a consolidated government were going on and the impression was being fostered that there was to be either a great empire or a chain of petty republics. "That we have it in our power," said Washington, "to become one of the most respectable nations upon earth, admits of no doubt, if we but pursue. a wise, just and liberal policy toward one another and keep good faith with the rest of the world. That our resources are ample and increasing, none can deny; but while they are grudgingly applied, or not applied at all, we give a vital stab to public faith and shall sink in the eyes of Europe into contempt . . . We have abundant reason to be convinced, that the spirit of trade which pervades these states, is not to be restrained. It behooves us then to establish just principles; and this cannot any more than other matters of national concern, be done by thirteen heads, differently constructed and organized. The necessity, therefore, of a controling power is obvious; and why it should be withheld is beyond my comprehension."

The men of the Convention, by way of preface, were familiar with the lessons of history and versed in science of government. They were more afraid of the people politically than of daring experiments upon which history shed no light. At the very beginning a majority voted to move toward a consolidated government, along a well trodden road. They declined the more difficult task of enlarging the Articles of Confederation so as to make it an amply efficient general government, kept in its orbit, not by a written constitution which might become a mere scrap of paper, but by sovereign states. This was done, with the warning in their ears that it was easier to grant more powers in the future than to take back what had been unwisely parted with. The encroaching tendency was like a screw working its way by slow degrees and holding fast whatever it gains. In pagan language they were driven on by Fate under the feeling of overwhelming necessity to do something to extricate themselves from an uncomfortable situation. Madison saw plainly that property was the main business of society, that in the event the new government should lose its equilibrium and be run by a majority united by a common interest, the rights of the minority would be in danger, that conscience is inadequate in individuals; in large numbers little was to be expected from it. Virginia's position and interests as well as his own equipoise made him prefer a government balanced so that neither the northern nor the southern states should have a supremacy and in trying to prevent that calamity he became an idealist and an optimist rather than a practical statesman. Among practical statesmen, the idealist fares badly.

The delegates from the states met at Philadelphia in May 1787 and after waiting eleven days for a quorum elected George Washington president. The representatives from South Carolina were C. C. Pinckney, Charles Pinckney, John Rutledge and Pierce Butler. They were all Federalists. Gen. Pinckney doubted at the opening whether the body had any right to formulate a government on principles different from those of the Confederation, but the body led by Gouverneur Morris' resolution that a national government ought to be established consisting of a supreme legislative executive and judiciary, prevailed. Gen. Pinckney showed also a disposition to make compromises where he could not obtain what he wanted. John Rutledge was a man of weight in the debates and in the select committee which wrought out the constitution into shape and form. Pierce Butler was always present, made brief remarks and showed impatience only when the assumption of state debts came up for discussion. Charles Pinckney was in his 29th year and out of 56 members he was the only one who had prepared a draft of a Constitution and brought it for consideration. It was however sent to the Committee of the Whole where it remained until it was needed by the Committee of detail. Charles Pinckney made the first motion after the credentials of the deputies were read—that a committee be appointed to prepare standing rules and orders. Edmund Randolph of Virginia opened the business by a long introductory speech in which he considered the defects of the Confederation, the sort of government needed and the danger of the situation. The remedy was offered in 15 resolutions, looking to the formation of a government of an executive, legislative and judiciary based on republican principles, but paramount to the states. These resolutions engaged the attention of the body from May 29 to June 13th. In the discussion the 15 abstract resolutions changed into 19. At this juncture Mr. Patterson of New Jersey, laid before the body a Federal plan as a substitute for Randolph's resolutions. It was ably advocated and opposed with equal ability and unequal numbers. Mr. Hamilton from New York, a West Indian by birth and not attached to a state, opposed it with great force. He was disposed to prefer a monarchical government but as that was out of the question, he thought the states should be abolished and the President hold office for life or during good behavior. He was one of the great quartette, viz. Hamilton, Gouverneur Morris, James Madison and Charles Pinckney who were in favor of an overwhelming United States government. Patterson's plan served only to show how impossible it was for that body to favor a mere revision and correction of the Articles of Confederation.[2] This impediment out of the way, the 19 resolutions occupied the time of the Convention until June 26 when the material was ready to be thrown into a constitution. What the South Carolina delegation stood for has to be gathered from the discussions which were almost unbridled. Charles Pinckney's draft, for instance, provided for the election of the first branch of the legislature by the people, but he yielded to the older members of the South Carolina delegation and opposed election by the people. Mr. Sherman and Mr. Gerry supported the motion, the former asserting that the people should have as little to do as may be about the government, the latter that the

---

[2]Madisoin's Papers and Notts' The Mystery of the Pinckney draft, p. 68.

evils of the day flowed from the excess of democracy, but the majority led by Madison defeated the proposed election by the legislature. Mr. Gerry insisted that the moneyed interest would be more secure in the hands of the state legislature than of the people at large. Much time was spent on the executive, his duties and limitations. How he was to be chosen, his term of office and his functions elicited a great variety of opinions. Mr. Pinckney wanted a vigorous executive but he thought too much power would make him an elective monarch. C. C. Pinckney thought it necessary for the president to affirm that he was worth $100,000, the judges $50,000 and the Senators and the members of the House correspondingly less. Mr. Rutledge seconded the motion. No other state favored a plutocratic element in the government, but others especially Gouverneur Morris, thought that wealth ought to be considered in the rates of representation inasmuch as property is the main object of society, to which Mr. Rutledge gave a hearty amen. It was also acknowledged in the debate by Gouverneur Morris that the moneyed interests would oppose the plan of government if paper emissions be not prohibited. It was left for Charles Pinckney to out—Hamilton Hamilton, by moving to give authority to the national legislature to negative all state laws which they should judge to be improper and was seconded by James Madison. Only Massachusetts, Pennsylvania and three Virginians voted aye. The good sense of the Convention was frequently made manifest by the sanity of a majority which rejected speculative extremes. A stand still occurred when the votes of the small states were reached. All the extreme Federalists were for representation according to size or population as a matter of justice, the representatives of the small states demanded an equality of votes in the second branch for protection. When the rift between the parties seemed to be widening, Benjamin Franklin reminded them when they were groping in the dark after political truth and could hardly distinguish it when found, that they had not humbly applied to the Father of light to illumine their understanding. He had lived a long time and the longer he lived he saw more convincing proof that God governs in the affairs of men. And with such further remarks as "if a sparrow cannot fall to the ground without his notice, is it probable that an empire can rise without his aid?" He moved that their sessions should hereafter be opened with prayer by one of the clergy in town. Hamilton and several others opposed it in vain.

The final result was the open refusal of the small states to budge from their demand of an equal vote in the senate. Charles Pinckney was among the first to show a weakening. He was extremely anxious that something should be done, considering this the last appeal to a regular experiment. Gen. Pinckney at once moved that a committee of one from each state be appointed to devise and report some compromise. Mr. Rutledge was one of this committee of eleven which agreed to allow one member to every 40,000 inhabitants of the description already reported and that money bills should only originate in the first branch and that in the second branch, each state should have an equal vote. This last part was especially displeasing to a majority who wanted to make the states dwindle into insignificance but it stood as the price of the entrance of the small states.

Another bone of contention was the question how the slaves would be regarded in the ratio of representation. Rufus King could not agree to let them be imported without limitation and then be represented in the national legislature. Gouverneur Morris moved to consider only free inhabitants but only New Jersey voted for his motion. All the South Carolina and Georgia delegation remained intact in making recognition of slavery in the constitution as the price of their entering into the union. If slavery is wrong, said Charles Pinckney, it is justified by the example of all the world. In all ages one half of the people had been slaves. Gen. Pinckney showed that Virginia would gain by stopping importations, it would make her slaves, now more than she wanted, rise in value. He considered the slaves imported subject to duty but he would consider the action proposed limiting the slave trade as an exclusion of South Carolina from the Union. Mr. Baldwin of Georgia thought "national objects alone to be before the convention; not such as, like the present, were of a local nature. Georgia was decided on that point." Gerry agreed that they had nothing to do with the conduct of the states with reference to slaves. Gen. Pinckney declared that he did not think South Carolina would stop the importation of slaves in any short time. Gouverneur Morris wished the whole subject to be committed, including the clauses relating to taxes on exports and to a navigation act. Mr. Sherman said it would be better to let the southern states import slaves than to part with them, if they made a *sine qua non*. Gen. Pinckney was of this committee of one from each state and in that committee a compromise was made by concessions to the eastern states in regard to navigation acts and to the southern states in regard to the importation of slaves and the rendition of runaways. This fact was brought out when Charles Pinckney moved that no act of the legislature for the purpose of regulating the commerce of the United States with foreign powers, among the several states, shall be passed without the assent of two thirds of both houses. He mentioned five distinct commercial interests besides the northern and southern interest. Gen. Pinckney opposed Charles Pinckney with the statement that it was the true interest of southern states to have no regulation of commerce etc. "An understanding on the two subjects, *navigation* and *slavery*," said Madison, "had taken place between these parts of the Union, which explains the votes on the motion depending as well as the language of Gen. Pinckney and others." Mr. Madison favored the compromise but Col. Mason with more sagacity declared that "the *majority* will be governed by their interests. The southern states are in a *minority* in both houses. Is it to be expected that they will deliver themselves, bound hand and foot, to the eastern states and enable them to exclaim in the words of Cromwell on a certain occasion, ' "The Lord hath delivered them into our hands?' " Virginia and North Carolina voted against it but the keenness of the New Englanders in clinching a good bargain extorted from the weaker states, outgeneraled James Madison with his idealism.

One other subject elicited no special opposition—the clause which clothed the United States with the power to assume the debts of the states—but it had in it the seeds of dissension which were soon to germinate. Mr. Butler was dissatisfied and dwelt on the division of opinion concerning the domestic debts, but it was finally agreed that "all debts contracted and engagements entered into by or under the authority of Congress shall be as valid against the United States under the constitution as under the confederation."

Madison left the convention with the conviction "that there never was an assembly of men, charged with great and arduous trust, who were more pure in their motives, or more exclusively or anxiously devoted to the high object committed to them." Pure disinterestedness is rarer than radium. Each brought to the task his past experience, his attachment to his locality and a desire to promote the welfare of his state and the United States. They were driven by fate to doubtful compromises in order to extricate themselves from their present situation. That invisible force was commercial necessity. Commerce called for a stronger government to curb the leveling spirit and to make uniform the laws of trade and the currency. The federalists represented this power behind the convention and they had less faith in the political virtue of the people than in their depravity. They looked the truth that they saw in the face and legislated so as to interweave man's love of money into the support and into the fabric of the government. In the new world, the last hope of mankind, one must recognize the key to its history to be the same as in the previous generations, in a theatre surpassing in magnitude of territory and prizes to be struggled for. Might makes right.

As the close of the task was reached on the 17th of September 1787, seventeen men who had shared in the deliberations did not sign the instrument, which unlike the Articles of Confederation, did not declare that the Union shall be perpetual. These were Caleb Strong, and Elbridge Gerry of Massachusetts, Mr. Ellsworth of Connecticut, Robert Yates and John Lansing of New York, William Houston of New Jersey, Mr. Mercer and Luther Martin of Maryland, Edmund Randolph, George Mason, George Wythe and James McClurg of Virginia, Alexander Martin and W. R. Davie of North Carolina, William Pierce and William Houston of Georgia. Thirty nine signed it. Mr. Madison, however said it was signed by all the members except Mr. Randolph, Mr. Mason and Mr. Gerry.[3] The South Carolina delegation signed in

[3] Madison's Papers, p. 565.

full and went back home thinking that they had done their best for the states and for South Carolina.

They could report that agricultural exports could not be taxed, that their slaves would be counted as three fifths inhabitants and that their right to import slaves was recognized until 1808. Another big item was that the general government would relieve the impoverished state of the debts due to the war. They had to defend themselves when under criticism for having passed a navigation act more favorable to New England than to the state, in return for the benefits of the Union arising to a weak state.

An interesting question to a South Carolinian is, What became of the Charles Pinckney draft? Its importance was obscured for many years by Mr. Madison's treatment of it, whose mild but effective way of discounting it, was accepted as final until Judge Nott in 1908 in "The Mystery of the Pinckney Draft" put the subject in a proper light. That patient, accurate and judicial minded investigator summed up the result of his inquiries as follows: "I was slowly forced to the conclusion that the young South Carolinian on whom I had placed no high estimate, had rendered a great service at a critical time, and that but for his needed work, the Constitution would be at least in form, a very different instrument from the one we revere. My slowly formed conclusion is that if wise and judicious forethought, and much patient work well done, and breadth of view commensurate with the greatness of the subject, and the production at a critical moment of a paper which all other men in or out of the Convention had neglected to prepare, entitle a man to a lasting recognition of his countrymen, there is no framer of the Constitution more entitled to be commemorated in bronze or marble than Charles Pinckney of South Carolina."

CHAPTER XXVII

Adopting the Federal Constitution

The four delegates from South Carolina were also members of the state legislature, to which body they reported by having the Constitution read and explained to them by Mr. Charles Pinckney in January 1788. He gave a concise history[1] of the occurrences at home and abroad which led to the calling of the Convention and a sketch of its proceedings in developing the three branches of the government and the compromises necessary between the small and large states. The ratio of representation, the structure of the House and Senate, the extensive powers given to the judiciary and executive, taxation and militia, called out his brief comments. Upon the whole, said he, he could not but join those in opinion who have asserted that this is the best government that has ever been offered to the world and that, instead of being alarmed at its consequences we should be astonishingly pleased that one so perfect could have been formed from such discordant and unpromising material. The tendency to disunion and its effects upon the people and upon public measures could only be remedied by a strong government. But after all he admitted that the Constitution was in a measure an experiment though he believed it would answer the great ends of public happiness better than any that has yet been devised. Hon. Robert Barnwell, Judge Pendleton, Mr. Pierce Butler, Gen. Pinckney and Mr. Rawlins Lowndes followed in the order of their names. The last named, Mr. Lowndes, started the ripples on the surface when he read the second clause in article sixth, and like a geyser threw out ideas in large jets against the Constitution. One of his criticisms was of sufficient force to call out a number of

---

[1] See Elliott's Debates, Vol. IV, pp. 253-263.

replies and among them elaborate ones from Chancellor Rutledge, Edward Rutledge and Gen. Pinckney. "This Constitution," said Mr. Lowndes, "and the laws of the United States which shall be made in pursuance thereof, and all the treaties made, or which shall be made, under the authority of the United States, shall be the supreme law of the land; and the judges in every state shall be bound thereby—anything in the constitution or laws of any state, to the contrary not withstanding. Now," said he, "in the history of the known world, was there an instance of the rulers of the nation allowed to go so far. Even the most arbitrary kings possessed nothing like it," etc. He also commented on the extensive powers given to the president who was not likely ever to be chosen from South Carolina or Georgia.

Gen. Pinckney thought the arguments thrown out were calculated *ad captandum*—If there was a man in South Carolina fit for the office of President he did not think the being a Southern man could be an objection. More than one president of congress had been taken from this state. The comparison between kings, who were hereditary, with the president who was elected by the people was not a proper one. South Carolina had a thirteenth share in his appointment. Chancellor Rutledge, Hon. Ralph Izard, Dr. David Ramsay and Gen. Pinckney a second time, replied on the subject of the treaty. Mr. Lowndes desired gentlemen to consider that his antagonists were mostly gentlemen of the law, who were capable of giving ingenious explanations to such points as they wish to have adopted and astonished some of his hearers by his eulogy of the old Confederation. "We are now under the government of a most excellent constitution, one that had stood the test of time and carried us through difficulties generally supposed to be unsurmountable; one that has raised us high in the eyes of all nations and given us the enviable blessings of liberty and independence; a constitution sent like a blessing from heaven; yet we are impatient to change for another that vested power in a few men to pull down that fabric which we had raised at the expense of our blood . . . It had been said that this new government was to be considered an experiment. He really was afraid it would prove a fatal one to our peace and happiness. An experiment! No, sir; if we are to make experiments rather let them be such as may do good but which cannot possibly do any injury to us or our posterity. So far from having any expectation of success from such experiments, he sincerely believed that, when this new Constitution should be adopted, the sun of the Southern States would set never to rise again." In proof of this he observed that six of the eastern states formed a majority. "Now was it consonant with reason, with wisdom, with policy to suppose, in a legislature where a majority of persons sat whose interests were greatly different from ours, that we had the smallest chance of receiving adequate advantages? Certainly not. He believed the gentlemen that went from this state to represent us in the Convention possessed as much integrity and stood as high in point of character as any gentlemen that could have been selected and he also believed that they had done everything in their power to procure for us a proportionate share in this new government; but the very little they had gained proved what we may expect in future—that the interests of the northern states would so predominate as to divest us of any pretentions to the title of a republic." Here he discussed the limitation imposed on the importation of negroes and stated that the Eastern states "had been particularly careful not to allow of any burdens—no tonnage or duties, all ports free and open to them. Why call this a reciprocal bargain, which took all from one party, to bestow it on the other?" Here Major Butler observed that they were to pay 5 per cent impost. This, Mr. Lowndes proved, "must fall upon the consumer. They are to be the carriers and we being the consumers, therefore all expenses would fall on us. A great number of gentlemen were captivated with this new Constitution, because those who were in debt would be compelled to pay; others pleased themselves with the reflection that no more confiscation laws would be passed; but these were small advantages, in proportion to the evils which he apprehended from the laws that might be passed by Congress whenever there was a majority of representatives from the eastern states who were governed by prejudices and ideas extremely different from ours ... Congress laboring under many difficulties, asked to regulate commerce for twenty-one years, when the power reverted into the hands of those who originally gave it; but this infallible constitution eased us of any more trouble for it was to regulate commerce *ad infinitum;* and thus called on to pledge ourselves and posterity forever, in support of their measure; so when our local legislature had dwindled down to confined powers of a corporation, we should be liable to taxes and excise; not perhaps payable in paper but in specie.

"However they need not be uneasy, since everything would be managed in future by great men and great men everybody knew, were incapable of acting under mistake or prejudice; they were infallible, so that, if at any future period, we should smart under laws which bore hard on us and think proper to remonstrate, the answer would probably be, ' "Go, you are totally incapable of managing yourselves, go, mind your private affairs, trouble not yourselves with public concerns—mind your business.' "

He was originally against the declaration of independence and the instalment law but when they received the approbation of the people, it became his duty as a good citizen, to promote their due observance.

Mr. Edward Rutledge dissected the old constitution and insisted that we had our full share in the House of Representatives and that fear of the northern interests prevailing was ill founded. Several of the northern states were already full of people; it was otherwise with us; the migration to the south was immense and we should in the course of a few years, rise high in our representation, whilst other states would keep their present position. The Southern States would be the last to raise objections to shipping and carrying trade which was to be vested in Americans. One more unreported speech by Chancellor Rutledge closed the first day and that night was largely drawn on by Gen. Pinckney in preparing an exhaustive reply on the subject of the treaty and in complimenting the force and variety of Mr. Lowndes' arguments and *ad captandum* spurts, by going over again the appointment of representatives, the argument about the importation of slaves, the weakness of the state, the strength of the eastern states and the agreement about the importation of slaves. "A committee of the States was appointed in order to accommodate this matter and it was settled on the footing recited in the Constitution." He could have entered into details here as a participant in the bargain but the members of the Philadelphia Convention were not at liberty to gossip about its proceedings. In Gen. Pinckney's own opinion the government could not under the constitution emancipate the slaves, nor prevent the return of runaways.

Mr. Lowndes was willing to give up his post, opposed by such a phalanx of able antagonists any one of whom was able to contend with him but further observations would be made at the request of respectable members, men of good sense, but not speakers, who wished him to state his sentiments on certain points. "Much had been said from different parts of the House against the old Confederation. He could not agree to this because there did not appear any evidence of the fact . . . Their prudence and their wisdom particularly appeared in the care which they had taken sacredly to guarantee the sovereignty of each state. The treaty of peace expressly agreed to acknowledge us as free, sovereign, and independent states, which privileges we at present lived in the exercise of. But this new constitution at once swept those privileges away, being severeign of all; so that this state would dwindle into a mere skeleton of what it was; its legislative powers would be pared down to little more than those now vested in the corporation; and he should value the honor of a seat in the legislature in no higher estimation than a seat in the city council." He developed the difficulties found in choosing a president and went over again the ground relating to the lack of reciprocity in the regulation of our commerce, which put us in the power of a set of men who may fritter away the value of our produce to little or nothing, by compelling payment of exhorbitant freightage. Mr. Lowndes concluded a long speech with a glowing eulogy of the Old Confederation and challenged his opponents whilst one state objected to get over that section which said: "The articles of this Confederation shall be inviolably observed in every state; and the union shall be perpetual; nor shall any alteration at any time hereafter be made in them, unless such alteration be agreed to in Congress of the United States and be afterwards confirmed by the legislatures of each state."

Much more was said but very little that was not a repetition was introduced. Gen. Pinckney was the chief antagonist. To Mr. Lowndes question "What harm had paper money done?", Gen. Pinckney replied that "Mr. Lowndes had already told the House that he lost 15,000 guineas by depreciation; but he would tell the gentleman what further injuries it had done—it had corrupted the morals of the people; it had directed them from the path of honest industry to the ways of ruinous speculation; it had destroyed public and private credit and had brought total ruin on numberless widows and orphans." In his last speech Mr. Lowndes still held his ground, kept reiterating his charges and came to the end with words that received more attention after 1861 than when they were spoken: "Popularity, said he, was what he never courted; but on this point he spoke merely to point out these dangers to which his fellow-citizens were exposed—dangers that were so evident, that when he ceased to exist, he wished for no other epitaph, than to have inscribed on his tomb, "Here lies the man that opposed the Constitution because it was ruinous to the liberty of America." Chancellor Rutledge perhaps voiced the impatience of a part of the Convention in the words, "I have often heard the honorable gentleman with much pleasure, but on the present occasion I am astonished at his perseverance."

Patrick Calhoun of Ninety Six thought that too great latitude was allowed in religion. James Lincoln of Ninety Six declared that the more he heard about the constitution, the more he was persuaded of its evil tendency. "What does this proposed constitution do? It changes totally the form of government. From a well-digested, well-formed democratic, you are rushing into an aristocratic government. What have you been contending for these ten years past? Liberty! What is liberty? The power of governing yourselves . . . was there ever an instance in the world that a people in this situation possessing all that heaven could give on earth, all that human wisdom and valor could procure—was there ever a people so situated, as calmly and deliberately to convene themsleves together for the express purpose of considering whether they should give away or retain these blessings?" He found fault with the president, "this mighty, this omnipotent governor general who might be elected years and years, with the total silence about the freedom of the press and the absence of a bill of rights." On the question being put for the Convention to assemble in Charles Town on the 12th of May, the ayes were 76 and the nays 75. Only two up-country votes went to make the majority, those of Patrick Calhoun and John Purvis. Of the parishes, of Prince Frederick, St. Stephens and St. Peters were all against the convention. St. David voted nay. There were altogether 18 of the lower parish votes cast against the convention. Among the worthy names opposing were Gen. Sumter and Judge Pendleton. Aedanus Burke was in the Charles Town delegation and went with the crowd. By so narrow a margin was the convention called. Had the two Abbeville votes been cast with the majority of that district, there would have been no convention.

Mr. Lowndes, the under dog that gets the sympathy of spectators who are in a place of safety, from this time disappears from the councils of the state. He had been unwittingly a representative of the unrepresented multitude. Had the people been consulted there would have been no revolution. Had they been fully represented in this convention the constitution as then worded would have been rejected. In point of time he was the first of that party that was called State Rights or Republican. The moral courage exhibited by him and the ability with which he withstood immense odds against him presents a figure majestic and imposing. Mr. Rutledge chided Mr. Lowndes because his arguments assumed that the people would choose the most worthless and most negligent to fill the office. That was a fact. He placed safety first, as a lawyer does when he draws a note and mortgage, as if an honest and wealthy borrower was as slick as an eel. When he subjected the constitution to a close scrutiny he saw the same flaws that Mr. Madison and Mr. Pinckney and first of all Wm. Henry Drayton had seen in it. Mr. Lowndes seeing the defects and prompted by his knowledge of what was in man, pointed out in what particular the constitution was dangerous to the liberty of the southern people and advised the calling of another convention. Not a piece of property but the happiness of a people free, and with a bright future before them, was at stake. As a patriot, he could not be silent, even if his intensity of feeling on the subject was adding to his unpopularity.

Mr. Lowndes declined to be a member of the convention which assembled at the appointed day in the hall of the custom house in Charles Town. A quorum being present on the second day, the debate under the presidency of Hon. Thomas Pinckney was opened again by Mr. Charles Pinckney. Judge Burke, who represented an inland township, Mr. Bowman, Dr. Fayssoux and others opposed; Judge Pendleton, C. C. Pinckney, Hon. J. J. Pringle and others favored the adoption of the constitution. Only two speeches made on this occasion were reported, one by Charles Pinckney and one by Mr. Tweed. The tone of Mr. Pinckney's speech is now quite different. Seven states had adopted and victory was in sight. He was among the first in that long line of orators that felt elated over the lessons youthful America had taught and was going to teach aged Europe in the science of government and over the enlarged liberty that had come to Ireland and other people. The people of the union, he divided into commercial, professional and agricultural, mutually dependent on each other; the thirteen states differed in constitutions, manners, population and products. These dissimilarities as he had observed them in puritan New England, among the Dutch in New York, Quakers in Pennsylvania and Catholics in Maryland, were striking but said he, striking as this difference is, it is not to be compared with the difference that there is between the inhabitants of the northern and Southern states. "Nature has drawn as strong marks of distinction in the habits and manners of the people as she has in her climate and productions." As the constitution was to operate on both states and citizens he had thought it necessary to dwell on these points; for, for a people thus situated, was this constitution intended. For the benefit of those who had not had time or opportunity for investigation, he began a disquisition on governments, separated into three simple forms, having their sovereignty in a person or in an assembly or in the people. The advantages and dangers of these three simple elementary forms of government being set forth, the speaker hoped that the president elected periodically would have all the advantages of a monarch—unity of council, vigor, secrecy, despatch without attendant evils; that a senate constructed on rotative principles for a term of six years, would have all the advantages of an aristocracy without its evils and being elected by the state legislatures would prove to be their safeguards as political associations; and that the House of Representatives being elected biennially would keep the purse strings in the hands of the people. "To the philosophic mind," said he, "how new and awful an instance do the

United States at present exhibit in the political world. They exhibit, sir, the first instance of a people, who being dissatisfied with their government—unattacked by foreign force and undisturbed by domestic uneasiness—coolly and deliberately resort to the virtue and good sense of their country, for a correction of their public errors."

In his last speech, Mr. Pinckney took for his text the 10th section of the 1st article of the constitution. This section he called the soul of the constitution. It contained the restraints upon the States which "will teach them to cultivate those principles of public honor and private honesty which are the sure road to national character and happiness." These restraints related to issuing paper money, tender-laws, and the impairing the obligation of contracts. In reference to the emission of paper money, he said, in conclusion, "How extremely useful and advantageous must this restraint be, to those states which mean to be honest and not to defraud their neighbors! Henceforth the citizens of the states may trade with each other without fear of tender laws or laws impairing the nature of contracts. The citizens of South Carolina will then be able to trade with those of Rhode Island, North Carolina and Georgia and be sure of receiving the value of their commodities. Can this be done at present? It cannot. However just the demand may be, yet still your honest, suffering citizen must be content to receive their depreciated paper or give up the debt. But above all, how much will this section tend to restore your credit with foreigners—to rescue your national character from that contempt which must ever follow the most flagrant violations of public faith and private honesty! No more shall paper money, no more shall tender laws, drive their commerce from our shores and darken the American name in every country where it is known, etc."

Within five previous years, the legislature in South Carolina had passed the pine barren act, issued paper money and was now moving the capital to a more central place and aiming to change the basis of representation. In the midst of this sea of uncertainty and misgiving, the new constitution appeared as a city of refuge. The aim of the general government was to preserve the states from foreign invasion and internal discord, to make and enforce treaties, protect and foster commerce. The constitution was made by and in the interests of the trading and commercial classes, a sort of harness for the people, and the great constitutional questions and the vast prizes at stake gave great importance to the study of law and lawyers whose legal talent was their stock in trade. The people, the source of all power and authority, without whom there could be no government nor commerce, were left to receive all the benefits which accrued to a well regulated commerce, to enjoy markets for produce and the privileges of furnishing the revenue and to paddle their own canoe, an uncommon privilege at that time. The agricultural classes were the great body of the nation and for their imporvement and prosperity nothing was done directly by this best government the world ever saw. On the eighth day of the convention, Gen. Sumter brought things to a head by moving to adjourn till the 20th of October. The motion was defeated by a vote of 135 to 89. This was decisive. The state which had a great future before it, under the guidance of a superabundance of wise and able men, decided to transfer certain sovereign powers to the United States and to receive in turn no small benefits from the United strength of the thirteen states. Looking back through seventy-one years, William Gilmore Simms said, "She entered the Confederation of her sister states, against the warnings of some of her great men and perhaps with some general misgivings. But she was naked, poor, struggling with disaster and debt; and still present to *her* eye, as to that of all the other states, was the dread of foreign invasion—an ever present fear, after the late experience of a seven year war—. The result of the Confederacy by natural laws was to abridge the independent energies of the Southern States; to cut off its trade and disparage its capacity for commerce and manufactures." The opposition dwindled from 75 in the legislature to 73 in the convention and the majority grew from 76 to 149. Part of this was owing to larger delegations from the parishes. Sixty two more votes were cast by them in the convention. Part of the increase was due to the campaign conducted about which little can be reported. St. David's for instance and the place lying between Savannah and the Edisto changed to the affirmative and other parishes which had been divided sent a solid delegation after the campaigns were over. The affirmative side was increased by two new voting precincts, led by Lemuel Alston and Samuel Earle on the Saluda, John Chesnut on the Wateree, John Harris of Ninety Six, Judge Henry Pendleton of Saxe Gotha, Rev. Francis Cummins of York were prominent individuals who separatel from their delegations in voting aye. Wade Hampton, John L. Gervais, Judge Burke, Gen. Sumter, Joseph Calhoun, William Butler, John Bowie, William Hill, Edward Lacy, Thomas Taylor and others were opposed to the constitution. In his History of South Carolina David Ramsay who was in the body relates that the vote indicating the adoption of the constitution caused a strong and involuntary expression of applause and joy to burst forth from the numerous transported spectators.

RECAPITULATION

1670-1790

The colony at Charles Town, founded in 1670, was more than any other the new England in America. Locke's Constitution provided an established church, barons, and baronies, and other lesser lights with large landed possessions, and guarded against any possible descent into democracy. In 1712, many of the statutes of the mother country were declared in force in the colony and the school system was modeled after English schools. Locke's Constitution, or its modification, was nominally in force till 1719, when the restless people threw off the yoke of the Lords Proprietors, who could not protect the people from the enemies of the colony. The colony had to struggle for existence against human enemies, as well as against the wild forces of nature and the fatal diseases of the tropics. From 1719 to 1775, the colony was under the Royal government and it shared abundantly in the rewards of peace and in the evil of wars. The peace of 1763 brought to South Carolina the security which came from the removal of Spaniards from St. Augustine and the hostile Indians in the north-west and from a place of refuge under the British lion's protection. Up to this time, there had been continued friction between the Commons House and the representatives of the crown. "The speaker of the House", said Gov. Glen, "had acquired almost the powers of a prime minister, the Governor had to consult him upon nearly all measures and take his advice —if he wished things to go ahead smoothly in his administration." Such was the predominance of the Assembly when the war ended and the stamp act followed. It was along this line that the antagonisms between the home and foreign element in the government were engendered. The Board of Trade, advised by royalists who saw the trend in the colonies, began to recover their lost power; but their efforts only excited more pronounced opposition. Economic causes underlay the trouble in Massachusetts, but in South Carolina, the highly favored colony, it was a mere love of self-direction, called the love of liberty.

The Assembly, up to 1769, was composed of representatives from below the Santee with the exception of one or two parishes. In the crisis which came from the government's double role—to stand against the crown for self-government and to restrain the angry democratic majority in the inland parts, the Assembly was equal to all emergencies. It yielded the minimum concessions to the up-country democrats by carefully weighing them beforehand so as to make no mistake in graduating the representation of the outlying parts. In 1776, the Assembly without consulting the people, changed their government into three branches, Governor, Assembly and Council, elected by the Assembly. It was a thoroughly centralized body, keeping in its hands the appointment of county officers. The only part the people had in it, was the election of the legislature. From this germinal idea must be traced the differences from the county arrangement in democratic states, and the gradual decentralization, as the sections became more assimilated and better understood, must not be overlooked.

Two years later, the larger dissenting element led by Tennent, Hart, Furman and assisted by Gadsden, William Henry Drayton, C. C. Pinckney and others, caused the disestablishment of the church and some strides toward a broader democracy. This so-called Constitution, made by the legislature, served the state till 1790, when under the urgency of Judge Pendleton and others, the capital was changed to Columbia and a more equitable representation was established. The Constitution was formed after the Convention had voted to be merged in the United States. The state had yielded to the great current of the day, set in motion by the greed of England and the perplexity of the trading and commercial interests of the states, caused by it. The backwoods people always conservative and stable as the Alleghany range, would have rejected the Constitution. William Henry Drayton, who was dead, and Rawlins Lowndes saw farther and more accurately into the future than the majority leaders. Charles Pinckney and James Madison saw with equal clearness the danger to the southern minority, but they were idealists, who were unable to cope with the leaders of the matter of fact, money loving beings which fill the world. If the testimony of the leading actors in the convention at Philadelphia is reliable, the mainspring of their actions was self-interest. Such appeared to be the key to the final compromise which allowed governmental aid to the north and protection of slavery to the south. That concession, frail as it was, buttressed the aristocracy of the south and left it the choice of three roads to pursue—To allow Virginia to hold the states in equilibrium, or to elevate the backward people in the south and the plebeians in other states, or to fall a victim to the more aggressive avaricious democracy, which, like stars in their courses which fought against Sisera, will fight against and pull down whatever is higher than itself. The Constitution had in embryo, its Esau and Jacob, one aggressive, the other asking only the protection of the government over its local affairs.

APPENDIX

I

MAJOR JAMES L. COKER[1]

FOREWORD

In making this effort to comply with the request of my esteemed friend, Dr. H. T. Cook, that I write a sketch of a great and good citizen, now dead, for Dr. Cook's book entitled "Rambles in the Pee Dee", I am likely to stretch the rambling privilege beyond the limits of the Pee Dee; and perhaps, in the opinion of some people, beyond the limits of good taste. However, I trust the reader will be sufficiently charitable to excuse any faults in presentation or in the selection of the material, for one cannot help writing in his own way even if it be a rambling or defective way.

J. W. NORWOOD.

MAJOR JAMES LIDE COKER
1837-1918

I came in contact with the late Major James Lide Coker over a period of nearly fifty years. He made a strong impression on me in my early childhood. After I was grown, I sought every opportunity to be in his company in order to observe him and to get his views on various subjects.

In addition to my own knowledge of him, I have gathered some facts from others which would throw light upon his character and attainments. One such source was my father, who was five years older than Major Coker but had known him from boyhood. They were interested in business enterprises together for thirty or forty years, and for six or seven years of that time were business partners. My father admired Major Coker more than any other of his friends or acquaintances. He told me that his first recollection of Major Coker was when they were boys going to school together at Society Hill. In playing ball and other games young Coker displayed noticeable energy, activity, and earnestness, my father said; and these characteristics were shown in his every undertaking throughout his life.

In addition to his energy and sound common-sense, Major Coker had remarkable natural intellectual ability, and was blessed with a noble, unselfish character, and a sound physical constitution. He was unusually versatile in his intellectual as well as his business talents and attainments. After finishing the course at the South Carolina Military Academy, as there were no great agricultural schools in America at that time, Major Coker took a special course in chemistry and botany at Harvard, with a view to using this knowledge in practical agriculture.

His studies at Harvard were pursued with uncommon thoroughness. He would take his lunch with him into the chemical laboratory, and spend hours in watching and studying every detail and change in his experiments. His knowledge of chemistry was so accurate and thorough that fifty years later he could give in correct chemical terms the composition of various substances. For many years, even after he was engaged in banking, mercantile, agricultural and manufacturing interests of magnitude for our state, he maintained a chemical laboratory in which he worked for more or less practical ends, and perhaps for entertainment. As a young man he became well, if not intimately acquainted with the great botanist, Asa Gray, at Harvard, and young Coker was pleased to learn that Dr. Gray corresponded with Dr. Curtis, the Episcopal clergyman of Society Hill, who

APPENDIX

was a botanist of attainment for his time. Major Coker stood among the first in all his classes, and in no exception to the well established rule, that boys who do thorough work in school and college make useful, honorable, and successful citizens.

While at Harvard Major Coker attended lectures in Cambridge and Boston on subjects other than botany and chemistry. Many years later, in 1906, he gave me an account of a lecture on slavery delivered by the great self-educated blacksmith and linguist reformer, Elihu Burritt.

Major Coker's father was a wealthy merchant and planter at Society Hill, having established a business there about one hundred years ago, which has been continuously and successfully operated since that time by his descendants. After Major Coker had finished his course at Harvard, his father purchased a large plantation in Hartsville township and gave his son an interest in it. Major Coker operated this plantation most successfully from 1857 to 1861. There is a popular idea that scientific farmers are not practical; that while they can grow farm products, they cannot "grow" money, as their products cost more than they yield in the markets. This idea is as fallacious as many other popular opinions. Scientific knowledge never fails to help any man in practical agriculture. If one should fail, after having acquired scientific knowledge, certainly he would have failed without such knowledge. Major Coker was not selfish in his success but organized an agricultural club, giving his neighbors the benefit of his wider knowledge.

His conspicuous agricultural success was interrupted by the Civil War. He promptly volunteered for military service when South Carolina seceded, and was elected Captain of Company G, Ninth S. C. Infantry, which later became Company E, Sixth S. C. Infantry. He took part

APPENDIX

in numerous battles in Virginia, sometimes as a field officer, but usually as captain of his company. He was frequently cited for bravery and skill. He was dangerously wounded in the left thigh, at Lookout Mountain, Tennessee, in October 1863, and was unfitted for further active military duty. His men, without exception so far as I can learn, were devoted to him. One of them said that Stonewall Jackson was not more beloved and respected by his men than Captain Coker was by the members of his company. The survivors had a reunion at his home annually for thirty years. At one of these reunions Major Coker made the following statement regarding his men:

"Shortly after our arrival at Manassas the 9th Regiment was attached to D. R. Jones' Brigade, and was ordered to cross Bull Run at Blackburn's Ford, to pitch camp with the rest of the Brigade at what was known as Camp Pettus. . . .

"On these Virginia hills we again betook ourselves to drill, and good work was followed by gratifying results. The company was noticeable for its fine drill and soldierly bearing. On the occasion of the first general review of the brigade, General Jones, who was a West Point graduate and a resigned United States army officer, sent for your captain after the parade, and after complimenting the company in high terms, insisted that so well drilled a company should be suitably clothed. He instructed me to go to Richmond to procure the goods for a company uniform, and have it made up and issued to the men.

"Surprised at this unsolicited commendation from so competent a judge, I obeyed the order with a pardonable pride, and endeavored to secure neat uniform suits with as little delay as possible. The best goods I could find for the purpose were purchased, a Richmond tailor made

APPENDIX

them up for me as best he could without accurate measures, and our first Confederate jackets and trousers, with military buttons and stripes, were made to take the place of our former nondescript apparel. This uniform served us well for many months, and certainly pleased General Jones, who took the credit for the improved dress of the company."

His company was actively engaged in Virginia almost continuously for two years, before he was wounded in Tennessee. The following refers to service rendered the latter part of his Virginia campaign:

"Headquarters Jenkins' Brigade,
April 29th, 1863.

"General Orders No.——.

I. The Brigadier General Commanding, announces with pleasure his satisfaction with the men and officers whose conduct has been brought to his immediate attention in the opening of the campaign.

III. The conduct of Captains Coker and Crawford, with their small corps of riflemen, the former openly engaging and repulsing the gunboats on the Nansemond River, has deservedly won the admiration of every one.

(Then follows a reference to Captain Crawford's death).

By command of Brigadier General M. Jenkins."

When Major Coker was wounded, Col. John Bratton (afterwards General) was commanding the brigade. In his report he stated:

"I have to regret the loss of the services of Captain J. L. Coker, 6th Regiment, South Carolina Volunteers, acting assistant Adjutant General on my staff. He was seriously wounded while nobly performing his duty."

At another reunion of Major Coker's company he made the following statement with reference to the engagement in which he was wounded:

APPENDIX

"Bratton's brigade lost about three hundred and fifty men in this engagement, out of fifteen hundred engaged.

"My active connection with the company now came to an end. As I was borne through our camp on the next day after this battle, I requested that the litter be set down for awhile, in order that I might take leave of my old company. Their affectionate concern and kind expressions that day I can never forget. For two years and a half we had been associated together under the trying experiences of a great war. I loved my comrades in arms, and valued the respect and affection they generously gave me, and never more so than on that day when our connection was severed.

"I will not go into detail as to my experience at the Hicks' House, where I lay wounded for over six months after falling into the enemy's lines, when Bragg was defeated at Missionary Ridge.

"Sergeant Nettles and Corporal Wilkins, at their own request, were detailed to nurse and care for me, and certainly no wounded soldier was ever favored with kinder friends.

"After Missionary Ridge, one of them was obliged to leave, and the lot fell to Wilkins. Sam Nettles remained with me and aided my devoted mother in nursing me. To their attention, with the blessing of God, I owe my life.

"Sergeant Nettles and myself became prisoners of war at the Hicks' House, where I was lying wounded, when the country near Chattanooga was taken possession of by the enemy after the battle of Missionary Ridge.

"It is very pleasant to relate the kindness received from the Federal surgeons. One of them, Dr. Taylor, of Indiana, proved himself a friend indeed.

"He seemed to enjoy the visits to the room where my mother, Sergeant Nettles and myself lived, and I am

APPENDIX

sure his thoughtful attention and professional skill contributed to our comfort, while his hearty friendship cheered and enlivened our dreary life. When he was promoted to full surgeon and ordered to another field, he rode to see me before leaving, to bid me good-bye, and to offer me money for my necessities.

"I did not take his money as I had other resources, but I was touched by his disinterested kindness. After the war I tried to find him, but learning from Washington records that he was dead.

"In May ('64), when it was thought I could be moved on a stretcher, I was sent to the rear to prison hospitals. At Louisville, where I was kept two weeks, many of the best ladies were our friends, as my mother found out. She was treated with great consideration by Mrs. Bridgeford, Mrs. Anderson, and others, who entertained her at their homes. When it was deemed safe to move me to Fort McHenry, several ladies came to the boat to see me off, and citizens, strangers to me, came to lift my litter and place me comfortably on the Ohio River steamer.

"We were, of course, under an armed guard; a sergeant wondered that I received more attention than a wounded Federal General, who was on the same steamer. I understood that the respect accorded me was due to my Confederate uniform.

"On the steamer a Kentucky girl called my attention to the buttons, 290 in number, with which her dress was trimmed in honor of Semmes' Confederate cruiser, then known as 'The 290', which was at that time a terror to the Yankee merchantmen.

"But there were Northern men who came to my stretcher with other feeling than sympathy. One hard looking man, after abusing the South in brutal fashion, said to me: 'Yes, you went to war to get your rights; you got part of them there', (pointing to my fractured thigh.) 'You should have them all, there', (pointing to my head.) Others behaved in similar fashion, plying me with argument for hours, until my mother protested. One fellow was greatly offended because I suggested that his ardent hatred could better be exhibited at the front with Grant.

"At Parkersburg, we were put ashore, and good Confederate sympathizers soon found us at the hotel where we were stopping for a few days, under the Federal surgeon's direction. They offered us money and showed us great kindness. The money was declined, as there were many needy Confederate prisoners; the kindness and sympathy were accepted as a gracious offering to our much loved cause.

"A friend of mine, a citizen of the town, whom I had been associated with at Cambridge, heard of me there, and loaded me with attentions. He was a Union man, but was married to a relative of Stonewall Jackson. She, of course, was a thorough Southerner in her sympathies.

"The hotel keeper at Parkersburg gave us the best rooms in the house, served us generously in every way, and when we were ordered away on our journey, he refused to accept payment for his lavish entertainment.

"These and other attentions we appreciated as some compensation for the trials incident to our condition. Perhaps the telling of them may encourage and strengthen the disposition to show mercy and kindness to those who are suffering and helpless.

"At Fort McHenry my devoted mother and my good friend were separated from me. Sam Nettles got back to me after a few days, thanks to his insistence, and to the interest in my condition which he awakened in the Provost Marshal, who had charge of the prisoners. This humane officer procured a special order from General Lew Wallace, then in command in Baltimore, who over-

APPENDIX

ruled the hospital authorities, and sent my good friend and nurse back to my bedside.

"Our guards at this place were 'hundred day men', from Ohio. They had never been in battle, and had none of the virtues of good soldiers.

"The best part of the food and delicacies sent to the hospital by our Baltimore lady friends, these fellows appropriated to their own use, and were abusive and insulting to the wounded prisoners, except when the Provost was around. That officer was a credit to his profession.

"In July, 1864, we were sent into the Confederacy on parole. When I reached Richmond an acquaintance at the War Department brought me my commission as Major of the Sixth S. C. Regiment, to which office I had been promoted shortly after I was wounded. At this time our regiment was in the throes of its hard labor about Petersburg and Richmond, and not one of them could get to Richmond to see me as I passed through."

Col. R. M. Sims, writing to Major Coker years after the war, said:

"I think that Jenkins', afterwards Bratton's Brigade, was one of the very best in the Army of Northern Virginia.

"It must be very gratifying to you and to the old members of your company, and to your families for generations to come to know that your's was one of the very best of all the companies in this brigade."

Colonel Sims and General Bratton were devoted friends of Major Coker the remainder of their lives. The former named a son in honor of Major Coker.

As to the conditions at the close of the war, Major Coker writes:

"I knew but little of the conditions at home until the last of July, 1864, when I was paroled, and sent through our lines from Fort McHenry. No exchanges were being

APPENDIX

made at that time, on account of General Grant's policy to retain our prisoners, but disabled men might be paroled, and my mother secured the parole of Sergeant Nettles, on the ground that I could not be sent back without his help, and so I had the happiness to bring him home with me. At home there were only women and children and old men, with such wounded and disabled soldiers as could procure furloughs. If there were a few able bodied men exempt from service for one reason or another, if they had not good cause, they got but poor encouragement from their neighbors, especially from the true Southern women, who looked upon all shirkers with contempt.

"What could be done by the people at home to supply food and clothing to the men at the front, was done, not only with cheerfulness, but with alacrity and pleasure. The women were untiring in working for the soldiers, and in caring for any sick and wounded who might come within their reach.

"The home people were under a constant and mighty burden of anxiety. Their sons, and brothers, and husbands were in danger, and every paper brought tidings of battles in which some loved ones were engaged. Hardly a family escaped the sorrow which the death of loved ones inflicted. Some of these instances were most pitiful. Let me recall a few. A widow, Mrs. Hudson, near Hartsville, sent three sons and a son-in-law into the army, all the male members of her family. All but one were members of Company E, 6th Regiment. One died of disease in camp, two were killed on the field of battle, the last one was mortally wounded, and was brought home in 1864 to die. Another widow, Mrs. Kilgore, had two sons in this company. Both fell on one field. Three other families sent two brothers each,— young men hardly grown,—to Virginia with the Harts-

APPENDIX

ville Light Infantry. All of them now lie under Virginia soil, having fallen victims to disease or battle.

"Many other instances almost as sad might be given, but let these suffice. Many young wives became helpless widows. Many tender children were orphaned by the cruel hand of unholy war. Sorrow and despair found seats in nearly every home.

"When I got back from Richmond, in March, 1865, the sight that met my eyes was appalling. That vindictive General, William Tecumseh Sherman, had passed along through our State, burning cities and homes, and desolating the country. His followers who believed in his vindictive maxims, terrorized the old men, and the women and children of Hartsville for three successive days. They bullied an old and feeble man, Mr. Joseph Norwood, and, without reason burned the gin house on the old Hart place, endangering the residence occupied by helpless women refugees. They came to Dr. Wilson's, upset the furniture from floor to garret, stole the clothing and silver, took all the food, and with threats demanded and obtained all valuables, even the rings from Mrs. Wilson's fingers. At the writer's house they burned all the cotton, except a few bales which were inaccessible, robbed the ladies of their watches and silver, gutted the residence, took all the farm animals and cattle, with every vehicle on the place, hauled away the corn and the bacon, and left the plantation a picture of desolation. These instances are not singular. Our experience was the common experience of the people all along Sherman's inglorious march. Some day his barbarous practices and spirit will be execrated by the good people of every section.

"The war left our people poor indeed, but they were proud of the splendid record of their armies. They continue so until this day. May God bless our Southland and its people forevermore!"

Mrs. Dr. Wilson, to whom reference is made, was a sister of Major Coker. I may be permitted to ramble here to show that Major Coker has not exaggerated Sherman's ruthlessness. Rev. Dr. John Bachman, aged 75 at the time, was beaten by Sherman's men for no offense. They erroneously supposed that he could tell them where private valuables were hidden. He requested them to kill him rather than bruise or maim an old man who could not live long. Besides being a minister, Dr. Bachman was a distinguished scientist. His close friend, Audubon, gives him credit for valuable assistance in the preparation of what is considered the greatest work ever written on birds. To a greater extent he assisted the sons of Audubon, who were sons-in-law of Dr. Bachman, in their work on quadrupeds. He was a correspondent, acquaintance and friend of Humboldt. Contrast Sherman's methods with those of Lee. When Lee invaded enemy territory he gave strict orders to his men not to damage private property. On one occasion when some soldiers in the regiment commanded by Col. D. G. McIntosh, a native of Society Hill and a boyhood friend of Major Coker, used fences on private property in building a fire with which to cook their provisions, General Lee reprimanded the Colonel for not being on the alert to prevent such a breach of orders.

Notwithstanding Major Coker's experience, and the subsequent inability of the best people of the North to prevent further injury to the South in reconstruction days, he was free from bitterness. He recognized that there were noble, patriotic men in the North as well as in the South, and that there were brutal men in the Confederate army as well as in the Union army. My father told me that when secession was agitated, Major

APPENDIX

Coker was one of the few men with whom he could talk who was thoroughly tolerant of differences of opinion. Major Coker did not believe in slavery, but he did believe that the tariff laws operated against the best interest of the South, and he accepted for the time being the popular idea in South Carolina that it was wise to secede, and that we had the constitutional right of secession. Such a view was probably due to the doctrine of Calhoun and Hayne that a State could nullify laws legally passed by specific constitutional authority. He expressed the opinion to me, over forty years after the war, that if the South had been successful it would have been a misfortune, and that long before the time at which we were talking, the South would have wanted to be back in the Union.

In the spring of 1865, though broken in body as well as fortune, he started cheerfully to rebuild his fortune, by having hired labor plow with a diseased horse, the only one left on the place, because Sherman's men considered it worthless; and one milch cow saved from Sherman's men by being hidden in the swamps. He did light manual work himself while directing others. He continued to farm on an ever increasing scale for more than fifty years after the war, and never failed to do so profitably. In January, 1895, he told me that 1894 was the least favorable year for growing cotton profitably he had ever experienced. That crop was sold by him for less than five cents a pound, but his net profits amounted to seven per cent on his investment at that time of one hundred thousand dollars in farming. Many large, as well as small, cotton farmers made serious losses that year. The cotton of Major Coker's grown before the war, which was burned by Sherman's men in March 1865, was an independent fortune for the time.

APPENDIX

A year or two after the Civil War, he started a small country store in order to sell farm necessities to his neighbors. This little country store, twelve miles from the nearest railroad station, has developed into one of the largest department store in South Carolina. After the Civil War there was in the rural sections of South Carolina very little business of any consequence except farming and small mercantile businesses. Practically all the cotton grown in the State was shipped to Charleston and sold through commission merchants. These commission merchants made advances to farmers and country merchants, charging them interest on advances and commissions for selling their cotton. Major Coker formed a partnership with my father in the cotton and naval-stores commission business in Charleston in January 1874, but continued for about three years to give his entire time to his Hartsville interests. The Charleston business grew to such proportions that he finally moved to Charleston and took an active part in its management for two or three years, when he sold his interest in the Charleston business to his partner, and returned to Hartsville in January 1881. The county seat of Darlington was fifteen miles away. In 1881, Major Coker organized the National Bank of Darlington, which was the first bank established in the Pee Dee section, or in the State north of Charleston and east of Columbia. He was practically the sole manager of the bank, and had to drive fifteen miles over country roads to direct its affairs. The bank at once became one of the most successful banks in the State. In 1886, after it had been in existence five years, its stock was worth forty per cent premium, although it had paid cash dividends for three or four years. Its capital was then doubled by having all shareholders take additional stock at par or sell the privilege of so doing. As no premium was paid

APPENDIX

in, the stock was reduced in value to $120.00 a share. In response to an inquiry from me, Major Coker expressed the opinion that under normal conditions the bank would make ten per cent per annum on a value of $120.00 a share, or twelve per cent on the par value. Most men overestimate the prospects of their own business, but knowing then that Major Coker was a rare exception to the general rule, I bought ten shares of the stock, the first stock I ever owned, at $120.00 a share, and made more than ten per cent per annum on the cost. He did not volunteer opinions, and was by no means free in expressing them when asked to do so, but his opinion in this instance was typical of the man. He was eminently conservative. He was no extremist except that he did everything he undertook "extremely" well. His prudence would not permit him to contract large debt, in the expectation of making big profits on borrowed money. He never bought stocks, or anything else, on margins. He never engaged in what is termed "speculation". In the course of a year or two after organizing the National Bank of Darlington, he organized the Darlington Manufacturing Company; was its first president; had the mill built and turned over to his brother, Captain William C. Coker, to manage. A year or two later he placed the bank in the hands of his brother, William C. Coker, and his young friend, Bright Williamson—the latter being the present successful manager of the bank.

About this time he advocated building a railroad from Darlington to Hartsville, and suggested to the Atlantic Coast Line that they build such a road and operate it. The Atlantic Coast Line declined to make the investment, as they felt that the profits of the business would not justify the outlay. Major Coker then suggested that the people of Darlington join him in organizing a company to build the road. Few people there were willing to invest in it, on the ground that the road would not be worth much to them, although it might help to build up the Hartsville section. Major Coker, therefore, formed a company and built the road himself. A few of his friends subscribed for small amounts of stock, but the outside investment was small. His son James had, in the meantime, graduated from Stevens Institute of Technology, and he, under his father's advice, did the engineering. The road was probably built as well and as economically as it could have been built by the Atlantic Coast Line or the Pennsylvania Railroad. Major Coker operated the road profitably for several years, and then sold it to the Atlantic Coast Line for a profit. I asked him why he sold the road, inasmuch as it was a paying investment, which would probably become more profitable as the section developed. He replied that the only connection of the little road was with the Atlantic Coast Line, and by them he had been treated with the utmost fairness and generosity. He stated that as long as Mr. Henry Walters, who was the controlling spirit in the Atlantic Coast Line, live, he felt no uneasiness as to the treatment he would receive at his hands, but, that in the course of time, Mr. Walters would cease to direct the affairs of the road, and it might fall into hands that would be illiberal, if not unjust.

About the time the railroad was built, Major Coker's oldest son, James, organized a corporation for the manufacture of wood pulp from Carolina pine, to be used in the manufacture of paper. (The Cokers were the first to successfully manufacture wood pulp from pine wood, which could be used in making paper.) Difficulties which seemed insurmountable developed in this enterprise, and it became necessary to invest three of four times as much in the plant as was originally planned.

APPENDIX

Finally the business became firmly established, and has been remarkably profitable. Major Coker's financial aid and business judgment were of vital interest to his son's business. After making the manufacture of paper profitable, Major Coker started in a comparatively small way to manufacture cones and parallel tubes from the paper to be used by yarn mills in winding yarn for shipment. This business has been developed into the largest and probably most profitable business of its kind in the United States. Almost all of the enlargement of their plant has been paid for out of the earnings of the business. They ship profitably some of their products abroad. This business is managed by Major Coker's youngest son, Charles.

About 1900, through the means and influence of Major Coker, the Hartsville Cotton Mill was organized, he being the largest stockholder. Under the management of Mr. C. C. Twitty, it has been one of the most successful cotton-goods manufacturing corporations in the South. Principally with Major Coker's capital, cotton-seed oil mills were also established, which have been constantly and profitably managed by his son-in-law, Mr. J. J. Lawton. In the meantime, he organized and managed the Bank of Hartsville, which has been one of the most successful banks in the State. In his later years, he did not undertake the active management of his mercantile, farming, banking, and manufacturing interests, but in a large measure directed all.

He accumulated one of the largest fortunes ever accumulated in this State, though he was practically insolvent when the Civil War closed. He was one of the most versatile business men the State ever produced. He was probably the most highly cultured intellectually of any man who has made a conspicuous business success in this State.

Appendix

He was eminently broad minded and kindly in his dealings with customers and competitors. After building the railroad from Darlington to his country store at Hartsville, he encouraged competitors, and lent them a helping hand, financially and otherwise. His business competitors were his friends. Every one had the most profound respect for him. On one occasion in the seventies, a neighbor who had a fine apple orchard and was in the habit of making quantities of apple cider, of which he was very fond, brought a keg of "hard" cider which was intoxicating to Major Coker's store. The Major was out at the time, but came in when the cider was being taken from the neighbor's keg. He said nothing, yet not one of his customers would partake of the intoxicating beverage while he was there, although if he had not been present possibly all of them would have imbibed. On one occasion while he was president of the National Bank of Darlington, a customer of the bank who had not been in Darlington long, paused to pass the compliments of the day with Major Coker, and in the course of his conversation, by way of making himself entertaining, told Major Coker a vulgar anecdote. The Major neither smiled nor made any comment, and the visitor awkwardly withdrew, feeling more embarrassed than if he had been rebuked by a bishop. I never heard of anyone taking liberties with him. No one indulged in loose, wild talk in his presence, yet the atmosphere about him, in business as well as in his home circle, was one of cheerfulness and kindness. Almost instinctively children, as well as mature people, respected him and were influenced by him.

Illustrations of such regard are many. W. E. Lucas, who organized, and successfully managed for years, the Laurens and the Watts Cotton Mills at Laurens, South Carolina, was reared a few miles from Major Coker's

APPENDIX

home, before Hartsville was a town. His father was a country physician and farmer, an educated gentleman of fine character, but not a good collector. He was deeply in debt to Major Coker in the late seventies, and was greatly worried about it. On one occasion Dr. Lucas was talking over his affairs with Major Coker, in the presence of young Lucas, a boy fifteen or sixteen years old. At the close of the conversation the Major put his hand on the boy's head, and told him he would soon be grown, and that he could be of great help to his father if he would look after the farm in his father's absence. Young Lucas went home determined to do all in his power to help his father. Through his attention to the farm the next year or two, he succeeded in getting his father entirely out of debt. After spending a time at college, he accepted a clerkship in the mercantile establishment of J. L. Coker & Company, which was managed by a junior partner. Young Lucas was surprised that Major Coker seemed to know all that was going on in the mercantile establishment, and was especially surprised when he told him never to promote a sale by misrepresenting the quality or value of anything in the establishment. The presence of Major Coker was an inspiration to young Lucas, as it was to many others.

Major Coker's intellectual attainments and talents were as varied as was his business interests. He was interested in chemistry, botany, zoology, and acquired such knowledge on these subjects as was taught in the American universities in his youth. He was interested in mathematics, and mechanical and civil engineering. He was fond of music, and was a good amateur vocalist. Late in life he had musicians of national reputation visit Hartsville. He was especially attracted by birds, and made a life long study of their habits. He was interested in architecture, and was also familiar with the works of great painters and sculptors. On one occasion, when I was visiting his home, all of his grandchildren, consisting of the small family of his oldest daughter and two of his sons, spent the day at their grandfather's. In order to help entertain them, an unmarried daughter in Coker-like fashion tried to instruct, amuse, and give pleasure to the absent, all at the same time. She had all of the children write a letter to their Uncle Will, the present head of the Department of Botany at the University of North Carolina, who was then a student in a German university. That night the Major was highly entertained reading the letters written by the children, and then added a few lines to his son in original rhyme. The Major was fond of poetry, and would often make little rhyming couplets for the amusement of his children. On one occasion a little child who was attracted by him wanted to make him a present, and presented him with a copy of the Rhymes of Mother Goose.

When he was nearly seventy years old, I accompanied Major Coker on a trip abroad, and was surprised to find that he could read French and translate it into English at sight. It had been nearly fifty years since he had studied French. I expressed surprise that he should remember his French so well, when he replied, with a smile: "I have kept up my French a little since my school days. I read a French novel occasionally." Here was this old gentleman, living most of his life in the country, reading French novels, when not many university professors, I venture to say, except those in a department of modern languages, could read a French novel ten years after leaving college.

On one occasion, I traveled for a few hours with Professor J. W. Gaines, President of Cox College of Atlanta. Major Coker was mentioned, his attainments were discussed at some length, and then Professor Gaines said: "I lived at Hartsville for years. Major Coker was one of the leading supporters and trustees of a boarding school of which I was principal, and I had many opportunities of seeing and knowing him. Do you know that Major Coker leads the medical thought of Darlington County?" I had to confess my ignorance. The Professor suggested that I ask Dr. Eggleston of Hartsville, or Dr. Robert Edwards of Darlington, and went on to tell me that Major Coker was greatly interested in medicine, took medical journals, and discussed medical subjects with young physicians, calling their attention to new ideas and methods. He was one of the first men in South Carolina to be posted as to the fact that the bite of certain kinds of mosquitoes causes malaria. He was the first man in the State to take steps to banish the mosquito from the town which he founded.

Dr. George Ben Johnson, of Richmond, a great surgeon, became acquainted with Major Coker late in life, and was so attracted by him that he made a visit to Hartsville. On this visit to Major Coker, Dr. Johnson became acquainted with young Dr. Robert Edwards of Darlington, a distant kinsman of Major Coker, was so impressed by his ability, character and attainments that he induced him to move to Richmond as an eye, ear, nose, and throat specialist, and gave him the hearty support of his wide influence. Dr. Edwards rapidly gained an enviable reputation, but died in a few years. A leading physician in Greenville, Dr. Davis Furman, who was chairman of the Board of Health in Greenville, told me that on one occasion he talked with Major Coker about what was being done by the Greenville Health Department, and seeing that he was interested, he offered to take the Major around and show him some of the things that were going on. The Doctor was greatly pleased with the Major's company, and told me that Major

APPENDIX

Coker talked on such subjects like a man trained at the Pasteur Institute.

Major Coker was one of the greatest philanthropists this State has ever produced. He was constantly thinking of ways to help others. On one occasion, I was spending a week-end with him, and some boy or girl was seriously ill in the boarding school of the town. He seemed more concerned about the condition of a poor, ignorant man's sick child, away from home, than most people would be about one of their own family. In a most unobtrusive way he would help others in need. On one occasion a scholar, with large family and small means, undertook some literary work for very small pay for a historical society. As the scholar doing the work lived in Greenville, Major Coker wrote me to pay this gentleman fifty dollars each month and charge it to his account. He thought the scholar should be paid more, but knew that the historical society had little or no funds. He said that he did not wish to send his personal check on his local bank, as it would be observed and his part in the matter might in a way be advertised. One of the friends of his youth who lived in another state wrote two or three historical or biographical works of note, but in his old age had not sufficient income to provide for the comforts of life. Major Coker, on hearing of his condition, had money sent to him indirectly every month thereafter until the man's death, and his boyhood friend died without knowing from whom the monthly aid came. I knew an ex-Confederate soldier who was unsuccessful, and left daughters unprovided for. Major Coker allowed these daughters to occupy his property without rent as long as they lived. I doubt if any member of his family knew the extent of such aid given to others. We cannot judge of philanthropy altogether in dollars and cents, but Major Coker gave to Coker College alone more than

APPENDIX

any other two men in South Carolina have ever given to any educational institutions, so far as is known to the public. At the same time he raised seven children, all but one married and have children of their own.

He was happily married early in life, and his wife was entirely in sympathy with him, intellectually, financially, and morally, or spiritually, if you please. When the Cokers lived in Charleston, it was the custom of my brother George and myself to take supper with James Coker, who was about a year younger than George and a year older than I, every other Friday night. Mrs. Coker would frequently bring out a book or a paper, and have us boys read aloud, greatly to my humiliation, because I was a very poor reader and would have to stumble over the simplest words and spell them out. If Mrs. Coker had considered her own pleasure, or mine either, she would have left that part of the entertainment out, but she was constantly on the alert to have children in whom she was interested do things that would improve them. She was gentle, kind, refined, cultured. She was the daughter of a highly respected Baptist minister, and accepted all of the doctrinal part of religion. Major Coker was reared in a similar atmosphere. When he was a young man he was superintendent of the Sunday School. Preaching service was held in the country church twice a month. On the Sundays when the preacher was not present, the Sunday School was prolonged and Major Coker made an ethical talk. I, who was reared to think the preacher was a direct representative of Deity, was surprised when plain people in the country said they had rather go to church on the Sundays when Major Coker spoke than when the preacher preached. As far as I know he never stressed religious doctrine. There was nothing in his surroundings to stimulate liberal thought, but I am confident that he questioned much of the doctrinal part of religion. Few men were as familiar as he was with the advance of science. He accepted as the most probable explanation of human development the Darwinian theory. He asked me on one occasion if I did not think the teachings of Darwin had more to do with causing people to question what is called orthodox religious opinion than anything else. Another time he mentioned that Dr. Osler had said that all of his scientific studies pointed to the idea that there is no future life, but he believed it anyway. He said to me on one occasion that denominational colleges helped the cause of education in the State, and that the teachings of the colleges tended to get people away from narrow and irrational religious opinions. He once told me that he enjoyed going to church, not so much for the sermon, but that he went in a spirit of worship, and he enjoyed seeing and shaking hands with people from all the country roundabout whom he had known for years, and many of whose parents were his friends.

He never engaged in heated disputes, but would promptly differ with a friend who might be prejudiced or unjust. On one occasion, a friend made unkind remarks about Roman Catholics in his presence. He immediately told of a kindness he received at the hands of Irish Roman Catholics in Baltimore who knew him to be a Protestant and a paroled rebel prisoner. His poise, common-sense and fair-mindedness were a cause of wonder. He appeared to me to be free from exaggerating the merits of friends or the faults of those distasteful to him. He never worked himself into a state of righteous indignation by discussing such people. He would sacrifice business interest unhesitatingly to protect a friend's interest or reputation. On one occasion a man of large business affairs, whose transactions with the Major brought him in contact with one of Major Coker's friends, complained to the Major of his friend's business methods. The Major heard him patiently, then caused the complainer to admit from his own statement that he was in the wrong. A year or two later this man of large affairs wrote the Major, again criticizing his friend's business methods. He received a prompt reply, informing him that it was not agreeable to the Major to receive letters from him containing criticisms of his friends, and that he preferred to discontinue their business relations, rather than to receive such complaints.

Professor Cook asked Major Coker to write a sketch of Mr. Bright Williamson for his "Rambles in the Pee Dee", the material for which he has been gathering for years. The Major replied: "I am incapable of writing in a way to do Bright justice," and I doubt if anyone could draw a word picture of Major Coker and do him full justice. He was especially fond of Mr. and Mrs. Frank R. Chambers, because of their generosity, kindness, and thoughtfulness of others. Mr. Chambers was a cousin of Mrs. Coker who went to New York as a boy just after the Civil War. He made a big fortune, for our people, and unostentatiously did much good with it. Few people in Greenville are aware of the fact that he gave the Margaret Home in Greenville to the Baptists, though not a Baptist himself, for a home for children of missionaries. He gave $80,000.00 towards the endowment of Coker College, because of his confidence in Major Coker's judgment and admiration for his character. He made this gift with the request that its source remain unknown. The information came to me through no betrayal of confidence, and I refer to it on my own judgment.

Major Coker was devoted to his brothers and sisters and their families, as well as to his own family, but he

APPENDIX

was especially devoted to his brother, William C. Coker. When the University of South Carolina conferred on the Major the degree of LL. D., he modestly said: "This degree is conferred, not on account of any intellectual attainment, but because I have shown some interest in educational institutions. If the degree had been conferred on my brother William it would have been very much more appropriate."

Dr. Gordon B. Moore, Professor of Philosophy in the University of South Carolina at the time this degree was conferred, told me that he suggested that the same degree be conferred on Captain W. C. Coker, but some of the faculty or trustees, I do not recall which, objected, not on the ground that the degree could not suitably be conferred on both, but on the ground that it was not good policy to confer this degree on two members of the same family. Dr. Moore, who lived in Darlington for years, was a neighbor of mine in Greenville after retiring from the professorship in the University, and often spoke of Captain W. C. Coker. Dr. Moore had the reputation of being one of the most scholarly citizens of this State, and he regarded Captain Coker as the greatest intellect with whom he had ever come in contact. He told me once that he was familiar with the lives of every man who had been president of the United States, and that he regarded W. C. Coker the intellectual and character superior of three-fourths of them. After pausing a moment he looked up and said: "Yes, and he would stand high in the remaining fourth." Another time he said that Captain Coker would have made a great teacher, and if he could have had such a man as instructor it would have been of inestimable value to him. He added "I have had some great teachers in my time. There was Dr. Harris, of Richmond College, afterwards Professor of Greek at the Southern Baptist Theological Seminary. Dr. Harris had what I would call a sharp mind as compared to W. C. Coker. There was Dr. J. L. M. Curry. He was considered a broad man, but he was narrow compared to W. C. Coker. There was Dr. Broadus. He is regarded as a thinker, but his thinking was picayunish compared to W. C. Coker." I repeated to Major Coker what Dr. Moore said of his brother, and he remarked that that he did not think Dr. Moore had an exaggerated idea of the intellectual ability of his brother.

On one occasion, Dr. W. W. Long, of Clemson College, was looking over a few acres of oats which I had planted. I told him that formerly I planted three or four bushels of oats to the acre, but since reading the result of the experiments of David R. Coker, Major Coker's son, I planted three pecks; and that I would rely on David Coker's statement before I would my own experience, because I knew Mr. Coker was accurate in surveying his land and measuring the quantity of seed, fertilizer, and yield, while mine was largely guess work. Dr. Long remarked that anybody could safely follow what David Coker said about agriculture; and that he considered the work of David Coker more valuable than that of any government agricultural experiment station in America, and did not cost any state anything either. He went on to say that he came to the State knowing something of the work of the Cokers, and he was prepared to think favorably of it, but it was far beyond his expectations. He said he had a neighbor in Virginia who came in contact with Major Coker during the Civil War, and visited him every year or two after the war; and that this neighbor would come to his home in Virginia and talk to Dr. Long about Major Coker, in terms of admiration beyond anything he had ever heard. His neighbor would usually end the conversation about his visit to South Carolina by saying:

APPENDIX

"I have had inspiration enough to run me for another year, after which I think I will visit Major Coker and get another dose."

Major Coker never held, nor was he a candidate for political office, with the exception of serving one term in the State Legislature at the close of the Civil War. Ten or twelve years before his death, Messrs. Lawrence Carrigan, Bright Williamson, James Coggshall, Dan McKeithan, and other leading citizens, tried to get him to consent to be elected to the State Senate. No one would be a candidate against him, but he declined. Later there was an unexpired term in the United States Senate to be filled by the South Carolina General Assembly. Thoughtful citizens from different parts of the State suggested the name of Major Coker, but he only expressed the hope that the Legislature would elect someone else.

Major Coker no doubt agreed with another of the Pee Dee's distinguished sons, Governor D. R. Williams, who said, in substance, that patriotism was manifested by making sacrifices for one's country, not by getting something out of one's country. An overwhelming majority of the population of South Carolina have an idea that the people who have held high political office are our great men. Brice, in his American Commonwealth, states that the best talent of America does not go into public life, and gives at length reasons for this unfortunate fact. This fact appears to me more pronounced in the South, and especially in South Carolina, than in any other part of the United States. Possibly the inhumanity of Sherman's raid through the State, and the wrongs heaped upon the South during the reconstruction period, have made the State a fruitful field for the demagogue. During the past generation, few governors, sen-

BRIGHT WILLIAMSON
Secretary-Treasurer Pee Dee Historical Society

ators, or congressmen have represented South Carolina, which I think could be classed as big men, free from appealing to prejudice. Honest, frank methods might be successful in public life, if persistently applied, just as such methods succeed in private life.

I do not know the history of any other native of South Carolina who would measure up to Major Coker in the combination of character, ability, culture, patriotism, usefulness, and business success. His admirers would be pleased if the influences of our politicians, or statesmen, if any can be so classed, our schools and our homes should produce others who are greater.

II

BRIGHT WILLIAMSON

The Williamsons came from Drewry's Bluff on the James River, Chesterfield County, Virginia, and settled on Black Creek about seven miles east of the town of Darlington about 1750. There are no accounts or records of those who came from Virginia or their Christian names. The Court House at Darlington with some public records were destroyed in 1784. Among the names of the Williamsons who owned land about 1800 were: Thomas, William, Abraham, Stephen, Shadrach and Jesse.

The records of the early settlers of that part of Darlington County and what was the lower part of Craven County and its early history were sadly neglected.

In Gregg's history of The Old Cheraws, Thomas Williamson is mentioned as voting for Claudius Pegues as a member of the General Assembly for the Parish of St. Davids in March 1769 (page 173) and on Jan. 23, 1776 he was commissioned Captain in Col. Powers' regiment. There were other Williamsons about the same

APPENDIX

age as Thomas Williamson. Some were no doubt brothers and some were near relatives.

On Jan. 31, 1778, Benjamin Williamson became a member of St. Davids Society (Gregg, page 281) and subscribed or paid £75 to the St. David's Academy fund, and among those whose names appear in an imperfect list taken from the archives of this State were: Shadrach Williamson, Lieutenant, Jesse, Stephen, Sterling, Willis and William, privates in Marion's brigade.

An ordinance passed by the General Assembly for South Carolina, March 27, 1776, opening up Black Creek for navigation, among the petitioners were James Williamson and William Williams. No doubt the latter was William Williamson who lived on Black Creek and owned land near Williamson's Bridge.

Thomas Williamson was paid £85 for provisions and military service in 1782 and on July 21, 1785, Thomas Williamson, Jr. was paid for services rendered in 1783 and on the same date Benjamin Williamson was paid £92-7s-3d for ferriages, provisions and sundries for continentals and militia for 1779-1780 and 1781.

The Williamsons at once, in accordance with a distinctive family trait, acquired lands and built homes. They have always proved their patriotism but have avoided political preferment and from one generation to another have possessed very good business ability. They have been inclined to attend more closely to their own business and to respond to the call of the State only when they were especially called upon to do so. They have been good livers and good providers and have taken a lively and timely interest in affairs around them for the advancement, welfare and betterment of their communities. The older Williamsons were particularly fond of hunting, sports of any kind and also of their grog and were quick to resent an insult or an injury.

APPENDIX

Thomas Williamson had several brothers. His sons were Bright, Thomas and one daughter, Mary. Very little is known of him or his history. His father was said by the older Williamsons to have been Thomas Williamson also.

Bright Williamson was born July 12, 1778 and died Nov. 20, 1854. He married Jane Rogers, daughter of Col. Ben Rogers who served with distinction in the Revolution. The mother of Jane Rogers was Margaret McAllester, daughter of Col. Alexander McAllester, who was a lineal descendant of Alester, eldest son of Argus Mor, Lord of the Isles and Kyntre, Scotland. (See Rev. E. D. McAllester's Life of Col. Alexander McAllester.) The children of Bright Williamson and Jane Rogers Williamson were Benjamin Franklin, Thomas Charles, Lownes W. and Lucius Williamson. Two children died in infancy and were buried on Meeting House Hill, Oaklyn plantation, on the North side of the old Charleston road.

Thomas Williamson, brother of Bright Williamson, married. He lived seven miles South of Society Hill at the residence of the late Samuel B. Goudy. He was the father of the following children: Samuel, Thomas, George, Lownes, Annie E., Caroline M., Sarah E., Joseph Wilds Horace, Mary Ann.

Bright Williamson lived at Brownsville, Marlboro County and walked four miles to a country school. Later on he plowed and worked on a farm for $6.00 per month. He returned to his home in Darlington County about 1798 and soon acquired land on Black Creek, north-east of Williamson's Bridge. He built a small dwelling on a little hill one-fourth of a mile from Williamson's Bridge, at the first bend, on the West side of the old Charleston road. Here he conducted and built up a large mercantile business and ran a line of pole boats from Georgetown

443

APPENDIX

where he brought his merchandise, up the Pee Dee River and Black Creek, to a point just above Williamson's Bridge. He was successful and soon made a large fortune for those days.

He was an exponent of that trait of the Williamson family of owning and acquiring land and he soon owned a tract of 2300 acres, comprising what is now "Oaklyn" plantation. He bought the southern part of this tract from one Coleman for about 300 acres and it turned out afterwards to contain about 1300 acres. He bought a part of the northern portion of the place at a Sheriff's sale. In addition to this place he acquired about 500 acres of land on Black Swamp, which is now a part of the place owned by A. J. Howard. In 1817 he bought land one mile South of Mont Clare where he was living at the time of the great storm in September 1822, which did much damage in Darlington district, destroyed a great deal of property and caused the loss of many lives on the Coast of South Carolina.

In 1818 he bought a large tract of land adjoining the above place from Jordan Sanders which includes the place where he afterwards lived known as Mont Clare. This place extended to the Pee Dee River and included the plantation known as Mexico, on both sides of Flat Creek and the Brick Culvert. Later on he acquired other plantations lower down on the Pee Dee River. He had a great propensity for building water mills for grinding corn.

He was interested in business affairs in this section of the State. He had an interest in the Bank of Georgetown and was a Director in the Bank of Cheraw, which was the principal financial institution in this entire section. On his way to Cheraw he frequently spent the night with his friend, J. Ely Gregg, who was also a Director in the Bank. He owned several corner lots in

APPENDIX

the town of Darlington, thinking that some of his boys might wish to engage in mercantile business.

His first attentions paid his wife, Jane Rogers were not favorably received but later on he was successful in his suit. A relative remarked that $50,000.00 made quite a difference.

In 1812 he was Captain of the Darlington Company in Col. Rutledge's brigade, which served throughout the war of 1812-14. His regiment was in camp at Haddrells point near Charleston and remained there for some two years. He was promoted to Adjutant, then to Major and on the resignation of Col. Rutledge near the close of the war he was made Colonel of the regiment.

He was a man of rather robust appearance and had a large physique, of great energy, physical strength and endurance. He often went to Georgetown and on one occasion he rode his famous horse of which he was so fond, named "Walker," from Georgetown to his home in one day.

Late in life Bright Williamson joined the Black Creek Baptist Church. The day he was immersed a great crowd gathered to witness the ceremony.

It is quite possible he had two or three brothers who emmigrated West.

His oldest son, Benjamin Franklin Williamson, named after the statesman, Benjamin Franklin, was born on the 3rd day of February, 1814 and died on the 20th day of October, 1887. He was born on the place where his father lived on Black Creek, one-fourth of a mile North of Williamson's Bridge. He first married Leonora Wilson, by whom he had five sons—Frank Rogers, John Wilson, George Dargan, Lucius Timothy (died in infancy) and Leon N. John Wilson married Bessie Sanders. George Dargan moved to Navara County, Texas, and

APPENDIX

married Sallie Dycus.   Frank and Leon never married. Leonora Williamson died in 1854.

In 1858 Benjamin Franklin Williamson married Margaret J. McIver, daughter of Gen. Evander Roderick McIver (see Cook's Life of David Rogerson Williams) by whom he had three sons and three daughters—Annie Eliza, Bright, Evander McIver, Mary Rogers, Benjamin Franklin and Meta J.

Thomas Charles Williamson first married ——————— Wilson by whom he had four children; Janie Rogers, Robert E., Lownes W., and Laurens E. Laurens E. married Adele Dargan. The others never married.

(Prepared by Mr. Bright Williamson, a leading banker of Darlington.)

III

K. KINLOCH

Francis Kinloch, of Wehaw and Rice hope plantations, Esq: T. P. was the only surviving son of Hon[ble].. James Kinloch, of New Gilmerton, President of H. M. Council, S. Carolina (who was a son of Sir Francis Kinloch, of Gilmerton (Scotland) Bart:).

He was born 1720. Inherited his fathers large estates, and was himself a successful planter, establishing extensive rice plantations "Rice Hope" on Santee River. He was a member of the Commons House for Berkeley and Craven Counties. He attended Gov. Glen, and later Gov. Littelton on their expeditions into the Cherokee nation. He married, 8 Feb'y 1751, Anne Isabella, only daughter and heiress of Hon: John Cleland (sometime Presid[t]: of H. M. Council S. C.) who inherited Wehaw plantations from her mother, Mary dau[r]: of John Perrie, of St. James' Westminster, Esq: (Provost Marshal General of the Leeward Islands) the grantee of the Wehaw lands. Mr. Kinloch died at his house at Santee 2 June

446

FRANCIS KINLOCH,
of Wehaw and Hope Plantations, Esq., J. P. President
of H. M. Council South Carolina

APPENDIX

1767. S. C. Car:) His sons Francis and Cleland Kinloch inherited Kensington and Wehaw plantations, and the latter was a large and successful planter, and erected at Wehaw one of the first improved rice mills in Carolina.

(Prepared by Mr. Langdon Cheves, of Charleston)

IV

An old Field School in time of the Revolution is described by A. Dromgoole Sims in his "Bevil Faulcon, A Tradition of the old Cheraw." This was the first book written and published in the Pee Dee Basin; its leading characters were Col. Abel Kolb, a Colonel under Marion, Rev. Jared Walters, a Methodist minister, and his ward, Bevil Faulcon. It is a work of fiction, and now existing in one Copy only, it is said, in possession of Prof. Henry C. Davis of the South Carolina College.

What Mr. Sims said of the School, in 1842, may be taken as a well authenticated description of the teacher, his methods and authority in his little Kingdom:

Some fifteen miles from the residence of Mr. Faulcon —Bevil's father—John Smith, of great reputation in the neighbourhood, taught a school. He was then the *beau ideal of* an "old-field school-master", and in the dialect of the surrounding country, expressive of his disciplinary excellence, "very tight". The largest, equally with the smallest scholars, female as well as male, (for all ages and sexes from five to twenty-five, frequented his school and received the enlightenment of his love (*lore) within the same pine log tabernacle of science), were subject to the wholesome restraint and encouraging stimulant of the rod.

So much had he risen above other pedagogues of the vicinage—that John Smith—that the honorary appellation of "school-master John Smith" distinguished him.

Appendix

The copies which he set, and the old cyphering books, which he made, are carefully preserved, even to this day, by the rustic pedagogues who now fill up his place in society . . . as standard specimens in the art to which he devoted himself.

Under the tuition of this distinguished master, at the juvenile period of eight years of age, Faulcon commenced his education, and continued its prosecution five or six years. . . . In the time, he was faithfully instructed in the fundamentals of reading, writing and arithmetic, the last of which was much better known, in school phrase, as cyphering.

A thorough acquaintance with these, added to a knowledge of practical surveying, was considered, by the master, as well as by most of his neighbors, as the *ultima thule* of human attainment. His pupil was, therefore, considered and pronounced "high larnt", when he quit the establishment.

Before any one, in the present improved state of schools and modes of instruction, condemns his proficiency as small, let him think of the manner in which he proceeded; in fact, in which all who walked the glades of learning's rudiments, in this his primary *alma mater*, were made to proceed.

I will say nothing of the time and importance given to the preparatory stages of orthography, penmanship, and a correct understanding of "point and pause", in reading; but remark a little on the inimitable mode, in which the pupil learned arithmetic; and this branch affords illustration ample of the whole method of instruction.

All the examples, called sums, illustrative of the various rules, from addition to cube-root, which was placed last in the series, were written down by the master, in what was denominated by a cyphering-book. The scholar, already versed in the contents of his "table-

APPENDIX

book" from many a Friday-night's task, and provided with a slate and pencil, would take these sums, one by one, and set down to their solution with all the importance and thoughtful gravity, with which Sir Isaac Newton or La Place ever approached the investigation of some abstruse principle in philosophy. A half dozen figures for a multiplicand, with a unit for a multiplier, would often engage the mighty cogitations of his laboring brain for days, and when, by some lucky chance, the product was found, the cunning art of "casting out the nines", and properly arranging the results in the forks of a cross-mark for proof, not frequently demanded a day or two more of his time and ingenuity.

All aid was strictly forbidden. Each sum was to be solved by the student himself, no matter if a month were required for it, and after the solution was examined and pronounced "right" by the master, it was carefully "set down" in cyphering book. Every sum, therefore, from the first to the last rule in arithmetic, was taken up as a business of importance, requiring time, and its solution looked upon as an epoch in the scholastic life of the pupil. When he reached the Rule of Three, which not unseldom, took a year or more, he was hailed as a wise man of the establishment; and to have passed sucseccfully through mulitiplication even, was not without its rewards of praise and wonderment.—But, to arrive at the distant goal of cube-root, brought to the fortunate adventurer the respect and applause of the school-master himself, and almost divine honors from the plebean spellers and tryo cypherers of the school.

When I call to mind other customs which obtained in his school, and the philosophy which he practised to rivet his instructions on the memory of his pupils, I own that it is with difficulty I suppress the risings of mirth, which a perception of the ridiculous excites within

APPENDIX

me; and, reader, I rather think that you will laugh right out, as did Mr. Danvers when Faulcon was detailing these things.

In its best order, when in full operation, the school exhibited the wildest uproar. All the scholars conned over their lessons at the top of their voices—some with the rapidity of an auctioneer vending merchandize—others, in the slow, solemn tones of a town-watch, singing out "half past one o'clock—all's well," and whenever the slightest symptoms of cessation appeared, the master, in a voice fearfully audible above the general buzz, would extend his order, "mind your books," and sometimes "say out".

Then again the hum of the tyrocinium would revive with redoubled animation. Mingled in loud and confused vociferation, might be heard the voices of those most advanced, chanting select pieces from Scott's Lessons, or the Psalter; others, in commendatory emulation of sound, making becoming respect to Thomas Dilworth,—his immortal rival, the venerable Noah Webster, was not yet in high vogue, as in our time; while the humble freshmen of the establishment, with suitable zeal and voice, would roar from their Horn-books, no inappropriate responses to their most advanced companions.

Fridays, particularly the afternoons, were the jubilees of the system. No slates, on these occasions, engaged the attention of a part of the scholars, or diminished, by the abstraction of a single voice, the mighty chorus raised in honor to the divinity of pedagoguism. All who could read or spell joined in the clamor, and the very monosyllabist, unwilling to contribute nothing to the stock of noise which the system called for, and not unmindful of the hortatory tones of the master, which ever and anon were heard cheering on his little subjects in their exercises, would sing out, letter by letter, t-h-e-

the; or, with the rapidity of a well practised tongue and ready memory, wind through the mazes of b-a—*ba,* b-e—*be,* b-i—*bi,* b-o—*bo,* b-u—*bu,* delighted with his part of the performance in this raging hurricane of articulate sound.

But his philosophy to fix his lessons of wisdom indelibly on the minds of his pupils, though it smacked something of cruelty, was perhaps, as good as the "say out system". He invariably enlivened the attention, and imparted adhesiveness to the memory, by a judicious employment of the ensign of his craft, whenever, from the intricacy of the subject, or the obesity of the scholar's perception, the assigned task was not acquired; and, again, whenever the scholar very easily learned what was proposed, a ponderous imposition of stripes was deemed necessary, lest "light come, light go," should be verified in the obliviousness of his recollection. But in both cases, the consolatory assurance, that when they came to a sufficient discretion, suitably to appreciate the bestowment benignly vouchsafed, they would be most grateful for it, invariably comforted, or rather was administered to comfort the victims.

I take not upon me, however, at this moment, to affirm how far this word of seasonable consolation was subsequently realized; or how far the awakened discretion of the urchins appreciated with gratitude the birchen blessings, which, with a most profuse munificence, school master John Smith bestowed upon them. Certain it is, that his philosophy, both in principle and practice, was in good keeping with the spirit of the times, and not unlike that of our matter-of-fact ancestors, who, in order the better to preserve the evidence of their boundaries and location of their respective territories, and thus escape the "glorious uncertainties of the law" in the strange work of a petty jury, were wont, periodically,

APPENDIX

to take the unsuspecting youth of the neighborhood round the lines, and diligently chastise them at all the corner trees; concluding, right enough, that a boy would not be prone to forget the spot at which the lassitude of his rambles were thus refreshed.

Peace to school-master John Smith! If uprightness of life avails ought in the grave, he sleeps quietly. That "goblin damned," a guilty conscience, which haunts the wicked, as it never disturbed him here, we may well conclude, will forbear its presence hereafter.

One Mr. Gregory, of North Britain, who had for several years been a successful instructor of youth in the United States,—the then British Colonies,—and whose reputation for classical attainment was deservedly high, next had our hero in charge.

In those days, and for years subsequent, the people of the South were much in the habit of filling their academies, where such things—institutions if you like the term better—did exist, with teachers from that land of industry and learning; and how far the literary proficiency of scholars, particularly classical accracy, has been promoted by the substitution of those from our own North country, or the young men of the South, considering how easily they may be tempted from the occupation, and how seldom they pursue it, except as a temporary business, I take to be a question, in the solution of which, the Caledonians have no great cause of apprehension.

One thing is indisputable, the teachers from Scotland were good scholars—not smatterers from some college, whose literary merit would reflect no superlative degree of credit on a grammar school, and who, after whiling away three or four years at scuh an institution, turn their attention to teaching for a short time, while in preparation for the profession of Law or Medicine,

APPENDIX

may be the Ministry, as that too is becoming a profession, and with the avowed intention of abandoning the business as soon as possible,—but they were men deeply versed in the subjects to which they made pretensions, and free from views of a profession ulterior to their then employment.

V

Warrants for Lands in South Carolina, 1692-1711, by A. S. Salley, Jr., Secretary of the Historical Commission and high authority in matters pertaining to the early history of South Carolina, was drawn upon in several chapters above. It throws light on the spelling, especially of words ending —ee. Such words as Copahee a sound, Combahee or Combee an island, Dachee a bluff, Dapontee a place, Dawhee a plantation, Holshewee, a place, Pedee and Santee, rivers, Wappitochee a place, Sewee a bay, Poshee a swamp, differed in the penult from such words as Caushee an island and the variant spelling Seawee and Seewee, the Assembly using the form Sewee in fixing the bounds of a parish, and Peedee from which the present Pee Dee arose.

The Indian name of Black river seems to have confused the words Winea, Wenia, Winnian, Weenee, meaning the Black River, with Winyaw, the name of the Bay and undefined neighborhood around it. In 1722, several ministers called the site of the Prince Frederick's church Winian, and Rev. Mr. Morritt called it Winnian and later Wenneyaw, combining, as it seems, Winea and Winyaw into one word. It is easier to tell how Winyaw got its name than to explain just what the word used to represent. "A good many years ago" says Mr. Walter Hazard, a leading lawyer of Georgetown, "I ascertained from the bureau of Ethnology at Washington, D. C., information as to the meaning of the name 'Winyaw'. This information was that the name Winyaw meant the 'people of the bend', which I have always understood to be a reference to the locality in which this tribe of Indians lived. They were located on the southern bank of Winyah Bay between that point and the North Santee River, where the Bay makes a 'bend' in the form of an elbow, running first to the South-west and then to the North-east. The name, therefore, seems to have a geographical origin."

It was used as the name of a bay, of a ferry, of a town, neighborhood and parish. It is now spelt Winyah, though Webster makes it 'Winyaw' Bay.

INDEX

Academy, Winyaw Indigo, 82, 107
Acadians, 99
Acres, granted 14, illegally 61, 66
Act, the Stamp, 238, 239, 240, 242
Act, Sheriff Sale, 350
Advertisements, 4, 215, 216
Agreements, non-importation, 247
Agriculture 72, 78, 408
Alison, Rev. Hector, 153
Allston, C. P., 4
Allston, John, 14, 32, 33
Allston, Wm. 13, 32, 33
Annapolis, Convention at, delegates, call for convention at Philadelphia, 387
Ardesoif, Capt., 298
Armistice, tacit, 230
Asbury, Bishop, 154
Assembly, 7, 13, 31, 91, 101, 146, 181, 219, 222, 223, 235, 236, 337, 363
Association, Charleston Baptist, 156
Association, an, entered into, 256
Ayer, Thomas, 293

Bassett, Rev. Nathan, 149
Baronies, 4, 13, 15, 61
Basin, People in Pee Dee, 106
Baxter, Rev. John, 100
Bay, Long, 30, 35
Beale, Othniel, 30, 57, 187
Beauty Spot, 66
Bedgegood, Rev. Nicholas, 158
Bellinger, Edmund, 1
Bill, Circuit Court, 301

Black Mingo, 45, 301
Bluff, Hunt's, 293
Bluff, Long, 64
Bluff, Mars, 62, 224
Bluff, Red, 66
Bluff, Sandy, 58, 63
Bluff, Wahees, 322
Boone, Gov., 236, 346
Botsford, Rev. Edmund, 162, 339n., 341
Braddock's Defeat, 99
Brittons, the, 26, 60
Brockington, Wm., 46
Brown, Rev. John, 162
Buford, at Waxhaws, 291
Bull, Lt. Gov. Wm., 102, 103, 186, 230, 246, 249
Bull, Rev. Tredwell, 114, 145
Burke, Judge Aedanus, 340, 343, 345, 370
Burrington, Gov. of N. C., running the line between the Carolinas, 23, 24

Calhoun, Patrick, 371, 404
Camden, battle at, 296
Campbell, Lord Wm., 276
Cannon, John, his letter, 272
Capital, at Friday's Ferry, 376
Captains, from the Pee Dee, 260
Carnes, Mr., 375
Carolina, South, indifferent about its northern line, 264
Cato, 241
Cattle, abundance of, 72, 73, 74
Ceremony, the marriage, 89
Chapels, 2, 27, 135, 243
Charleston, 75 meeting of its citizens, 274, 275, its fall 283

INDEX

Charraws 11, Cheraws
Cheraw, 64, 132, companies raised, 260, 261, 274, 358
Cheves, Langdon, 8n.
Chicken, Col. George, 46
Child, James, 2
Church, Aimwell, 153
Church, Black Mingo, 151
Church, Brick, 148
Church, Cashaway, 163
Church, Circular, 41, 149
Church, Prince Frederick, 2, 6, 14, 43, 59, 73, 115, 122, 127, 135
Church, Hopewell, 153
Church, Indian Town, 151
Church, new, on Lower Pee Dee, 132
Church, Prince George, Winyaw, 113, 136n, 137
Church, St. David's, 244
Church, St. Marks, 141
Church, Welsh Neck, 88, 156
Church, Williamsburg, 151
Churches, Baptist, 156, 161
Church Discipline, 88, 161
Circulars, 77
Circulation, Medium of, 349
Civilization, rude substitutes for, 172
Cleland, John, 30
Clergy, letter from, 114
Clinton, Sir Henry, 275, 289
Coker, Thomas, 163
Coker, Maj. J. L., 164
College, Rhode Island, 164
College, State, proposed, 111, 112
Commander, Saml., 43
Commissioners, Indian, 9; church, 114, 243; King's Commissioner, 50; to run the line, 24; to form a compact, 386; build church, 137

Commissions, military, 262
Committees, General, 254, 255; Secret, 255; Special, 256; of three Judges, 366; to remove the capital, 374; Compromise Committee, 376; lots in the new city and compensation, 377; Madison's Committee, 384; to bring in a new plan of government, 267
Complaints, as to taxation, 184, 220
Confederation, Articles of, 278; the governors of S. C. during the, 382
Congress, Continental, 251, 255, 266
Congress, Provincial, 256, 266, 269, 271
Constitution, State, 268, 272, 273n; convention called, 373
Constitution, U. S., 382, 389, 396; adopted, 408; made by, 408
Constitution, Locke's, 223
Convention of Indian Chiefs, 97, 98, 100, at New York, 239
Conyers, Capt., 316, 318
Cooper, Dr. Thomas, 109
Cornwallis, Lord, 306, 328
Counties, laid out, 365
County, Craven, 13; Anson, 74, 365
Courts, Circuit, 187; rooms, 378
Cowpens, 74; battle of, 311
Crackers or poor whites on the sand hills, 173
Creek, Black, 63, 66, 294
Creek, Black Mingo, 7, 13, 44
Creek, Brown, 261
Creek, Bull, 31
Creek, Caanan, 41, 42
Creek, Catfish, 58, 61, 321

INDEX

Creek, Cedar, 27
Creek, Collins, 33
Creek, Cuffeetown, 327
Creek, Gravelly, 41
Creek, Green, 43
Creek, Hard Labor, 327
Creek, Hurricane, 65
Creek, Jeffries, 62
Creek, Jericho, 32
Creek, Lynch's, 60
Creek, Muddy, 64
Creek, Naked, 64
Creek, Peter's, 45
Creek, Pidgeon, 65
Creek, Sampit, 13, 28, 41, 42
Creek, Schooner, 32
Creek, Squirrel, 32
Creek, Thompson, 66
Creeks, Three, 261
Creek, Toby's, 62
Creek, Turkey, 41
Creek, Wadbaccon, 26
Creek, Wando, 32
Creek, Wehaw, 2
Creek, Wittee, 27
Cunningham, Robert, 262
Cunningham, Patrick, 262
Currency, the early, 5

Dargan, John, 103, 104
Dargan, Timothy, 164
Debt, public, 234; of the States, 394
Debtors, 343
Dictatorship, 283
Disestablishment, 270, 273
Divorces, 90
Dissenters, 145, 150, 185
Dobbs, Gov. of N. C., 98
Drayton, William Henry, 247, 251, 252, 256, 257, 258, 279
Dwight, Rev. Daniel, 32

Edwards, Rev. Joshua, 161
Emigration, causes of, 48
England, the crafty policy of, 383
Euhany, 11
Ervin, Col., 320
Estates, large, 66; real estate, 377
Eutaw, battle of, 331
Evans, Thomas, 270
Eveleigh, Saml., letter of, 47, 48
Exchange, papers posted at, 216
Expenditures, exploring, 34, 35-39.
Exports, from Georgetown, 29

Family, in Colonial times, 87, 90
Farmers, attempted legislation by, 83; petitions of, 85; failure, 86
Fayerweather, Rev., 138
Ferguson, Col., 302
Ferry, Le Nud's 3, 283; Wineaw, 34; Potato, 45; Cashaway, 63, 65; Nelson, 299; Haly's, 308; Manigault, 316
Fledger, Robert, 59
Forces, the disposition of, 305; relative, 305
Ford, Timothy, 345-348
Fordyce, Rev. John, 60, 90; his letters, 128-133, 158
Fox, James, 29
Franklin, Benjamin, 392
Freeman, James, 4, 175
"Freeman", 251, 253
French, the Neutral, 99
Furman, Rev. Dr. Richard, 164

Gadsden, Christopher, 232
Gage, Gen., 250, 257
Gaillard, Bartholomew, 1, 9

INDEX

Gaillard, Peter, 301
Gainey, Maj., 299
Game, abundance of, 76
Garth, agent of S. C. Assembly, 237
Gates, Gen., 296, 298
George III, King, 236
Georgetown, 2, 25, 28, 35, 105, 135, 290, 315
Germans, the, 95, 259, 285, 327
Glen, Gov., 61, 70, 82, 96, 97, 99, 225, 235
Government, Colonial, 70, 99, 225; new plan of, 267
Graham, the historian, 241
Gregg, Bishop, 220
Green, John, 4, 6, 9
Green, Richard, 356
Greene, Gen., 304, 308, 310, 322, 328, 331, 333, 335, 337, 342
Grievances, made by Jury, 177, 247, 378

Hampton, Col. Wade, 329
Harrington, Gen. H. W., 82, 293
Harrison, Rev. James, 141
Hart, Charles, 26, 32
Henry, Patrick, 238
Heron, Rev. Robert, 152
Hewatt, Rev. Alex., 241
Hicks, Maj., 262
Heyward, Judge, 371
Hill, Hobkirk's, battle of, 323
Hill, Col., his losses, 305
Horry, Col. Peter, 300, 314
Horry, Col. Daniel, 362
Horses, 75
Hospitality, 7, 91
Howe, Rev. Dr., 1
Hughes, Meredith, 11, 13, 46
Huguenots, the, 15, 16, 26, 83, 92
Hume, Robert, 66-67

Hunter, George, 14
Hunter, Rev. Samuel, 151

Imports, into Georgetown, 29
Indians, Cherokees, 336; Pee Dees, 10; Senecas, 22; Tuscaroras, 6, 21; Vocarnas, 11; Waccamaws, 10; Charraws, 11
Indigo, 81
Inflation, 83
Insurrection, 69; consequent legislation, 70
Intoxicants, 79
Island, Bull, 32
Island, Snow, 302, 318

James, Maj. John, 298
James, Gavin, 318
James, Rev. Philip, 157
Jenkins, Rev. James, 60, 85, 315, 320
Jenkins, J. R., 217
Johnson, Gov. Robert, 19, 22, 177

Keith, Rev. Alex., 138
Kennedy, Rev. Thomas, 153
Justices Chief, 251; Associate, 251, 253
King's Mountain, battle of, 303
Kingston, 35, 38
Kinloch, Francis, 8, 44
Kinloch, James, 15
Kirkland, Capt. Moses, 220
Knox, Rev. Wm., 153
Kolb, Col. Abel, 308, 324, 325
Kolb, Johannes, 65, 69, 94

LaFayette, 278
Landowners, 14, 67
Lane, John, 6
Laroche, Daniel, 30, 44, 45

INDEX

Laurens, Col. Henry, 215, 256
Law, Lynch, 183
Lawlessness, 186
Laws, Blue, against blasphemy, 67; bastardy, 68; desecration of the Lord's Day, 68; bigamy, 68; divorce, 68
Lee, Gen., 274, 277, 315
Legislature, 342, 364, 408
Lewis, Rev. Joshua, 162
Lide, Robert, 163
Lincoln, Gen., 282, 283
Lincoln, James,
Lincoln, President A., 266n.
Line, the State, dissatisfaction over, 265
Look, a backward, 381
Lowndes, Rawlins, 274, 279, 397, 398, 401
Lowry, Wm., 56
Lucas, George, 33
Lynch, Thomas, 25
Lynch, Jr., Thomas, 239
Lyttelton, Gov., 96, 101, 102

Madison, James, 386-388
Map, Mosely's, 22; Hunter's, 14, 15, 28, 60, 327
Marion, Gen. Francis, 297, 300, 302, 304, 312, 318, 323, 329, 336, 337
Marion, Gabriel, 315
Marks, Conrad, 78
Mason, Col. 394
Matthews, Gov. John, 342, 364
McArthur, Maj., 293
McCullough, Henry, 14, 53
McDonald, 319, 323
McGlothlin, Dr. W. J., 170
McIntosh, Col. Alex., 280, 281
McKee, Rev. David, 153
McLeroth, Col., 308, 317

Men, the great, of S. C., 237, 283, 388; captured, 283, 369, 405
Meeting Houses, 148
Methodists, Armenian, 166; Early polity, 167
Merchants, British, 346
Meriwether, Colyer, 107, 110
Militia, 70, 101
Mills, Wm. Henry, 295
Mitchell, Thos., 292
Montagu, Gov., 220, 246, 248, 249
Montgomery, Col., 102-103
Morgan, Gen., 308; at Cowpens, 310, 311
Morris, Gouverneur, 293
Morritt, Rev. Thomas, 42, 108; letters of, 117, 127
Motte, John Abraham, 8
Moultrie, Gen. Wm., 388
Moultrie, battle of Fort, 274, 338
Murphys, the, 15

Neck, the, 15
Nicholson, Gov., 27, 113

Oxen, 74

Parish, All Saints, 242
Parish, Prince Frederick, 107, 127
Parish, Prince George Winyaw, 13, 27, 42, 113, 117, 137
Parish, St. David's, 146, 147, 219, 222, 242
Parish, St. Matthews', 242
Parish, St. Mark's, 138, 139
Party, Exploring on Waccamaw, 34
Pawley, Percival, 16, 24, 32
Pawley, Adj. Gen., 97
Pawley, George, 30, 41

INDEX

Pea, cow, 78
Pearce, Rev. Offspring, 138
Pee Dee, the Great, 3n, 69; Little, 60; Soldiers of the, 106, 280
Pegues, Claudius, 214, 244
Pendleton, Judge Henry, 366, 367, 368, 369, 370, 372, 374
Petitions, disregarded, 181, 219
Perrie, John, 2, 3, 8
Pickens, Gen. Andrew, 336
Pillmoor, Rev., 166
Pinckney, Charles, 255, 374, 389, 393, 397, 405, 407
Pinckney, Thomas, 405
Pinckney, C. C., 370, 389, 391, 392; a costly compromise, 393, 394, 398
Pines, virgin, 8
Pioneers, 67, 72
Plantation, the Windsor, 4, 44; Thomas', 309
Poor, the, 172, 174, 175, 178, 180
Postell, Capt. John, 313, 316
Posts, British, 290, 305
Powder, 257
Powell, Col. George Gabriel, 101, 260
Pownell, Rev. Mr., 115
Presbyterians, 132, 154
Prevost, Gen., 281
Prioleau, Rev. Samuel, 1
Privateers, near Georgetown, 105
Problem, a political, 231
Proclamations, 239
Proprietors, the Lords, 18, 21, 176, 177
Province, 9, 24
Pugh, Rev. Evan, 162, 291, 293, 297
Purry, Mr. Peter, 75
Queries, 232

Races, the blending of, 91
Rae, Rev. Mr., 152
Ramsay, David,
Randolph, Edmund, 390
Rawdon, Lord, 294
Read, Mr., 372, 373
Recapitulation, 410
Reese, Rev. Joseph, 165
Refugees, 294
Regiments, 257, 277, 322
Registers, Church, 90
Regulators, 186, 215, 221, 224, 229
Remonstrance, 187
Representatives, 234, 342, 389; Revolutions, causes of, 86
Rice, 79, 80, 81
Richardson, Gen. Richard, 104, 262, 263, 303, 362
River, Black, 7, 23, 41, 46
River, Little, 34
River, Little Pee Dee, 59
River, Great Pee Dee, 31, 57
River, Sampit, 23, 41
River, Santee, 1, 13
River, Waccamaw, 13, 21, 22, 31, 33, 38
Royalists, 78, 185
Rutledge, Edward, 371, 401
Rutledge, John, 268, 277, 285-288, 305, 308, 334, 335; Chancellor, 373, 389

Safety, Council of, 357, 259, 266
Salley, Jr., A. S., 79, 81n
Savannah, battle at, 282
Schools, 107, 109, 110, 111, 112
Scotch-Irish, 47, 92, 93, 94, 259, 299
Screven, Aaron, 2
Screven, Elisha, 17, 30
Screven, Robert, 3

INDEX

Screven, Rev. Wm., 3, 7, 16, 17, 31
Sectionalism, in S. C. Shaper's, 20
Separates, 164
Servants, indented, 4, 6
Settlements, 79
Sheriffs, 269
Sickness, endemic, 153
Sims, A. D., 166
Simms, Wm. Gilmore, 409
Skirmishes, 295, 306, 307, 308, 312, 323, 326, 333
Slaves, insurrection of, 69, 81
Smith, Thomas, 3, 4, 9, 32, 149
Smith, Capt. George,
Smith, Rev. Hezekiah, 162
Smith, Rev. Josiah, 44
Smith, Rev. Josias, 150
Smith, Rev. Michael, 133-134
Smith, Capt. Richard, 26, 27, 41
Society, for the propagation of the Gospel, 150, 188
Society, main business of, 391
Spain, 105
Spangenburg, Bishop, 74
Stewart, Rev. James, 138
Stokes, Dr. J. L., 169
Strategy, British, 327, 328
Stub Entries, 351-363
Sumter, Gen. Thomas, 296, 302, 304, 318, 329, 334
Swinton, Wm., 28, 30

Tanyard, reputed settlement at, 60
Tarleton, 283, 303, 304, 306
Taxation, the genius of, 184
Tea, 246, 249, 250
Teachers, competent, few, 108
Tennent, Rev. Wm., 258, 270
Territory, French, 96

Tynes, Col., 301
Tories, 303
Townships, 19, 21; Kingston, 35; Queensboro, 57, 58; Williamsburg, 47, 139, 151, 178
Tract, the Welsh, 61, 63, 68
Trade, Board of, 18, 21; a letter to, 39, 145, 181, 236
Traditions, 60
Travelling, in 1734, 34-35
Treaty, with Indians, 278
Turbefield, Rev., 63
Tweed, Mr., speech of, 405

Vestrymen, Prince Frederick, 127, 135

War, its ravages, 330; aftermath, 89, 339-341; preparation for, 96; against the Cherokees, 102; cost of, 234, 339; debts, 396
Washington, Col., 306, 308
Waties, Wm., 10, 32, 33, 34
Watis, Capt., 21
Watson, Col., 318, 319, 320, 321
Watson, Fort, 315
Waxhaws, 155, 291
Welsh, the, on the Pee Dee, 63, 94, 259
Wemyss, 291, 292, 300, 304
Wesley, Rev. John, 170
White, Capt. Anthony, 43
Whitefield, Rev. George, 7, 170, 188
Wilds, Abel, 270
Williams, D. R., 93, 180 n
Williams, Rev. Robert, 160
Williamsburg, Colony of, 47, 48; town laid out, 48; first owners of land, 49; petitions from, 51-56; soldiers of, 103, 332
Williamson, Maj. Andrew, 276

INDEX

Winchester, Rev. Elnathan, 162
Winyaw, later Winyah, 2, 4, 7, 16, 22, 39
Winyaw, Indigo Society, 77, 107
Wise, Capt. Samuel, 282
Witherspoon, Gavin, 93
Woodmason, Rev. Charles, 61, 140, 142; letter of, 143-144, 181, 229, 242

Wrangling, Council and Assembly, 245, 248
Wye, Rev. Wm., 12

Yamassee, War by, 9

Zamba, an African King, enslaved in Charleston, 76n, 172

www.ingramcontent.com/pod-product-compliance
Lightning Source LLC
Chambersburg PA
CBHW020633300426
44112CB00007B/99